Administering a Supervising Programs for Young Children

First Edition

Early Childhood Education

Jane Humphries, Ed.D.
Creative Educational Strategies
& Services
Oklahoma City, Oklahoma

Kari Rains, M.S.
Creative Educational Strategies
& Services
Oklahoma City, Oklahoma

Linda Nelson, Ph.D.
Professor Emerita of Child
Development and Family Relations
Indiana University of Pennsylvania
Indiana, Pennsylvania

Alan Nelson, Ed.D.
Professor Emeritus of Child
Development and Family Relations
Indiana University of Pennsylvania
Indiana, Pennsylvania

Publisher
The Goodheart-Willcox Company, Inc.
Tinley Park, IL
www.g-w.com

Preface

Administering and Supervising Programs for Young Children is designed to help students understand what goes in to running a child care program. As you consider a career in early childhood administration, this text informs you about what goes into organizing and administering a program, including budgeting, finding appropriate physical spaces, staffing, and curriculum development. Understanding what is needed to craft an effective program that engages children, their families, and the community helps create programs that enhance learning down the line and enriches communities. In *Administering and Supervising Programs for Young Children*, Unit 1 discusses what is required to set up an effective program, such as costs, marketing, and types of programs. Unit 2 covers educational programming, health and safety issues, how to manage people, and program assessment and accreditation.

Administering and Supervising Programs for Young Children supports constructive dialogue about complex issues such as anti-bias education and does so with intellectual humility and compassion. Each chapter offers multiple points to reflect on learning and respond to application questions to help students gauge their understanding of the material. An abundance of study aids—such as learning outcomes matched to key chapter summary content—and application and assessment opportunities increase students' ability to succeed in this rewarding course.

About the Authors

Jane Humphries' experience in the early care and education field has included being a child care director of an NAEYC accredited program, child and parenting specialist, college instructor, researcher, program administrator of several government-funded initiatives in Oklahoma, and national speaker. Dr. Humphries earned undergraduate degrees in Family and Child Development, a master's degree in Early Childhood Education, and a doctoral degree in Occupational and Adult Education from Oklahoma State University. She has taught undergraduate and graduate students for over 25 years and has authored several articles to include a book co-authored with Kari Rains titled *A Fighting Chance: Supporting Young Children Experiencing Disruptive Change*. Dr. Humphries serves as an adjunct instructor at the University of Central Oklahoma and National Louis University, which includes work as the Aim4Excellence Specialist at the McCormick Center for Early Childhood Leadership. She also founded her own company, Creative Educational Strategies & Services, dedicated to providing educators, administrators, parents, and other caregivers with the knowledge and research that supports best practices when working with people, especially those who need to fiddle to focus, talks and learn.

Kari Rains is a Child Development Specialist with decades of clinical work in the field of child development. She earned her undergraduate degree in Communication Sciences and Disorders and her master's degree in Child Development, both from Oklahoma State University. Working as a clinician for the early intervention program provided in the state of Oklahoma, Kari gained insight and experience working with families in their homes of children born with disabilities or children living with a developmental delay. In this work, Kari has continually striven to find practical solutions for families and early childhood teachers and directors who have few resources within the rural areas of Oklahoma. This includes providing practical solutions to those living and working with children struggling with social and emotional regulation issues. She currently provides early childhood education consultation and in-service training for programs across the state of Oklahoma. Kari is also a mother of a child who was diagnosed with ADHD/Sensory Processing, which has allowed her to see first-hand the realities of being a parent and an early childhood professional. She has served as an adjunct instructor, and has published two books and numerous research articles in the field of child development. Since teaming up with Dr. Jane Humphries in 2013, their mission has been to assist those who work with children and adults who struggle with social/emotional regulation issues.

Linda Nelson, Ph.D., taught at Indiana University of Pennsylvania for 35 years and is now professor emerita. Her educational background included degrees from Penn State, Cornell University, and the University of Pittsburgh. These degree programs involved experiences working in or observing each of the university's laboratory preschools. She also studied at the Merrill-Palmer Institute in Detroit, Michigan, and was head teacher of a three-year old group in the Wimpfheimer Nursery School of Vassar College. During her years at IUP, she was a professor of Child Development and Family Relations and authored numerous grants in the Family and Consumer Services area. For several years she was chair of the Human Development and Environmental Studies Department. She was also a training consultant for child care and Head Start programs throughout Pennsylvania and served as a guest speaker and workshop presenter at regional and national conferences.

Alan Nelson, Ed.D., is professor emeritus of Child Development and Family Relations at Indiana University of Pennsylvania. His education included degrees from Grove City College, Westminster College, and Indiana University of Pennsylvania. He served as the Executive Director of the Indiana County Child Care Program, a Pennsylvania Title XX model program. He also was a member of numerous child care committees at the state level and authored/co-authored successful state and national grants, including a federal Department of Education Child Care Access Means Parents in School grant for IUP. Earlier he worked for the Pennsylvania Department of Educational Research as an Early Childhood Advisor and Field Researcher in language development. Alan also worked for Nova Southeastern University as a Cluster Coordinator for Child and Youth Studies doctoral students. Prior to that, he was a summer preschool teacher in the nursery school at Chautauqua Institution and later established a kindergarten through third grade elementary school guidance program at the Kiski Area School District in western Pennsylvania. He has traveled internationally to study philosophies of preschool programming that relate to the importance of developmentally appropriate play opportunities.

In retirement, the Nelsons continue to contribute to their community as advisors and volunteers with programs for young children.

Reviewers

The author and publisher wish to thank the following industry and teaching professionals for their valuable input into the development of *Administering and Supervising Programs for Young Children*.

Maria Abercrombie
Chattahoochee Technical College
Dallas, GA

Amanda Beacham
Carroll Community College
Westminster, MD

Andrea Boberg
Ivy Tech Community College
Evansville, IN

Sulema Caballero
Coastal Bend College
Pleasanton, TX

Tamara Calhoun
Hudson Valley Community College
Troy, NY

Jill Carey
Mendocino College
Ukiah, CA

Linda Carlson
Aims Community College
Greeley, CO

Erin Clifford
Valley View School District
Bolingbrook, IL

Katie Craddock
Tyler Junior College
Tyler, TX

Traci Daniel
Danville Community College
Danville, VA

Erika Davis
Hinds Community College
Jackson, MS

Jennifer Dews
Florida State College at Jacksonville
Jacksonville, FL

Julie Ehle
Mid Michigan College
Harrison, MI

Joyce Fair
City Colleges of Chicago
Chicago, IL

Student Tools

Student Text

Administering and Supervising Programs for Young Children is a comprehensive text that focuses on the organizing and administration of child care programs for future and current administrators.

G-W Digital Companion

- For digital users, e-flash cards and vocabulary exercises allow interaction with content to create opportunities to increase achievement.

Online Learning Suite

- Provides easy-to-use access and navigation
- Includes accessible resources for all learners
- Encourages exploration and discovery (or practice and repetition)

Video Library

- Video assets enrich learning by capturing authentic examples of physical, cognitive, and social-emotional development of children. The videos were created in a developmentally appropriate learning environment and are rich in examples of child care best practices and effective classroom design. Videos are accompanied by assignable quiz questions that challenge students to identify the skill, stage of development, or best-practice endeavor that is being displayed in the video and think critically about the content.

Instructor Tools

LMS Integration

Integrate Goodheart-Willcox content within your Learning Management System for a seamless user experience for both you and your students. EduHub LMS–ready content in Common Cartridge® format facilitates single sign-on integration and gives you control of student enrollment and data. With a Common Cartridge integration, you can access the LMS features and tools you are accustomed to using and G-W course resources in one convenient location—your LMS.

G-W Common Cartridge provides a complete learning package for you and your students. The included digital resources help your students remain engaged and learn effectively:

- **Digital Textbook**
- **Videos**
- **Drill and Practice** vocabulary activities

When you incorporate G-W content into your courses via Common Cartridge, you have the flexibility to customize and structure the content to meet the educational needs of your students. You may also choose to add your own content to the course.

For instructors, the Common Cartridge includes the Online Instructor Resources. QTI® question banks are available within the Online Instructor Resources for import into your LMS. These prebuilt assessments help you measure student knowledge and track results in your LMS gradebook. Questions and tests can be customized to meet your assessment needs.

Online Instructor Resources

- The **Instructor Resources** provide instructors with time-saving preparation tools such as answer keys, editable lesson plans, and other teaching aids.
- **Instructor's Presentations for PowerPoint®** are fully customizable, richly illustrated slides that help you teach and visually reinforce the key concepts from each chapter.
- Administer and manage assessments to meet your classroom needs using **Assessment Software with Question Banks**, which include hundreds of matching, completion, multiple choice, and short answer questions to assess student knowledge of the content in each chapter.

See www.g-w.com/administering-and-supervising-programs-for-young-children-2025 for a list of all available resources.

Professional Development

- Expert content specialists
- Research-based pedagogy and instructional practices
- Options for virtual and in-person Professional Development

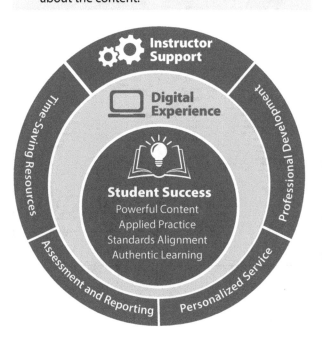

Guided Tour

The instructional design of this textbook includes student-focused learning tools to help you succeed. This visual guide highlights these features.

Chapter Opening Materials

Each chapter opener contains a list of learning objectives, a list of key terms, and a NAEYC/DAP correlation. The **Objectives** clearly identify the knowledge and skills to be gained when the chapter is completed. **Key Terms** list the key words to be learned in the chapter. **Introduction** provides an overview and preview of the chapter content. The **NAEYC/DAP standards** correlate what you will be learning to the important industry standards.

Director's Showcase

The **Director's Showcase** features provide you with the opportunity to explore different aspects of administration of child care programs, large and small, for-profit and non-profit, as well as in-home child care. The **Reflect** questions expand upon concepts in the Showcase features using information you learned in the text.

CHAPTER 4

Facilities, Equipment, and Curriculum

Aluxda/iStock/Getty Images Plus

Learning Outcomes

After studying this chapter, you will be able to:

4.1 Review guidelines for indoor and outdoor environments when determining facility and space needs for children.

4.2 Examine equipment needs that influence the organization and arrangement of successful indoor and outdoor learning spaces for young children.

4.3 Distinguish equipment differences for infants and toddlers, preschoolers, school-age children, and family child care home programs.

4.4 Evaluate curriculum recommendations for infant, toddler, preschool, out-of-school-time, and family child care home programs.

---

60 Unit 1 Establishing a Quality Child Care Program

Key Terms

block center
creative art area
curriculum
dramatic play area
housekeeping area
literacy and writing areas
math and science areas
sensory area

NAEYC/DAP standards

Standards covered in this chapter:

NAEYC

4c, 5a, 5b

DAP

1D, 4C, 5B

Introduction

No matter what age group of children is being served in a center- or home-based program, they will all have state-mandated practices and expectations. NAEYC Program Standards 2 and 9 (2021) specifically focus on the areas of equipment and curriculum when developing and maintaining a high-quality early childhood program. These standards concentrate on providing well-maintained indoor and outdoor physical environments that facilitate child and staff learning and development. This includes providing learning opportunities with appropriate equipment that is developmentally appropriate and exhibits a commitment to equitable outcomes for all children.

4.1 Guidelines for Indoor and Outdoor Environments

There are many sites where early childhood programs are housed, including buildings specifically designed for the care of children, small or large areas of space that are donated for program use, or a designated area within a home. Whether the program is center specific or a home, there are many space considerations to keep in mind, including

- location and accessibility;
- licensing standards;
- planning room arrangement needs;
- kitchen and storage space;
- space for staff;
- interior elements;
- outdoor space; and
- security.

Location and Accessibility

The location of the center must be convenient for busy families (Figure 4.1). Accessible routes to primary businesses, shopping, or housing areas are helpful to parents and guardians. This includes consideration based on

Director's Showcase

Zara

Zara was the director of a large child care facility in the city. Based on a recent improvement survey completed by staff and parents, Zara decided to update and upgrade the outdoor play areas at the facility. The outside spaces had only been maintained in the 12 years since she was director of the facility. She applied for and received a grant for funding of the remodel. Zara decided to update fencing around the outdoor play areas by replacing a chain-link fence with privacy fencing for greater security. She then decided to replace all of the large motor-skill play structures. This was expensive, but she felt it was important to find an outdoor play system that was safe and secure for all ages.

Asha

Asha was a home child care provider in a small town. She had recently added two new toddlers to her home and was struggling with managing behaviors. While preparing meals or brushing teeth, the children would run circles around the table and play areas while they were waiting. She tried to engage them in activities to help them wait for their turn but had not been successful. She wondered if the environment or room arrangement might be factors in the problem. Asha decided to rearrange the play areas and meal area to see if that helped with the behavior issues she was having. When she looked at how the tables, play area, and kitchen were arranged, she found that there was a connecting oval, which was perfect for children to run; she had a built-in racetrack. Asha was hopeful that by rearranging the space, the children would not be tempted to run around.

Illustrations

Illustrations have been designed to communicate the specific topic clearly and simply. Photographic images have been selected to reflect the diversity of children, families, communities, and classrooms.

End-of-Chapter Content

End-of-chapter material provides an opportunity for review and application of concepts. A concise **Summary** provides an additional review tool and reinforces key learning objectives. This helps you focus on important concepts presented in the text. **Review** questions enable you to demonstrate knowledge, identification, and comprehension of chapter material. **Showcase Your Skills** questions extend learning and develop your abilities to use learned material in new situations and to break down material into its component parts. **Matching** questions help enforce vocabulary learned in the chapter.

Figure 3.7 Child care programs must support safe and healthy environments to protect children and staff from injury or illness.

director or owner of an early childhood program, you are responsible for the well-being of the children in care. It is generally accepted that young children cannot be responsible for themselves. Those who care for them must be aware of basic safety and health precautions. If a child is injured or becomes ill because of negligence or deliberate actions by staff, your program will be liable (Figure 3.7).

Careful adherence to all licensing and local safety requirements can provide some legal protection. Any type of child care program operating illegally would be at a substantially greater risk for both civil and criminal legal action if an accident were to occur. Staying current with the required training and constant oversight of the established responsibilities of staff is imperative. Careless or poorly trained staff members are less likely to spot potential hazards. Alert supervision minimizes the likelihood of accidents. Liability resulting from an accident may be lessened if it is clear that the early childhood program's leadership and staff have been diligent in trying to keep children safe.

Insurance Protection

No matter how cautious a program is nor how well trained its employees, accidents can and will happen. Insurance provides protection against financial loss for an early childhood program. Many times, the size and location of a program will determine the need and type of insurance protection that will be necessary. This cost will vary based on the types of protection and what area of the country the program is located. Even those who provide care in their home to children must have additional insurance added to their homeowner's insurance. Assuming that all types of incidents would be covered is a dangerous expectation to have. Often, insurance packages are offered to members of professional and child care trade associations. Check these costs since discounts might be given to offset the cost of membership dues.

The insurance company that provides the policy may insist that the program adheres to additional requirements. These requirements are usually designed to minimize the chance that a claim for insurance reimbursement will be expected. For example, some insurance companies will not insure a family child care home if they are located in what is deemed as a "high-risk" area by the insurance program. Insurance companies know that family child care homes are harder to supervise. They present a greater risk for the company than a larger program would. Some companies may not insure a center if it has a swimming pool or body of water on the premises.

Director's Showcase

Lora

After doing more research, Lora has been learning more about the expectations that come with overseeing a larger program. Research on government websites has been very helpful in better understanding what is required for her non-profit program. In addition, because she is located within a church, the different types of liability insurance coverages have different expectations. She also has uncovered that insurance discounts have been applied due to the size of the policy already purchased by the church. She has double-checked that all state coverages were already in place and that the program appeared to be fully covered. She is starting to feel much better about this part of her responsibilities.

Petra

Petra, on the other hand, has decided that staying with a small program that cared for seven children is the best choice for her. She would only need to purchase an additional policy on top of what she is already paying for homeowner's insurance. After discussing dividing this expense among the interested parents who want her to care for their children, Petra and her friends have agreed that making sure that Petra, her family, and her friends' families are properly protected is important. They all also have become more aware of what this business venture would mean for Petra. The friends renewed their commitment to each other and to supporting Petra in opening her own family child care home business.

Reflect

There is so much to consider. In the case of Petra and the liability opening a child care program creates, would this be something that you would be willing to do?

Showcase Your Skills

As we discussed in this chapter, Johanna and David are beginning a new business by leasing an established center. That business is to provide an early childhood program to their community. As a hired consultant there are many things that need to be considered as next steps. Determining trends in an area as well as defining best practices to support children already in care, their families, developing procedures, and implementing new ideas are part of the consultant's job. After two years of leasing the program, the current owner has offered the option to purchase the business and building. Johanna and David are considering the buying process.

Based on the information shared in each section of this chapter, it is now your turn to serve in the role of consultant. Write a proposal using the following points as your guide.

1. Choose a strategy you would use to gather information about the child care needs of the community and surrounding area.
2. List pros and cons of Johanna and David to continuing to lease the program versus purchasing the program.
3. Create a list and rationale as to what additional programming needs they might consider, including cost considerations and likely sources of income.

Matching

Match the following terms with the correct definitions:

A. blended family	G. Montessori programs
B. child care cooperatives	H. nursery schools
C. drop-in care	I. out-of-school-time care
D. entrepreneur	J. sick child care
E. kith and kin care	
F. laboratory schools	

1. Type of child care that provides care for children when they are out of school.
2. Type of care program often located in or near shopping centers or recreational areas that allows parents to have a few hours to themselves while their children receive care in pleasant, well-supervised settings.
3. Person who is willing to expand an opportunity and invest their own time, money, and skills to get either their service or product in place.
4. Type of child care that provides supervision for children with mild conditions and low fevers related to illness not allowed within a child care setting.
5. New model of child care programs that are sponsored by parents, a business, or multiple businesses interested in providing care for a designated group of children.
6. Type of family that brings two unrelated families into one household.
7. Half-day programs that typically provide scheduled activity and curriculum opportunities for young children.
8. Child care programs that utilize special equipment designed to help children develop their sensory awareness and cognitive skills at their own pace.
9. Programs that exist for the primary purpose of training future teachers and studying child development and education.
10. Informal care of a small group of children provided by relatives or a friend that is mostly unlicensed.

Brief Contents

Unit 1

Establishing a Quality Child Care Program 2

Chapter 1	Quality Child Care: A Critical Need	3
Chapter 2	Child Care Programs	24
Chapter 3	Governance of Child Care Programs	43
Chapter 4	Facilities, Equipment, and Curriculum	59
Chapter 5	Staffing Costs and Considerations	79
Chapter 6	Budget and Finance	100
Chapter 7	Marketing and Planning for Enrollment	124

Unit 2

Administering a Quality Child Care Program 142

Chapter 8	Educational Programming	143
Chapter 9	Maintaining a Safe and Healthy Program	167
Chapter 10	Engaging and Supporting Families	194
Chapter 11	The Complex Role of Leading Others	212
Chapter 12	Supervising and Supporting Program Staff	236
Chapter 13	Managing People and Setting Expectations	251
Chapter 14	Supports for Director Success	268
Chapter 15	Program Evaluation to Support Quality Improvement	287

Contents

Unit 1

Establishing a Quality Child Care Program 2

Chapter 1
Quality Child Care:
A Critical Need 3

1.1 Societal Trends and the Need for Child Care 5
1.2 Community and Economic Considerations 7
1. 3 Types of Early Childhood Programs 12
1.4 The Early Childhood Program Leader 17

Chapter 2
Child Care Programs 24

2.1 Characteristics of a Quality Child Care Program. 25
2.2 Universal Program Practices 28
2.3 Elements of Age-Appropriate Programming 34
2.4 Family Child Care Home 38

Chapter 3
Governance of Child Care Programs 43

3.1 Why Is Regulatory Oversight Important? 44
3.2 Legal Concerns and Obligations of Operating a Program. 48
3.3 Quality Rating Systems 51
3.4 National Accreditation 54

Chapter 4
Facilities, Equipment, and Curriculum 59

4.1 Guidelines for Indoor and Outdoor Environments 60
4.2 Equipment Needs for Successful Indoor and Outdoor Spaces 67
4.3 Choosing Equipment for Varying Ages 70
4.4 Curriculum Considerations for Varying Ages 74

Chapter 5
Staffing Costs and Considerations 79

5.1 Characteristics of Quality Child Care Staff. 81
5.2 Organizational Structure. 84
5.3 Job Descriptions 86
5.4 Staff Recruitment 88
5.5 Selecting the Best Applicant 90
5.6 Staff Orientation 96

Chapter 6
Budget and Finance 100

6.1 Financial Planning for a New Program. 102
6.2 For-Profit and Not-For-Profit Status. 105
6.3 Developing a Budget 109
6.4 Budget Analyzing. 112
6.5 Financial Management 114
6.6 Needed Financial Services. 116
6.7 Purchasing Decisions 117

Chapter 7
Marketing and Planning for Enrollment 124

7.1 Public Relations and Marketing 125
7.2 Making the Program a Welcome Place for Parents. 131
7.3 Helping Parents Help Their Children 134
7.4 Helping Children and Families Adjust 136

Unit 2

Administering a Quality Child Care Program 142

Chapter 8
Educational Programming 143

8.1 Program Strategies Supporting Developmentally Appropriate Curriculum 145
8.2 Learning for All Ages Through Play 153
8.3 General Principles When Planning Daily Schedules 156
8.4 Appropriate Guidance Strategies for Young Children. 159

Chapter 9
Maintaining a Safe and Healthy
Program **167**
9.1 Planning for a Healthy and Safe
Environment 169
9.2 Establishing and Following Child Care
Health Policies and Practices 173
9.3 Food Safety and Proper Nutrition 177
9.4 Meeting the Special Health Needs of
Children and Staff 181
9.5 Preparing for Emergencies 183
9.6 Policies Concerning Child
Endangerment and Abuse 186
9.7 Why Does the Program Need a
Health and Safety Committee? 190

Chapter 10
Engaging and Supporting Families **194**
10.1 The Communication-Engagement
Connection 195
10.2 Strategies for Effective
Communication 197
10.3 Supporting Your Families
and Caregivers 203
10.4 Engaging Families and Caregivers 205

Chapter 11
The Complex Role of Leading Others **212**
11.1 Leadership Skills and Characteristics 214
11.2 Building and Maintaining a Healthy
Organizational Climate 223
11.3 Roles and Responsibilities of
the Early Childhood Leader 227
11.4 Utilizing the NAEYC Code
of Ethics 231

Chapter 12
Supervising and Supporting
Program Staff **236**
12.1 What Are Personnel Policies? 237

12.2 What Kinds of Personnel Actions
May Be Necessary? 242
12.3 How Can I Support a Positive
Working Environment? 243

Chapter 13
Managing People and Setting
Expectations **251**
13.1 Workplace Relationships 253
13.2 Conflict in Healthy Workplace
Environments 256
13.3 Conflict-Resolution Partnerships 258
13.4 Establishing Policies and
Procedures 260
13.5 Workplace Gossip and Bullying 263

Chapter 14
Supports for Director Success **268**
14.1 Establishing Professional Boundaries . . . 269
14.2 Recognizing the Daily Stress
of Managing Programs 273
14.3 Creating a Healthy Program
Environment for All to Thrive 277
14.4 Health and Mental Wellness
Supports 281

Chapter 15
Program Evaluation to Support
Quality Improvement **287**
15.1 Program Benefits for Children 289
15.2 Meeting the Needs of Families
and the Community 290
15.3 Supporting Staff in Their
Professional Development 293
15.4 Measuring Administrative Success 297
15.5 Quality Rating System Initiatives 298

References 302
For Further Reading 306
Glossary 309
Index 316

Feature Contents

Director's Showcase

Chapter 1 . . . . 5, 7, 12, 17, 18, 21

Chapter 2 . . . . 25, 28, 33, 34, 38, 39, 40

Chapter 3 . . . . 45, 48, 49, 50, 51, 54, 56

Chapter 4 . . . . 60, 67, 70, 71, 74, 75, 76

Chapter 5 . . . . 81, 84, 85, 86, 89, 90, 97

Chapter 6 . . . . 102, 105, 109, 112, 117, 120, 121

Chapter 7 . . . . 125, 130, 131, 134, 136, 139

Chapter 8 . . . . 145, 153, 155, 156, 159, 163, 164

Chapter 9 . . . . 168, 172, 173, 177, 181, 182, 183, 186, 190, 191

Chapter 10 . . . . 196, 197, 199, 200, 201, 202, 203, 205, 209

Chapter 11. . . . . 213, 222, 223, 227, 231, 233

Chapter 12 . . . . 237, 241, 243, 248

Chapter 13 . . . . 252, 255, 256, 257, 258, 259, 260, 262, 263, 265

Chapter 14 . . . . 269, 273, 277, 278, 280, 281, 284

Chapter 15 . . . . 289, 290, 292, 293, 296, 297, 298

UNIT **1**

Establishing a Quality Child Care Program

Chapter 1   Quality Child Care: A Critical Need

Chapter 2   Child Care Programs

Chapter 3   Governance of Child Care Programs

Chapter 4   Facilities, Equipment, and Curriculum

Chapter 5   Staffing Costs and Considerations

Chapter 6   Budget and Finance

Chapter 7   Marketing and Planning for Enrollment

lithiumcloud/iStock/Getty Images Plus

CHAPTER 1

Quality Child Care: A Critical Need

Learning Outcomes

After studying this chapter, you will be able to:

1.1 Identify the main factors that have led to a critical need for quality child care in America.

1.2 Analyze community and economic factors when determining the need for child care services in an area.

1.3 Distinguish the types of early childhood programs.

1.4 Describe the role of the early childhood program leader.

Key Terms

blended family
center-based care
Child Care and Development Fund (CCDF)
child care cooperatives
Child Care Resource and Referral (CCR&R)
Child Development Associate (CDA)
cohabitating parents
consortium model
director's credential
drop-in care
Early Head Start
elementary school
employee model
entrepreneur
Family and Medical Leave Act (FMLA)
Head Start
home-based care
kith and kin care
laboratory schools
Montessori programs
NAEYC Code of Ethical Conduct
networking
nursery schools
out-of-school-time care
parent model
preschool care
sick child care
staff-to-child ratios
subsidy voucher
Universal Pre-K

Introduction

The field of early childhood has come a long way since the 1960s. The care of young children evolved into an area of great interest to society as individual states attempted to license facilities caring for large groups of children to ensure that basic needs were met. In 1987, the National Association for the Education of Young Children (NAEYC) began to identify developmentally appropriate practices, better known as DAP. At the same time, accreditation standards were formulated by NAEYC that identified quality practices that programs must follow to be nationally recognized. As this trend continued to evolve, so did the research on early childhood settings and brain development of young children. On April 17, 1997, the importance of quality early childhood experiences for young children caught the attention of the

NAEYC/DAP standards

Standards covered in this chapter:

NAEYC

2c, 6b, 6c

White House. President Bill Clinton and First Lady Hilary Clinton hosted an event that focused on the brain development of young children. With the backing of significant research findings, it was then that society began to learn more about the importance of children's earliest experiences and how they must get off to a strong and healthy start.

Broad participation began sweeping across the nation. Federal and state funding was allocated to enhance basic licensing requirements for child care programs. This allowed for states to begin developing and launching Quality Rating and Improvement Systems (QRIS) better known today as Quality Rating Systems (QRS). It was these standards that the cost of quality discussions began resonating within the field of early childhood. More recently, in the past few years, the national spotlight has been placed on the need for child care to support parents' ability to work, while still providing quality care. This combination promotes parents' confidence in their child's care and made it so they could focus on successfully completing their own jobs.

At the beginning of each chapter, you will be introduced to early childhood leaders of varying program types and circumstances. It is through the experiences of these leaders who come from a variety of backgrounds and different stages in their careers, you will learn more about

- establishing and maintaining quality child care programs;
- different types of early childhood programs;
- necessary facility equipment and curriculum;
- staffing costs and considerations;
- budget and finance;
- marketing and planning for enrollment;
- educational programming;
- maintaining a safe and healthy program;
- engaging and supporting families;
- complexity of leading others;
- supervising and supporting program staff;
- managing difficult people and situations;
- supports for leadership success; and
- program evaluation to support quality improvement.

All of these areas will be discussed at length to help you better understand the complexity of becoming an administrator of an early childhood program. In addition, the balance of principles and practicality will provide the necessary information to you as you either determine whether this is a career you would like to pursue or to support you as a current early childhood leader.

1.1 Societal Trends and the Need for Child Care

Families of all kinds and sizes require child care in order to be productive and stable. They often depend on the support of relatives, neighbors, and friends to help care for their children. However, changing family structures, financial demands, and expanding career opportunities have made quality licensed child care a necessity for many families. The structural change of families; the type of jobs available to working parents; the lack of affordable, quality child care; and the pressures of modern life, including a global pandemic, have made successful parenting challenging.

Women Fully in the Work Force

Until the mid- to late 20th century, most women in the United States stayed home to care for their children. Women who did work usually gravitated toward what were considered to be traditionally female careers, such as nursing, teaching, or office administration. Most other choices were male-dominated and not readily accessible to women. Today, women are employed in every career field imaginable. World War II, the women's movement of the 1970s, federal antidiscrimination legislation, and

Director's Showcase

Johanna and David

Johanna and David have recently taken over a small child care center in the suburbs of a big city. They both have experience in child care and previously worked together at a large child care center. Johanna will be in the director's role, and David will be in charge of maintenance, transportation, and any other areas of need. They are excited to be small business owners. However, they feel pressure to succeed and provide quality child care to their community. They are aware many new businesses have opened in their area and want to better understand what type of care families need.

the need for women in the workforce are some of the factors that brought about this change. Expanded opportunities for jobs in fields that had historically been closed to women are now providing them with challenging and financially rewarding opportunities (Motherly, 2019). However, the flexibility and support needed for working mothers is still a major social and political issue in the United States.

As more women are continuing their education beyond the secondary level, women who have spent time and money to prepare for a challenging career still face the problems of finding affordable, quality child care and balancing work and family life (Matthews & Hamilton, 2016). There has been some movement in Congress to help working parents, including the **Family and Medical Leave Act (FMLA)**, which entitles eligible employees of covered employers to take unpaid, job-protected leave for the birth of a child, to include the care of a newborn child within one year of birth.

At the other end of this spectrum, women with little education or low socioeconomic backgrounds have fewer job opportunities, even at an unskilled level. Without adequately paying jobs, single mothers may receive public assistance and participate in job training programs. Trainees who have young children may require child care in order to participate in these programs. Introduced in 1996, the **Child Care and Development Fund (CCDF)** is a consolidated fund of multiple federal dollar streams that go directly to states. These funds support low-income families and are administered by the Office of Child Care within the Department of Health and Human Services in each state.

Women and their role in the workplace have certainly shifted over the decades. Each time women's care of their children has become a social issue, this has been highly debated within the political landscape. For the family unit, this becomes a tough decision made by the woman either on her own or with a significant other. Having quality, affordable, child care options allows women to develop interesting, satisfying careers. Some are reluctant to risk losing opportunities by staying home when their children are young. This issue and the growing cost of living has placed the burden on the home that requires two incomes to support basic needs.

Two-Income Families

Economic conditions have made it more difficult for young families to establish comfortable standards of living. Many of the new jobs created are minimum wage jobs with costly health insurance options. Young families, especially those headed by individuals without special job skills or advanced education, find it difficult to survive financially without income from both partners.

Even when both parents are working at minimum wage jobs, the family will still have an income level that is below the federal poverty standards (Rnaji & Salganicoff, 2014).

Many Americans have dreams of home ownership, a college education for their children, adequate health and retirement benefits, a comfortable lifestyle, and financial stability. These have become increasingly difficult to achieve on a single income. Young adults find it difficult to succeed in paying for living and household expenses while paying off student loan debt. For many young families, building a family life similar to what they experienced growing up requires the income of two working parents. When both parents work similar hours outside the home, reliable child care becomes a necessity (US Census Bureau, 2018).

Many college-educated, dual-income couples choose to delay parenthood until their careers are well established. It is not uncommon for couples in their thirties to start families. At this point in their lives, these families often have an established lifestyle and financial security that they are unwilling to jeopardize. Although the "juggling act" required to balance career and parenthood is difficult and stressful, these families feel it is worth it. These families rely on a quality, reliable child care provider to care for their children while both parents continue working.

Modern Family Structures

Many children are growing up in single-parent households either as a result of separation, divorce, death, or legal and life circumstances. Single head of household, same sex parent families, and grandparents raising grandchildren make up the modern family structure as well. In these cases, the custodial parent often has to work outside of the home, creating a necessity for child care. Death of a spouse, either due to long-term illness or unexpected event, creates many pressures for the remaining parent. Life circumstances may create family separations whether due to a job transfer, frequent travel obligations, or the need to care for elderly family members. In addition, military commitments, job training opportunities, or parental incarceration may also separate families. In some of these cases, children will spend their entire childhood with only one parent available to them. This parent must provide family income, nurturance, guidance, and basic care. Under the best of situations, single parenthood is hard work and partnering with the program is essential. It can often be stressful for both parent and child.

There has also been an increase in the number of families with cohabitating or unmarried parents. **Cohabitating parents** are those individuals who share a biological child, or one parent is the biological parent of the

child, and live with a significant other, but are not necessarily married. For example, in 2016 the number of cohabitating parents raising children has contributed to the overall growth in unmarried parenthood (Livingston, 2018). Further, four in ten births were to women who were either single mothers or living with a non-marital partner (Livingston, 2018). Typically, cohabitating parents are younger on average than married parents and have lower levels of educational attainment (Livingston, 2018). This includes having a high school diploma or less education in comparison to solo parents and married parents. However, the economic situation for these parents is dependent on their circumstances and support of those around them to include family and friends.

Blended families are very common in today's society. A **blended family** is one that brings two families together into one household. These families do not "blend" overnight, and many times it takes several years for the growing pains of coming together to be resolved. Parents in these situations are often dealing with child attention issues, sibling rivalry, and differences between how each parent chooses to discipline. Typically in these households, there is opportunity for bonding between the blended family members.

Grandparents are oftentimes the "safety-net" for grandchildren when parents cannot care for them (**Figure 1.1**). This may happen due to hardships or an unsafe environment in relation to a parent's substance abuse or violent behavior. Stressors that may affect these grandparents include legal issues, financial strain, a lack of understanding of modern child development, behavioral issues, and a safe place to express the emotions involved in raising grandchildren. While potentially overwhelming, grandparents should have access to resources in their community, including child care, to

PeopleImages/iStock/Getty Images Plus

Figure 1.1 Grandparents provide care for grandchildren when parents are not available to care for them.

help support them in their role as caregiver. Due to the structures of today's modern family, there is an obvious need for care of young children.

Shortage of Skilled Workers

The population aged 65 and older increased 36 percent between 2009 and 2019 (Administration for Community Living). People are living longer, and many are moving out of the workforce into retirement. In contrast, fewer young people are approaching adulthood and moving into the workforce. This creates a knowledge gap and a need for those entering the workforce to participate in ongoing education and professional development. A labor shortage means that there simply won't be enough trained people to fill all of the jobs that will need to be done (Panday & Bovino, 2017). At the same time, young adults with little education, job skills, or training who find work fulfilling the most menial of jobs at the lowest wages will encounter challenges accessing and paying for quality child care.

Census statistics and school enrollments are sources that portray a reasonably accurate representation of the number of people at each age level. These statistics indicate how many people are growing up, going to school, pursuing advanced education, or dropping out each year. For example, 90 percent of the American population aged 25 and older completed high school or higher levels of education in 2017 (Schmidt, 2018). While these statistics reflect many who are pursuing an advanced education or skilled workers such as those who work in trades as an electrician or plumber, there is concern that the shortage of skilled workers in these and many other fields will harm the vitality of the US economy (Banday & Povino, 2017). Should that take place, the need for child care within the community could potentially drop.

Another trend that has created a shortage of skilled workers is one parent choosing to stay home and care for their young children, partially due to the high cost of quality child care. Employers recognize these parents as a valuable labor source. However, due to either inadequate child care choice or the cost of quality child care in the area, many parents are unable or unwilling to return to work (Matos, Galinsky, & Bond, 2017). As employers begin to consider ways to bring these skilled workers back into the workforce, child care has been identified as a major draw. This has resulted in many employers taking an active role to partner with local early childhood programs. In addition, employers often access their state-funded **Child Care Resource and Referral (CCR&R)** agency to locate child care services within the community and in many regions of a particular state that participate in the program.

Director's Showcase
Reflect
What are the trends in society that Johanna and David need to consider as they better understand the need of families seeking child care in their community?

1.2 Community and Economic Considerations

Before decisions are made about the type of service offered at a child care facility, it is important to carefully gather information about the community and local families. Questions about location, hours, tuition, and type of services to offer cannot be answered until more information is available. Accurate information is essential to start a successful early childhood program. This includes considering the economic geography, the area's economic factors, family characteristics, and the tools necessary to gather this information.

Geographically, there are several factors to investigate about the community, starting with a detailed map. Use a map to gain knowledge of the area and locate sites that will influence the demand for child care. Utilize internet searches to uncover the location of major employers, housing within the area, **elementary school** locations that typically serve children ages Pre-Kindergarten to fourth grade, and existing early childhood programs (**Figure 1.2**).

Director's Showcase
Johanna and David
Since Johanna and David leased an existing child care center, they had an established client base and many experienced staff who remained after the transfer of leadership. They had to evaluate the needs of their community in order to fill open enrollment spots and hire a few new teachers and support staff. Because of recent economic growth and new business in their area, they needed to discover the child care needs of their community. They needed to know more about the community surrounding them before making changes to the existing program and making it their own.

FreshSplash/E+/Getty Images

Figure 1.2 Performing in-depth internet searches assists with uncovering important information when making decisions about where to locate a child care program.

Area Employment Opportunities

Begin by identifying the location of the main business areas and other major employers. Consider the following questions:

- Where are the shopping districts or restaurants?
- Where are the large factories, call centers, industrial and office parks, warehouses, or professional buildings?
- Where are the hospitals or nursing homes?
- Where are the grocery stores and schools?

These are the areas in a community where numerous people work. Consider the hours when these sites are open or in operation. Any type of early childhood program will need to match the hourly needs of working parents who use the program. You may also check with the local Chamber of Commerce for facts about businesses and agencies in the community. The chamber or a thorough internet search may provide population

data, spending patterns, current and anticipated business activity, and local census data. This information will help you identify growth in certain sections of choosing to locate. New businesses will be hiring workers as well as attracting families to the area, many who may need child care.

Neighborhoods

When considering the location of a child care facility, identify the housing areas and which neighborhoods have young families. First, look at average home prices. Neighborhoods even with a town or small city vary widely according to the average age and income of the residents. The average home prices in a particular area can provide clues as to whether that neighborhood attracts dual-career families, first-time buyers, or young families. Some neighborhoods are popular choices for commuters who travel daily to jobs in nearby cities. Others may appeal to low- to moderate-income families. To learn more about the local population and neighborhoods, you may also search the state education department public records for information concerning school enrollments (**Figure 1.3**). This will provide you with data on where families with young children are currently living within an area.

Area Child Care Programs

Choosing the best spot for your children's care facility also depends upon identifying where other child care centers are located. You will need to determine what types of care are offered and whether or not each program has a waiting list. If possible, tour each facility and meet and network with the child care administrators in your prospective area. **Networking** allows professionals in the same field to exchange information, offer advice, and provide referrals to other resources within your area

Mark Baldwin/Shutterstock.com

Figure 1.3 Identifying neighborhoods within an area assists with determining geographic locations to consider when setting up a child care program.

or field. The goal when networking is to build relationships that have the same common goal—to care for the children and families in the area together. Network contacts can serve as sources of new information, can help identify trends, and may even help identify trouble areas before they become larger issues. Keeping in touch with others who have the same types of responsibilities, frustrations, and concerns can give new ideas and help keep problems in perspective.

To research the size of child care facilities in the area and if they are participating in state-supported initiatives, go online and check the child care licensing. Your search results will inform you whether quality child care is a staple within the community and what the expectations will be for your program as well.

Economic Opportunities

Any type of early childhood program is an expensive service to provide, especially infant and toddler care, due to the small group size and low staff-to-child ratios. The cost incurred by parents can be upwards of a mortgage payment per month (Bump, 2018). Infant and toddler care is typically in high demand, but also a service that programs struggle to balance within their budgets. Child care facilities must balance the cost of providing services with what families in their area can afford.

As you consider facility locations, research the overall economic conditions of the local community. Some areas are booming, while others are not. Some areas may be experiencing a period of high unemployment, low incomes, and depressed job opportunities. Other communities may be growing with increasing demands for workers, the development of new shopping facilities, and a healthy housing market. A community where young families are leaving because there are no job opportunities for them may not be the ideal market for a new child care facility. The Chamber of Commerce is a helpful resource for information about the local economy.

Keep in mind the long-term employment possibilities in the area. Questions to consider include

- What can you find out about the job stability in the target area?
- Will the program attract employees of a particular industry and is that industry doing well?
- Will employees need around the clock shift care for their children?
- Have the employees just had a recent contract settlement?
- Is this an industry that has a history of going on strike?
- Does it appear the industry is growing, or is it laying off workers?
- Is the industry attracting new families to move into the area because of the availability of jobs?

- Do the jobs provided by the local industries pay high salaries, or are they mostly minimum wage jobs?
- Who are the major employers in the area, and what is the outlook for them?
- What are the major roads that people use to get to their jobs?

When considering whether or not to start a child care program, it will be key to learn about the financial capability of the residents in the area. Many programs are fully funded by tuition. Determining if there are enough families who will be able to pay that tuition will be essential. In a lower income neighborhood, there may not be enough families who can afford the cost of care. A higher income neighborhood may be populated by older families with no need for child care. If the program is located where it can draw from families who represent a broader spectrum of income levels, it is more likely to have a clientele that can afford the program cost per week.

An additional area of consideration is the ability to recruit and employ staff to work within the program. While this will be discussed in later chapters, it is common knowledge that salaries within the field are typically lower and it is often difficult to attract personnel. Many times the benefits seen by those who work in early childhood is the discount in care for their own children, ability to be where their children are cared for, and an overall interest in serving family and children in the local community (Thomason et al., 2018). Overall, if the labor market is generally healthy, there will be interested people in the area who are seeking opportunities to work within the early childhood field.

Family Requirements

Planning a program to meet family needs requires knowledge about the families in the area (**Figure 1.4**). Accurately determining their needs and wants increases

Figure 1.4 There are many types of families looking for child care. This includes one- and two-parent households.

your likelihood of planning a successful program. You will want to create a clear picture of the variety of services families desire and an estimate of how many children are likely to participate. For example, if you plan to open a preschool center for children ages three to five, but most area families need care for infants or toddlers, you may have trouble filling your program. If there is a high demand for before and after school care, your program could miss out on a potential enrollment opportunity if you do not offer this service.

Preferred Types of Care

Parents have definite preferences for the child care their children receive. Some parents favor a family child care home, while others look for the stimulation of extensive daily programs usually found in a large early childhood program. Some parents like to be involved in the program, while others do not have the time for consistent in-person participation. Some parents prefer large, multiple-age centers so they can enroll all their children at the same location. In other situations, parents may not mind having their preschool child at a child care facility while their toddler is enrolled in a nearby family child care home. Families are more likely to utilize school-age programs that are located in or near the children's schools.

Amount of Care Needed

Some families need full-time child care. Others need care only on a part-time basis. Some parents are employed on weekends or evenings, but others may work varying shifts. If you can determine there is a clear indication of need for a center with weekend hours, you may want to consider this option. However, if there is almost no demand for weekend care, the decision is easy to not offer it. Some centers are open 24 hours. Checking into other programs' operating hours in the area can assist with this process. State Resource and Referral agencies can assist with identifying local employer's needs for employee child care. To be successful, the hours must match the needs of parents who will use the program.

Program Service Needs

The needs of families vary. A program that can provide services to meet a variety of these needs will be popular. Some families might sign their children up for special lessons or use occasional evening care for special events. If parents have no way to get their children from the school to the location of an after-school program, transportation to and from the school would be a desired service. If a competing child care center provides transportation and your program does not, then there will be a probable loss of children to the other center. On the other hand, if only one family requires school transportation service, it may not be profitable to offer it.

SDI Productions/E+/Getty Images

Figure 1.5 Many child care programs provide parent education events. Child development topics assist parents as they learn more about how to best care for their child.

Parent education classes can be popular (**Figure 1.5**). Parents often feel a need for more information about effective parenting. Trying to work and balance family demands can be difficult and frustrating. For many parents, having a chance to meet with others who are experiencing the same feelings, or whose children are the same ages, can be a helpful experience. Some centers sponsor parent education programs during lunchtime. For example, a parent educator could lead group discussions either in-person or via video conference about various topics of concern. Because the event can be open to the community, events like this could serve to introduce families to the early childhood program, which may lead to future enrollment.

There are a number of other services that can be offered to meet the needs of busy, working families. Some programs have cooperative arrangements with local dance or karate schools. Centers may link up with the local scouting and 4-H programs to provide these activities for school-age children. Music lessons, gymnastics, dance, tutoring, dry cleaning service, and meal catering can also be offered. Working families often have a difficult time scheduling all of the things they want for their children. A program can facilitate lessons and special activities for the children in their care.

Tools to Use When Gathering Necessary Information

It is crucial to find out about the needs and resources of the families interested in using the early childhood program. A successful program must be developed around the needs of the families you want to serve. This includes financial considerations such as interested families' ability to afford the tuition charged for their children. If the program will depend solely on tuition, there must be enough interested families who will be able to pay the fees.

A program may serve families who receive state-issued **subsidy vouchers**, which are vouchers provided by the government, typically through the state's Department of Human Services, as support for part of the tuition that a parent qualifies to receive, the amount of which is typically lower than the rate charged by the program. The subsidy program would determine if the parent would pay a copayment to the program based on a sliding fee scale. The principle of this program is that families receiving subsidies should have "equal access" to child care that is comparable to the care available to non-subsidized children. Participation by the early childhood program means following the government regulations and policies and receiving the tuition after the child care services are rendered which could be a 30- to- 45-day lag in time.

In addition to researching economic factors, it will be useful to determine specific background information about the area where the program will be located. Using tools such as questionnaires, online surveys, or public meetings where the program will be located will require some effort to obtain useful information about patterns and trends in an area along with parents giving information about their family needs.

Background Research

Begin your background research by identifying the agencies or businesses within the community that are responsive to local patterns and trends. The local newspaper, internet sources with city and state data, school district personnel, the community planning agency, the regional Cooperative Extension office, and the local Chamber of Commerce are good sources of information. All of these have an interest in the characteristics of the community and its families. Analyzing data from the most recent government census indicates patterns of growth and decline in various geographic areas. The census also provides information on family size and economic data. Interviewing local health officials may be able to give you insights into the characteristics of their clients. Religious leaders can offer information about their organization. Neighborhood store owners often have insights into the needs of families in their area. While it takes time and effort to set up interviews, the information gained can be very valuable information with which to make decisions.

Network with the early childhood programs in the area. Many quality programs have waiting lists with names of children for whom there is no room. Program leaders in this situation find it frustrating to know there are children needing care who cannot be placed in their program. While some program leaders may be threatened by the possible opening of a new program, explaining the overall intent of the program often assists in building the relationship. Once established, the program leader is more willing to help get the program started. A word of caution, if there are several centers in a community and no waiting list, attracting enough children to be successful in a new program might be challenging.

Questionnaires, Online Surveys, and Parent Meetings

Two strategies to consider are the use of a questionnaire or online survey. These are often a helpful tool in determining whether there is a need for child care services. Contacting businesses in the area to inquire if they would distribute the information to their employees is a great starting point when using these methods. Other considerations are specific neighborhood associations, religious organizations, clubs, or stores. Be prepared to provide up-front information about the desire to provide an early childhood program to serve families in the area and to determine if the need exists.

Keep in mind that responding to a questionnaire or online survey is voluntary on the part of the participants. Therefore, questions should reflect concern for children and their families, sensitivity, anti-bias, and commitment to quality care. If parents feel they will be criticized for their answers or be pestered for a commitment, they are unlikely to respond. If parents feel that the questions are too personal or too "nosy," the information gathered will be limited. Even families who need child care may be reluctant to answer a questionnaire or survey if they know nothing about who is planning to operate the center.

After describing the intent of the questionnaire or online survey, questions must be written carefully so that the responses are meaningful. Questions should be clear, concise, and user-friendly so that parents are willing to answer them. Items to address in a typical questionnaire or survey include

- number and ages of children in the family;
- information about parent work hours;
- type of care needed;
- location of employer and hours worked;
- need for a program's location, hours, and tuition;
- the number of wage earners in a family; and
- schools that older children attend.

Once this information is collected, compiling the information gives another data point, which is very helpful when determining next steps for the placement of an early childhood program within a community.

Another strategy is public meetings or hosting a community event. Many employers, homeowner's associations, local libraries, community centers, rotary clubs, and religious organizations are willing to host a meeting for all those who are interested in child care. The meeting should be organized so it will be convenient, both in

Director's Showcase
Reflect
What strategies might Johanna and David use to find out more about the needs of their community? How would they use this information to help them build enrollment within their program?

Director's Showcase
Johanna and David
The small child care center that Johanna and David took over did not offer care to children under the age of one. Based on feedback from community surveys and information they gathered from meeting with new business owners in their area, Johanna and David decided to add an infant room to their center. To add a new room, they had to re-evaluate their current setup and utilize all the space available in the building.

Using his skills in carpentry, David made a suitable space for the new classroom. Johanna received positive feedback from the many parents and caregivers with children enrolled in the program. There was a need for infant care for siblings of the children in the program and quite a few pregnant mothers were relieved not to have to find another place for care after the birth of their babies.

time and location, for potential client families to attend. As with questionnaires or online surveys, gathering the same types of information mentioned would help to identify the kinds of programs or services families need.

Considerations When Analyzing Needs and Predicting Future Trends
Once the research and all the necessary data points have been gathered, this input can be used in the next phase of the decision-making process. When reviewing the data, keep in mind that it reflects a snapshot of information. Data always changes due to the many influences and variables in and around each of us. For example, not everyone who responds to surveys or attends meetings will actually follow through by enrolling children in the program. There is a time lapse where a family may have already found suitable care. Due to many factors, these families may have based their decisions on a change in employment situation or child care may be needed for different hours than what was originally indicated. While data is important, use it as one of the many tools described in this section when making decisions about the future of opening a child care program.

1.3 Types of Early Childhood Programs
Early childhood programs in the United States exist in many different formats. NAEYC uses the term, "early childhood programs" in reference to all types of care provided for children ages newborn to eight. In addition, they are strong advocates for creating equitable learning opportunities for young children. When these opportunities are provided, children thrive based on their uniqueness, family strengths, cultural backgrounds, respect for home languages, experiences, and abilities. In addition, NAEYC has worked to create a national accreditation system for programs, established professional principles and ethical standards, to provide opportunities to empower the early childhood profession for teachers and directors, to supply guidance to state systems, and to support the field of early childhood.

Types of Care
There are early childhood programs that operate for profit, and those that are organized as not-for-profit. Some programs depend financially on the tuition charged. Others receive public funds, referred to as subsidies, that are designed to assist low-income parents who have trouble finding affordable child care. These payments are provided directly to the program by the state on a monthly basis. Programs may be privately owned, sponsored by religious organizations, community organizations, or the government. They can be organized by a group of parents or provided by an employer. In some parts of the country, parents have many choices when searching for infant and toddler settings while in other locations there may be very few options for parents. In some areas of the country, quality child care for children is scarce.

Programs for young children can differ in a variety of ways. The goals of the program, hours of operation, age of children enrolled, and location of the program (either home- or center-based) may vary. **Staff-to-child ratios** and group size are mandated by state regulatory agencies that measure the number of children for whom each adult in the classroom is responsible (**Figure 1.6**). Within a community, there may be many different types of early childhood programs for young children. While each type of program has some specific characteristics, the basic components of quality programming and good care for children are basically the same. For the purpose of this discussion, the types of care will be classified as home-based or center-based. Special-purpose programs will also be described.

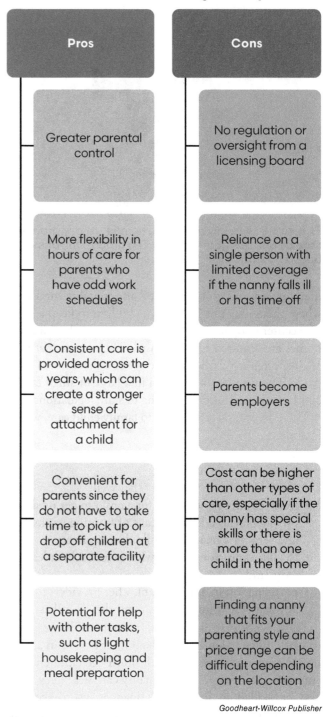

Lostinbids/E+/Getty Images

Figure 1.6 All states require that children be cared for in limited group sizes by designated adults based on the age range of the children being supervised.

Home-Based Care

Many parents prefer **home-based care**, which is care provided in a home setting. This typically is care for infants and toddlers due to the feeling of warmth and intimacy. Upholstered furniture, drapes, and good smells from the kitchen all create an atmosphere of nurturance. Home-based care is less likely to have an "institutional" feel to it. Types of home-based care include nannies, family child care homes, and kith and kin arrangements.

Nannies

Most parents of very young children would prefer having professional nannies come to their homes to care for their children (**Figure 1.7**). This way, the child has one consistent caregiver, avoids long commutes, and is always in a familiar environment. If a family has several young children, in-home care can prevent the early-morning pressures of trying to get everyone up and ready to leave the house. The caregiver can take care of breakfast and early-morning routines in a more relaxed manner. Many nannies stay with a family until the children are all in school. They may become lifelong friends of the family. Parents often hope to find someone who will also prepare meals and do light house cleaning.

Most child care experts agree that when in-home care works well, it is highly desirable for families and young children. Nanny-training programs have been developed in schools and community colleges. A nanny provides the benefits of in-home care along with specialized training in the child development field. Placement agencies exist to screen both the family who is recruiting and the potential nanny. Good agencies review the qualities that the family wants, find suitable candidates, and review backgrounds and references. The agency also develops a contract that provides protection for both the family and nanny. Many families opt for nannies who provide

Pros and Cons of Hiring a Nanny

Pros	Cons
Greater parental control	No regulation or oversight from a licensing board
More flexibility in hours of care for parents who have odd work schedules	Reliance on a single person with limited coverage if the nanny falls ill or has time off
Consistent care is provided across the years, which can create a stronger sense of attachment for a child	Parents become employers
Convenient for parents since they do not have to take time to pick up or drop off children at a separate facility	Cost can be higher than other types of care, especially if the nanny has special skills or there is more than one child in the home
Potential for help with other tasks, such as light housekeeping and meal preparation	Finding a nanny that fits your parenting style and price range can be difficult depending on the location

Goodheart-Willcox Publisher

Figure 1.7 Choosing child care is a tough decision for many parents. Some look at the pros and cons of hiring a nanny.

scheduled in-home care, but may or may not live with the family, and may be paid hourly or by salary.

Family Child Care Homes

This type of care takes place in a provider's home. The family child care home provider usually cares for several children possibly of varying ages. Family child care is often

kate_sept2004/E+/Getty Images

Figure 1.8 A family child care home typically provides care by one designated adult. The group size varies based on state regulations.

used for very young children. It is also found in rural areas where there may not be enough children to keep a child care center in operation. In many states, family child care homes are required to be licensed. This means that they are inspected regularly and held to state-determined standards. The number of children in a large or small family child care home varies according to state regulations.

There are several advantages to family child care, which include

- a homelike atmosphere;
- a low number of children;
- children get to know each other well;
- fewer children and adults for a child to get used to;
- providers who take advantage of training workshops and seminars related to child development;
- flexible hours for parents whose work schedules vary; and
- participation in a network of other providers to advocate for young children and their families.

Those who serve in this role must be skilled enough to work independently or with another person in a large home situation, work well with multi-age children, and committed to maintaining a quality care site. They must also be skilled in budgeting, finance, record-keeping, maintenance, and repair. A family child care home provider is typically on their own to maintain all aspects of this small business (**Figure 1.8**).

Kith and Kin Care

In some states, relatives, friends, or neighbors can legally care for a small number of children—usually no more than three—without any type of registration or state license. These arrangements, referred to as **kith and kin care**, are typically relatives or a friend who provide informal care for a small group of children which, in most states, is unlicensed care. There is no oversight by any licensing

agency and the parent must monitor the care that the child is receiving. The caregiver usually has no specific training in child development, nor are they linked to any ongoing training opportunities that state-licensed facilities are mandated to obtain on a yearly basis. Many times, these arrangements are made by parents for their children due to limited funds to pay for someone to take care of their child. In some states, subsidies will pay for the care of the child and this support and process is typically managed by the Department of Human Services within a state.

Center-Based Care

Care for larger groups of children in settings that have been organized specifically for their use is classified as **center-based care**. These facilities are licensed by the state in which they operate and provide daily programming of appropriate activities carried out by trained staff members who work within environments that have adequate equipment, and safe, healthy routines. The typical term referred to within society is child care centers. Types of center-based care include

- infant-toddler care;
- preschool;
- out-of-school-time care;
- nursery school or parents-day-out;
- laboratory schools;
- child care cooperatives;
- Montessori;
- Early Head Start and Head Start;
- elementary school; and
- sick child care.

Infant and Toddler Care

The demand for quality center-based care for infants and toddlers is high (**Figure 1.9**). However, families typically

ibnjaafar/E+/Getty Images

Figure 1.9 Quality care for infants and toddlers is very costly to parents and also to the program providing the care due to the small group and ratio of adults to care for them.

Ratio of Children to Adults and Group Sizes Based on Age*				
Infants	Toddlers (ages 12 to 36 months)	Children (ages 30 months to five years)	Kindergartners	School-age Children (ages six to eight)
Ratio: 1:4	Ratio: 1:6	Ratio: 1:10	Ratio: 1:12	Ratio: 1:15
Max group size: 8 children	Max group size: 12 children	Max group size: 20 children	Max group size: 24 children	Max group size: 30 children

* Numbers based on NAEYC standards, and can vary from state to state. Be sure to locate accurate information from the state in which your program resides.

Goodheart-Willcox Publisher

Figure 1.10 Staff-to-child ratios vary from state to state. It is important to access state licensing regulations to obtain correct guidance.

struggle to afford the true cost of this care in most communities (Workman & Jessen-Howard, 2018). Typically housed within a child care center that provides preschool and school-age care that offsets the cost, these programs have small group sizes and the ratio of adults to children must be low. While state guidelines provide minimum care standards and vary in ratio and group size specifications, NAEYC (2018) standards recommend a 1:4 ratio for infants with a maximum group size of eight children. For toddlers aged 12 to 36 months, the expectation is 1:6 with a class size of no more than 12 children (NAEYC, 2018). (**Figure 1.10**) This makes the cost of staffing high. Many advocates continue to push for a significant and ongoing public investment to pay for the true cost of providing high-quality care for infants and toddlers.

Preschool Care

As an extension to the care of infants and toddlers, centers provide **preschool care**, which is programming for children ages three to five years. Minimum staff to child ratios are also set by state requirements, while NAEYC has expectations that children who are 30 months to five years of age be cared for with a 1:10 ratio and a maximum group size of 20 children (NAEYC, 2018). While manageable from a fiscal perspective, cost for this programming can also be expensive for parents. In addition, there has been a sweeping movement across the nation to provide Pre-K programs in public schools for children who are four years old by the state cut-off date. Since this service is offered for "free," and in most cases are "full-day" programs, most parents choose this option to assist with their family budget. In response to this, some programs have had to change their programming to provide transportation to the schools and provide before-and-after school care or collaborate with the local school district and house a Pre-K program at their child care center location. Savvy directors partner with their local school districts to support their community needs.

Out-of-School-Time Care

The need for **out-of-school-time care**, which provides care for children when they are out of school, has risen significantly over the years. The typical school day does not usually match the workday of employed parents. Growing concern over the well-being of children in self-care has led more families to recognize the value of organized school-age child care (**Figure 1.11**). This care can be provided at a child care center that provides transportation to and from the local school. This programming helps to defray the costs incurred by providing infant and toddler care. Also regulated by state minimum standards, NAEYC (2018) supports a 1:12 ratio for kindergarten-age children with a maximum group size of 24 children, and school-age children ages six to eight years, a 1:15 ratio with a maximum group size of 30 children. During summer break and other days when elementary schools are closed, the program can expand to function on a full-day basis for an extra fee.

NickyLloyd/E+/Getty Images

Figure 1.11 Care for school-age children is important. It allows children to be supervised, and to participate in scheduled and safe activity rather than going home to be unsupervised until a parent arrives.

Nursery School

Nursery schools are half-day programs that typically provide scheduled activity and curriculum opportunities for young children. They have existed in the United States since the early 1900s and are chosen by parents who do not need full-day child care. Most nursery schools use tuition as the main source of income. The types of programs found in nursery schools are generally play-based and consistent with the principles of NAEYC's developmentally appropriate practices statement. Preschool children, ages three to five, are the typical age served. This is why the term "preschool" is often used interchangeably with the term "nursery school."

Drop-In Care

Many families do not need care on a regular basis. **Drop-in care** programs, such as parent-day-out, meet the need for occasional care and are popular. Centers with these programs are often located in or near shopping centers, fitness clubs, or other recreational areas. They allow parents to have a few hours to themselves while their children receive care in a pleasant, well-supervised setting. Resorts, hospitals, or convention centers often provide these services to support clientele utilizing their facilities. Depending on the hours and location, such as a program located at a school or college and the caregiver is on campus, that the service is open, state licensing is necessary.

Laboratory Schools

Laboratory schools or "lab schools" are programs that exist for the primary purpose of training future teachers and studying child development and education. Since they are affiliated with colleges, universities, vocational schools, high schools, community colleges, or other training and research institutions, they have a reputation in the community for offering high-quality programs. These model programs demonstrate appropriate ways of working with children. Some lab schools offer full-day programs and also may serve a child care role for parents. Others operate on a half-day basis and serve as nursery schools.

Child Care Cooperatives

Child care cooperatives are a new model of child care programs that have surfaced in the past several years that are sponsored by parents, a business, or multiple businesses interested in providing child care for a designated group of children. These programs can be offered in a variety of different structures, including a parent model, an employee model, and a consortium model.

- The **parent model** involves parents who have formed a cooperative to provide care for their children. Membership fees are typically applied to the capitalization of the facility, including setting up a board to oversee the professional management of the program.
- In the **employee model**, a business provides the space and initial financing to make a child care facility operable. Then, the operation and ownership of the facility are given to the employees of the business.
- The **consortium model** is composed of multiple businesses working together within industrial parks or commercial developments to establish a child care facility as a benefit for the employees within these areas. The program is essentially owned by a group of employers or organizations that provide start-up capital, a designated space, and the hiring of outside management to operate the program.

Cooperatives have flourished across the United States with the goals of supporting the workforce, allowing flexibility, and enhancing benefits to support parents while attracting and maintaining the employee base.

Montessori School

Many Montessori schools are privately owned and operated. They follow the philosophy and curriculum developed by Dr. Maria Montessori in Italy around 1908. **Montessori programs** utilize special equipment designed to help children develop their sensory awareness and cognitive skills at their own pace. Montessori teachers have specific training, and the Montessori approach has some similarities to NAEYC's developmentally appropriate practices. Both emphasize respect for each child as a unique individual and view children as eager learners. However, the two philosophies differ considerably in their approach to daily programming. Montessori programs allow and encourage children to explore the world around them and is a child-led program, differing from other types of care that are more structured.

Early Head Start and Head Start

The **Head Start** program began in 1965 and receives funding from the federal government. It is specifically designed to provide a preschool experience for children from families of low income. It can be a full- or half-day program that includes breakfast and a hot lunch, medical and dental services, parent education and involvement, and educational programming designed to help prepare children for school. **Early Head Start**, launched in 1995, serves children from birth to three years old, and provides the same benefits as the Head Start program, including developmentally appropriate programming.

Depending on the community and sponsor organization, some Early Head Start and Head Start programs are year-round or may operate only on the local school schedule. Both programs have proven to be successful in helping children from families of low income successfully transition to school programs.

Universal Pre-K

Many school districts have **Universal Pre-K** programs, which offer no-cost programming at schools for children four to five years old, kindergartens, and grades first through third, which typically serve children ages four to eight years old. These programs are paid for through federal and state government dollars and housed in school buildings staffed by school district teachers. Or, in some cases, community partnerships with local centers are formed and Universal Pre-K or kindergarten classrooms are housed within the child care center. Universal Pre-K began as a movement by early childhood education experts and advocates who wanted to make preschool available to every child in the United States. Supported by NAEYC, the intent is to provide opportunities for all children to achieve their potential by engaging them early within educational systems. However, the debate continues about providing necessary developmentally appropriate programming for four- and five-year-olds rather than some of the recent trends to "push down" higher-grade course curriculum. Private schools also provide Pre-K and kindergarten programs through tuition-based funding.

Sick Child Care

Another type of program that exists in some areas across the United States are programs that provide **sick child care** for particular groups of children and families. This care provides supervision for children with mild conditions and low fevers related to illness not allowed within a child care setting. Most parents find their child care arrangements break down when their children are sick. Their usual center cannot handle children with illness. This has led to the growth of centers for sick children (**Figure 1.12**). Some of these are housed in hospitals and staffed by nurses. In general, they do not provide care for seriously ill children. Some resemble a hospital setting while others have made an effort to look like a regular early childhood classroom. Overall, they play a role in helping parents who cannot be absent from work. Sick care usually charges a very high fee. Employers who cannot afford to have their employees miss work are sometimes willing to share the cost of the care. While there are not a lot of sick child care centers, they can usually be found in urban areas and are typically licensed by state and local regulations.

FatCamera/E+/Getty Images

Figure 1.12 Care for sick children allows for parents to go to work and for their child to be cared for in a safe and supervised setting.

Director's Showcase
Reflect
What, if any, potential drawbacks would there be to Johanna and David when adding an infant/toddler classroom? Why do you think parents would choose a small child care center over home-based care or a large child care center? Compare and contrast each type.

1.4 The Early Childhood Program Leader

There are many titles that are used for early childhood program leaders when it comes to providing administrative oversight at a program. The terms *administrator, school principal, preschool headmaster, owner*, or *site coordinator* can signify a leadership role. However, the most common term used is *director* and the one that will be used most often throughout each chapter. Directors of child care programs have certain responsibilities that are necessary to ensure the center can operate effectively. The difficulty in carrying out these tasks may be affected by the nature of the center. Small centers with few classrooms are usually easier to administer than large ones. Centers that offer a wide variety of services to families will be more challenging to direct than less complex programs. Perhaps you hope to open a center of your own. This can bring a great deal of personal satisfaction, but it may also entail additional work and commitment. Some of the personal characteristics and resources needed to successfully own a center may be different from those needed when working for someone else.

Director's Showcase

Johanna and David

Johanna and David retained many of the staff after they took over the center. They did hire new teachers and staff, but the core group of teachers remained. Johanna recognized the need to establish clear expectations and build relationships with their staff. As director, Johanna excelled at organization and communication. She met with the staff as a group to discuss expectations and what her vision was for the program each year. As a group, they chose goals for the next year for the center.

To build relationships with each team member, Johanna also met individually with them to find out their wants and needs to build relationships with each member of her team. She discovered what her staff needed and then set clear expectations for their jobs and provided consistent guidance.

She also learned that many of her staff wanted to further their careers in child care and helped them to the next step in their education. Johanna would tell her staff that she "had their back," and the staff learned that she did.

Recently, the owner of the center approached Johanna and David about purchasing the center rather than continuing the lease-to-own arrangements. Over the past couple of years, they had implemented all of the changes and improvements they set out to make when they leased their small child care center. While Johanna had focused on building relationships with everyone, David made many upgrades to the building and had become something of a celebrity to the children due to his goofy personality and the tool belt and hardhat he wore. While they took a risk when leasing the center from the owner, they now had the opportunity to purchase the business and knew it would not be an easy undertaking.

An early childhood program leader should have a broad overview of the total program, whether it is large or small. The director "holds things together" and understands how the different parts of the program relate to one another and has knowledge of all aspects of the program to keep it functioning each and every day. From dealing with daily teacher absences and coordinating coverage, to how the budget relates to the cost of keeping the program in operation, it is the director who must be goal-oriented and able to guide the program toward a successful future.

Global Responsibilities

In general, the responsibilities of a child care director are vast. In a typical large business structure, there are departments such as human resources, maintenance and repair, facilities and cleaning services, payroll, and other specialty areas to manage the overall functioning of a business. However, most of these duties fall squarely on the shoulders of the director. A successful director has a working knowledge of all parts of the child care program. A general listing of responsibilities includes

- providing leadership and overall organization for the program.
- finding ways to provide adequate funding for the center.
- recruiting and hiring, orienting and evaluating qualified staff who can create a quality program for the children.
- maintaining an awareness of community trends and family needs to plan future direction for the program.
- communicating clearly with staff and being aware of how things are going throughout the program.
- engaging and communicating with families that attend the program.
- marketing and public relations.
- managing conflict and difficult situations.
- representing the program at various meetings within the community.
- maintaining state and local regulatory rules and working with regulatory agencies.
- evaluating and improving weak areas of the program.
- guiding overall curriculum choice and delivery.
- maintaining all aspects of emergency preparedness.
- establishing program budget and collecting tuition fees.
- maintaining a safe and healthy environment to include necessary maintenance.
- preparing and maintaining all paperwork for governmental programs.

Necessary Personal Skills and Abilities

Examining your personality and abilities may prove helpful as you consider pursuing a career in child care administration. In a small center, you may be handling the administrative tasks and working directly with the children. The administrative work may become much more complex and the time spent in a classroom may decline. Characteristics of a successful director include

- excellent interpersonal skills;
- demonstrated respect for all people;
- knowledge about child development programming;
- knowledge about business practices;
- cultural responsiveness;
- familiarity with technology;
- knowledge about administrative responsibilities;
- leadership, problem-solving, and team building skills;
- self-confidence to be an independent decision maker;
- the ability to organize multiple projects;
- excellent time-management skills;
- a willingness to take on responsibility;
- a willingness to work hard, even beyond actual working hours when necessary;
- flexibility when adjusting to necessary, but unexpected, interruptions; and
- an understanding and dedication to the ethical standards and principles of the profession.

While many find friendship with coworkers, the director of a program has to be very careful of perceived friendships. The director must maintain the unique role of leading others. As its leader, you will find it necessary to develop outside personal friendships with people who are not involved with the program. This provides healthy boundaries for you, your staff, and reflects an environment that is perceived as everyone being treated equally (**Figure 1.13**).

Educational Requirements

Many young people start their education for child care administration in high school vocational and/or technical programs. There is a trend for these programs to provide

SDI Productions/E+/Getty Images

Figure 1.13 Successful directors are friendly, responsive, kind, respectful, and knowledgeable about business practices.

supervised work experience in child care settings as a part of their program curriculum. The competencies attained and the completion of coursework may support entrance into a junior or community college or a four-year college degree program. Strong knowledge of core early childhood competencies along with work experience may prepare students to apply for the **Child Development Associate (CDA)**. This credential is approved as acceptable preparation for a variety of early childhood-related jobs according to state-mandated regulations. However, most states have specific education and experience regulations that mandate expectations for directors.

The qualifications for being a child care program director vary from state to state. They are determined by licensing regulations. The number of children enrolled in the center may influence the required qualifications of the director. Larger programs may require a director with more education. Each state may also set different educational requirements for various types of programs. Currently, in states where Quality Rating Systems (QRS) are in place, there are multiple levels of education and experience referred to as a **director's credential**. This credential spells out specific educational requirements for leaders of early childhood programs, including ongoing professional development expectations.

Qualifications for directors of part-day or specialty programs, such as sick care, may or may not be recognized in state regulations. The leader of these programs must research and adhere to these regulations. In addition, depending on the ages of children served, there may be specialty training expected. Find out what the specific requirements are in your state in order to plan your career path.

Code of Ethical Conduct

Did you know that physicians, lawyers, and architects are some of the many professions that have a code of ethical standards? The field of early childhood education does as well. Adults in child care must make multiple decisions each day when working with young children and their families. The **NAEYC Code of Ethical Conduct** offers guidelines for behavior that is responsible and sets a common ground for resolving ethical dilemmas. This code of ethics is reviewed and updated regularly by early childhood experts based upon feedback received from the field. This code guides early childhood leaders and teaching staff to provide safe environments for children, uphold regulatory rules, communicate effectively with each other, remain accountable, act professionally, and have trust and mutual respect for families and one another. This code is the foundation upon which quality early childhood leaders uphold best practices for the profession and a useful guide if considering program ownership.

Owning an Early Childhood Program

You may have a dream of leading and owning your own child care center, or you may admire someone that is currently doing the work and have an interest in making the field your career. You probably like the idea of being independent and working with children. If you plan your own child care business, you will be considered an entrepreneur. An **entrepreneur** is a person who is willing to expand an opportunity and invest their own time, money, and skills to get either their service or product in place. This includes taking on all of the risk as well. The entrepreneur also expects the new business venture will be successful and earn a profit. In most new child care businesses, the owner works as the director.

whyframestudio/iStock/Getty Images Plus

Figure 1.14 Successful early childhood program directors are motivated, self-directed, and are always looking for ways to create a successful program.

Being an Entrepreneur

There are many things to think about when considering opening up your own center. Having the knowledge and expertise, finding out if there is a demand for the area you are wishing to target, start-up costs, locating capital, determining who the competition is, and lastly, the location, are just a few of the many tasks that will need to be successfully completed. Keep in mind that there are many individuals out there that have been successful and locating a successful business owner in your area is a great place to start. They can serve as a mentor as well as provide advice and guidance to you.

There are likely many successful entrepreneurs in the community where you live. Successful entrepreneurs typically have many of the same characteristics, such as being

- willing to take a reasonable risk.
- knowledgeable about business practices.
- knowledgeable about the field of early childhood.
- hardworking.
- responsible.
- goal-oriented.
- self-confident.
- innovative.
- highly motivated.
- self-directed.
- disciplined.

Keep in mind that a business involves the risk that it may not be successful. Risk, in itself, is often scary. Obtaining capital may mean signing for a loan and being responsible for paying back a large sum of money. If the business closes, what will you lose and how will it impact your ability to recover financially? How long can you operate your business before it turns a profit? How much tuition needs to be charged to cover operating costs? These are key questions to ask yourself. Your chances of success are much greater if you know about what it takes

to operate a successful center. Contacting resources such as the local bank and taking courses in business, child development, and child care administration are essential. In addition, experiences working directly with children and families improve your chances. The risk of opening a center would be high for someone with no training in the field. However, having knowledge about child care administration will make the risk a more reasonable one.

It is well known that the work is hard and has long hours. Having set goals, maintaining confidence, and thinking "outside-of-the-box" is helpful when you come to the many roadblocks of issues that will arise. Keeping yourself motivated, self-directed, and disciplined are keys to meeting the challenges of each day. Most successful entrepreneurs are very definite about their goals for center ownership within a specific time frame and they believe in their own abilities to succeed. They are creative in finding new and better ways to create a successful program and they are not afraid to try out new ideas (**Figure 1.14**).

Advantages and Disadvantages

There are both advantages and disadvantages to starting your own business. Some very capable individuals decide business ownership is not for them. As you progress through this course, your own personal goals for a career in early childhood will probably become clearer.

Know that when entering into any venture, it is always vital to do your research and to seriously consider the advantages and disadvantages. A few advantages to owning your own program include

- *Independence and personal satisfaction.* Owning your own center gives you the freedom to create the very best center you can. As long as you conform to all licensing and regulatory requirements, you can bring your own ideas to the program operation. The decisions made about the program are your ideas. You can take pride in the success of the program. There is usually a deep sense of satisfaction in seeing families and children benefit from a program you created.

- *Profit.* As the owner, you will benefit from any income left over after expenses have been paid. The time and effort you put into making the center successful will come back to you in the form of increased profit.
- *Job security.* As an entrepreneur, you are not subject to the whims or business practices of others above you. You cannot be fired, transferred, or forced to retire. As long as your center is financially healthy with a strong enrollment, you will have a job.
- *Freedom.* Business ownership allows you to decide your own hours, arrange your life around your priorities, create a career for yourself, and establish a work culture that supports your values.

There are also several significant reasons why you may choose *not* to own your own center and become an entrepreneur. These reasons include

- *Low or unpredictable income.* Child care is an expensive business to operate. Tuition must be kept low enough to attract families. Salaries must be high enough to attract qualified staff and teachers. Supplies and equipment must be adequate to support a quality program. If the center has low enrollment for a period of time, the profit may be minimal.
- *Loss of investment.* As an entrepreneur, you will have to invest your own time and money to start the center. If the center is not successful, you may lose all of the money and effort you have put into it including the loss of your own job.
- *Hard work.* Most business owners work long hours and do whatever is necessary to establish their business. Successful child care centers usually offer care for more than eight hours a day. Your staff may only work part of that time. As the owner, you may find yourself performing cleaning and other unskilled tasks, required reports, and even equipment repair. Hiring others to do these jobs requires additional cash outlay.

- *Accepting that mistakes will be made.* Along the journey you will make mistakes. The key will be to keep going and to seek out others to network with and ask for support when you need it as well as to provide support when they need it.

Considering these factors along with others will help you. When completing a full investigation based on the many insights shared, it is these factors that help you to determine if owning your own center is really for you.

Director's Showcase
Reflect

What are some considerations that Johanna and David might have for purchasing the existing child care program from the owner? List and explain some of the risks they might have.

Director's Showcase
Johanna and David

Johanna and David faced many challenges when they decided to lease the child care center. The driving force behind their decision was their passion to provide quality child care in their community. While their approaches to providing child care may vary from others in the industry, the end result is the same—quality child care programs for all children.

David and Johanna succeeded in part because they involved all staff in decision making, using the staff as valuable resources, and did diligent background work in the community. They were open and honest about expectations and clearly defined roles. Johanna and David provided the "what" they wanted to happen, but also provided the "how" and the "why and when." These characteristics are imperative to becoming a successful director in a quality child care program.

Chapter 1 Review and Assessment

Summary

1.1 Identify the main factors that have led to a critical need for quality child care in America.

- Major societal changes, starting in the late 20th century, have increased the need for child care services based upon the multiple types of families and their needs that has contributed to this trend.
- Women make up nearly half of the American workforce and though protections are in place, pay gaps, stagnant wages, and lack of affordable quality child care has led to a need for two-income families.
- There is a serious shortage of available quality child care services, especially for infants and toddlers due to the cost. Although the benefits of a good preschool experience are recognized, many families flock to the free Pre-K programs offered in their communities, which has impacted the day-to-day operations and financial future of early childhood programs.
- Projections for the future indicate there will be a significant lack of educated and skilled workers. This means even more parents with young children will be taking jobs that will not always cover the costs of a two-income family.

1.2 Analyze community and economic factors when determining the need for child care services in an area.

- Programs are needed to support care for school-age children after the school day ends and local schools are closed at varying times throughout the year. It is necessary to do investigative research to gain valuable insights regarding child care operational needs. There are multiple ways to obtain information when supporting the growth of new and established programs.

1.3 Distinguish the types of early childhood programs.

- Quality programs for children have many similarities. While they may be located in home- or center-based situations, they are governed by state regulations.
- Adult-to-child ratios and overall group sizes must be age-appropriate. Programs funded by state and federal dollars can target specific children and their families, or can be in cooperation with local employers.
- Centers are led by early childhood leaders called *directors*. The director must be familiar with all of the program aspects and ensure all licensing and regulatory requirements are met. The director must plan for the future, guide the program toward financial security, and ensure quality care is being provided.

1.4 Describe the role of the early childhood program leader.

- Individuals who decide to own and operate their own centers are defined as *entrepreneurs*. Not everyone has the personality or resources to become an entrepreneur.
- Successful center owners must be knowledgeable about the field of child care, sound business practices, children and families, and have confidence in themselves. They are willing to work long hours and to take the risk of investing their own money.

Review

1. Identify four trends in society that have led to the need for more child care. (1.1)
2. Explain why the quality of child care varies widely. (1.1, 1.2)
3. List and explain the factors that have contributed to the increased need for child care. (1.1)
4. Explain the different types of child care programs available to families. (1.3)
5. What is the purpose of NAEYC (National Association for the Education of Young Children)? (1.1)
6. What act supports families that need to care for children while also providing protections so that the parent can return to their job? (1.1)
7. Explain the economic factors that must be considered when determining the need for a child care program within an area in a community. (1.2)
8. Identify the two major types of care, list the program types, and explain each. (1.3)
9. Summarize the many roles and responsibilities of a director of a child care program. (1.4)
10. List three advantages and disadvantages of becoming an entrepreneur. (1.4)

Showcase Your Skills

As we discussed in this chapter, Johanna and David are beginning a new business by leasing an established center. That business is to provide an early childhood program to their community. As a hired consultant there are many things that need to be considered as next steps. Determining trends in an area as well as defining best practices to support children already in care, their families, developing procedures, and implementing new ideas are part of the consultant's job. After two years of leasing the program, the current owner has offered the option to purchase the business and building. Johanna and David are considering the buying process.

Based on the information shared in each section of this chapter, it is now your turn to serve in the role of consultant. Write a proposal using the following points as your guide.

1. Choose a strategy you would use to gather information about the child care needs of the community and surrounding area.
2. List pros and cons of Johanna and David continuing to lease the program versus purchasing the program.
3. Create a list and rationale as to what additional programming needs they might consider, including cost considerations and likely sources of income.

Matching

Match the following terms with the correct definitions:

A. blended family
B. child care cooperatives
C. drop-in care
D. entrepreneur
E. kith and kin care
F. laboratory schools
G. Montessori programs
H. nursery schools
I. out-of-school-time care
J. sick child care

1. Type of child care that provides care for children when they are out of school.
2. Type of care program often located in or near shopping centers or recreational areas that allows parents to have a few hours to themselves while their children receive care in pleasant, well-supervised settings.
3. Person who is willing to expand an opportunity and invest their own time, money, and skills to get either their service or product in place.
4. Type of child care that provides supervision for children with mild conditions and low fevers related to illness not allowed within a child care setting.
5. New model of child care programs that are sponsored by parents, a business, or multiple businesses interested in providing care for a designated group of children.
6. Type of family that brings two unrelated families into one household.
7. Half-day programs that typically provide scheduled activity and curriculum opportunities for young children.
8. Child care programs that utilize special equipment designed to help children develop their sensory awareness and cognitive skills at their own pace.
9. Programs that exist for the primary purpose of training future teachers and studying child development and education.
10. Informal care of a small group of children provided by relatives or a friend that is mostly unlicensed.

sturti/E+/Getty Images

2 CHAPTER

Child Care Programs

Learning Outcomes

After studying this chapter, you will be able to:

2.1 Identify the major characteristics of quality child care programming.

2.2 Examine universal early childhood program practices.

2.3 Distinguish program elements specific to age-differentiated care.

2.4 Investigate considerations when providing a family child care home.

Key Terms

behaviorist
child-directed play
constructivist
developmentally appropriate practices (DAP)
inclusive environment
interactionalist
maturationalist
NAEYC 10 Program Standards

NAEYC/DAP standards

Standards covered in this chapter:

1c, 2b, 2c, 4a, 4c

1A, 1B, 1D, 2A, 4D, 4H

Introduction

Many families require care for children as young as six weeks of age. The difference between parents' work hours and their children's school day can create a gap in care for many families. As a result, many child care programs offer care for both younger and older children. Many families need full-time child care, while others only need part-time care. Parents working weekend, evening, or varying shifts typically have a difficult time locating care that accommodates their needs. For a program to be successful, the hours must match the needs of the families who will use the program. In addition, the type of care provided for varying age groups creates certain administrative challenges. Out-of-school-time care is not the same as preschool care. Infants and toddlers have very specific care needs. In order to offer each of these types of care successfully, you must be aware of the pitfalls and plan carefully. You may begin by exploring the costs in conjunction with state licensing requirements and quality rating standards. This knowledge will help you determine staffing needs for each age group, proper space allocation, and the supplies and equipment necessary to operate the program successfully. Let's turn now to learning more about characteristics of quality programs while learning from early childhood leaders working in the field.

2.1 Characteristics of a Quality Child Care Program

In the United States, the quality of child care varies widely. While basic state licensing regulations for child care services are different in each state, there are minimal health and safety standards of caring for young children of different ages. Research indicates there are positive outcomes for children who attend quality early childhood programs. Many families have the option of choosing private or public programs. However, there are families living in areas where choices are limited. The COVID-19 pandemic

Director's Showcase

Johanna and David

Johanna and David purchased the program from the owner of the child care center. They worked to achieve the 3-Star level of the 5-Star quality rating system provided by their state. After discussions, they decided to make their center the very best by pursuing national accreditation through NAEYC. After reading more about accreditation, they started to realize that they may need to do more work before starting the process.

Halima

Halima, a long-time family child care home provider, wants to be the first in her area to participate in the state quality-rating system. While other providers are interested, she wants to be the trendsetter. In the past couple of years, she earned her Child Development Associate (CDA) credential and began taking child development courses at the local community college. The children's parents have been supportive and are urging her to consider participation in the program. She begins to do research to find out where to start in the process.

revealed that access to quality care options was not equitable across the United States. Parents, who were caring for others or trying to return to the workforce, found that many programs were struggling to keep their doors open or had to shut down completely. Quality child care standards and needs became front and center in the national spotlight. This included funding child care systems as it was apparent they were "essential." This furthered the national discussion on how to best fund early care and education systems across the country (**Figure 2.1**).

gawrav/E+/Getty Images

Figure 2.1 The NAEYC Standards are important for leaders to utilize when imagining their early childhood program and how it will best serve children and families.

Development of Universal Program Standards

Over the years, the **National Association for the Education of Young Children (NAEYC) 10 Program Standards** were established for all types of early childhood programs to use as guides and to help families be better informed when selecting child care. Experts and educators applied research regarding the development and education of young children to create the 10 NAEYC Program Standards (2021). These standards have been accepted in the field as the basis for high-quality early childhood programs (**Figure 2.2**).

Guided by these standards, it is important for a program leader to actively work to instill principles of fairness and justice that reflect the goals of anti-bias educational opportunities. It is through this lens these standards, which are all essential elements, culminate as a program's philosophy becomes apparent.

NAEYC 10 Program Standards	
NAEYC Standard	Explanation
Standard 1: Relationships	Adults working with children to provide warm, sensitive, and responsive relations to help them feel safe and secure.
Standard 2: Curriculum	Implementation of curriculum is consistent with the program's goals for children and promotes learning and development in the areas of social, emotional, physical, language, and cognitive.
Standard 3: Teaching	Practices use developmentally, culturally, and linguistically appropriate and effective teaching approaches that enhance children's learning and development in the context of the curriculum goals.
Standard 4: Assessment of Child Progress	Informs by ongoing systematic, formal, and informal assessment approaches to provide information on a child's learning and development within the context of reciprocal communications, sensitive to a family's cultural context.
Standard 5: Health	Promotes nutrition and health of children and staff and protection from illness and injury.
Standard 6: Staff Competencies, Preparation, and Support	Employs and supports staff with educational qualifications, knowledge, and a professional commitment that supports children's learning and development and to support a family's diverse needs and interests.
Standard 7: Families	Collaborative relationships are essential to foster children's development in all settings and must be a relationship based on mutual trust and respect while being sensitive to a family's composition, language, and culture.
Standard 8: Community Relationships	Relationships are established with resources of children's communities to support the achievement of program goals and to connect families with resources that support children's healthy development and learning.
Standard 9: Physical Environment	Well-maintained indoor and outdoor physical environments are safe and healthful environments facilitate child and staff learning and developing.
Standard 10: Leadership and Management	Those who lead programs effectively implement policies, procedures, and systems that support stable staff and strong personnel, are fiscally responsible, and program management that all children, families, and staff deem high quality.

Goodheart-Willcox Publisher

Figure 2.2 The NAEYC Program Standards set forth expectations for early childhood programs to follow.

Program Philosophy

While NAEYC's 10 Program Standards brought about a collective understanding in the field about standards of care, there are also many philosophies that do not always agree on what is best for children. Across time, many researchers and theorists have developed concepts and ideas to support the understanding of how children grow and learn. Some of the philosophical elements from major theorists are

- **Maturationalist.** Children develop according to predictable biological patterns and increase in competence when the environment supports this development.
- **Interactionalist**. Children learn through their interactions with the environment.
- **Constructivist**. Children construct their knowledge of the world through having a wide range of concrete experiences in a variety of areas.
- **Behaviorist**. Children's learning is believed to occur as they have more complicated interactions with the environment that is either positively or negatively reinforced in a highly structured and teacher-controlled environment.

These varying ideas about how children learn have led to several different philosophies found in early childhood programs today. A program's philosophy is important because it affects

- the mission and goals of the program;
- the value of serving diverse groups of children;
- the role of the teacher in the classroom;
- the choice of equipment and activities;
- the daily schedule;
- expected behaviors of the children; and
- interactions between staff and children (**Figure 2.3**).

The director and staff must all share the same philosophy for a program to operate smoothly. Most trained adults find it impossible to work in a program that is in conflict with their beliefs about what is good for children. As a program owner, you must decide on the type of philosophy your program will offer. If you are hired to operate a program, the philosophy may have already been chosen by the owner or board of directors. Your satisfaction in working with children will be greatly affected by how comfortable you are in implementing the program's philosophy while using developmentally appropriate practices.

Developmentally Appropriate Practices

Stemming from the maturationalist, interactionalist, and constructivist philosophies came a collective agreement on a developmentally based concept of embracing

Tips for Creating a Program Philosophy

1. Begin with writing down ideas of what you see as important when providing programming for young children.
2. Use terms that everyone understands.
3. Engage your staff to assist with developing your ideas further.
4. Remain open to ideas, suggestions, and critical thinking.
5. Be prepared for change and adjustments to the philosophy developing process.

Goodheart-Willcox Publisher

Figure 2.3 Developing a program philosophy is important as this is the foundational belief that the program director and staff utilize when serving children and families.

children's individual learning and is woven into many philosophies supporting programs. **Developmentally appropriate practices (DAP)** utilize methods that promote optimal development and learning through a strengths-based, play-based approach to joyful, engaged learning (NAEYC, 2020). While constantly evolving, DAP views children as unique individuals who learn in designed learning environments across all domains of learning—physically, cognitively, socially, and emotionally to include practices that are culturally, linguistically, and ability appropriate for each child (**Figure 2.4**).

Planning developmentally appropriate activities for young children requires that a teacher

- know age characteristics of the children in the group;
- know the types of equipment and activities preferred by the age group;
- know how to prepare the classroom and activities for optimum use;
- know how to plan concrete, "hands-on" experiences;

energy/E+/Getty Images

Figure 2.4 Working with young children can be challenging. Teaching staff must be ready to carefully plan curriculum and classroom activity.

- understands the progression of development, so activities can be matched to children's developmental readiness;
- know each child's unique characteristics;
- know where to go to get new ideas;
- understands how to create a positive, supportive learning environment; and
- is sensitive to the social and cultural context in which each child lives.

A program that offers a variety of quality, developmentally appropriate activities each day requires careful planning. It doesn't just happen. There must be a match between what the children are ready for and the activities available to them. Teachers need to plan the room arrangement, select appropriate equipment, plan the daily schedule, and include special activities and group time activities. A quality program for young children will fascinate and challenge them (**Figure 2.5**). It will not bore or frustrate them. When children are enrolled within quality program practices, they will look forward to the day's activities and end the day feeling successful and good about themselves.

filmstudio/E+/Getty Images

Figure 2.5 All of the toys and equipment that children play with daily should be cleaned and sanitized to prevent the spread of disease.

common elements set the bar for essential standards and create a springboard for ongoing evaluation and improvement, which all starts with the education and training experiences of the director and teaching staff.

Director's Showcase

Reflect

As Johanna, David, and Halima begin to learn more about the application of universal program standards, there are so many other areas to think about. Where would you start in the process of developing your program?

2.2 Universal Program Practices

No matter the ages of the children served in a center- or home-based program, they will all have state-mandated practices and expectations. The common elements include

- education and experience levels of teachers;
- regular professional development opportunities;
- staff-to-child ratios;
- group size expectations;
- health, safety, and nutrition;
- importance of play;
- curriculum and equipment;
- use of appropriate behavior and guidance strategies; and
- necessary partnership with a child's family.

Each are important when planning a quality program. This includes providing learning opportunities that exhibit a commitment to equitable outcomes for all children. These

Director's Showcase

Johanna and David

Johanna and David realized that incorporating the universal standards into their daily practices was needed after spending time observing in the classrooms. In addition, they realized that the program philosophy from the previous owner had not been updated since they purchased the program. When they began talking more with the staff, it became evident that not everyone knew what the program philosophy was and some of the staff were not sure what developmentally appropriate practices involved. Johanna and David decided that they needed to get a plan to address these issues but were unsure where to start.

Halima

After more reading, Halima was relieved to find out that the universal program practices applied to the family child care home environment. In addition, she also decided to update her program philosophy. The classes that she was taking at the local community college talked about how important it was to share with parents the program's approach to the children's learning. She was also intrigued to learn more about developmentally appropriate practices because she could think of instances where she was utilizing these practices with the children throughout the day.

Education and Experience Levels of the Director and Teachers

Standard 6 of NAEYC's Early Learning Program Standards (2021) emphasizes the importance of specialized education and experience expectations as well as state-mandated training for staff members. Pre-determined qualifications are those standards that a program, of any size, must follow. Typically, the number of children enrolled in a center may influence the required qualifications of the director. Programs with larger numbers of children and staff may be required to have a director with more education. Each state may also set different educational requirements for various types of programs. Currently, in states where Quality Rating Systems (QRS) are in place, there are multiple levels of education and experience referred to as a *director's credential*. This credential spells out specific educational requirements for leaders of early childhood programs to include ongoing professional development expectations. Local community colleges or vocational schools will specialize in these areas to build leadership capacity in their areas.

Hiring teaching staff has a range of possibilities. While program leaders are charged to recruit and retain these individuals to meet state standards, they must carefully select staff who reflect the diversity of children and families served, including staff who speak the languages of the children and families served. Teachers are expected to earn or be in the process of earning a Child Development Associate (CDA) credential. This credential is approved as acceptable preparation for a variety of early childhood, related jobs according to state-mandated regulations. For programs that have achieved higher recognition within state systems, a two- or four-year degree in child development or early childhood education is required. In some states, a combination of child development coursework and on-the-job experience is acceptable. In general, no matter at what level a staff member is hired, they must always be encouraged to grow in the field by participating in ongoing professional development opportunities to enhance their skill set.

Professional Development Opportunities

Teaching staff must have a working knowledge of the stages of child development and learning. Participation in ongoing professional development opportunities such as college courses, seminars, or workshops prepare individual staff members to work with groups of young children and continue to support the ideals behind *Standard 6 of NAEYC's Early Learning Program Standards* (2021). Courses in child development or early childhood education prepare teachers for working in lead positions to

meet children's needs. They are better able to make decisions about program activities, curriculum, and overall behavior and guidance strategies carried out within the classroom. Trained staff also understand that working with young children is a challenging job requiring careful thought and planning (**Figure 2.6**). Attracting and retaining staff who specialize in working with certain age groups to include infants, toddlers, and preschool age are important considerations.

States vary in terms of the training required for different positions. To assist with this, many state programs offer scholarships and wage supplements specifically designed to support ongoing professional opportunities for staff. As director, knowledge and use of these programs assist with the program's budget, the ability to recruit, and retain staff. Overall, the teaching staff is the backbone of the program and its operations. Care for them includes worthy compensation along with opportunities to learn and grow.

Staff-to-Child Ratios and Group Size Expectations

Young children need warm, supportive, ongoing relationships with consistent, caring adults. They need adults who know them well and understand them. If an insufficient number of adults are assigned to a group of children, the overall quality of care is diminished. When the adult-to-child ratio is too high, each caregiver has a larger number of children under their care. As a result, more time must be spent on basic care routines and the staff has less time to spend interacting with each child. When the adult-to-child ratio is low, there are more adults for the group and each child has individual attention from an assigned primary caregiver. Program activities can be planned with individual children in mind. State licensing requirements identify adult-to-child ratios

Wundervisuals/E+/Getty Images

Figure 2.6 Program staff provide developmentally appropriate activities for the young children in their care.

for the different age groups of children, and these vary from state to state. In general, younger age groups require more adults than older age groups.

Standard 10 of NAEYC's Early Learning Program Standards (2021) holds leadership accountable to state licensing standards and regulates the maximum number of children that can be in a group based on ages of the children in the group. Young infants and toddlers must be in smaller groups and older preschoolers can be in slightly larger groups. As the group becomes larger, each child must try to cope with both more children and adults. Even when the adult-to-child ratio is low, large groups result in a more chaotic environment. Chances are greater that a child's needs will not be responded to appropriately in a larger group. This also impacts the overall health, safety, and nutrition expectations if adults have too many to care for at one time.

Health, Safety, and Nutrition Requirements

Standard 5 of NAEYC's Early Learning Program Standards (2021) addresses the areas of health, safety, and nutrition. From a wide array of rules and regulations that oversee food handling and nutrition expectations, there are plenty more that prevent the spread of disease. Local regulatory agencies will check these areas on a regular basis. Toys must be carefully cleaned daily. This includes spraying, wiping, or immersing the toy items in a state-approved cleaning solution. Classroom tables, chairs, storage areas, and floors require constant upkeep. From diapering procedures to toileting expectations, routine tasks have rules and regulations that must be monitored and attended to every day. Handwashing is a must! (**Figure 2.7**) This, by far, is one of the most effective ways to limit the spread of disease for both children and staff. Finally, the program must keep records regarding children's immunizations,

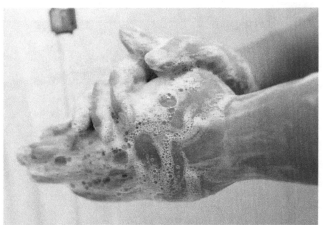

Sucharas wongpeth/iStock/Getty Images Plus

Figure 2.7 Handwashing is key to keeping everyone in the environment safe from the spread of germs and disease.

notes from doctors supporting why a child does not have immunizations, or a child's release from care due to a contagious illness.

These standards further identify the importance of how the facility must be continually monitored for safety concerns. This includes the removal of broken toys or equipment, the constant upkeep of the grounds, playgrounds, and inside areas. Anything that could be a hazard must be removed and include safe flooring that avoids slips and falls. Fencing and impact-absorbing materials under large playground equipment is a daily monitoring process. Outdoor surfaces must be safe for children to run and play. Indoor cabinets must have the correct safety locks, and table tops must be without cracks and tears. Doorways and doors must be kept in good repair and the paint within the facility lead-free. Fire extinguishers, smoke alarms, and other building inspections by city and local codes certainly are a part of the safety concerns.

Food must be stored and served safely and monitored by local regulatory agencies such as the health department. This includes the locations where food is stored, for dry and refrigerated items; how it is labeled; and the monitoring of expiration dates. Human milk, baby formula, and juices used with infants and toddlers must be stored and used by expiration dates. Any prepared foods must be delivered to the children at the right temperatures, in clean cookware and utensils, and served using appropriate tableware. Many programs participate in government food subsidy programs that have additional expectations to include portion and serving sizes along with specific menu planning for all ages of children served (**Figure 2.8**).

Importance of Play

Research has shown that play is a key to a child's development. It helps them to discover, build, and reinforce knowledge about their world (Tayler, 2015; Langford 2010). Children will naturally engage in play activities that are appropriate to their developmental level. Young children benefit from being able to make choices and pursue their own interests. Classrooms must allow many opportunities for children to set their own pace when they play. Children engage in many types of play throughout childhood. Children benefit from unstructured and other types of play in many ways, including

- fostering social skills (Ramani & Eason, 2015; Ramani, 2012).
- enhancing executive function to include self-regulation (Cavanaugh et al., 2017; Becker et al., 2014; Savina 2014; McCrory, De Brito, & Viding, 2010; Christie & Roskos, 2009).
- increasing coordination, maintaining a healthy body weight, creating appropriate sleep habits, and

Daily Recommended Amounts for a Child, Aged 2 to 3 Years, with Moderate Activity

In the chart is the daily recommended amounts of food for a child two to three years of age who gets 30 to 60 minutes of moderate activity per day. A child care facility may serve one meal and several snacks throughout the day and should be aware of how each food fits into a healthy diet for the children in their care.

Food Group	Daily Recommended Amount	Sample Foods
Fruit	1 ½ cups	1 cup from this group counts as: • 1 cup raw, frozen, or canned fruit • ½ cup dried fruit • 1 cup of 100% fruit juice
Vegetables	1 ½ cups	1 cup from this group counts as: • 1 cup raw, cooked, or canned vegetables • 2 cups leafy salad greens • 1 cup 100% vegetable juice
Grains	5 ounces	1 ounce from this group counts as: • 1 slice of bread • 1 ounce ready-to-eat cereal • ½ cup cooked rice, pasta, or cereal
Protein	4 ounces	1 ounce from this group counts as: • 1 ounce of seafood, lean meat, or poultry • 1 egg • 1 Tbsp peanut butter • ¼ cup cooked beans, peas, or lentils
Dairy	2 ½ cups	1 cup from this group counts as: • 1 cup dairy milk or yogurt • 1 cup lactose-free dairy milk or yogurt • 1 cup fortified soy milk or yogurt • 1 ½ ounces natural cheese

Courtesy of the USDA

Figure 2.8 Accessing government links can assist with excellent, healthy meal planning.

reducing stress and anxiety (Levine & Ducharme, 2013; Wenner 2009).

• improving language skills (Cohen & Emmons, 2017; Stagnitti et al., 2016; Ramani & Eason, 2015; Ramani, 2012).

• creating opportunities to begin foundational math and science concepts (Cohen & Emmons, 2017; Travick-Smith, Swaminathan, & Liu, 2016; Bulotsky-Shearer et al. 2014).

Play affects every aspect of development and learning. Teachers assist with guiding and initiating play with children. The role of the teacher is to playfully combine a child's interests with learning opportunities and goals addressed in *Standards 1 and 3 of NAEYC's Early Learning Program Standards* (2021). This is a skillful act on the part of the teacher and an important skill set that is constantly developed from ongoing professional development opportunities for teaching staff. Like we have experienced as adults, if learning is a joyful experience, it deepens the overall learning of new concepts. The same can be said for children. They, too, will have different interests and talents along with different growth rates and varying attention spans. As we begin to explore the

different age groups later in this chapter, it will become evident that there are distinct needs when supporting programming. Overall, play considerations should always be at the forefront of all classroom planning by teaching staff who are supported by their director.

Curriculum and Equipment

Programs are characterized by a clearly defined curriculum. The curriculum utilized by the program should be in harmony with the way that the program leadership and staff believe children learn and the role that teachers play in that learning (Frede & Ackerman, 2007). While it is important to have knowledge about the age characteristics of the group of children, everyone must agree on the basic principles of how young children learn, what they need to know, and how they should be taught. *Standard 2 of NAEYC's Early Learning Program Standards* (2021) supports that curriculum is the blueprint for planning and implementing a program; it is deciding what to teach and how (Dodge, 2004). The content of the curriculum is building the whole child from a physical, cognitive, language, and social-emotional perspective. While guided by the curriculum, classroom teachers should have a level of independence to implement curriculum programming within their lesson plans and activities.

Equipment varies with age groups and the class size. While states regulate the amount of equipment needed indoors and outdoors, these are always considered as minimum standards. Regulations will also set forth expectations of the number of certain pieces of equipment, their placement within the classroom, and how often this equipment must be serviced and/or replaced. The director's role is to maintain inventory as well as budget for the replacement or addition of certain equipment pieces. The equipment used in the classroom assists teachers as they facilitate learning and the day-to-day structure of a program. Much more about this topic will be shared in Chapter 4.

Positive Behavior and Guidance Strategies

Programs need teaching staff who use age-appropriate strategies when guiding children. Children need gentle guidance to help them grow. As established within *Standard 1 of NAEYC's Early Learning Program Standards* (2021), positive guidance helps children learn what behaviors are acceptable in a safe and secure manner. This guidance is matched to the age level and understanding of children. This contrasts with negative forms of guidance that focus on what the child does wrong. Negative guidance is often based on unrealistic expectations of children's behavior. It is often harsh and makes children feel worthless and incompetent. Shame, humiliation, embarrassment, threats, and physical punishment are examples of negative guidance.

Children thrive in programs where staff provide guidance based on each child's needs, rather than responding to children's behaviors emotionally (**Figure 2.9**). It is sometimes an adult who overwhelms children with rules when limits are really what is necessary. Children should be given simple explanations that help them to understand the logic of the adult world. Positive guidance is a "teaching tool" in the classroom. Children are always treated with respect that helps them grow in self-confidence and self-control. Harsh, demeaning types of control and punishment have no place in any early childhood program. This type of behavior works against the goals of a quality program.

Establishing an Inclusive Program

Programs must be prepared to care for children living with special needs by providing inclusive environments (**Figure 2.10**). **Inclusive environments** enhance the abilities of all children to cooperate and work together in a space that accommodates all abilities and requirements.

sturti/E+/Getty Images

Figure 2.9 Children display lots of emotions. Staff are expected to provide appropriate guidance and support.

Community supports are crucial to this need, which substantiates *Standard 8 of NAEYC's Early Learning Program Standards* (2021). This can be a wide range of diagnosed medical conditions or disabilities to include

- allergies;
- physical challenges;
- chronic medical issues;
- asthma;
- diabetes;
- autism;
- sensory issues; and
- developmental delays.

While these are only a few of the possible conditions that programs may encounter, it is important to recognize that working with these children is a commitment to learning more about their needs. Whether it be swallowing challenges, a child's reactions to certain foods and awareness of what they can or cannot have, to the administration of special medication, the director and staff must be open to the care necessary. Classroom space,

IvanJekic/E+/Getty Images

Figure 2.10 Small adaptations can be made in the environment to assist children living with special needs.

equipment, and the staff acquiring the knowledge and skills necessary to assist the child in their everyday care is a must. Programs should access state resources as needed (**Figure 2.11**). This includes early intervention programs whose role is not only to come into programs to provide services, but also to assist staff in providing the necessary education and insights when providing appropriate care for the child over time. A strong partnership with health professionals strengthens the best possible outcome for the child and their family. In addition, the director and teaching staff must realize that a key to this success for not only these children, but *all* children served in the program, is a partnership with parents.

Partnership with Parents

A young child's concerns focus primarily on their family as this is the most important factor influencing them. *Standard 7 of NAEYC's Early Learning Program Standards* (2021) addresses relationships with families.

Director's Showcase

Reflect

Now that you have learned more about what universal program practices are, if you are currently employed in a program, what is going well or needs to be changed? If you were starting a new program, how would you approach each area so that you are implementing best practices?

State Resources for Early Intervention Services

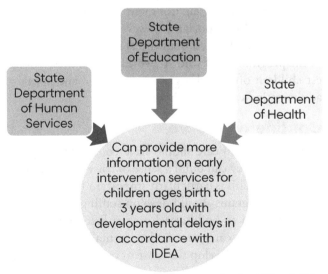

Goodheart-Willcox Publisher

Figure 2.11 Accessing state resources begins by checking with potential branches of state departments that are tasked with providing early intervention services.

Any program that wants to have a positive impact on children must include parents or the child's caregiver. The expert on any child begins with the significant adults in their lives. Parents and staff need to share pertinent information regarding the children. Children benefit most when their family members and staff communicate with each other. For example, parents need to share if a child has had an upsetting experience outside of school or at home. In turn, teachers need to share if a child has had a difficult day or is not feeling well (**Figure 2.12**). This shared partnership to work toward the benefit of the child is always the goal.

Quality programs involve parents in many ways. Some have parents represented on the governing board or committees. Others plan special activities for children and parents together. Parents can help with fund-raising activities and providing ideas for future planning. There may also be opportunities for parents to volunteer in the classroom or to attend parent education classes. Parent involvement helps parents feel they are an important part of the center. It allows for additional interaction between the staff and parents. Parents are more likely to share important information about their child if they feel comfortable with the teachers. They will feel a sense of commitment to the center if they understand its goals and methods.

What Your Child Did Today!

Name: _____ Date: _____

Ate or Drank (ounces):

Formula _____ Juice _____ Baby food _____

Other _____

We changed wet diapers _____ times.

Number of bowel movements _____

Consistency and color of bowel movements was

_____

Any fever? Yes   No

Napped from _____ to _____

Went to sleep easily? Yes   No

Interesting things your child did today.

_____

Concerns _____

Signature _____
(staff member in room)

Goodheart-Willcox Publisher

Figure 2.12 A simple form like this one provides an easy way to share important information with parents of infants and toddlers.

2.3 Elements of Age-Appropriate Programming

Necessary considerations must be made when learning about the elements of age-appropriate programming. For example, having an infant and toddler classroom located right by the rooms housing a summer school-age program would not be ideal. Conversely, school-age classrooms would not benefit by having small spaces to move their bigger bodies around in. While licensing regulations assist with learning more about the specifics, let's begin by learning more about infant and toddler programming.

There has been a dramatic increase in the need for quality infant and toddler care, specifically children birth to age three, which has led many states to support and enhance the expectations. From a community awareness perspective, having a reputation for quality infant and toddler programming is an excellent way to introduce new families to your program. As the child grows within the program, the family who is happy with the

Director's Showcase

Johanna and David

As Johanna and David continued their observations throughout the program as they were learning more, they began focusing on the infant and toddler classroom. First, they determined that they needed to be sure that they were implementing best practices so that the classroom was providing high-quality care. Keeping ratios in mind, Johanna sat down with the infant and toddler staff to determine ideal routines, schedules, classroom furniture, health and safety practices, and play. It was important to Johanna and David that each infant and toddler form a bond with an adult working in the classroom. This included the implementation of classroom activities that were age appropriate.

Halima

Halima felt strongly that her care of infants and toddlers already met the standards. However, working with preschool and school-age children was not an area of comfort for her. She wondered how she could best meet their needs keeping in mind that she cared for one infant and two toddlers throughout the day. She certainly wanted to provide age-appropriate activities, but also needed to keep in mind the safety of the infants and toddlers when the older children were participating in activities.

care provided for their infant or toddler is likely to stay with the same program as long as there is a need for child care. If this need is not met, many times families will go elsewhere. While the cost to provide this care is high, it is an important consideration so as not to lose the potential enrollment to another program that provides comprehensive infancy through school-age services.

Infants and Toddlers

Recent research in brain development gives a fascinating look at how the young child's brain develops. It confirms what child development specialists have been saying for many years—infancy and toddlerhood are critical times for brain development. A program for these children must make a commitment to providing a high-quality, nurturing, interesting, and supportive program environment. This environment must be both physically and emotionally safe in order to help children grow to their full potential. While each state has specific licensing regulations for these programs, our focus will be to address them from a management perspective, and how to provide a quality infant and toddler program based upon the overall program practices we learned about.

Location

When considering placement of an infant and toddler classroom, it is best to locate the room away from the rest of the center if possible. A separate wing of the building would be ideal. This placement can help to reduce the spread of illness from older children to younger ones. It can also reduce the noise level reaching the infant and toddler classroom. Nearby preschoolers or school-age children need a lot of physical activity and often engage in loud play. This can be stressful for infants or toddlers who need a calmer environment with fewer startling noises. It is also important, however, to be sure that the infant and toddler staff doesn't feel isolated from the rest of the program. Staff who are working with these youngest children often feel a great need to see and speak to adults periodically throughout the day.

Continuity of Care

Children in child care should have consistent caregivers with whom they can build a sense of trust and emotional attachment. This is particularly important for very young children. Programs should develop staffing patterns that allow children to build attachments. Frequently changing or rotating caregivers is detrimental to children. It will not help to develop the sense of trust that is the basis for a healthy personality.

Some staff may not like working with babies, while others love it. You will need to find a match between those adults who love the infants and their placement in infant classrooms. As staff members receive additional training in the developmental characteristics of infants and toddlers, the children become more interesting to them. As staff learn to recognize the importance of developmental milestones, they begin to view development as a fascinating process to be supported with enthusiasm. This leads to better care and to more satisfaction for the adults providing that care.

Grouping

The placement of infants and toddlers in specific groups is an important consideration. Toddlers who have just learned to walk are thrilled with themselves. They are so busy practicing this new skill that nothing in their way will stop them. Unfortunately, it may be a baby on the floor who gets in their way! Toddlers, who have no sense of themselves as a force, are likely to walk right over anything on the floor. The baby has no way to get out of the way, and the toddler has no sense of obstacles in the way. This is a dangerous combination. Toddlers are unsteady. They can be doing just fine, and then suddenly fall over their own feet. A 20-pound toddler falling on top of a 10-pound infant can cause serious injury. Think of yourself being landed on from above by a 250-pound squirming weight. Not a pleasant thought!

Most experts feel strongly that walkers and non-walkers should be in separate groups. While safety is one reason, another reason has to do with cognitive development. The ability to walk is often viewed as a signal that children are ready for more active exploration of the world. This newfound freedom opens the doors for greater exploration. The ability to walk is also followed quickly by a desire to climb. Toddlers need these expanded opportunities. Babies need to be protected from the enthusiasm of the toddlers. States will vary in their licensing requirements regarding this age group. Some states specify that walkers and non-walkers cannot be in the same area. Other states have no restrictions.

Daily Schedule and Activities

The daily schedule of infants and toddlers must reflect their needs. While there should be some general pattern and sequence to the day, the schedule should be flexible. Rather than following a rigid minute-by-minute, preplanned routine, caregivers must be sensitive to the individual needs of each child in their care. If one child gets hungry early, he or she should be fed. If a child is not quite sleepy at the usual time, he or she should be rocked and quietly helped to relax.

Caregivers need to be actively and emotionally involved with the babies in their care. Every interaction is important as the infant begins to recognize the warm, caring faces of the staff members and the predictability of their

behaviors. These interactions, whether they take place during routines such as diapering, toileting, or during playtime, are an important part of the program in a quality center (**Figure 2.13**).

Activities should always be developmentally appropriate and should be matched to the developmental levels and individual interests of the children. Infants need items they can grasp, mouth, and examine. They like simple patterns and bright colors. Safe, interesting objects to look at, hear, and touch fascinate them and help them learn. As they learn how to reach, they need items to grasp. They need toys that they can control. It is a wonderful discovery for infants and toddlers to find that when they pull, or squeeze, or shake, something in the toy responds. They also need to see themselves. Mirrors in several spots around the room will fascinate young children.

Toddlers need even more items to help them develop muscle control and coordination. Kiddie cars, beach balls, toy trucks and cars, and large, soft blocks are valuable additions to the toddlers' toy supply. They need the opportunity to run, roll, jump, and laugh heartily. Cruising around the room, looking at the adult to confirm the names of objects, is also a valuable use of a toddler's time. A simple game of "Ring Around the Rosie" can be a fun way to encourage balance and coordination. Toddlers also enjoy soft stuffed toys and dolls as they begin to develop an interest in pretend play. For both older infants and toddlers, walks around the center or outdoors expand their awareness. In a developmentally appropriate program, children are never bored.

Preschoolers

While the care of infants and toddlers is a significantly growing sector, the movement to provide Pre-K

filadendron/E+/Getty Images

Figure 2.13 Learning routines such as toileting takes time, practice, and patience by staff members working with children who are toilet training.

programs in public schools for four-year-old children has significantly impacted programs that offer care for pre-school-age children. Many parents flock to these "free," government-supported, and in many cases full-day, programs as a convenient, budget-friendly option. This limits many center-based preschool programs to three- to four-year-old children who do not meet the state age cut off. Many programs have shifted to providing onsite Pre-K programs in collaboration with the local school district, coordinating transportation to and from local schools to facilitate before and after school care, or offering full-day care when Pre-K programs are out of school.

Opportunities for Structured and Unstructured Play

The benefits of play for this age group are tremendous. Play not only reflects but also contributes to children's cognitive and social skills. Preschoolers should spend a tremendous amount of their time participating in dramatic play. Make-believe strengthens a wide range of mental abilities, including attention span, memory, logical reasoning, language and literacy, imagination, creativity, emotional understanding, and understanding their own as well as others' perspectives. For example, several children are playing "restaurant" in the housekeeping area. One child is taking orders, another is cooking the ordered food, while others might be placing and changing their orders. The interactions provide a rich opportunity for imaginative play and realistic interactions for the children. The teacher can encourage this learning by supplying the area with interactive props, such as an order pad, pencils, pots and pans, cooking utensils, a chef's hat and apron, placemats, menus, and other assorted items. In this example, the children are engaging in learning through structured and unstructured play.

Teacher's Role

Jones (2004) has written extensively about the roles that teachers assume when supporting children's play. Noting that teachers who provide a variety of activities, observe what unfolds, stay nearby to help as needed, and acknowledge children's actions and words are more successful. Preschool-age children need aware and engaged teachers to work with them each day. **Child-directed play**, or allowing the child to choose their activities during free play, allows for exploration and enrichment (**Figure 2.14**). Involving young children in the planning and development of their structured play activities also increases participation and learning.

Daily Schedule and Activities

This age thrives on daily schedules and activities that are routine. Teachers working with this age group assume that

South_agency/E+/Getty Images
Figure 2.14 Children playing with multiple materials provides lots of opportunities for exploration and learning.

change to the daily schedule is "no big deal." However, it is a big deal and many times results in a teacher experiencing a classroom of frustrated or difficult-to-manage children. Knowing what comes next allows a continuity of daily functions and supports the sense of security that preschool children need to be successful. Anxiety decreases in children who are aware of upcoming transitions and know what to expect next. Repetition and consistent routines are hallmarks of a successful classroom.

Because play is such a significant part of every preschool classroom, make it a primary focus in program planning. Incorporating learning objectives into structured and unstructured play is a way to enhance child development while keeping children engaged in the classroom around them.

Developmental Considerations

A typical preschool classroom is made up of children of the same or close to the same age. This is necessary for curriculum and planning as well as child development. When placing a child within a classroom, take the developmental age of the child into consideration along with chronological age. Skill development and achievement happens rapidly in this age group. One child may be speaking in complete sentences at 20 months of age, while another child may just be combining two words at 24 months. A child who is not yet communicating effectively may not be ready to move up with same-aged peers at the same time. Allowing for differences while also considering what is best for each individual child will benefit the child and the program.

Out-of-School-Time Care

Working parents frequently find that the hours of school do not match the hours when they are working and commuting. While elementary schools typically start at

8 a.m. or 9 a.m., parents must often begin their work-day by 7 a.m. or 8 a.m. They worry about leaving their children to eat breakfast and get to the bus or school on time independently. The same problem occurs at the end of the day. The typical school day ends by 2:30 p.m. or 3:30 p.m., yet parents frequently work until 5 p.m. Some parents work evening or night shifts, while others have shifts that change every few weeks. Rather than having children come alone into an empty house and be on their own for several hours each day, many early childhood programs have developed out-of-school-time programs. Before, after, and out-of-school care alleviates a stressful situation for both children and parents.

School-age programs also tend to be cost-effective for centers. Because the groups of older children can be larger, the cost of providing staff is not as high as it is for other age groups. Many home- and center-based programs include school-age programming for children. It is important that the program be suited to their age group. By creating an atmosphere and program that is appealing to older children, it is successful.

Location and Facilities

Locating a suitable facility for school-age care may be difficult. In many cases, elementary schools have been reluctant to have these programs in their buildings. The licensing requirements for school-age programs are some-times in conflict with school procedures and safety reg-ulations. Only recently, primarily in response to parent requests, have schools become more willing to allow their facilities to be used for after-school child care programs.

If school rooms are unavailable, it may be difficult to find space suitable for school-age programs. Often reli-gious buildings or community centers have rooms that meet licensing standards. The facility must have running water, bathrooms, a small kitchen area for fixing snacks, access to an outdoor play space, and ideally, a gym for indoor active games. A vehicle and driver may be neces-sary to transport the children to and from school.

Hours

School-age care hours must be established around the school schedule and the needs of families. Some children may need care for an hour or so before school starts in the morning. Because children who have to be up and out of the house so early may not have time to eat a healthy breakfast at home, breakfast is often provided in before-school programs. Early morning activities may be less active and quieter to give children a chance to pre-pare for the school day.

For after-school care, children may arrive from several different schools. They will need a snack and time for activities. Typically, programs do not extend beyond the

dinner hour. Most children are picked up by 5:30 p.m. or 6 p.m. However, if your community has a factory or other major employer with hours that extend into the evening, there may be a demand for extended evening hours. Parents who commute long distances may also require later pickup times. During summer break or on days when the schools are closed, the program should be open all day.

Program

The needs of school-age children are different from those of preschoolers. Because they have been in school all day, many are ready for lively after-school activities (**Figure 2.15**). An outdoor playtime, organized games, and a nutritious snack are essentials for an after-school program. Some children will be tired after the school day. They need opportunities for quiet activities. Crafts, board games, opportunities for dramatic play, and quiet reading may appeal to them. Children will also need a quiet space to focus and complete homework. If a child needs the help of a tutor, this may be coordinated with a local tutoring agency. Because an after-school program is only open for a couple of hours, activities must either be short or must be ones that can extend over several days.

During summer and winter breaks, or days when schools are closed, most programs expand into full-day service. The summer months can offer lots of opportuni-ties for more-involved projects and activities. One large center divides children into age groups. The counsel-ors then have children sign up in advance for particu-lar project areas. One year, a group dismantled an old, discarded engine; another group designed and decorated house plans using a computerized program and old mag-azines. There have been groups who have spent the week exploring colonial crafts, making jewelry, taking bowl-ing lessons, learning the fundamentals of cooking, and

SolStock/E+/Getty Images

Figure 2.15 Being outdoors is a great release for school-age children who need to release energy and relax after a structured school day.

preparing and then performing a play. Each week, children can change their choices. New activities are constantly added. In addition, each group has opportunities every week to visit the local swimming pool and park. There is always lots of time for outdoor play.

Working with the Schools

It is important to develop good communication with the school district personnel for your program to run smoothly. Be sure you are on the school's mailing list and receive a copy of the school-year calendar. You must be able to plan ahead for your program to be open on teacher in-service days, parent conference days, or breaks when the schools are closed.

You may also request some way to be alerted if the schools are unexpectedly closed. In areas where snow days are common, announcements are usually made online, through an emergency closing service, and on the radio, TV, and the district's website. However, in order to have your staff ready to go, you may want to ask the district to add you to their emergency closing call or email list or for an advanced early morning phone call from the school district administrator in charge. One local center director always gets a phone call at 5 a.m. on snow days as an advance warning that the school-age program will need to be open all day.

2.4 Family Child Care Home

Opening your home to children and their families can be a daunting task and sharing private spaces can be overwhelming (**Figure 2.16**). Creating a welcoming, warm, and safe environment for children in your home is vital to the success of the program. Some home providers have found that using designated space for child care activities and keeping some rooms as personal spaces works well. Others have used all the space in their home for child care activities. Using labels, pictures, daily routines, and schedules prominently placed in the areas used for

Nikola Ilic/E+/Getty Images

Figure 2.16 Having designated spaces in a family child care home allows for family members to still have their own private spaces. Activities can be carried out in these safe and secure spaces.

Director's Showcase
Reflect
What would be considerations for Johanna and David as they assisted the infant and toddler teachers with program planning?

Since Halima is in a home, all of the children are cared for in the same space. How could she best meet the needs of the older children in her care while also keeping the space safe for infants and toddlers?

Director's Showcase
Johanna and David
As Johanna and David continued their work with the infant and toddler teachers, it became evident that one of the toddlers was really struggling with transitions, especially when mom left each day. What everyone thought would be a few weeks of adjustment had not changed and it had been almost two months. The mom mentioned to one of the teachers that maybe a large program was not best suited for her child. The teacher knew of a couple of the family child care home providers in the area and mentioned this as a suggestion to Johanna and David. They wanted to learn more about what a family child care home was.

Halima
As she continued her progress to become a highly rated family child care home, word was getting out in the community. Phone calls requesting care and to get on her waiting list became more frequent. She also realized that all of her hard work was paying off! While she certainly wanted to care for as many children as possible within regulations, she also knew that recruiting more interested people to provide the same type of care was needed. She decided to talk with her instructor at the community college about her next steps.

care helps distinguish what is child care space and what is personal space. Family pictures and personal decorations add to the warmth of a family child care home.

Child safety and security need to be considered when opening your home to child care. State guidelines for child care homes must be addressed. Fenced yards, secure play structures, as well as other household dangers need to be considered before children are enrolled.

Opening Your Home to Regular Inspections

As in center-based child programs, child care homes are required to meet specific standards and to pass inspections. Regulations regarding health, safety, and nutrition as well as child development will be monitored by state and local agencies. Opening your home to inspection can be a time of anxiety and worry. Following guidelines and communicating and developing a relationship with your local agency staff can help alleviate some anxiety and help with a smooth inspection. Plan a dedicated space in your home for written procedures and parent information, and maintain it as a place where families can receive vital information. Some home care providers have a designated space with children's cubbies and a bulletin board containing information and state-required regulations for all to see.

Working Alone

Many child care home providers operate independently, which can be rewarding but challenging at times. In many areas, there are networks of providers that share resources, ideas, activities, and problem-solving strategies that are inclusive to the family child care community. These networks often meet in person or within online social platforms and networks. While larger early childhood programs typically steer their staff members

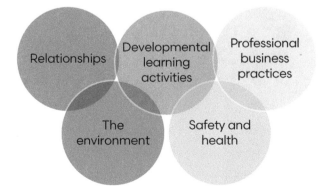

NAFCC Standards Content Areas*

Relationships

Developmental learning activities

Professional business practices

The environment

Safety and health

*Content areas are subject to updating and change. Be sure to always have access to the most up-to-date information from NAFCC.

Goodheart-Willcox Publisher

Figure 2.17 NAFCC sets content standards for family child care home providers to follow as they plan their day-to-day programming for the children in their care.

PeopleImages/iStock/Getty Images Plus

Figure 2.18 Operating a family child care home not only means sharing living space but also, more importantly, a parent. It is important to set aside time each day, after the children in your care have left for the day, to spend with your children.

to have professional memberships with NAEYC, the National Association for Family Child Care (NAFCC) works in collaboration with NAEYC but is very aware of the differences and the particular needs of home-based providers (**Figure 2.17**). Belonging to this organization connects the individual to a network of others who are doing the same work on a daily basis. Because this work can be isolating for the child care provider, fostering connections with other home providers benefits all involved.

Caring for Your Own Children While Caring for Others

Another benefit to running a family child care home is being able to include your own children in work (**Figure 2.18**). This may be an adjustment for your family. Your children may have difficulty sharing their mom, space in their home, and even their own toys. When assisting your own children with making the adjustment, allow them to have a space of their own in the house, separate toys that are not shareable, and set aside time in the day just for your children.

Director's Showcase
Reflect
Do you believe that some children are better suited for family child care home environments? Why?

Director's Showcase

Johanna and David

Since the purchase of the child care center, Johanna and David have learned so much! Serving the varying ages certainly opened their eyes to all of the many considerations for each age group. It also made them realize that pursuing national accreditation was important, but they needed to slow down their pace and work on several identified areas to best support the teachers in their classrooms. They were excited for the future and all of the possibilities that could best serve the children and families in their care.

Halima

After talking with her instructor, Halima found a group on social media that she was able to refer families to, as well as gain support through new friendships. She shared ideas with the other members of the group. Halima was also able to gain insight into state agency inspection staff and shared her experiences as she continued to exceed within the rating system provided by the state. She also found a child care home provider in her own neighborhood and was able to schedule trips to the park and activities around their community together. This became a strong professional friendship that provided support during times when they needed to share ideas or talk about challenging issues they were dealing with.

Chapter 2 Review and Assessment

Summary

2.1 Identify the major characteristics of quality child care programming.

- Over the years, the National Association for the Education of Young Children (NAEYC) has established 10 Program Standards for all types of early childhood programs to use as guides and to help families be better informed when selecting child care and recognizing quality child care programming. These standards have been discussed and reviewed by experts in the field.
- This has included each being extensively researched in the support of development and educational needs of young children. As these standards have evolved, they have been accepted in the field as the basis for high-quality early childhood programs. The 10 standards include: relationships; curriculum; teaching; assessment of child progress; health; staff competencies, preparation, and support; families; community relationships; physical environment; and leadership and management.

2.2 Examine universal early childhood program practices.

- All early childhood program practices are universal, whether a program is large or small, housed in a child care center, or provided within a home.
- Utilizing the 10 NAEYC Program Standards, those providing care in any type of program can develop appropriate program philosophies. These philosophies are determined based on theory and research that supports what is good for children.
- This includes providing developmentally appropriate practices within classrooms specific to the age groups served in an early childhood program environment.

2.3 Distinguish program elements specific to age-differentiated care.

- The ages of children served help to distinguish the necessary program elements that provide quality classroom environments. Elements that are necessary for infants and toddlers have different considerations as do those for preschool and school-age children.
- Although the types of child care programs vary in many ways, it is essential to all programs to provide a secure and safe environment, developmentally appropriate activities, warm nurturing staff, and ample opportunities for play.
- The facility where child care is offered may differ—a church, a shopping center storefront, a freestanding building, a community center, or a home—but the core values and principles are the same.

2.4 Investigate considerations when providing a family child care home.

- Providing a family child care home does have its own set of differences. Unlike a child care center where you lock the door and walk away each day, when care is provided in the home, that is not the case.
- In addition, family members must share their spaces as well as their mom or dad with others receiving care in the home. In addition, there are liabilities to consider as well as the many benefits when providing care out of the home environment.

Review

1. When caring for infants and toddlers, what special classroom specific considerations must be made to best support a quality environment? (2.1)
2. What caregiving characteristics are essential for teachers who work in the infant and toddler classroom? Why? (2.3)
3. What specific physical development needs do toddlers have and how can this be supported in the classroom? (2.3)
4. Describe opportunities for structured and unstructured play opportunities for preschool-age children. (2.3)
5. How would the term "developmentally appropriate practices" apply to caring for infants, toddlers, preschool, and school-age children? (2.1)
6. List possible considerations when creating an inclusive environment serving children with special needs. (2.2)
7. Describe several parent involvement opportunities and state why they would be important to implement. (2.2)
8. What considerations need to be made when providing out-of-school-time programming for school-age children? (2.3)
9. Why is it important to work with local schools when providing care for school-age children? (2.3)
10. Many family child care home providers work alone. List the advantages and disadvantages and include your thoughts on each. (2.4)

Showcase Your Skills

As we discussed in this chapter, Johanna and David became owners of a previously established child care program. Halima, on the other hand, opened her home to care for children in the community. Each have high quality care expectations for their programs and want to aspire for national accreditation.

Based on the information shared in each section of this chapter, it is now your turn to serve in the role of consultant either for Johanna and David's child care center, or Halima's family child care home. Write a proposal using the following points as your guide.

1. What considerations need to be made for the infants, toddlers, preschool, and school-age children being served in either program environment?
2. List professional development topics that would be helpful as the team of teachers or Halima learn more in the pursuit of national accreditation.
3. Determine a proposed list of next steps at either program to include a suggested timeline to begin the process of national accreditation.

Matching

Match the following terms with the correct definitions:

A. behaviorist
B. child-directed play
C. constructivist
D. developmentally appropriate practices
E. inclusive environment
F. interactionalist
G. maturationalist
H. NAEYC 10 Program Standards

1. Children develop according to predictable biological patterns and increase in competence when the environment supports this development.
2. Environment that enhances the abilities of all children to cooperate and work together in a space that accommodates all abilities and requirements.
3. Play that allows the child to choose their activities during free play.
4. Standards established for all types of early childhood programs to use as guides and to help families be better informed when selecting child care.
5. Theory stating that a child's learning occurs as each child has more complicated interactions with the environment that is either positively or negatively reinforced in a highly structured and teacher-controlled environment.
6. Methods that promote optimal development and learning through a strengths-based, play-based approach to joyful, engaged learning.
7. Theory stating that children construct their knowledge of the world through having a wide range of concrete experiences in a variety of areas.
8. Theory stating that children develop through their interactions with the environment.

yacobchuk/iStock/Getty Images Plus

3 CHAPTER

Governance of Child Care Programs

Learning Outcomes

After studying this chapter, you will be able to:

3.1 Examine the role of state licensing and other state regulatory agencies or program boards and committees that impact the care of children in early childhood programs.

3.2 Review the legal concerns and obligations of operating an early childhood program.

3.3 Distinguish the role of quality rating systems and their support of continuous quality improvement of early childhood programs.

3.4 Discover what national accreditation is and why it is important to the early childhood field.

Key Terms

accreditation
accreditation performance criteria
advisory board
American with Disabilities Act (ADA)
bonding insurance
child medical and accident insurance
Civil Rights compliance
Department of Labor Fair Wage and
     Standards Act
directors and officers insurance
disability insurance
governing board
I-9 Illegal Aliens Act
liability insurance
national accreditation
Occupational Safety and Health Act (OSHA)
program standard
property insurance
Quality Rating Systems (QRS)
Right to Know Act
Title VII of the Civil Rights Act of 1964
zoning codes

Introduction

Many factors will affect the decisions made when operating an early childhood program. Regulatory agencies are in place to protect the welfare of children when they are not in the care of a parent or legal guardian. Whether your program is a larger facility or housed within a home, you will be contacting and working collaboratively with regulatory agencies. As a program owner or director, it is important to understand that when designing and running a facility, dictated regulations are put forth by the state in which the program operates. While these are minimal standards, they will be determined based on each individual state. In addition, other state regulatory agencies are often involved due to the health and safety aspects of caring for children and a program's need to employ individuals who assist with the care of children.

Operating an early childhood program, large or small, has liabilities. There are multiple state regulations and agency expectations. As a leader, one must be continually aware of and adhere to state regulations and policies. This includes those who work directly with a board, advisory committee, or other established entity within some program types. There are many concerns to be considered, and state expectations and regulatory obligations to provide care for certain age groups can be costly.

NAEYC/DAP standards

Standards covered in this chapter:

NAEYC

3b, 3c

DAP

3A, 3C, 3E

When opening and operating a program, it is important to weigh all of these considerations very carefully.

Infant and toddler care is particularly costly. Because of this, finding quality infant and toddler care is often difficult. To help assist with these costs, many states have implemented quality rating systems, or QRS. These systems have expectations that are above the state minimum standards. However, if these standards are met consistently, programs can receive a higher reimbursement rate for children receiving subsidized child care. In addition, community and local area agencies will provide services to these higher-rated programs at a discounted rate.

As part of these state quality initiatives, programs that have achieved national accreditation status often receive the highest rating that a program can receive. Set forth by recognized national organizations, these have established program standards based on research and dialogue with early childhood experts. Implementing these standards comes at a higher cost to the program. However, parents are typically willing to pay the higher cost of tuition so that their children receive the highest quality care possible.

3.1 Why Is Regulatory Oversight Important?

Each state establishes regulations designed to protect children's health, safety, and general well-being while they are in child care (**Figure 3.1**). Programs that meet those requirements are granted a license. This license gives a program legal permission from the state to operate. Without a license, a program is operating illegally and may be fined and shut down by the state. With a license, there is confidence in knowing that the program meets the minimal legal requirements of the state. The license assures parents, insurers, and the community

Director's Showcase

Lora

Lora has accepted a position as director with a non-profit, church-affiliated program. Coming from two years of experience as an assistant director in a for-profit, corporate-based early childhood program, she has had little interaction with state and local regulators and is unfamiliar with the expectations of a non-profit organization. In addition, she has never worked with an advisory board before now.

Petra

Petra recently became a mom and decided to stay home with her baby due to the high cost of child care in her area. After talking with a few friends, they decided that having Petra care for their children as well would be cost saving for them and would make all of them feel better about the care their children would be receiving. While Petra cared for children in various babysitting jobs in her high school years, she just left a career working in a call center providing customer service support. This is a completely new adventure for her, and she has decided that finding out more information about caring for others' children would be a good starting point.

Reflect

Both Lora and Petra come from different backgrounds and experiences, but both want to provide a child care program. What do you think will be most important for each of them to understand about program operations in a center and home environment?

itaesem/E+/Getty Images

Figure 3.1 All states have minimal licensing requirements that must be met to operate a program legally.

that your program has met state standards. The National Association for the Education of Young Children (NAEYC) Code of Ethical Conduct guides early childhood leaders and teaching staff to provide safe environments for children by upholding regulatory rules.

For certain programs, due to their financial structure or business status, a board or oversight committee is either required or simply helpful. This group of people are intended to not only provide guidance to the program's overarching purpose of providing child care services to the community, but they also lend their expertise and insights to aid in the success of the program. In most cases, early childhood program leaders are responsible for the day-to-day operations of the program. The board or committee should serve as a sounding board to assist the director in making significant decisions necessary to keep the program viable.

What Licensing Regulates

Some states allow for certain child care providers to be exempt from child care licensing laws, such as care by relatives, better known as kith and kin care; half-day nursery schools; limited out-of-school-time care; and drop-in or sick care (due to its limited hours of operation). Child care licensing requirements will vary from state to state. The following aspects of child care may be subject to licensing requirements:

- the number of square feet of space necessary in the classroom for each child enrolled;
- the number of square feet of space necessary on the playground for each child enrolled;
- the ratio of adults to children in each age group;
- the minimum age, the required training, and education of the adults in the program;
- the nature of the daily program;
- the maximum group size;
- the type of equipment and materials utilized with different age groups;
- the structural, health, and safety components of the building and outdoor areas;
- the nutrition and food delivery to children;
- the required health exams and immunization status of children and staff; and
- the criminal background checks on staff.

Some states may require a higher quality of care than others do. Overall, obtaining a license is required and viewed as a starting place when providing early childhood services. Programs striving for higher-quality care have additional options and benchmarks to strive for and will be discussed later in the chapter.

Preparation for Licensing

Getting ready for a visit from a licensing representative is a serious activity. It requires thought and preparation. While each state varies in its requirements, the following steps are typical of what needs to be done:

- complete application and additional compliance forms
- organize staff records to be sure they include any required tests, background checks, fingerprint checks, yearly physicals, evaluations, professional education and/or training documentation, and other required clearances
- secure insurance policies that meet all required liability protections for individuals, property, and any vehicle use
- update children's records to be sure they include yearly physicals, immunizations, developmental records, emergency contacts, court records necessary for custody disputes, and record of parent contacts or conferences
- review plans for emergencies and evacuation, including notification of local authorities
- perform a visual inspection of center and playground with staff
- review key areas of concern, such as plug covers, water temperature, required postings of items such as evacuation routes or emergency numbers

While these steps are general, all states provide a checklist on their websites and/or the licensing representative will provide this information for preparation purposes (**Figure 3.2**).

Responsible Agencies

Every state has an agency or division that is responsible for the licensing of child care programs either in a center or home environment. These are typically housed in the Department of Human Services, State Department of Health, or the State Department of Education. In some

Delmaine Donson/E+/Getty Images

Figure 3.2 As a program director, it is important to stay current regarding the minimal licensing requirements for centers or homes by visiting your state's child care regulation website for more information.

states, there is a designated State Department of Early Childhood Education. Organizational structure is often not the same from one state to another. Carefully researching state agencies helps to determine which is responsible for licensing in your state. Then, it is important to check local regulations for any additional regulators in the area. This can include building and code inspectors, the fire marshal, and local health department's environmental, food safety, nursing, and sanitation divisions.

While the large state agency will have the responsibility of issuing the state license, the local government divisions will vary from area to area in a state. An awareness that another division may be responsible for determining the basic safety and occupancy status of the building is important. This inspector may be different from the one that inspects the kitchen facilities and food program. A health department nurse may monitor whether immunization records are up-to-date and serve as the reporting institution should there be a severe outbreak of a communicable disease. A half-day nursery school program may be subject to a completely different regulatory process from that of a full-day program.

Before proceeding, become familiar with the state licensing regulations by doing a thorough internet search and making phone calls to local agencies. Being unaware of state and local requirements can lead to costly mistakes, such as starting on building renovations without the proper permits and approvals or making hiring decisions that are not in compliance with regulations. In addition, some homeowner's associations have limits on the type of businesses that can be conducted within a home. Exceptions or variances, which grant special permission to operate without exactly meeting the licensing standards, to the requirements are sometimes possible. However, it is risky to count on an exemption. Assuming that officials will be willing to grant an exception or variance is risky and could be much more costly than what was budgeted.

Local Ordinances

In addition to state and local agencies, child care programs may also be subject to local regulation. You will need to determine what city, township, county, parish, or other legally organized governance structures has jurisdiction over the area where your early childhood program is located. Local governing agencies include:

- Zoning Commission
- Fire and Safety Commission
- Borough or Township Governing Bodies
- Local Planning Commission

Each of these types of agencies may have the power to impose restrictions on a program with little opportunity for a program to negotiate. They may also require compliance to regulations that are very specific to your local community. For example, property easements, number of parking spaces required for the occupancy of the building, the location of wheelchair ramps, and kitchen codes could all fall under local regulations. As mentioned before, if operating out of a home, it is important to check local regulations and with a homeowner's association, if applicable.

Zoning

Many communities have **zoning codes**, which are rules that specify the types of permitted land use. Size and type of building, nature of commercial activities, and number of occupants may all be regulated by zoning codes. A center's outdoor play space may have to meet certain local requirements. The site plan may have to include a water and/or flood run-off plan. Zoning codes may also require an examination of the environmental impact of your program. Scrutiny may be directed toward the energy use and conservation efforts of your building plans. The size of the parking area and entrance-exit traffic flow may also be of concern if the building is located on a busy road or highway. If it is a program located within a home, traffic flow and parking on the street may be an issue (**Figure 3.3**). It is always a good idea to check with neighbors and the local police about traffic expectations.

Fire and Safety Codes

Local communities have fire and safety regulations, which may be more or less strict than state regulations. These regulations may indicate the type and nature of wiring, plumbing, and heating used in a building to meet specific local standards. The location of certain alarms, who monitors them, and how often they are checked are sometimes a part of these local codes. In addition, the type of building materials, type and placement of sprinkler systems throughout the facility, and access to safety exits may all be subject to local as well as state regulations. Many times the home environment does not have as many regulations applied to it, but the use of smoke detectors and other devices may be warranted.

cmart7327/iStock/Getty Images Plus

Figure 3.3 Zoning for a business, whether it be a center or a home, must include considerations for traffic flow and parking options to best serve families and the surrounding community.

Governing Boards and Committees

Privately owned programs can be operated at the discretion of the owner(s) as long as they meet licensing standards and do not violate any applicable laws. However, not-for-profit programs or those who receive government or charitable support require a more complex type of governance structure. This structure is in addition to the state and local regulatory agencies mentioned and may take the form of an advisory board or governing board. The role of an **advisory board** is to study issues and make recommendations but are not required to see that those recommendations be carried out. A **governing board** is a legal entity that is authorized to actually operate the program. Decisions requiring legal and financial commitments must be made by the governing board. When a program has a legal governing board, the director is an employee of that board. While on a day-to-day basis the director will make decisions for the program, overall policies that govern the activities and direction of the program will come from the governing board.

An advisory board has no legal authority to set policy, make commitments for the program, hire staff, or spend money. Its function is strictly to offer ideas and advice to the director. Many private programs have advisory boards to help the director gain insight into the concerns and ideas of community leaders or client families. Head Start programs have both a parent advisory council that offers suggestions and ideas while the executive board has legal authority for the program (**Figure 3.4**).

Advisory Boards	Governing Boards
• Study issues and make recommendations, but have no legal authority to carry out suggestions	• Legal entities that are authorized to operate a program
• Cannot hire staff	• Make decisions about legal and financial commitments
• Cannot spend money	• Provide additional insights into program issues that are brought to the board members attention
• Provide oversight to support the company status with the Internal Revenue Service (IRS)	• Serve as thought partners as the director pursues different ideas or potential opportunities for the program

Goodheart-Willcox Publisher

Figure 3.4 Governing boards and advisory boards are responsible for providing guidance to the early childhood director based on the expectations set forth by rules and regulations.

Director's Showcase

Lora

Now that Lora is more aware of the regulatory expectations for the new area that she will be working in, she wants to know more about the legal aspects of caring for children in a non-profit organization. When she worked in corporate-based child care, there were lengthy manuals that provided many company-wide policies and rules to follow. In her new role, Lora has been advised that she is expected to be the program expert on the legal regulations and expectations using her background knowledge as well as talking with board members to build the program.

Petra

After checking state and local regulations, Petra has learned that caring for her friends' children will be much more than just helping each other out with child care costs. She will be operating a business in her home. This means liability concerns as well as protections for her family should something happen while the children are in her care. Petra has decided to continue researching home child care before making a final decision.

Reflect

The decision to open or assume responsibility for a program is a major decision. Based on what you have learned so far, which program type would you opt to open and why?

Relationship Between Director and Board

When a program has a board of directors, the program director is legally the employee of the board. The working relationship with the board will vary according to how knowledgeable the board is about issues of child care. If the board members know little about child care, the program leader will need to advise, guide, and educate the members about the early childhood program. If the board is made up of individuals with expertise in related areas, these members provide valuable assistance. At one time or another, program leaders will deal with legal, personnel, medical, financial, and programming issues. A strong board can be a great help when formulating policy and making decisions.

Ideally, the board and the program director support each other (**Figure 3.5**). Each works for the benefit of the program. The director acts as a resource person, bringing ideas and plans to the board. The board offers suggestions and additional ideas. When a decision is reached, the director can be trusted to carry out the actions that the board has approved. This relationship needs to be a positive one, where board members and the early childhood program leader feel good about their involvement with the program. Board members should be recognized for the valuable role they play. In turn, the program director should feel that the board is supportive and trusting in the difficult role of administering an early childhood program.

3.2 Legal Concerns and Obligations of Operating a Program

When providing care to children either in a school, center, or home environment, you are providing a public service and must abide by the federal, state, and local laws that apply to your program (**Figure 3.6**). These laws differ throughout the United States, in urban and rural areas, and sometimes from town to town. No matter what type of program or where it is housed, doing due diligence to find out every possible aspect of expectations is of upmost importance. While caring for children is a joyful job, it comes with significant responsibility that must be taken seriously. Finding out more about federal laws that apply to any type of child care program is a great starting point.

Federal Laws and Regulations

There are several federal laws and regulations that relate to child care programs.

fotodelux/E+/Getty Images

Figure 3.5 As a director works with the board, it is important to bring ideas, share resources, inform, and collectively plan to benefit the overall early childhood program.

Director's Showcase

Lora and Petra

Both Lora and Petra have been feeling overwhelmed by the enormity of the responsibility to care for children. Lora, who is overseeing a program that is state licensed for 150 children, is busy learning every detail about her new program. Petra has found out that because she may be working from her home, she actually has two choices. She could establish a small family child care home that could care for up to seven children or a larger home that could care for up to 12 children but would require an aide. No matter the size of the programs, the liability and obligations are real considerations for both women.

NataBene/iStock/Getty Images Plus

Figure 3.6 It is important to stay current with all federal, state, and local laws. This comes from carefully tracking this information and creating systems to assist with monitoring and changes that will impact the early childhood program.

- **Civil Rights compliance**—Prohibits discrimination in hiring and program policies.
- **Americans with Disabilities Act (ADA)**—Provides for building access for all persons (e.g., children, parents, and employees) with disabilities and handicaps. This covers restrooms and fire/safety exits. It also prohibits discrimination in hiring or enrollment policies.
- **Right to Know Act**—Requires posted information regarding storage and use of cleaning materials or other hazardous chemicals.
- **I-9 Illegal Aliens Act**—Requires employers to see proof of employees' citizenship status.
- **Department of Labor Fair Wage and Standards Act**—Identifies minimum wage and employment conditions.
- *The Family Medical Leave Act (FMLA)*—Requires employers to provide eligible employees with up to 12 weeks of job-protected, unpaid leave during

a 12-month time period. The leave may be taken for the birth of a child, the adoption of a child, providing foster care, an illness of a close relative, or a disabling health condition of the employee.
- **Occupational Safety and Health Act (OSHA)**—Requires employers to maintain a safe and healthy workplace.
- **Title VII of the Civil Rights Act of 1964**—Requires employers to not discriminate against job applicants based on race, color, religion, sex, and national origin.

Because new laws frequently go into effect and existing ones may change, staying current with the requirements may affect program decisions and overall budgetary needs of the program. More information can be found on federal government websites on pending legislation and changes in applicable laws. Monitoring these areas on a regular basis are highly advised.

State Laws and Regulations

Many states have a governor's hotline or other offices, including the Department of Commerce, that can provide helpful legal information for small or large businesses. As a program administrator, you may contact these resources to seek advice and stay current on regulations and requirements, such as:

- *Out-of-state registration requirements*—If the decision is to buy in to a franchised child care program, the business may need to register as a "foreign entity" if the company's headquarters is located in another state.
- *Unemployment taxes*—States often require an account to withhold and remit state unemployment taxes as a protection to the employer and employee.
- *Income tax and payroll benefit withholdings*—Businesses with employees must set up accounts with state commissions for withholding and remitting state income taxes from wages and salaries paid to employees.
- *Worker's compensation insurance*—While personal insurance is different, this insurance is required by states that provide it through an insurance agent. This insurance protects individuals who are hurt on the job and are unable to perform their regular duties set forth by their employers within their job descriptions.

These state laws and regulations are in addition to those laws, regulations, and agencies states have established to provide oversight specifically for the care of children.

Liability Concerns

A major concern in the operation of child care programs is the need to provide a safe, healthful environment for children and staff. Strict adherence to licensing regulations is an important part of ensuring safety. As the

rollover/E+/Getty Images

Figure 3.7 Child care programs must support safe and healthy environments to protect children and staff from injury or illness.

director or owner of an early childhood program, you are responsible for the well-being of the children in care. It is generally accepted that young children cannot be responsible for themselves. Those who care for them must be aware of basic safety and health precautions. If a child is injured or becomes ill because of negligence or deliberate actions by staff, your program will be liable (**Figure 3.7**).

Careful adherence to all licensing and local safety requirements can provide some legal protection. Any type of child care program operating illegally would be at a substantially greater risk for both civil and criminal legal action if an accident were to occur. Staying current with the required training and constant oversight of the established responsibilities of staff is imperative. Careless or poorly trained staff members are less likely to spot potential hazards. Alert supervision minimizes the likelihood of accidents. Liability resulting from an accident may be lessened if it is clear that the early childhood program's leadership and staff have been diligent in trying to keep children safe.

Insurance Protection

No matter how cautious a program is nor how well trained its employees, accidents can and will happen. Insurance provides protection against financial loss for an early childhood program. Many times, the size and location of a program will determine the need and type of insurance protection that will be necessary. This cost will vary based on the types of protection and what area of the country the program is located. Even those who provide care in their home to children must have additional insurance added to their homeowner's insurance. Assuming that all types of incidents would be covered is a dangerous expectation to have. Often, insurance packages are offered to members of professional and child care trade associations. Check these costs since discounts might be given to offset the cost of membership dues.

The insurance company that provides the policy may insist that the program adheres to additional requirements. These requirements are usually designed to minimize the chance that a claim for insurance reimbursement will be expected. For example, some insurance companies will not insure a family child care home if they are located in what is deemed as a "high-risk" area by the insurance program. Insurance companies know that family child care homes are harder to supervise. They present a greater risk for the company than a larger program would. Some companies may not insure a center if it has a swimming pool or body of water on the premises.

Director's Showcase

Lora

After doing more research, Lora has been learning more about the expectations that come with overseeing a larger program. Research on government websites has been very helpful in better understanding what is required for her non-profit program. In addition, because she is located within a church, the different types of liability insurance coverages have different expectations. She also has uncovered that insurance discounts have been applied due to the size of the policy already purchased by the church. She has double-checked that all state coverages were already in place and that the program appeared to be fully covered. She is starting to feel much better about this part of her responsibilities.

Petra

Petra, on the other hand, has decided that staying with a small program that cared for seven children is the best choice for her. She would only need to purchase an additional policy on top of what she is already paying for homeowner's insurance. After discussing dividing this expense among the interested parents who want her to care for their children, Petra and her friends have agreed that making sure that Petra, her family, and her friends' families are properly protected is important. They all also have become more aware of what this business venture would mean for Petra. The friends renewed their commitment to each other and to supporting Petra in opening her own family child care home business.

Reflect

There is so much to consider. In the case of Petra and the liability opening a child care program creates, would this be something that you would be willing to do?

There are different types of insurance available. In some states, the licensing requirements dictate certain types of insurance coverage. There are several types to consider depending on your specific program:

- **liability insurance**—protects against financial loss due to a lawsuit against program
- **property insurance**—protects against loss of equipment or building
- **child medical and accident insurance**—provides medical and hospital costs for an individual child injury
- **disability insurance**—protects program workers from lost income if they become disabled and cannot work
- **directors and officers insurance**—provides protection of personal assets and legal fee coverage in case of a lawsuit against a director or officer of a program
- **bonding insurance**—protects program against financial loss due to actions of officers or staff who are authorized to handle program money

There is so much to consider based on the needs and characteristics of your program. For example, a program housed within a government-owned building has different insurance needs than a rented facility. All facilities, no matter what size, must consider insuring the program's more costly equipment, such as the playground equipment. Liability insurance is also generally considered essential to protect the individuals providing care to young children. While you may be highly competent, feel that you have sought out competent staff, and have done everything possible to have a safe environment to care for children, accidents can happen. A judgment against you or staff members could wipe out any available financial resources. Seeking out professional consultation from resources, such as an attorney, accountant, and insurance agent, is a wise time investment.

3.3 Quality Rating Systems

The field of early childhood has come a long way over the past few decades. During this time, states have worked to license facilities caring for large and small groups of children so that basic needs are met. In the mid-1980s, the care of young children evolved into an area of great interest to society and the NAEYC began to identify developmentally appropriate practices, better known as DAP. As this trend continued to evolve, so did the research on early childhood settings and brain development of young children. Based on significant research findings, society learned more and began to take notice about the importance of children's earliest experiences and the need to get off to a strong and healthy start.

With this focus on the importance of quality child care, many states began to launch voluntary Quality Rating and Improvement Systems (QRIS), more commonly

Director's Showcase

Lora

After about six months of getting a better handle of her responsibilities, one of the board members approaches Lora about the program striving to become a part of the quality rating system provided by the state. She thinks that this might be a great marketing tool for the program as well as recognition of the great care that she and the program staff are providing to the children each day. A little overwhelmed by the request, Lora decides to check into it a little more.

Petra

Petra is able to open her home as a family child care business. Within weeks, she has several women in her community who also provide home-based child care reach out to her. She is excited to discover that these women want to be considered more than just "babysitters." They belong to a local family child care association and are participating in the state's quality rating system. She is very interested and wants to learn more!

known today as **Quality Rating Systems (QRS)**. These systems, which are federally and state funded, have built-in criteria that support early childhood programs of all sizes and types with the intent of increasing the quality of care of children beyond basic state licensing requirements. Examples of the areas of focus include lower staff-to-child ratios and group sizes, enhanced education and professional development expectations for staff and program leadership, enhanced daily programming expectations, and heightened health and safety

Thinkstock Images/Getty Images

Figure 3.8 Lower staff-to-child ratios and group sizes support more one-on-one time between the teacher and children in the classroom.

considerations (**Figure 3.8**). Many times, these areas are measured by a variety of assessment scales that are performed by a trained individual who often provides either written and/or on-site consultation services.

Early Childhood Program Assessment

The word *assessment* is often perceived as intimidating, and the process of an assessment may seem scary. However, the intent of a program assessment is to engage early childhood leaders and their staff in thinking about continuous improvement of their services. Some states have utilized self-developed checklist criteria that assist programs with this process. Other states have made large investments in specific tools that are valid and reliable. Not only have these states invested in developing and purchasing assessment tools, but they also provide training to professionals with specific credentials and experience who will eventually go out to programs and complete the assessment. While there are multiple tools used by different states for different purposes, the idea is to engage the program staff by completing the self-assessment portion, have opportunities to make changes or adaptations, and learn more about criteria that supports quality care of young children (**Figure 3.9**).

Sense of Space or a Place I Belong?

What does your classroom radiate?

Directions: Select A, B, or C for each item listed below.
A = Strongly Agree; B = Agree; C = Strongly Disagree

1. _____ There is an open space where children are free to manipulate materials and equipment, and have input to design the area to transform the *space* into a more personal space or *place*.

2. _____ At least 60 minutes is provided each day for children to play freely in the open space to allow social interactions and relationship building.

3. _____ Children's artwork is displayed using unique ways to frame their work with natural textures such as wood, straw, or fabrics to frame children's creations.

4. _____ Child-created artwork is displayed that represents at least three different types of art, such as drawings with colors, watercolors, or designs made with a variety of collage materials.

5. _____ At least three local natural elements are accessible to children for exploration and are frequently refreshed and changed such as dried wild flowers, plants, woods, or rock.

6. _____ There are very few laminated posters in the classroom that reflect current events or community-related information.

7. _____ At least five authentic and child-created objects, per enrolled child, are purposefully and intentionally placed on the walls.

8. _____ Classroom walls are painted with neutral colors and natural elements that include baskets, woven placemats, marble, slats of wood, or bowls.

9. _____ Classroom promotes the connection between past and present by reflecting the people who live in the community by displaying real photographs of community workers and common places that children recognize.

10. _____ There are images in the classroom that reflect the uniqueness of each child enrolled in the program.

11. _____ At least three items in the classroom reflecting the rich history of the community or region.

12. _____ At least five examples of authentic materials opposed to plastic or commercial materials are used in the classroom.

- If you responded frequently with an "A," you are well on your way to creating a *place* which is an environment with a feeling that is beautiful and respectful to children.
- If you responded frequently with a "B," you may have some additional items needed to enrich your *space* in order for it to be considered a *place*.
- If you responded frequently with a "C," you may want to consider implementing some of the ideas to transform your classroom *space* into a *place*.

While there are no "correct" answers, use this as a guide in program and classroom planning. Make a commitment to providing a place that children in your care can relate to and call home.

Goodheart-Willcox Publisher

Figure 3.9 Use the above checklist to evaluate how your classroom reflects a sense of space or a sense of place. A classroom with a sense of place helps children feel safe, loved, and reflects their own culture, heritage, and community.

The use of these types of assessment tools can be costly. However, many states provide a variety of initiatives to support early childhood leaders and their staff to be successful in the process. Many of the initiatives include incentives for participating programs to receive free copies of the assessment tools, on-site technical assistance by experts in the tools, and mini-grants or stipends to purchase necessary equipment. Leadership in state-established early childhood education efforts understand the need for early childhood programs to be successful as they know that investment in the earlier years pays off as children grow and support the workforce one day.

State System Recognition

Programs that achieve success in the quality state rating initiatives oftentimes receive higher reimbursement for children who receive subsidy payments. Families who qualify for subsidy child care may either pay little to nothing for care or may be awarded minimal co-payments (**Figure 3.10**). This enables parents and caregivers to go to work or school while their children are cared for in quality programs. Since programs typically only receive payment when the child is in attendance, receiving a higher level of reimbursement helps to offset the true cost of the child's enrollment in the program. While these payments are not the full cost of care, the rates are constantly reviewed and adjusted as state system budgets allow to assist programs in meeting their budgetary requirements to provide care to their community.

States also provide several marketing and public relations outlets to promote quality child care. Informational campaigns educate the public on what quality child care should look like. For example, in Oklahoma, when the

JohnnyGreig/E+/Getty Images

Figure 3.10 Care for children living with disabilities often receives higher reimbursement to help offset the cost of the child's enrollment in the program. Those higher costs can be due to the need for more adults in the classroom and lower staff-to-child ratios.

state launched its quality rating system in the late 1990s, the program was named "Reaching for the Stars." Why? Drawing upon the crafted rating system of the hotel and restaurant industries, the higher the star level, the better the establishment. People will seek out a program with a higher-quality rating and will also be willing to pay a premium for higher-quality care. Years later, "Reaching for the Stars" is still going strong in Oklahoma, and its star system continues to be refined and additional levels created to better inform the public and recognize quality programs.

Some states require participation in these programs when receiving higher reimbursement, and others do not. These determinations are made by a collective group of people in state and local government entities that do research in the area of early childhood. In addition, they talk with state and local leadership to get an idea of which child care system would work best in areas throughout the state. This concentrated effort allows the government and the local child care industry to work together to best serve the citizens in the area and receive reimbursement.

State System Reimbursement

The true cost of care has long been debated and certainly has never been resolved. The cost to provide child care services vary based on areas of the country, cost of living, wages paid to working parents, industries that support those wages, and the overall economic climate. These varying costs make it difficult to accurately calculate the true cost of care. For example, the cost for infant care in the Washington, D.C., area can be upwards of $400 per week, while in a small town in Arkansas, the average rate is $125 per week. As you can imagine, the types of wages for working parents have the potential of being much higher in a large city with multiple opportunities for work. Whereas in a small town, these communities typically thrive on a handful of industries. Wages in these areas are spread among a large group of people doing the same type of work with very few receiving executive-level salaries. An example of this would be a tire or food-processing plant. State systems keep these variables in mind when setting reimbursement rates for their urban and rural communities.

State System Levels

Each system level varies on a variety of benchmarks. As mentioned earlier, some state systems utilize program assessment tools to determine the level of quality a program is providing. Individual states have differed in their thinking when putting these systems together. For example, in some states, programs must achieve a certain score on an assessment tool to receive higher reimbursement. This score is typically tied to a time frame and means that additional future assessments will be required. On top of maintaining the score, the program must meet basic state licensing requirements. If a program is written up for failure to meet state regulations and is unable to correct the issue, states will demote the program to a lower level until it deals with its issues. While this sounds punitive, it also builds in a safety net to stop those who are only willing to try and meet the expectations for the purposes of more money instead of believing in and implementing higher-quality practices on a regular basis.

The highest level for any of the state systems is that of **national accreditation** and from a reimbursement or incentive program standpoint provided by quality rating systems, this can assist with income for accredited programs.

One of the most highly sought-after accreditation systems is the one provided by NAEYC. Launched in the mid-1980s, this accreditation system has worked hard to educate the public and government officials about what quality child care looks like and should be. NAEYC, along with other early childhood associations and entities that award recognized systems of accreditation, have found a collective voice to include an accreditation system for homes. This voice has worked to better inform government officials and the public as to what standards are necessary for a quality early childhood program. These standards have been highly researched, and feedback has been sought from the field to help best define the quality inter-workings necessary to support children's learning and development.

3.4 National Accreditation

National **accreditation** officially recognizes that a program meets certain standards of quality and has successfully completed the accrediting organization's evaluation process and met its criteria. National accreditation in early childhood programs began in the mid-1980s. One of the first was the formulation of accreditation standards by NAEYC. These standards identified quality practices that programs must follow to be nationally recognized. Other

Director's Showcase

Lora

After talking more with her licensing worker and hearing his encouragement, Lora decides to apply for the Two-Star rating that was created by her state system. This means that she not only has to make sure that basic licensing regulations are met but that she and her staff need more professional development training and must participate in an assessment process. When she takes the information to the board for a vote, the members unanimously throw their support behind her to pursue the higher star rating. After she meets with the staff to share the news of what this means for the center, the staff are excited to do this as well!

Petra

Petra also wants to participate in the quality rating system provided by her state. She discovers that mini-grants are available to assist her with purchasing a few more pieces of equipment and the state has provided an on-site technical assistance person who provides training for her. Within weeks the equipment pieces that she needs are delivered and installed, and the on-site technical assistance specialist has helped her to rearrange her space to be more functional to care for the children in her home. She is looking forward to learning more about the assessment process.

Reflect

Now that you have learned more about being a quality-rated program, how likely would it be that you would pursue this higher rating and why?

Director's Showcase

Lora

Within a year, Lora and her staff are delighted to achieve the Two-Star rating. They feel recognized for the effort they all contribute each day to the children in their care. Upon attending a state conference, staff heard more about an accreditation support project that is being offered by the state. Not only would it provide money to help purchase the tools, but it also would provide access to an expert who knows more about what accreditation means for their program. Excited, the interested staff members and Lora begin to find out more.

Petra

Petra recently participated in the assessment requirement her state mandated. It was performed by a trained state consultant who came to her home. After feedback was given by the consultant regarding her scores, the consultant urged her to think more about getting her home nationally accredited. At first, Petra was hesitant. She cannot believe that she has come such a long way in a short period of time. The consultant continues to urge her to find out more.

Figure 3.11 The cost of quality infant and toddler care can range based on the state, size of the city or town, and the need of the community.

national groups developed quality benchmarks and standards for early childhood programming to include family child care homes and preschool programs, including the National Early Childhood Program Accreditation (NECPA) and the National Association for Family Child Care (NAFCC). Program accreditation helps parents to determine if a program is committed to quality child care services by participating in a rigorous process. These accreditation entities base their quality benchmarks on what research and practice says is best when providing quality programming for young children (**Figure 3.11**).

Accreditation Standards and Performance Criteria

While there are several organizations providing program accreditation, NAEYC has spent years working with experts and educators to develop 10 Program Standards that have become essential components. A **program standard** defines the level of functioning and sets the expected

benchmark in areas that research has found to support high-quality programs for young children. Today, these standards have been accepted in the field as the basis for high-quality early childhood programs (NAEYC, 2021).

In addition to meeting the standards, programs must also be observed implementing these practices based on a set of specific indicators. Commonly known as **accreditation performance criteria**, these are the activities a program must demonstrate in order to prove it meets the program standards (**Figure 3.12**). This is done by collecting evidence from various points within the program. Evidence includes a detailed report with supporting documentation from administration, a lengthy survey completed by staff and parents, classroom observations, and many other action steps and items that are eventually placed within a program's portfolio. The documents within the portfolio are intended to give a clear, well-defined picture of the characteristics of excellent early childhood programs.

On-Site Accreditation Visits

As part of the portfolio review, there is an on-site visitation that coincides with the process. The site visit allows for trained experts in the accreditation criteria and process to observe the operations of the daily program. Oftentimes these experts will observe classrooms, parent-staff-child interactions, and administration interchanges within the program throughout the day. Lesson plans, meal service, and aspects related to the health and safety practices of the program are reviewed. Identified staff and administration, as well as parents, may be interviewed. The visit might be as little as a couple of days or longer for larger programs. While a stressful process, the accreditation visit is an opportunity to celebrate the hard work that it takes to operate a quality program while identifying any areas where the program can continue to grow.

Shortly after the visit, the program will hear whether it has been awarded the accreditation status or deferred. If deferred, the program is provided information on

Child Care Accreditation Groups			
Organization	Abbreviation	Website	Description
National Association for the Education of Young Children	NAEYC	www.naeyc.org	Provides program accreditation for early childhood programs serving children birth to 8 years.
National Early Childhood Program Accreditation	NECPA	www.necpa.net	Provides program accreditation for center-based child care.
National Association for Family Child Care	NAFCC	www.nafcc.org	Provides program accreditation for home-based child care.

Figure 3.12 There are three main accreditation organizations that are recognized by state quality rating systems across the nation.

identified areas of weakness. These areas are intended to assist the program in developing an action plan with a reasonable timeline to address the areas. Depending on the identified areas either more visits are scheduled and/or documentation is submitted when the enhancements are completed. Once this process takes place, a final determination of program status is awarded.

Accreditation Long Term

The process is lengthy as well as costly. Many programs struggle to find the funding to pursue national accreditation. Over the years, in conjunction with the state quality rating systems, parents are becoming increasingly aware of what program accreditation means and how it impacts the care of their child. Communities, as well as businesses, are beginning to provide grant dollars to support programs in the accreditation process. Employers have repeatedly found that if an employee is happy where their child is receiving care they are a much more productive, long-term employee. Making the investment is smart for today's business world, and program accreditation is highly sought after in these instances.

Overall, program accreditation by reputable organizations is highly encouraged. This established status recognizes programs that have achieved the characteristics of high-quality programs that have been based on years of research, literature, findings of field tests, and input from thousands of professionals who care about children. This developed procedure ensures programs are effectively committed to the provision of quality programming. From a marketing and public relations aspect, programs are permitted to identify themselves as accredited centers in advertising and for other professional recognition purposes. Programs that receive accreditation can be justifiably proud. The recognition represents approval by experts in the field that the program has achieved a high level of quality (**Figure 3.13**).

Maintaining Accreditation

All accreditation entities have a length of time that the status is awarded. Then, the expectation is for the program to go through the process again. Award of the accreditation can vary over a series of years. Oftentimes there have been changes in staffing, program orientation, and educational or curricular programming. Part of the role of the agency is to continually work to enhance their standards, revise if necessary, and inform the field of changes. While quite the balancing act for everyone involved, this allows for best practices to continue to evolve and for practices that have become outdated to be excluded from the criteria expectations. With over 40 years of accreditation experience, NAEYC updates its program standards on an ongoing basis. It is in

FatCamera/E+/Getty Images

Figure 3.13 High-quality programs provide many opportunities for children to play and learn. Music is one of the many activities provided to young children.

their best interest to maintain standards that reflect the current values and research-supported data on what high-quality programs should promote for optimal learning and development for all children.

Director's Showcase

Lora

Lora has researched the different accreditation bodies recognized by her state and discussed the process with the board. While the NAEYC accreditation is a little more costly than the others, the board has committed to doing fund-raising as well as looking into ways to ask for financial assistance from the church to support the effort. Because the idea came from the staff, they chat regularly about it and have already started doing their homework on what the expectations would be for the different ages of children that they care for.

Petra

Petra has talked to her husband and the parents that have been supporting her and entrusting her with the care of their children. The home child care provider friends that she has made have started to talk more about accreditation. Recently at an association meeting, Petra and two of the ladies decided that they would work together on the national accreditation process. The very next day, one of them called to find out what the state provided to assist them, while Petra called NAFCC to find out more about the accreditation materials.

Reflect

Should you decide to be a center director or home provider, would you pursue national accreditation? Why or why not?

Chapter 3 Review and Assessment

Summary

3.1 Examine the role of state licensing and other state regulatory agencies or program boards and committees that impact the care of children in early childhood programs.

- There are many factors that affect how a program operates. All states require some sort of licensing for any early childhood programs—both home- and center-based—that operate a minimum number of hours per day. Meeting these licensing requirements is essential if a program is to operate legally. These licensing regulations vary from state to state. Oversight can come from federal, state, and local municipalities. Researching each is highly recommended as well as seeking out appropriate expertise to assist with understanding all of the requirements. Depending on the size and business structure of the program, program boards or committees may be required to assist with the overall oversight of the operating early childhood program.

3.2 Review the legal concerns and obligations of operating an early childhood program.

- There are also many legal concerns and obligations that come with operating an early childhood program. These legal concerns and liabilities can be safeguarded by the many forms of coverage and professional insurance choices available to the field. While this could become costly, it is necessary and an area that must be constantly monitored to make sure that the program is covered to the best of its ability when caring for the children each day.

3.3 Distinguish the role of quality rating systems and their support of continuous quality improvement of early childhood programs.

- Many states are now recognizing the significant investment made by early childhood programs in their communities. This recognition has come from developed quality rating systems that have been in existence since the late 1990s and enhanced across time. These systems have distinguished those programs that have striven to provide consistent quality to the children in their care and show ongoing commitment to maintain this quality. Those who participate in these programs value continuous quality improvement of their early childhood program and are often times recognized by state programs and reimbursement for the care of subsidy children.

3.4 Discover what national accreditation is and why it is important to the early childhood field.

- The highest level of quality rating systems is a program's participation in national accreditation. The accreditation process recognizes those programs that meet high standards of quality. Programs receiving the accreditation are permitted to use the designation in advertising and press releases. In addition, program perks such as incentives and higher reimbursement for subsidy care children assist with the cost of maintaining this national recognition.

Review

1. List five aspects of child care that may be subject to licensing requirements. (3.1)
2. List five agencies or divisions that may provide regulatory oversight to child care programs. (3.1)
3. What do zoning codes specify? (3.1)
4. Why is insurance protection important? (3.2)
5. How are an advisory board and a governing board different? (3.1)
6. What is the expected relationship between a board and a director of an early childhood program? (3.1)
7. Who is the contact to find out more information about state specific information for small or large businesses? (3.3)
8. What is the difference between liability and property insurance? (3.2)
9. What is the purpose of quality rating systems? (3.3)
10. Why is national accreditation an important achievement for an early childhood program? (3.4)

Showcase Your Skills

As we discussed in this chapter, Lora and Petra had a lot to consider when either leading a large early childhood program or one that is housed within a home. Either way, the amount of time to research each choice is an overwhelming process. A hired consultant must consider numerous factors as they make a recommendation for next steps. Assisting with understanding the state regulation criteria as well as knowing local contacts such as attorneys, accountants, and insurance agents are all important.

Based on the information shared in this chapter, it is now your turn to serve in the role of consultant. Write a summary resource for either Lora or Petra using the following points as your guide based on information that can be located within your state.

1. Where can the child care licensing standards be found for a center and for a home?
2. What is the state and local contact information for child care licensing in your area?
3. Where can zoning information be found related to operating a child care center or home?
4. What are the local agencies that must be included in the regulatory oversight of a child care center or home?
5. What, if any, are the different licensing capacity requirements for a center or home?

Matching

Match the following terms with the correct definitions:

A. accreditation performance criteria
B. advisory board
C. bonding insurance
D. child medical and accident insurance
E. disability insurance
F. governing board
G. national accreditation
H. program standard
I. property insurance
J. zoning codes

1. Defines the level of functioning of a program and sets the expected benchmark in areas that research has found to support high-quality programs for young children.
2. Legal entity that is authorized to actually operate a program, including making legal and financial commitments for the program.
3. Type of insurance that protects a program against financial loss due to the actions of officers or staff who are authorized to handle program money.
4. The highest level of accreditation of any of the state systems; examples include NAEYC.
5. Activities a program must demonstrate in order to prove it meets the program standards.
6. Rules that specify the types of permitted land use.
7. Type of insurance that provides medical and hospital costs for a child who is injured.
8. Board that studies issues and makes recommendations to a program, but those recommendations are not required to be carried out.
9. Type of insurance that protects against loss of equipment or building.
10. Type of insurance that protects program workers from lost income if they become disabled and cannot work.

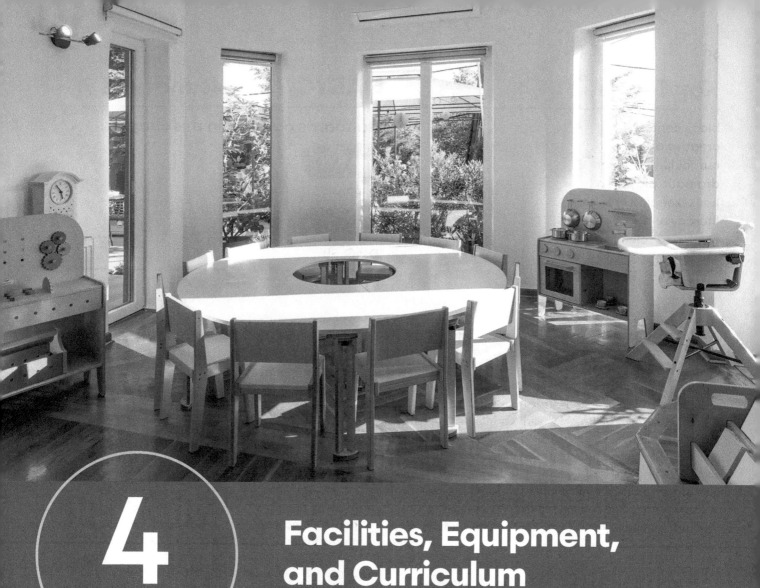

rilueda/iStock/Getty Images Plus

Facilities, Equipment, and Curriculum

Learning Outcomes

After studying this chapter, you will be able to:

4.1 Review guidelines for indoor and outdoor environments when determining facility and space needs for children.

4.2 Examine equipment needs that influence the organization and arrangement of successful indoor and outdoor learning spaces for young children.

4.3 Distinguish equipment differences for infants and toddlers, preschoolers, school-age children, and family child care home programs.

4.4 Evaluate curriculum recommendations for infant, toddler, preschool, out-of-school-time, and family child care home programs.

Key Terms

block center
creative art area
curriculum
dramatic play area
housekeeping area
literacy and writing areas
math and science areas
sensory area

NAEYC/DAP standards

Standards covered in this chapter:

NAEYC

4c, 5a, 5b

DAP

1D, 4C, 5B

Introduction

No matter what age group of children is being served in a center- or home-based program, they will all have state-mandated practices and expectations. NAEYC Program Standards 2 and 9 (2021) specifically focus on the areas of equipment and curriculum when developing and maintaining a high-quality early childhood program. These standards concentrate on providing well-maintained indoor and outdoor physical environments that facilitate child and staff learning and development. This includes providing learning opportunities with appropriate equipment that is developmentally appropriate and exhibits a commitment to equitable outcomes for all children.

4.1 Guidelines for Indoor and Outdoor Environments

There are many sites where early childhood programs are housed, including buildings specifically designed for the care of children, small or large areas of space that are donated for program use, or a designated area within a home. Whether the program is center specific or a home, there are many space considerations to keep in mind, including

- location and accessibility;
- licensing standards;
- planning room arrangement needs;
- kitchen and storage space;
- space for staff;
- interior elements;
- outdoor space; and
- security.

Location and Accessibility

The location of the center must be convenient for busy families (**Figure 4.1**). Accessible routes to primary businesses, shopping, or housing areas are helpful to parents and guardians. This includes consideration based on

Director's Showcase

Zara

Zara was the director of a large child care facility in the city. Based on a recent improvement survey completed by staff and parents, Zara decided to update and upgrade the outdoor play areas at the facility. The outside spaces had only been maintained in the 12 years since she was director of the facility. She applied for and received a grant for funding of the remodel. Zara decided to update fencing around the outdoor play areas by replacing a chain-link fence with privacy fencing for greater security. She then decided to replace all of the large motor-skill play structures. This was expensive, but she felt it was important to find an outdoor play system that was safe and secure for all ages.

Asha

Asha was a home child care provider in a small town. She had recently added two new toddlers to her home and was struggling with managing behaviors. While preparing meals or brushing teeth, the children would run circles around the table and play areas while they were waiting. She tried to engage them in activities to help them wait for their turn but had not been successful. She wondered if the environment or room arrangement might be factors in the problem. Asha decided to rearrange the play areas and meal area to see if that helped with the behavior issues she was having. When she looked at how the tables, play area, and kitchen were arranged, she found that there was a connecting oval, which was perfect for children to run; she had a built-in racetrack. Asha was hopeful that by rearranging the space, the children would not be tempted to run around.

Interglossa/iStock/Getty Images Plus

Figure 4.1 When building a child care program, it is important to choose locations that are close to local businesses and easy for parent to access either by car, bus routes, subways, or other public transportation options.

bus routes, use of the subway, personal car, or carpool. Families with children of multiple ages need a program that is as convenient as possible for them.

Safety of the location is a vital consideration. It should be free of lead-based paint, and flaking or chipped wallpapers or plaster on the walls. Deteriorating asbestos can also be a significant hazard to anyone in the building. If you suspect your location may contain asbestos, use a local testing service and then a professional cleaning company to assist with asbestos removal or mitigation. Finally, the overall ventilation, wiring, plumbing, and heating systems must all be in adequate and working condition.

Adults or children with disabilities will need modifications to any program site. Considerations and adaptations must be made to include ramps, entry/exit access, parking, and adjustments inside and outside the program area. For example, swing seats must have high backs, extra support, safety belts, and impact-absorbing materials. Additional railings in hallways or grab bars in bathrooms can assist an unsteady child or adult. Space and storage for wheelchairs, walkers, hearing aids, breathing aids such as nebulizers, or other necessary items must be considered. Working with staff to meet their needs as well as the needs of a child's parent or guardian ensures that overall accessibility requirements are met when attending the program.

Licensing Standards

As discussed in earlier chapters, child care programs must be licensed. One of the most important aspects that the standards set forth is the indoor and outdoor space requirements. This includes the determination of the amount of available space that must be available to serve the number

of children in the facility (**Figure 4.2**). NAEYC (2019) recommends 35 square feet of usable space per child and 75 square feet of outside space for each child at any one time. Therefore, a room for a group of 15 children should ideally have 750 square feet or be about 25 feet by 30 feet in size. Most states do not require this amount of space per child, but the size of your group will be limited by the size of the space available. Most states specify such items as the number of sinks and toilets per group, the structure of the space housing the furnace and hot water tank, or the type of sink (three-compartment) in the kitchen. Programs must have a license to keep the doors open to serve children. It is always important to remember that licensing requirements dictate minimal acceptable standards in each state. Striving to exceed those standards only increases the level of quality for the children in care.

Planning Room Arrangement Needs

The arrangement of the rooms within any building or home should be a consideration when planning a child care facility, as well as any state and local regulations. While many different floor plans can work well, there are some that are less desirable than others. Spaces with a series of small rooms may have enough square footage per child but can only manage one or two activities, which require adult supervision. Enrollment patterns may also vary from year to year. Depending on the age of the children in the room, access to sinks and toilets will be necessary. If opening new classrooms or increasing enrollment, facilities will have to be added. Facilities that have movable walls, a combination of large and small rooms, and several bathrooms provide greater adaptability.

In a center environment, several factors are important when deciding which group to put into each available

Ivan-balvan/iStock/Getty Images Plus

Figure 4.2 Architects and other consultants can be very helpful when creating and reviewing building plans for new facilities.

room. A good match between the room location and the characteristics of the groups can create a more workable, comfortable building. The size of the rooms, their access to fire or playground exits, and their water supply and distance from restrooms have an impact on these decisions. Decisions regarding classrooms are also based after reviewing the ages of the children to be in each group. Keep in mind that younger children are in smaller groups while larger groups of lively preschoolers or school-age children will need more space to move around. Having groups of similar-aged children grouped in the same area is ideal. This allows for easy sharing of equipment from one classroom to another.

In a home environment, local and state regulations will also apply. It is important to choose spaces where the adult can supervise all angles of the room. Keep in mind that the kitchen space for cooking and serving meals as well as bathrooms and sinks will all need to be readily accessible (**Figure 4.3**). While less equipment and supplies may be needed, storage for these items must be in proximity. This includes individual items that children bring from home as well as supplies such as diapers, wipes, and extra children's clothing in various sizes. Last, but by no means least, consider how to restrict other areas of your home from children wandering off into areas that are unsupervised.

Kitchen and Storage Space

In any child care facility, provisions for food service are an important consideration. Kitchens must have adequate space, plumbing, and wiring. In addition, shelving is needed to keep all foods off the ground to meet state and local regulations. Refrigeration and freezer space must all fit within the usable space and adequate storage and placement for all of the cookware and utensils.

Figure 4.3 The location of sinks is important and often specified in various state regulations. This includes separate spaces for handwashing, diaper-changing, and meal preparation.

Oven space must be able to handle the heating needs of foods, and the space must include a sink designated for handwashing and another area for washing and cleaning food-specific items. Some programs use a commercial dishwasher, while others hand wash. Areas for handwashing food items typically incorporate large deep sinks that are separate from the hand-washing area. The safe handling of food requires a lot of attention either within a center or home environment.

Storage space must be thoughtfully planned out in any home or center environment. Many times, this is an afterthought for early childhood leaders. With the wide range of items necessary to operate an early childhood program of differing sizes, storage requirements must be met and planned accordingly. Materials and equipment not currently being used in the classroom must be stored and available for later use. If there is planning of a variety of activities, easy access to stored items is needed. Art supplies and food can be purchased more economically in large quantities. Without enough storage space, bulk purchases may not be possible. Problems can develop if the storage space is damp or too hot. Ruined paper supplies or spoiled food products will wipe out any savings that might have occurred from bulk purchasing. Storage is necessary for seasonal equipment as well as cleaning equipment and supplies that must be carefully locked away from the curious investigations of children.

Large Programs Need Space for Staff

Regardless of a child care center's size, the needs of its staff are an important consideration. A large program will have a variety of staff members in different positions, often working on different schedules. A child care leader must provide suitable spaces to meet their needs. Designate secure places for their coats and personal belongings as well as a place to relax during breaks. Restrooms that provide privacy for adults are also necessary. Administrative staff sharing a large office may be more comfortable with sound-absorbing room dividers. These dividers can also help to direct the traffic flow through a busy office. In addition to the classroom areas, you should plan comfortable areas where staff members can work. A workroom space for classroom staff provides an area where they can prepare materials needed for daily activities, keep records, and lesson plan. A water supply is useful in this area as well.

Office space is necessary for the administrative functions of the program (**Figure 4.4**). Large programs usually employ many staff, care for large numbers of children, and receive support from a variety of sources. The administrative responsibilities to keep such a program functioning smoothly require a team of people who do not ever work directly with the children. Their work is

evgenyatamanenko/iStock/Getty Images Plus

Figure 4.4 All program leaders in center and home environments need designated office space. This comfortable space should support the administrative paperwork and conversations necessary when performing the administrative role.

performed primarily in offices. This space, like the other areas of the center, should be attractive and comfortable. It should be set up so each person can work with a minimum of distraction from others. Some of the administrative work, such as conferences with parents or interviews regarding personnel issues, require privacy. Some of the work requires close cooperation and communication among several of the staff. Complex programs also require a large amount of paperwork. In setting up an office, consider which staff members will

- often work together;
- need privacy to carry out their responsibilities;
- require substantial storage space; and
- need to greet the public on a regular basis.

Staff members also appreciate an area where they can get together to share information, work on group projects, or just relax. Pleasant working conditions for staff are extremely important. Working in child care requires concentration, commitment, and long hours. When staff members feel respected and appreciated, it can encourage stability and loyalty among personnel.

Interior Elements for Early Childhood Programs

Whether an early childhood program is housed in a center or home, there are many interior elements to be considered. Working walls, ceilings, and floors can be used for communication, display, storage, and activity (Greenman, 2017). Interior space in a facility or home is the atmosphere that creates the first impression that families and visitors have of the program. Anyone coming in to the program should have the feeling that children and families are respected. The look of the program should

convey a sense of warmth and nurturance. The interior elements that must be considered include

- floor treatments
- wall, window, and ceiling treatments
- lighting

These interior elements receive a lot of usage within any program setting, so selection is important to include how they will be maintained and cared for.

Floor Treatments

Young children in child care settings typically spend a lot of time playing on the floor. In some centers, they nap on mats on the floor as well. Children are also hard on floors. Spills occur frequently. Floor coverings must be chosen not only for appearance, but for features that make them function well in child care centers. This includes factors such as:

- the use or purpose of the area (eating, sand play, block building, napping, etc.)
- ease of cleanup and stain-resistance
- quality of construction and durability

One of the first considerations is the use of carpeting, rugs, or some type of resilient flooring. Many centers and homes use a combination of both in each program area. Each type has advantages and disadvantages.

Carpet or Large Rugs

Carpeted floors and large area rugs provide warm, pleasant surfaces on which children can play. The texture and fiber of those surfaces can affect both the durability and ease of cleaning. Carpeting designed for commercial use usually holds up well but may be rough. Rough surfaces can cause skinned knees and brush burns as children play actively on the floor. Thick loops or shag carpet can be fun to play on but may be difficult to clean. Some types of carpet require padding between the floor and the carpet, while large area rugs need nonslip backing to avoid accidents. On a normal day, paints spill, food splatters, children get upset stomachs, and mud is brought into the building. Stain-resistance and washability are important characteristics to consider before purchasing carpeting or large area rugs.

Resilient Flooring

Flooring such as linoleum, vinyl, or tile provides resilient, flowing options. Its durability and cleaning ease make it desirable for many areas of an early childhood program. It creates a harder surface than carpet, but is generally not abrasive, and will not snag children's clothing. Although each kind has its own unique characteristics, resilient floor coverings wear well and are easy to maintain. They can be damp-mopped, washed, and waxed. Some new products do not require waxing to stay shiny. Before making any decisions on resilient flooring, consider the amount of traffic and play the flooring will receive. Some products are more suitable for heavier use. Examine the subfloor, or the floor that will be covered by the new material before ordering flooring. Not all resilient flooring can be used on concrete or basement floors, or on top of other resilient flooring. Frequently, old resilient flooring must be removed before the new can be installed.

Wall, Window, and Ceiling Treatments

Wall and ceiling treatments should be both functional and aesthetically pleasing (**Figure 4.5**). The most common wall coverings include paint, paneling, wallpaper, and carpeting. Paint that does not include lead is the quickest to apply and is less expensive than the other coverings. Latex, flat-finish paints are recommended for classroom use. Semi-gloss finishes are preferred in bathrooms and kitchens for ease of cleaning. Decisions regarding wall coverings can affect the level of noise in the centers. Hard surface walls reflect sounds and seem to magnify them. Walls with fabric coverings or decorated with drapes and fabric wall hangings tend to absorb and minimize sound.

Ceilings come in a variety of heights and shapes. While frequently unnoticed, the height and material of ceilings can affect the lighting, temperature, and sound control within a room. If ceilings are high, as in an older building or warehouse, they can be lowered with a framework that holds sound-absorbing panels. This can help make the room less overwhelming to children and reduce the noise level. Open ceilings that show the interior construction of the roof can be dramatic, but they are costly

miodrag ignjatovic/E+/Getty Images

Figure 4.5 Classrooms can contain many types of colors and textures. Wall coverings, the use of color, and types of floor coverings all combine to provide warm, welcoming, and durable space for young children to thrive.

in heat loss. When making decisions about the walls and ceilings, consider how they will look from the children's viewpoint. Pictures, posters, chalkboards, and bulletin boards that are at an adult's eye level will be too high for children to look at comfortably. If you want children to notice the interesting things hanging on the walls, place these items at their eye level.

Windows provide light, ventilation, and views. The more children can experience natural light, the calmer the classroom will be. When choosing window treatments, it is important to choose curtains or drapes made from flame-retardant fabrics. Keep in mind that rooms are typically darkened when children are napping. When using window blinds, shades, or drapes—it is critical that these items do not contain strings that children could potentially become trapped, suffer strangulation, or hurt themselves or others by pulling them down. Many products on the market meet these safety concerns.

Lighting

The location of a center can make a difference in the kinds of lighting needed. Centers with south-facing windows will get more natural sunlight than centers with windows facing other directions. If your center is located in a climate where winters tend to be long, cold, dark, and dreary, pay special attention to the lighting. Using a combination of fluorescent lighting and ambient lighting can be a solution to rooms that lack natural lighting.

There has been a tremendous amount of technology created in the lighting arena, and the possibilities are endless (**Figure 4.6**). Energy-efficient, economical fluorescent lighting is commonly found in public buildings, but can be very hard on the eyes as well as difficult to turn down or off in some instances. Opportunities to allow children to control the lighting as well as the adults in the space adds more possibilities within a classroom. Light can influence activities and moods, it can brighten spirits, or create a glare. Thus, you should consider the lighting from all angles, such as an infant lying on their back looking at a ceiling, a toddler trying to see as they are taking their next step, and a preschool child wanting more light to discover a bug that they brought in from outside to put in the science area. Lighting can create a warm, welcoming, and productive atmosphere. The wrong lighting can be harsh and uninviting to students, families, and staff and can affect mood and behavior.

Outdoor Elements for Early Childhood Programs

Early childhood programs must have outdoor play space (**Figure 4.7**). Outdoor activities provide exciting

A

B

Figure 4.6 (A) Classrooms need to reflect natural light, natural elements, small pops of color, durable flooring, natural elements, and interest centers appropriate for the age group served. Classrooms like this are inviting and provide a sense of order and welcoming play. (B) It is important to avoid bright lighting, lots of plastic toys, and classroom equipment lined up against walls. These types of classrooms are not welcoming for children and create confusing messages regarding classroom expectations.

learning opportunities for children and should provide first-hand experiences with many natural elements of the outdoor environment. While programs almost always have access to an outside play area, special care should be taken to ensure that children have the opportunity to go on walks and to have vigorous, large muscle activity indoors. This might include access to a large gymnasium or classrooms that are big enough to be equipped with indoor climbers and wheel toys; options such as these are appropriate substitute activities. It is important to have year-round outside activities regardless of the climate or weather. A covered porch area also provides a protected area when the direct sun or wind is too intense to allow for comfortable outdoor play.

Figure 4.7 Daily outdoor play allows children of all ages to experience natural elements and participate in large muscle activity.

As Greenman (2017) pointed out so eloquently, access to nature provides

- a universal and timeless space
- a place that is unpredictable and bountiful
- space that is beautiful and alive with sounds
- a multitude of spaces to explore
- an awareness of how nature is real, and how it nourishes and heals

Do be aware that there are states that will not license an early childhood program that does not have easy access to a safe and secure outdoor space. Regulations will have expectations for space that is adequate for the amount and age of children served, the use of impact-absorbing materials, and secure areas where children can play safely. In addition, storage for outside equipment must be included. Teachers are more likely to use equipment if it is conveniently located. An outdoor storage shed, treated to withstand the weather should be large enough to hold a variety of items such as trikes, sandbox toys, and water activities. It should be secured to avoid theft or children's access to a space that is likely unsupervised.

Size and Location

Outdoor space should be divided into zoned areas, if possible. A space designed for infants and toddlers, preschoolers, and school-age children is ideal. These outdoor spaces should incorporate activities for children to use small and large muscles as well as wide open space for lively play. Spaces designed to foster less energetic play, such as sand and drama activities, should be separated from the more active play areas. Plant gardens away from active play traffic patterns. Plan trike paths on a harder surface, such as concrete, patio blocks, or packed dirt paths, to roll around on and separate from climbers and swings. NAEYC (2019) recommends providing at least 75 square feet of outside space for each child outside at any one time. The ideal playground space is accessible immediately outside the early childhood program facility. With a close playground, teachers can easily bring indoor activities outside as well as access and supervise children's restroom breaks.

Safety and Accessibility

As with any space in a child care facility, children must be protected from any hazards while outdoors. The center staff should evaluate the area for and eliminate, if possible, access to streets, exposure to auto exhaust, equipment that may splinter or break, and natural materials that are poisonous. Considerations must include serving children with disabilities so that they, too, can fully participate. Easy access to play areas, wide sidewalks, and appropriately sized equipment should be incorporated in the design. Ideally, the playground will have shaded areas to protect from the sun. Teachers should ensure children have sunscreen on and DEET-free bug sprays when needed. It is important to have year-round outside activities regardless of the climate or weather. A covered porch area also provides a protected area when the direct sun or wind are too intense to allow for comfortable outdoor play. Finally, adult supervision in all areas is key to creating a safe and adventurous outdoor space.

Surface Treatments

A variety of surface treatments makes the outdoor area more interesting. Variation in surface textures and heights, such as large grassy areas and trees, provides a natural feeling (**Figure 4.8**). Children love to sit and

CreativeNature_nl/iStock/Getty Images Plus

Figure 4.8 Many options are available for playground surfaces. Dirt, sand, and grass are a few of the surfaces that are regulated to meet state licensing regulations.

play on soft grass. A shaded area allows for gardening. The playground area should be a space of wonder and sensory experiences. This includes smooth and rough textures. While playground equipment such as climbers and swings need to be rooted in concrete, the outdoors provides so much more. Surface areas under climbers may require impact-absorbing materials for insurance or licensing regulations, such as sand, wood chips, rubber mulch, or mats made from recycled materials. There are many products on the market to explore that are cost-conscious, durable, provide good drainage, and have a cushioned surface. Look to state licensing regulations, local codes, or insurance regulations to assist with your choice of the types of surfaces that are acceptable.

Security

Adequate security, including emergency preparedness, that protects children's safety cannot be compromised. It is important that all early childhood program staff can monitor who is entering and leaving the program areas at all times. This includes having secure areas with locked doors and panic bars, electronic key card entry systems, or coded keypad systems to unlock doors. Installation of intercoms and security cameras allow staff to identify visitors before permitting entrance. While most programs will not experience the tragedy of someone coming in with the deliberate intent to harm children, there are unpleasant custody disputes and other outside threats that must be identified and assessed. Administrators must also evaluate their facility to ensure that young children cannot easily wander from the building or outside areas. Plans for dealing with these types of emergencies and others should be developed and communicated. Russell (2018) suggests asking the following questions when reviewing safety plans and emergency procedures:

- Do you have adequate supplies for emergencies?
- Have you developed both a nearby and more remote relocation site, and have you determined how you will travel to those sites if an emergency requires it?
- Do you have the ability to quickly alert staff of an emergency via an intercom system that also works on the playground?

Making an investment to have a security professional come consult periodically is important. A parent may volunteer their expertise, or the program may bring a security consultant in to assess the facility's safety. This look through a high security lens can help to point out vulnerabilities at the site. Child safety will be discussed in further detail in Chapter 5.

4.2 Equipment Needs for Successful Indoor and Outdoor Spaces

Taking the time to plan equipment needs for indoor classrooms and space outdoors is important. Keep in mind that these are places where memories are made and children's first educational experiences take place. Learning blooms in these spaces. Curtis and Carter (2014) have several considerations when planning indoor and outdoor play spaces for children. The spaces should

- foster connections and a sense of belonging;
- have flexible space and use open-ended materials;
- provide natural materials that engage the senses;
- create wonder, curiosity, and intellectual engagement; and
- display symbolic representations, literacy, and the visual arts.

Well-designed spaces that are equipped appropriately for young children do not happen by accident. They require careful planning.

A program leader is responsible for every aspect of the program. Knowing the basic principles of classroom and outdoor space organization and planning is important. This supports the teaching staff and their ability to plan effectively. It also allows staff to have an awareness of the classroom furniture, and the needed equipment for indoors and outdoors that best serve the age groups of children within the program. Infant rooms require more floor room and a sleeping space for each child. For toddlers, preschoolers, and school-age children, the room arrangement has an important impact on classroom activities and children's behavior.

Classroom setup encourages involvement and opportunities to learn self-control for children. This includes open space as well as interest centers that focus on a particular type of play. Some of these areas will need tables and chairs appropriately sized for the specific age group. The tables and chairs should be sturdy and have smooth, washable surfaces. Classroom equipment should be stain-resistant so spilled food or messy creative projects will not be a problem. Rounded corners and edges are an important safety design feature. When tables are placed on a hard, washable floor surface, spills are easy to clean up. Consider using vinyl covering to protect carpeted floors.

Every classroom needs an open area that can be used for lively movement or full-group participation (**Figure 4.9**). Activities such as circle time, music, and games are activities that require space for everyone to participate. However, wide-open spaces invite running or

zeljkosantrac/E+/Getty Images

Figure 4.9 Open areas in classrooms are important. They provide for activities such as circle time, music, and games that require space for everyone to participate.

chasing around aimlessly. An area where shelves or tables can be easily moved aside may work better than totally open space. However, spaces should not be too cluttered. Teachers should be able to easily supervise all the spaces where children are busy with activities. The following are smaller areas that should be located within a classroom based on the age of children served:

- a dramatic play area
- a block-building area
- a literacy and writing area
- a creative art area
- a math and science area
- a sensory activity area

The program leader and teaching staff should regularly discuss the effectiveness of room arrangement for the age of children being served in each space, including the teachers' line of sight within the space and the location of doors, windows, electrical outlets, lights, and water supplies. Ongoing evaluation of the classroom layout creates interesting environments to foster learning while keeping children safe.

Dramatic Play

The **dramatic play area** is designed to encourage and enhance children's pretend play. It includes toys and equipment that have been used for many years to appeal to young children and to stimulate dramatic play. This is one of the primary areas of the room. It should be large enough for several children to play together comfortably. The area should be located in a central, yet protected, area where traffic patterns will not cross through it. This area is often referred to as the **housekeeping area** because it contains many replicas of familiar items found at home. The child-sized

kitchen equipment, such as sink, refrigerator, and range, remind children of their home and help them to feel comfortable in the center. Some centers even include a small file cabinet, desk, and calendar since many children's families have home offices. The following items are basic to this area:

- child-sized kitchen equipment including sink, range, and refrigerator;
- household phones;
- dolls, doll buggies, and doll beds;
- dress-up clothes;
- dishes and plastic food; and
- a small table and chairs set.

Items such as empty food containers or old kitchen utensils can often be added to this area. Care must be taken that sharp, heavy, or rusted items are not included. Items that have held real food must be carefully washed. Utensils and dishes in this area will need to be washed weekly or even daily should there be a contagious health issue taking place between the children in the classroom. Children often put these props in their mouths during play. Dress-up clothes should be replaced or washed regularly to avoid the spread of contagious disease.

Block-Building

Materials in the **block center** need to reflect what works best for children's ages and abilities (Giles & Tunks, 2013). Unit blocks of all shapes and sizes arranged on low shelving provide an excellent space for block-building. The space should be fairly large and allow several children to build without interference from others. Blocks are typically sold in sets of multiple shapes. Facilities should purchase enough blocks for deep involvement and complicated building projects by children (**Figure 4.10**). The very nature of blocks helps children begin to see

FatCamera/E+/Getty Images

Figure 4.10 The block area is an essential designated classroom space. Playing with blocks teach mathematical relationships, shapes, and space.

the mathematical relationships of the different shapes to each other.

Adding accessories such as handheld cars and trucks, road signage, roadway carpets, community-helper accessory sets, and other materials only enhance the opportunity for learning more in this area. Teachers must decide what the expectations will be when children are playing together in the space. For example, teachers will need to determine how high they will allow children to build. They must also consider whether roofs on block buildings with children inside them will be safe. The age of the children and how crowded the area may influence this decision.

Literacy and Writing

The **literacy and writing area** provides children with a quiet space that contains an interesting selection of developmentally appropriate books and materials to learn more about the written word. Materials should be multicultural, represent the community being served, and appropriate in content and attitude for young children. Keep this area away from the noisier areas of the room and include a wide selection of children's books available, changing them periodically to complement seasons, interests, and curriculum. Some programs incorporate fluffy rugs, large soft pillows, a beanbag chair, or a small sofa, table, and chairs. This area should not only provide a variety of developmentally appropriate books, but also serve as a warm, cozy place for a child to snuggle up.

To support writing, add storyboards and other writing instruments that are age-appropriate to the space. During early childhood, children begin to learn the basic foundation of literacy. Teachers can encourage the children's exploration by including and explaining how to use a variety of writing props. While this area may only support one to two children at a time, it provides indirect encouragement and support for writing and promotes writing as part of a daily routine (Schickedanz & Casbergue, 2004). From basic scribbles to eventually creating lines of words, children have access to the necessities for learning to read and write.

Creative Art

Every classroom should have a **creative art area** where children can engage in multiple types of art activities (**Figure 4.11**). Young children should have daily opportunities for creative expression (Copple & Bredekamp, 2009). This should include having access to a wide variety of art supplies such as paste, child safety scissors, watercolors, glue, wood pieces, envelopes, markers, and crayons. Placed on low shelving, the teacher can set out a

Figure 4.11 Access to art supplies such as paint, watercolors, markers, and crayons allow children to plan, create, and work together with others.

variety of open-ended art materials that allow children to plan and solve problems as they create. Access to child-sized tables and chairs along with a water source and ability to work within a space that has washable surfaces supports opportunities for various projects. Care must be taken that all materials used are nontoxic.

Easel painting should be available to the children every day. It gives them a chance to explore dimensions of color, as well as to try out different kinds of paints and paper. Working with paints can be relaxing for children. Painting should be available throughout the free play time, so children feel invited, not pressured, to be creative. If two easels are available side-by-side, two children can have a social experience while painting. The easels and supplies should be located close to a water supply along with smocks to cover children's clothing. Because paints sometimes spill, and creativity is sometimes messy, the room arrangement should help make cleanup as easy as possible. Easels should not be placed on carpeted areas unless some washable surface can be put down under them.

Math and Science

Another fun consideration is opportunities for children to explore **math and science areas**, which contain materials for engagement that support the foundations necessary when learning about these subjects in the early childhood classroom. Every day, all day, indoors and outdoors, children are learning about math and science through a multitude of experiences. While these designated areas only enhance these areas of learning, it is important to understand that equipment, materials, and planning by teaching staff contribute even more to children's foundations of math and science.

NAEYC (2015) provides a basic overview of math and manipulatives that should be included in a math area:

- self-correcting, structured toys like puzzles, self-help frames, and nesting cups;
- open-ended toys like Legos™, sewing cards, magnetic letters and numbers, parquetry blocks, small building blocks, puzzles, bristle blocks, or stringing beads;
- collectibles like large buttons, bottle caps, and keys; and
- group games like lotto, dominoes, and simple board games.

These are all items that allow children to learn about numbers, shapes, and patterns.

A science area should incorporate interesting items for children to explore, such as prisms, magnifying glasses, an aquarium, live plants or animals, eyedroppers, scales, and displays of rocks or leaves. Displays should be placed on a table and located at an easily visible spot where children passing by will stop for a look. Science can be extended into other interest areas and outdoor spaces. High-quality science programs are based on an understanding of how children learn, what they are capable of learning, and appropriate science content (Worth & Grollman, 2003).

Sensory

The **sensory area** allows children to participate in activities involving many types of textures. Sand and water play are mainstays of early childhood programs. While not always presented in the same way, quality programs make some provision for them to occur. These activities are soothing and can be used in various ways by the different age groups. Some programs have designated tables or tubs of varying sizes where children can sift through the textures placed out for discovery. Some come with a cover and a plug in the bottom for ease in cleaning.

A selection of toys for use in the sensory tables is necessary. Spoons, small shovels and pails, squeeze bottles, measuring cups, floating and sinking toys, and other items make the play more interesting. These objects should be available on a nearby shelf. This area should be near a water supply and located on a hard surface for ease in clean up. Be sure that no electrical items are near the water and sand play areas.

Outdoors

The outdoor space is an extension of indoor learning. The space should allow children to immerse themselves in nature. In addition, Greenman (2015) recommends supporting these outdoor activities by purchasing an array of equipment that allows children to

- swing, slide, roll, climb, jump, and dance;
- run, throw, kick, bounce, and balance;
- dig, grow, and observe bug and animal life; and
- read, discover, eat, and rest.

SolStock/E+/Getty Images

Figure 4.12 Gardens incorporated within early childhood playgrounds cultivate children's wonder as they learn more about the natural world.

Director's Showcase

Reflect

Based on Zara's plans for the outdoors, what could be some additional outdoor opportunities for her teachers to plan to provide the children with more learning opportunities? After doing more research, what could be some additional considerations for Asha to begin implementing within her home environment?

Research has found that natural environments help to restore focus and provide opportunities for increased attention by young children (Amezquita, R. & Tagawa, D., 2021). Clearly, outdoor spaces filled with opportunities and a variety of play surfaces allow children's overall development to thrive (**Figure 4.12**).

4.3 Choosing Equipment for Varying Ages

There is no doubt that purchasing equipment for use with varying ages is a cumbersome task. With so many state and local regulations to consider, a child care leader must not only stay in budget, but also ensure that the correct items are being purchased. Any program leader will describe the investment in outdoor play equipment as one of the largest in terms of time and money. In addition, ongoing maintenance, repair, and replacement of equipment is a massive undertaking. Equipment must be monitored to ensure that it stays

Because young children put almost everything into their mouths, disinfecting equipment and materials are necessary. A conveniently placed laundry basket, out of reach of the children, can serve as a collecting point for toys that have been in someone's mouth.

Larger pieces of furniture and equipment needed for the classroom include

- several rocking chairs;
- plastic storage bins for each child's diapers and supplies;
- small storage trays for each child's food or formula in the refrigerator;
- shelves that can be closed off when not in use;
- foldable gates to close off hallways or other areas;
- step stools and toilet seat inserts;
- strollers, preferably the type designed for child care centers that hold six children;
- high chairs;
- cribs; and
- a changing table.

Infants and toddlers need environments that are engaging without being overstimulating. Providing a variety of opportunities to explore the outside world enhances learning and development. Equipment must be maintained and secure. You must also stay current with any safety recalls and repairs. Adults provide the overall space for learning while also role-modeling appropriate behaviors and being responsible for the safety of the children.

with the correct age groups, is in proper working order and available to children, and is rotated on a regular basis for higher engagement. Unintentionally, smaller items may end up in little pockets never to be returned, a tricycle left out on the playground over the weekend may be absent by Monday morning, or a windy day may blow several playground balls away. Budget and time are a constant consideration when making the initial investment to purchase equipment as well as replacing it as needs arise. It is important to first understand the different needs of each age group.

Infants and Toddlers

Equipment in the infant and toddler areas must be designed for this younger age group. Simply moving preschool toys into this classroom can lead to injuries. Educational companies have created lines that specialize in sturdy equipment and materials designed for infants and toddlers. While smaller in scale, this equipment is designed to be sturdy so it will not tip if a wobbly toddler grabs onto it for support (**Figure 4.13**).

Basic Materials Needed for Younger Groups Include ...

Stacking rings · Unbreakable mirrors · Push-pull toys · Dolls · Puppets · Soft, cuddly toys · Rubber or sponge balls · Rattles for infants · Easily washed chew toys · Small-scale climbers · Toy cars and trucks · Busy box toys · Toy phones · Soft blocks

Goodheart-Willcox Publisher

Figure 4.13 State licensing regulations list the types of equipment and materials required for each age group cared for within the program.

Preschool

Equipment and materials become much more extensive for preschool-age children to include

- art materials
- table toys
- cars and trucks
- sensory table
- dramatic play clothing and accessories
- books
- manipulatives
- writing materials
- math and science materials
- low shelving units to display materials
- appropriate-sized tables and chairs for preschoolers
- cubbies to store children's belongings (**Figure 4.14**)

Preschool children use materials and equipment in the classroom to explore and learn more about their world and to investigate their own thinking of how things work, or do not work. Through their inquiry, children continue to learn more as their teacher engages and guides them.

Equipment and Materials Needed for Preschoolers	
Equipment	**Examples**
Art materials	paper; crayons; glue; safety scissors; large, blank paper; markers; chalk; play dough or clay; variety of nontoxic paints and brushes; textured collage materials—scraps of ribbon, yarn, buttons; easel surface; papier-mâché materials
Blocks	unit blocks of all sizes and lengths; accessories to include hand cars, larger trucks, community helpers, dump trucks; connecting blocks; boats; planes; trains; animals; people
Sensory table	sensory items such as sand, water, and accessories such as shovels, buckets, and funnels; large spoons; small rakes; items to put sensory items in and dump out; squirt bottles; turkey baster; items that float; items that sink; food coloring; bubbles
Dramatic play	dresses, shoes, hats, purses; pots and pans; community helper uniforms; everyday items used by children and families: kitchen appliances—stove, sink, refrigerator, microwave; sets of dishes and utensils; sets of pots and pans; sets of clean-up toys—brooms, dust pan, mop; doll bed or cradle; child-size rocking chair; lawn care equipment—lawn mower, wheelbarrow, gardening tools; prop boxes designed around themes reflecting a child's life experiences—doctor office, barber shop, veterinarian office, shoe store, donut shop; water play equipment
Math manipulatives/Table toys	bristle blocks; stacking blocks; pegs and pegboards; matching games; simple board games; connecting blocks; counting beads; seriation activities; lacing boards; puzzles
Science exploratory play	magnifying glass; bug catcher; prisms; balance scale; nature items—plants, leaves, rocks; aquarium; light table and accessories; nature items—ant farms, plants, animals, rocks, shells; chemistry sets; science kits; marble runs; simple machines—pulleys, pendulums, gears and levers
Language and literacy	picture books from a variety of genres: alphabet, counting, informational, look and find, wordless, folk and fairy tales, nursery rhymes, fantasy fiction, rhyming stories, realistic fiction; books that reflect the ethnicities of children and their family; flannel or magnetic board with accessories; listening tapes; puppets; finger puppets; puppet stage
Outdoor play	soccer balls; soccer nets; basketballs; baseballs and bats; balls for kicking; jump ropes; riding toys; swings; slides; areas to dig and garden; accessories for digging; riding toys

Goodheart-Willcox Publisher

Figure 4.14 There are so many equipment options for teachers to plan with and to create engaging interest centers for preschool-age children to play with and discover.

Out-of-School-Time

Typically, centers separate school-age children into two or three age groups, depending on enrollment. Developmental recommendations as well as state requirements guide how you determine age groups within a program. Age-group designated areas will have equipment and materials appropriate for their size, development, and interests (**Figure 4.15**). Equipment and materials tend to create a more relaxed environment:

- structural art materials
- table toys
- table games
- comfortable seating areas
- technology to assist children in tutoring or have homework needs
- large game items
- shelving units to display materials
- appropriate-sized tables and chairs for children

Daniel Balakov/iStock/Getty Images Plus

Figure 4.16 Older school children need access to board games as they learn more about working with others, following rules, reading, and learning strategy.

Gear project areas toward the typical interests of the age group (**Figure 4.16**). One project area might provide tools to dismantle an old engine; another might focus on designing and decorating a house using a computer program; and still another might encourage building with large boxes. Groups might spend a week exploring colonial crafts, making jewelry, learning the fundamentals of cooking, or preparing a play for the whole group. Planned field trips contribute to learning new information and make project interests come alive (Nadelson & Jordan, 2012; Scribner-MacLean & Kennedy, 2007; Kisiel, 2003). These trips are a valuable part of out-of-school-time program planning and learning experiences. High-quality field trip experiences lead to increased interest in and a deeper understanding of a subject matter (Tunks & Allison, 2020; National Research Council, 2009). During the summer months, create opportunities for varied outdoor play with trips to a waterpark, swimming pool, splash pad, forest preserve, playground, ball field, or local park.

Many communities have other organizations and agencies that provide services and activities for school-age children. It is helpful to develop cooperative relationships with these agencies. Many times, their offerings can enhance or enrich your programming. Organizations, such as Boy Scouts, Girl Scouts, Boys and Girls Clubs, the local library, the YMCA, community centers, museums, or local dance or martial arts schools, frequently offer school-age programs and lessons (**Figure 4.17**). Some require a fee, while others are free. You may negotiate agreements with some of these services so that all children in the out-of-school-time program can participate. Ultimately, school-age children want to be where their friends are and can become engaged in the community alongside their friends.

Out-of-School-Time Equipment Needs	
Larger Equipment Needs	**Examples**
Tables	tables must be adjustable to the size of the children served in the classroom
Comfortable seating areas	beanbag chairs, floor pillows, or sofas to lay around and relax on
Chairs	chairs must be size appropriate for the age of children served
Shelving	shelves must be durable, child height, easily supervised, cannot be tipped easily
Technology	often strictly guided by state regulations, this can include computer stations, tablets, or gaming devices
Diaper-changing stations, rocking, and climbing toys	for classrooms serving infants and toddlers, diaper-changing stations must be available as well as structural sound, appropriate height climbing structures for toddlers

Goodheart-Willcox Publisher

Figure 4.15 Depending on the ages of the children served, large equipment purchases will be necessary and guided by state licensing requirements.

Organization	Website	Examples
Boy Scouts of America	www.scouting.org	Boy Scout troop opportunities based on child's age, but can include camping, matchbox cars, and community service projects
Girl Scouts of the USA	www.girlscouts.org	Girl Scout troop opportunities based on child's age, but can include crafting, science projects, and community service projects
The YMCA	www.ymca.org	May provide classes to encourage swimming, exercise, or team sports such as baseball, soccer, basketball, and football
The YWCA	www.ywca.org	May provide classes to encourage swimming, exercise, cooking, hand arts, or team sports such as baseball, soccer, basketball, and softball
Boys and Girls Clubs of America	www.bgca.org	Out-of-school-time programming often provided in local community centers
Big Brothers and Big Sisters of America	www.bbbs.org	Non-profit organization that works to engage children who need a significant male or female role model in their life besides immediate family members
JCC Association of North America	www.jcca.org	Provides Jewish Community Centers across the nation with a wide array of programs and activities for people of all ages

Goodheart-Willcox Publisher

Figure 4.17 During out-of-school-times, children can participate in programming offered by many different organizations.

Family Child Care Home

Equipment will vary based on the ages of children who are within the family child care home. Keeping in mind general categories, considerations include

- art supplies;
- books;
- gross motor-skill equipment;
- blocks and accessories;
- dramatic play materials;
- manipulative toys;
- science materials; and
- outdoor equipment such as swings, slides, and climbing apparatus with appropriate levels of impact-absorbing materials.

Extending children's play experiences involves asking and answering questions. All of the interactions between the provider and the children offer a rich opportunity for language and dialogue that is sometimes lacking in a much larger group of children. Within a home child care setting, there is a need for opportunities to explore the community and have access to robust play experiences. These needs can be met with neighborhood walks, having family of staff or children come and share recipes and cook with the children, or exploring the neighborhood and various local activities at the library or other community agency.

4.4 Curriculum Considerations for Varying Ages

Curriculum is the framework for play for all ages of children cared for in an early childhood program environment. It serves as the framework that pulls together developmentally appropriate practice—the what, why, and how to plan, implement, and evaluate the program (Dombro, Colker, & Dodge, 1999). High-quality, developmentally appropriate programs contain three interwoven elements: age appropriateness, individual appropriateness, and cultural/social appropriateness. These three elements steer the necessary activity for each individual child, at any age, in the early childhood program environment.

Director's Showcase
Zara

With the implementation of the community garden, improved outdoor play areas, and the opportunity to purchase more equipment for the infant and toddler classrooms, the staff shared their concerns about the curriculum that they were using. While it had been used by the program for years, it lacked individual and cultural appropriateness. Many of the staff seemed excited about updating it, but others were leery of new activities and how they would best "fit" into their lesson plans. Zara decided that she would work with the staff but was unsure on how to start the process of searching for the most appropriate curriculum choice for their program.

Asha

After making changes within her home environment and securing new and thrifted equipment, Asha decided to take the next big step and began researching curriculum options for family child care home environments. Tired of downloading the ideas from the internet, Asha wanted a plan of ongoing activity and something that she would be proud of and supported the children's learning.

Because Zara and Asha had such success working with the consultant at the local Child Care Resource & Referral agency, they each decided to reach out to her again to get her opinion on how to choose an appropriate curriculum for their programs.

Dodge (2004) provides excellent guidelines for program leaders who are considering a curriculum to choose. Those guidelines include making sure that

- the curriculum matches the program vision and mission.
- the curriculum choice supports the program philosophical beliefs.
- state regulatory mandates and requirements are met.
- the teaching staff has the stability, formal education, and experience to implement the curriculum.
- professional development opportunities are available for teaching staff to learn more about the curriculum.
- resources are readily available to support the implementation of the curriculum.

The choice of curriculum may also come from the direction of either federal or state funds that a program receives. For example, federally funded programs such as Head Start and Early Head Start are required to use a high-quality, research-based curriculum that promotes measurable progress toward children's development. While there are many different curricula that meet the program's standards, it is up to the program leader and their staff to choose the best choice for their particular program.

There are different ways to explore a curriculum to understand its purpose as well as use within a program environment. Some of the basic elements include

- the description of its approach to teaching and learning;
- how it addresses learning domains;
- how learning goals are defined;

- the design and organization of the learning environment and daily schedule;
- the planning and implementation of learning experiences; and
- how family engagement is supported.

Whether you are a program director with teaching staff to assist with making the decision or a family child care home provider, there are also considerations when choosing curriculum appropriate for infants and toddlers, preschool, school-age, and multiple ages typically served in a home environment.

Infants and Toddlers

Curriculum for infants and toddlers includes every interaction and experience that supports the child's natural desire to explore and learn (Petersen & Wittmer, 2013). Activities should always be developmentally appropriate. Infants need items they can grasp, mouth, and examine. Safe, interesting objects to look at, hear, and touch fascinate them and help them learn (**Figure 4.18**). As they learn how to reach, they need items to grasp. They need toys that they can control. It is a wonderful discovery for infants and toddlers to find that when they pull, or squeeze, or shake, something in the toy responds. They also need to see themselves. Mirrors in several spots around the room will fascinate young children.

Toddlers need even more items to help them develop muscle control and coordination. They need the opportunity to run, roll, jump, and laugh heartily. Cruising around the room, looking at the adult to confirm the names of objects, is also a valuable use of a toddler's time. A simple game of "Ring Around the Rosie" can be a fun way to encourage balance and coordination. Toddlers also

FatCamera/E+/Getty Images

Figure 4.18 Infants enjoy interactions with their teachers and classroom activities that allow them to grasp, mouth, and examine safe objects.

enjoy soft stuffed toys and dolls as they begin to develop an interest in pretend play. For both older infants and toddlers, walks around the center or outdoors expand their awareness. In a developmentally appropriate program, children are never bored. Curriculum for infants and toddlers emphasizes the social and physical environment of learning rather than the content focus, which most people relate to elementary school.

Preschool

Curriculum is all the educational experiences provided for children by the early childhood program. For infants and toddlers, it consists of every interaction and experience that supports the child's natural desire to explore and learn. When providing educational experiences to preschool-age children, five critical core practices developed by Curtis & Carter (2008) should be the specific principles utilized to guide administration and teachers as they determine the framework of curriculum utilized within the program:

- Create a nourishing classroom culture.
- Enhance the curriculum with a wide array of materials.
- Teachers participate in the teaching and learning process.
- Coach children to learn about learning.
- Teachers dig deeper to learn with children.

Rather than offering a step-by-step set of lessons or activities, the teaching staff should champion children by planning curriculum that relates to children's lives, their learning styles, culture, and everyday experiences.

Out-of-School-Time Care

The needs of school-age children are different from those of preschoolers. Because they have been in school all day, they are ready for lively after-school events.

Outdoor play time, organized games, and a nutritious snack are essentials for an after-school program. Some children will be tired after a long day. They need opportunities and space for quiet activities. Crafts, board games, opportunities for dramatic play, and quiet reading may appeal to them. Programs should provide a quiet working space for those children who have homework. If a child needs the help of a tutor, you may coordinate these services with a local tutoring agency. Because the after-school program usually is only open for a couple of hours, activities must be either short or extend over several days at a time. During the summer, or when school is closed, most programs expand into all-day service. The summer can offer many opportunities for more involved projects and activities.

Family Child Care Home

Any high-quality early childhood program environment has adults who are knowledgeable about child development. Since family child care home providers are often working on their own with children of various ages, they need to be especially aware of how children learn in order to meet the individualized need of each child in their care. All children benefit from being in an organized and consistent environment with rituals and routines. Depending on the ages of the children, space is a consideration as well as the type of activity offered. A home is a natural environment for learning, and it must feel safe and secure. When the learning space is working, children are engaged and frustrations among and between children are limited.

No matter the age group served in any program environment, the early childhood leader provides the guidance for the best choice of curriculum for the program. It is up to the teaching staff to bring the curriculum to life within the classroom environment and this comes from having a program leader that supports them. This includes making sure that the teaching staff have what they need to provide developmentally appropriate environments that are fully equipped and supplied in facilities that promote children's individual learning.

Director's Showcase

Reflect

If you were in the consultant role, what guidelines and suggestions would you provide to Zara and Asha to assist them with choosing an appropriate curriculum?

Chapter 4 Review and Assessment

Summary

4.1 Review guidelines for indoor and outdoor environments when determining facility and space needs for children.

- When setting up indoor and outdoor environments, several factors must be carefully considered. This begins by choosing a location that is convenient for families. The building should not be too difficult or expensive to bring into compliance with state licensing standards. It should be free of asbestos and lead-based paint and be designed so it can be kept secure from unauthorized persons. The building must be accessible to people with disabilities, and it must be suitable for the types of services to be offered.
- Allocation of space must be appropriate for older children who require larger rooms, while space for infants, toddlers, and preschool-age children vary based on state requirements.
- Adequate utilities and storage space must be available. Interior elements such as windows, doors, flooring treatment, and lighting are just a few of the considerations. Outdoor elements must be safe, secure, and provide a strong connection to nature for children to experience.

4.2 Examine equipment needs that influence the organization and arrangement of successful indoor and outdoor learning spaces for young children.

- Equipment for different age groups is expected. Basic principles of classroom and outdoor space organization is guided by state and national standards. This allows for the appropriate planning for the different age groups and support of the many activity spaces necessary to support children's learning. Each one of these activity areas are designed to enhance children's self-discovery and ability to learn through play.
- The outdoor area is a classroom that provides opportunity for discovery and ongoing learning opportunities. Both the indoor and outdoor environments are key to children's everyday learning experiences.

4.3 Distinguish equipment differences for infants and toddlers, preschoolers, school-age children, and family child care home programs.

- All classrooms need to be equipped with age-appropriate equipment. This includes having extra inventory to rotate within or between classrooms to support children's individual interests and learning.
- The type of equipment chosen should be based on developmentally appropriate considerations for the children within the classroom, and it is important that a variety of equipment be available within a home program environment due to the multiple ages being served.
- Activity areas that must be equipped include dramatic play, block-building, easel/art, library, and table activities. Science and nature displays and activities, music, sand and water play, and lively large muscle activities must also be accommodated. General guidelines for room arrangement should be followed.

4.4 Evaluate curriculum recommendations for infant, toddler, preschool, out-of-school-time, and family child care home programs.

- Developmentally appropriate curriculum incorporates age appropriateness, individual appropriateness, and cultural/social appropriateness. It is the framework for play and the what, why, planning, implementation, and overall evaluation of the program.
- Curriculum guides the activities for each individual child, at any age, in the early childhood program environment.

Review Questions

1. List five factors to consider before making a commitment to open a child care center on a specific site. (4.1)
2. What type of standards for child care facilities are dictated by licensing requirements? (4.1)
3. How can child care centers be made accessible? (4.1)
4. Why would a school-age program require a larger room space than an infant or a toddler program? (4.1)
5. List five factors to consider when choosing a floor treatment for a child care center. (4.1)
6. What type of paint is recommended for classroom use? (4.1)
7. What type of lighting do experts recommend for child care centers? (4.1)
8. How much outdoor space do experts recommend per child? (4.1)
9. List four factors to consider when setting up an office. (4.1)
10. Describe the major considerations when choosing a curriculum for a center or home program. (4.4)

Showcase Your Skills

As we discussed in this chapter, Zara and Asha were able to improve their programs by adding a variety of equipment and activity opportunities in the indoor and outdoor environments provided by their programs. This further ignited interest in either enhancing or choosing a curriculum to best support the children in their programs. While the local Child Care Resource & Referral Consultant provided some great insights, you have been contacted to assist them with the research and recommendations of some possible curriculum choices for a large center and home program.

Based on the information shared in the chapter, it is now your turn to serve in the role of consultant. Write a proposal using the following points as your guide.

1. Research a curriculum choice for a center and a home program. Select and provide justification for each curriculum. (4.4)
2. Provide an overview on how each curriculum provides developmental, individual, and societal/cultural appropriateness for children. (4.4)
3. Explain any professional development or training to assist the staff or home provider when implementing the curriculum choice. (4.4)
4. List cost considerations for each curriculum choice. (4.4)

Matching

Match the following terms with the correct definitions:

A. block center
B. creative art area
C. curriculum
D. dramatic play area
E. housekeeping area
F. literacy and writing areas
G. math and science areas
H. sensory area

1. Quiet spaces that contain an interesting selection of developmentally appropriate books and materials to learn more about the written word.
2. Play area designed to encourage and enhance children's pretend play.
3. Play area that contains blocks of all shapes and sizes, which encourages children to create complicated building projects.
4. Classroom space that allows children to participate in activities involving many types of textures, including sand and water.
5. Space where children can engage in multiple types of art activities and create opportunities for creative expression.
6. Framework that pulls together developmentally appropriate practices for all ages of children cared for in an early childhood program environment.
7. Play area that contains replicas of familiar items found at home, including kitchen equipment, dolls, plastic foods, and furniture.
8. Spaces that contain materials for engagement that support the foundations necessary when learning math and science concepts in early childhood classrooms.

PeopleImages/E+/Getty Images

5 CHAPTER

Staffing Costs and Considerations

Learning Outcomes

After studying this chapter, you will be able to:

5.1 Define characteristics of quality early childhood teachers and staff.

5.2 Develop an organizational structure.

5.3 Prepare early childhood job descriptions.

5.4 Recruit qualified job applicants.

5.5 Interview and select qualified staff members.

5.6 Establish an employee orientation program to welcome new hires.

Key Terms

administrative staff

classroom staff

class size

contract

employment at will

job description

labor-intensive

mentor

organizational chart

orientation plan

portfolio

positive self-esteem

probationary employment period

staff-to-child ratio

support personnel

Introduction

Selecting staff to work with young children is serious business. Not just anyone can step into the role of early childhood teacher. The National Association for the Education of Young Children (NAEYC) has worked diligently over the years to establish six areas within their accreditation standards that reflect areas of expected competency, preparation, and support that should be provided. According the NAEYC's rationale for *Standard 6: Staff Competencies, Preparation, and Support*:

> Children in early learning programs benefit most when teaching and administrative staff have high levels of formal education and specialized professional preparation. Staff who have specific preparation, knowledge, and skills in child development and early childhood education are more likely to engage in warm, positive interactions with children, offer richer language experiences, and create higher quality learning environments. Opportunities for teaching and administrative staff to receive supportive supervision and to participate in ongoing professional development ensure that their knowledge and skills reflect the profession's ever-changing knowledge base.

The Staff Competencies, Preparation, and Support standard is made up of four topic areas:

- 6.A—Supportive Work Environment
- 6.B—Professional Identity and Recognition
- 6.C—Qualifications of Teaching and Administrative Staff
- 6.D—Ongoing Professional Development (NAEYC, 2022).

Each one of these areas provide significant insights as to why it is important to hire and maintain quality early childhood teachers (**Figure 5.1**).

Marcy Whitebook, director of the Center for the Study of Child Care Employment at the University of California, Berkeley, made a very specific comparison in relation to teachers working within the field and in elementary grades: "Teaching preschoolers is every bit as complicated and important as teaching any of the K-12 grades, if not more so. But we still treat preschool teachers like babysitters. We want them to ameliorate poverty even as they live in it themselves" (Interlandi, 2018).

Successfully supporting young children and appropriate guidance of behavior through the early childhood years will lead to more successful adults. Quality child care providers apply the necessary knowledge, skills, and dispositions when working with young children. These are defined as competencies: specific, measurable, and observable behaviors that reflect a practitioner's knowledge and ability to apply that knowledge to meet needs and expectations for roles ranging from teacher's assistant to lead teacher or center director.

In 2018, Catherine Main and Karen Yarbrough explained in their *Transforming the Early Childhood Workforce* report, the quality of adult-child interactions has the greatest impact on the health, overall development, and future success of young children before they enter school. It is these relationships between adults and children that provide the stability and security to grow and learn.

The National Academy of Medicine (2015) report recommends that early childhood educators across age ranges and settings have the following competencies:

- A core knowledge of developmental science.
- The mastery of practices that help children learn and develop on individual pathways.

Drazen Zigic/iStock/Getty Images Plus

Figure 5.1 Early childhood programs must be staffed with quality teachers who have appropriate education and experience working with young children.

- A knowledge of how to work with diverse populations of children.
- The ability to partner with children's families and professional colleagues.
- The ability to engage in ongoing professional development to keep up with new knowledge and developments in the field of early childhood education and continuously improve their professional practice.

The quality of your program will be determined, in large part, by the skill of your staff. Well-trained teachers are essential to a successful program. Child care is a **labor-intensive** field, requiring a large workforce for a quality service to occur, so "people power" is the most important part of the program structure. Without a good staff, the program no matter what its size cannot be a quality center for children.

SDI Productions/E+/Getty Images

Figure 5.2 Program leaders must invest time in potential job applicants. This includes a thorough interview and background check process.

5.1 Characteristics of Quality Child Care Staff

Staffing the program is one of the most important parts of a director's job. It takes time. Good staff may be hard to find. Hiring top-notch employees is a process that involves both careful screening and intuition (**Figure 5.2**).

Working with children and families requires a special type of person. Each staff member's personality will have an impact on the program. An encounter with an irritable, critical individual can set the tone for the day for coworkers, children, and family members. It can also cause parents to question whether this is a place they want their children to be. For a successful, happy program, it is necessary for staff members to display the following characteristics (**Figure 5.3**).

- *Kindness and nurturance.* Children need to be nurtured and treated with kindness. The world can be a scary place. Children feel secure with adults who treat them kindly, and adults who are tender in their interactions with children are usually kind in their dealings with adults also. They go out of their way to reassure and help others. This characteristic is a necessity in the personality of anyone working with children and families. Being able to nurture others and help them grow and develop requires being able to support children in their efforts, applaud their successes, and soothe

Director's Showcase

Loren

Loren is the director at a large child care facility that is located close to a major university. Many of the children enrolled in the facility are children of parents employed by the university. She also works closely with the early childhood education (ECE) program at the university, employing students and allowing observations and research projects.

Loren has had success when employing students but has experienced problems with turnover. Students graduate and move away, change majors, or decide a different path. While she would like to continue to work with the ECE program, she feels that she needs to hire more teachers and staff who will be a more permanent fixture in her program.

Kevin

Kevin is the director of a small child care center in a small town. He recently accepted the position as director at this facility after many years of working at a large center in a metropolitan area. He had to deal with high turnover at the last facility but seemed to have a larger pool of applicants to pull from when hiring. In his new center, he has struggled to find teachers and staff and has been told that high turnover is to be expected at this facility. Kevin is trying to figure out ways to find quality teachers and staff in a limited pool of available applicants.

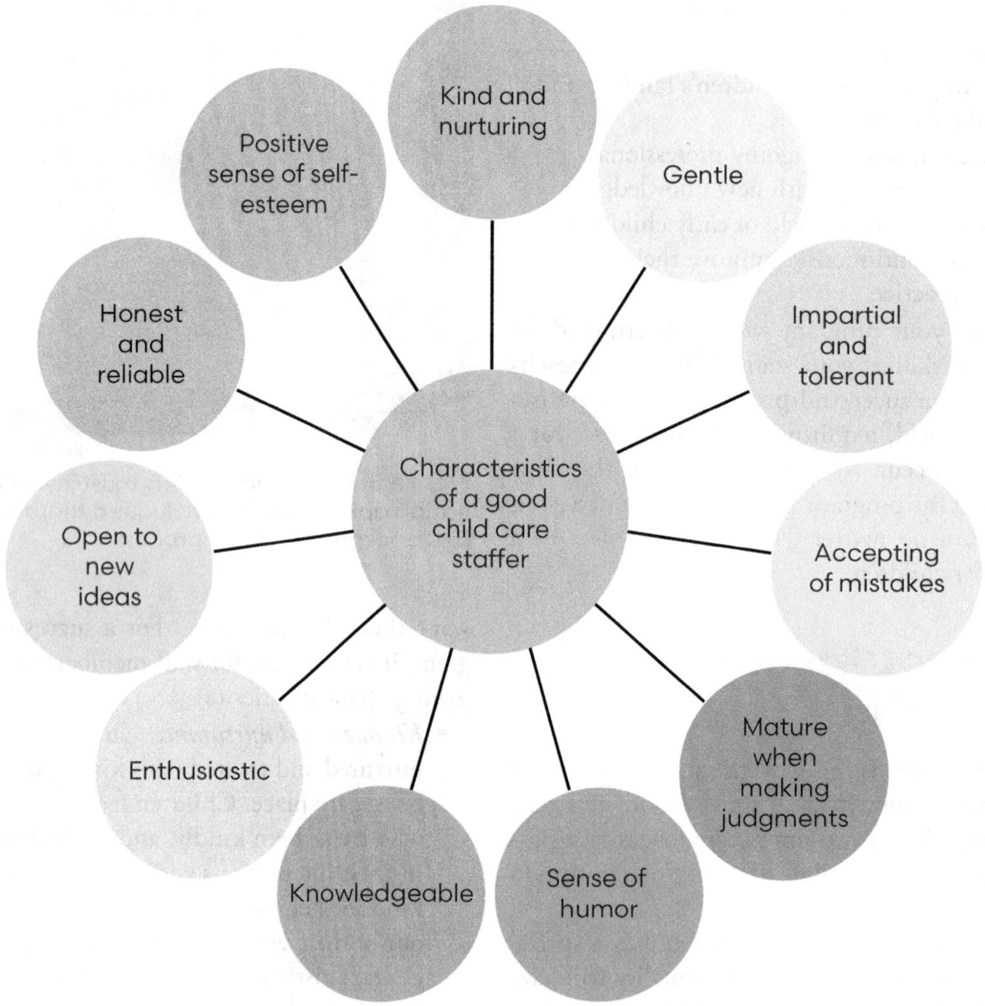

Goodheart-Willcox Publisher

Figure 5.3 It is important to find just the right person to work with young children. Listed are the many characteristics that adults need when working with young children.

them in their disappointments. Adults who are nurturing can leave their own problems outside the door. They can give love and warmth that children need whenever it is needed.

- *Gentleness.* Staff members must treat children gently, both physically and emotionally. Washing a toddler's face, helping a child get into a heavy snowsuit, or soothing injured feelings should all be done with gentleness. Not only are children appreciative of the sensitivity and often more willing to cooperate, but they also have a role model to guide them as they interact with others. This is crucial when building relationships and learning to care for others.
- *Impartiality and tolerance of differences.* Everyone has a set of values and beliefs that guide behavior. It is sometimes difficult to accept others whose values and beliefs are different. Working with families

requires the ability to remain impartial and avoid judging others who may view the world differently. A staff member who is always critical of others and behaves with a superior attitude will quickly be avoided by others. Staff must also be aware of the need to maintain a tolerance of differences. An early childhood program is a busy place with many people. It is common to have a mix of personality types, clothing styles, food preferences, cultures, attitudes, and lifestyles in the people who visit or work in the center. Children's families may be quite different from those of the teachers and staff. Staff must work comfortably with a diverse array of families, children, and other center personnel (**Figure 5.4**).

- *Acceptance of mistakes.* Children are beginners in every aspect of life. They are just beginning to know how to control their bodies, interact

Lordn/iStock/Getty Images Plus

Figure 5.4 All staff members who work within an early childhood program must interact with a diverse array of families, children, and coworkers.

socially with others, solve problems, and learn all they will need to know. A good staff member encourages children and supports their efforts to learn. Parents and caretakers of young children may also feel overwhelmed and occasionally forget a deadline or a request. Everyone makes mistakes occasionally. Coworkers also need an atmosphere that is relaxed and free from harmful criticism.

- *Mature judgment.* Every day, teachers are required to make decisions about how to handle situations in the classroom. For example, they must help children learn to deal with conflicts and take turns while playing with others. Teachers must know when to give extra love and support to a child who is upset. Staff members must also be able to judge how to handle conflicts with other staff. Mature judgment includes knowing when to stick up for yourself and when to back off.

- *Sense of humor.* A kind sense of humor is helpful to anyone working in a child care center. Levity helps children to relax. It also helps them to know that the adults here are fun; they are not just waiting to pounce on mistakes. Gentle humor can help defuse confrontations between children and adults as well as between the adults themselves. It can help everyone keep the day's events in perspective and minimize stress. Sarcasm, a tendency to ridicule, laughing at others, and using a joking style to embarrass or attack someone are not examples of gentle humor. They are hurtful, destructive characteristics to avoid when hiring staff members.

- *Knowledgeable about child development.* Teachers must have an education that provides a good working knowledge of children's development. This allows them to plan activities that are developmentally appropriate and match the needs of each individual child and the group. Teachers who possess this specialized training can create a quality day-to-day experience for the children. Current research clearly shows that trained staff provide a better program for children than staff with no training (Snyder, 2018). All staff members need to have knowledge about the developmental characteristics of the children in the center. Everyone who encounters the children should have some understanding of their needs and behavior patterns.

- *Enthusiasm for learning.* Good staff members are always eager to learn more. They find the world an interesting place that is full of new things to explore and want further education and experiences. An office staff member who is enthusiastic about mastering a new computer software system is an asset to a program. A teacher's aide who wants to know more about child development may have the potential to become a lead teacher one day. Teachers who are always looking for new ideas and learning more about child development pass that enthusiasm for learning on to the children. The children, in turn, model themselves after these important adults in their lives.

- *Openness to new ideas.* As a program leader, being alert to new ideas for the program is crucial. Your teaching staff should also have an openness to new ideas. This may be as simple as a willingness to try a new room arrangement. It may involve acceptance of a move to a different classroom. In a growing program, change is inevitable. Children grow old enough to leave the program and new ones arrive. Staff may change. The needs of the program, in terms of adding new classrooms or providing additional services, may require that all staff members need to adjust to changes and try new ideas. The staff member who approaches new ideas with confidence and enthusiasm is pleasant to work with and helps others. The individual who complains to everyone and resists change is a negative influence that can stall or make progress difficult.

- *Positive sense of self-esteem.* Many of the characteristics already discussed are related to **positive self-esteem**, or the knowledge that a person is a good and worthy individual.

Positive self-esteem supports one's sense of being a successful person and that they can make thoughtful decisions and can care for others. Being able to relax with a gentle sense of humor, having an openness to new ideas, and the ability to deal with others in a nonjudgmental, tolerant, and accepting manner, are all linked to a positive sense of self-esteem. Staff hired for the center are more likely to possess all the other characteristics if they have a positive view of themselves.

- *Honesty and reliability.* Anyone hired to work in the center must be honest and reliable. Staff must be dependable and come to work on time. They must complete records carefully and honestly. Some staff may be responsible for handling money. Others maintain the waiting list for enrollment and interact with parents. Some positions may require filling out time sheets for wage calculation. Teachers must be role models for the children and staff in their classrooms. The center cannot function effectively if some staff members are deceptive and dishonest. Parents will not choose a center if they are aware that essential staff are not at work on time. Honesty and reliability are essential requirements for all jobs in the program.

One of the most important tasks of a program leader is the selection of staff. This includes the positions necessary for the program and the plan for how to find the appropriate individuals for each position.

5.2 Organizational Structure

Before a center begins to hire or add more employees, the program needs a clear organizational structure (**Figure 5.5**). In a small center, one person may handle

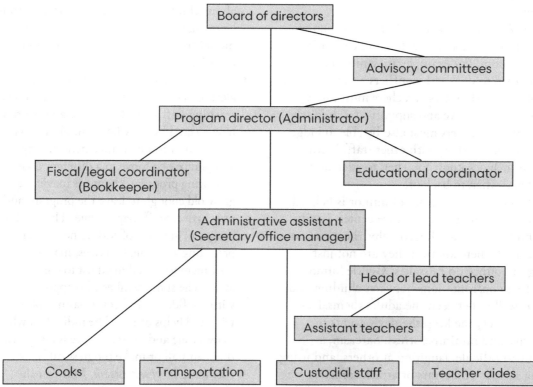

Goodheart-Willcox Publisher

Figure 5.5 Small and large centers have a staff organizational structure. This structure helps to designate responsibilities within all individuals that support the early childhood program.

several sets of responsibilities. For example, a family child care home provider is the teacher and the director and performs teaching and administrative duties. In larger programs, there may be several people who handle strictly administrative tasks, while the teachers focus on working with the children in the classrooms.

Developing Organizational Structure

When looking at your organizational structure, you can group program staff into three categories: classroom staff, administrative staff, and support personnel. **Classroom staff** are those people who work directly with the children. Staff in each classroom can be viewed as team members. The lead teacher is the organizer and planner for the team. Many classrooms have an assistant teacher, who helps with decision making in the classroom and can take over if the lead teacher must leave. Since most programs are open 11 to 12 hours a day, there are typically afternoon assistant teachers who cover when the lead teacher goes home for the day. They, too, play a valuable role by helping the classroom run smoothly.

Administrative staff are those employees with organizational and planning skills who provide direction for the total program. They seek funds, pursue licensing, recruit and enroll children, and handle other managerial duties. Administrative staff do not usually work directly in the classroom but may provide coverage as needed.

The third group consists of **support personnel**, which includes administrative assistants, bookkeepers, receptionists, cooks, van drivers, and maintenance staff. Their work provides essential support to program activities. They help others do their jobs. They also provide key customer service to parents and caregivers.

When organizing your program, map out an **organizational chart**, creating a visual image that indicates job titles and the lines of authority within the program. The organizational chart displays how many job classifications there are in the program and shows which staff positions are responsible for overseeing others. Employees can see how their positions fit into the overall organization. In general, positions on the higher levels of the chart

- require more training and/or experience;
- involve managerial responsibilities;
- demand more planning and organizational abilities;
- include greater responsibilities;
- have more authority;
- have more flexibility in when and where their work is done;
- are responsible for lower-level positions; and
- earn higher salaries.

Factors That Influence an Organizational Chart

A number of factors will influence a program's organizational pattern. Consider the following when deciding the best way to organize your program.

Director's Showcase

Loren

Loren has been revising an existing organizational chart for her center. It is sadly out of date, as the program has grown since the chart was last updated. She has discovered that clear job descriptions, roles, and expectations are areas where she needs to focus her attention. Because of the fluid and ongoing employment of university students, Loren sees that additional information needs to be added to the chart specific to these employees. She has noted much confusion and chaos occur at the end and beginning of a new school semester. This chaos leads to disruptions in the classroom with the children and staff. She will focus on clearly defining roles of university students to begin her reorganization.

Kevin

Kevin held a meeting with the center staff to address the high caregiver turnover and filling the vacant positions. He asked if any existing staff had an interest in moving from a support role into a teaching role. Two staff members have expressed interest but are concerned about not being qualified. Many other staff members have expressed an interest in further education. He has learned that the previous director offered few continuing education opportunities to the center's teachers and staff. He has also found information about members of the small community that may be interested in a career in early childhood through current staff and parents.

Size of Program

Smaller programs have fewer children enrolled, fewer teachers and staff, and a less complex budget than a larger program. In a larger program, staff may take on dual roles and consolidate tasks for each staff member.

Program organization should be designed to group components of the program logically together. Larger programs will need more staff in each area, although the areas of organization may be the same as in smaller programs.

Types of Services Offered

The types of services offered will affect the organizational structure of a program. If a program only offers full-day child care, the organization will be simpler than if it offers before-and-after school care as well as full- and half-day care. Varied hours with school breaks need staff who are hired to work varied work schedules which may not be ideal. The organizational chart will reflect the size and complexity of the services a program offers.

State Regulations

State regulations need to be considered in the organizational chart. The chart should reflect specific rules and regulations, including staff-to-child ratios and group size limitations. **Staff-to-child ratios** are the number of children compared to the number of adults responsible for a designated group of children. All teaching and support staff must be aware of and maintain these rules and regulations. **Class size** is also a consideration and makes up all of the children assigned for the majority of the day to a specific teacher or group of teachers within an assigned classroom space.

Skill and Training of Available Employees

Hiring experienced and educated teachers and staff allows for the program leader to focus more on other areas of the program. However, if hired staff have little to no experience, the director's focus will also need to be on the growth of each individual employee.

5.3 Job Descriptions

Once you have identified the many roles in your organizational structure, every role in the program needs a

Director's Showcase
Reflect
Now that you have learned more about the necessary characteristics for filling positions and a need for an organizational structure, do you believe that Loren and Kevin are doing the right "next steps" to deal with the issues they are experiencing? Why or why not?

written *job description*. A **job description** spells out the duties, qualifications, and experience needed to perform the position successfully. Job descriptions clarify each job's purpose for everyone in the program (**Figure 5.6**). Jobs in the same job category, such as master teacher positions, will be identical or very similar. This is because each of the master teachers handles almost the same responsibilities and requires similar training. The job description also identifies other positions that report to the role and specify to whom the role is responsible. As the program grows or changes, job descriptions might have to be changed according to program needs.

A job description helps a potential applicant decide whether to apply for a position (**Figure 5.7**). Anyone reading the job description should be able to tell how that position fits into the organizational structure. A clear explanation of duties is essential. Applicants want to know what their potential duties would be. Knowing what their duties will be allows them to decide if the position is a good fit for their skills, experience, and interests even before they apply. For example, all teachers in the program may have basically the same types of responsibilities. The teacher's duties may include

- planning classroom activities and daily schedule;
- setting the classroom atmosphere;
- providing expertise in determining appropriate guidance for assistants, children, and families;
- planning the schedules and responsibilities of the aides in the classroom; and
- ordering classroom supplies.

Job descriptions take time to develop. They are essential, however, to ensure that the responsibilities of each position are clearly identified. Small programs may function quite well with an "everybody pitch in to get the job done" philosophy. However, in larger programs, confusion over responsibilities is likely to occur. Some important tasks may not get done at all because

Job Description—Master Teacher

Qualifications: B.S. degree in Child Development, Early Childhood Education, or related field that includes a minimum of 18 hours of coursework relevant to work with children and families or an A.A. degree that includes 18 hours of coursework in child-related studies and two years of successful experience in child care.

A Master Teacher in the child care program is responsible for supervising the total program of the individual classroom.

Responsibilities:
- **Responsible to the Program Director.** Master Teachers are responsible for conducting the program in the classrooms in accordance with the policies established by the Board of Directors and interpreted by the Program Director. The Master Teachers are to inform the Program Director or appropriate coordinator of the needs of the children, parents, and classroom staffs. They are to suggest improvements and discuss problems. The Master Teachers are to help maintain the budget control as established by the Program Director.
- **Supervision of Staff.** Master Teachers are to participate in the interviewing of Aides and Assistant Teachers and in the assignment of classroom staff responsibilities. They are responsible for scheduling the hours of the classroom staff, assigning duties, and sharing information with the classroom staff. Master Teachers should meet frequently with their classroom staff members both individually and as a group to discuss plans and problems. Master Teachers will participate in the evaluation of their classroom staff members and will be evaluated by the Program Coordinators.
- **Development and Implementation of the Daily Program.** Master Teachers organize all aspects of the daily program. They are primarily responsible for the preparation of materials and the organization of developmentally appropriate activities. They will have a large part in the establishment of program goals and the ongoing process of program evaluation.
- **Primary Responsibility for Children.** Master Teachers will have the primary responsibility for the welfare of the children who are in the care of the center. They should know all the children in their classroom well. They should be aware of the special needs of the children and plan for ways to meet these needs. They should cooperate with the appropriate Division Coordinator to arrange for consultant services for those children needing them.
- **Responsible for Health and Safety Decisions Within the Classroom.** Master Teachers maintain healthy and safe classroom practices, use universal precautions, and are prepared to respond appropriately to emergency situations. Master Teachers have and maintain CPR and First Aid certifications.
- **Maintenance of Facilities and Equipment.** Master Teachers are responsible for seeing that their classrooms are in order and that equipment is kept in good condition. They are responsible for keeping the Director up-to-date on equipment and supplies needed to carry on the daily program.
- **Maintenance of Records and Reports.** Master Teachers are responsible for keeping time sheets and vacation information for their classroom staff. They are to maintain lists of needed equipment and supplies, classroom attendance, and daily plans. They are to contribute to records involving the children in their classroom.
- **Interpreting the Program to Parents.** Master Teachers are responsible for working with their Division Coordinator in interpreting the program to their classroom parents. They share responsibility with the Coordinator for giving parents information about their children. They are responsible for keeping parents informed about the center calendar and special events.

Goodheart-Willcox Publisher

Figure 5.6 All programs have job descriptions for the variety of roles that individuals fill to support the program. These descriptions spell out the education and experience requirements for each position and include expected job duties.

no one feels responsible. People may be spending time on tasks that are not matched to their expertise or salaries. In addition, employee evaluations are often linked to the performance of assigned duties. If an employee does not understand what their job entails, this may result in a poor evaluation and affect their potential pay increase.

Whenever a position becomes vacant, examine the job description. It may need to be changed to reflect changes in the program and the expertise of staff members. It should be updated periodically. As you are posting a job opening, you may also consider including information about your center, its philosophy and mission, any employee benefits, and a salary range to attract suitable applicants.

Job Description—Teacher Aide

Qualifications: High School diploma or G.E.D. is required for this position. Aide must also have personal qualities, interests, abilities, and potential for effective functioning in this position.

A Teacher Aide in the Child Care Program is responsible for carrying out the duties as assigned by the Master Teacher and/or Assistant Teacher. Aides are responsible for sharing ideas and suggestions in a manner supportive of the Master and Assistant Teachers.

Responsibilities:

- **Responsibility to the Classroom Master Teacher and Assistant Teacher.** The Aide is directly responsible to both the Master Teacher and Assistant Teacher. Aides carry out duties and assignments in accordance with instructions. They are responsible for informing the Teachers of observations on the needs of the children.
- **Implementation of the Daily Program.** The Aides assist classroom teachers with daily activities and routines. They may conduct special activities in line with interests and abilities. Aides may be assigned some kitchen duties and clean-up duties as well as activities directly with children.
- **Responsibility for Children.** Aides with the help of another Aide may supervise groups of children for brief periods upon direction of the Teacher. Aides may give special attention and help to children needing it.

Goodheart-Willcox Publisher

Figure 5.7 Those who serve in the role of a teacher aide require the least amount of education and experience. Their job duties are less complex than the role of teacher.

5.4 Staff Recruitment

The search for good staff requires a thoughtful recruitment process. Finding qualified people and attracting them to an early childhood program can be a difficult task. Because salaries in the child care field are low, many talented and qualified people leave the field. Teachers often move into administrative positions or take positions in the pre-K programs offered at local schools. Many programs experience high turnover rates among staff members. Even relatively stable programs find it necessary to recruit new staff members at some point in time.

Established programs should first look within their own staff for employees who are ready to move up into higher positions. Promoting from within has the advantage of providing an incentive to hard-working, loyal employees. The possibility of moving into a position of increased prestige, responsibility, and salary can be an encouragement to a staff member. Of course, this leaves the director with the problem of filling the spot left vacant by the promoted employee.

First, let qualified people know when a position is open. Prepare the job description and include the qualifications that are necessary. Indicate the procedure for applying for the position.

Develop an overall recruiting plan based on the position available. Post positions on your website, on social media, and in the local newspaper (**Figure 5.8**). Notify employees, parents, and board members of any openings. Use community contacts to share openings. Local community college and vocational school career centers are ideal partners for recruiting and posting positions.

Positions requiring higher levels of education and experience in child development or early childhood

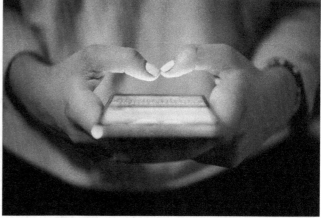

diego_cervo/iStock/Getty Images Plus

Figure 5.8 Use of the internet and social media help to spread the word about open positions within an early childhood program.

education may be harder to fill. Advertise these positions more widely on online job boards and using job recruitment websites. Work with local university career centers and utilize organizational resources, such as National Child Care Association or NAEYC. Child Care Resource and Referral (CCR&R) and other government agencies may have insights into obtaining qualified staff members. Using web-based job search engines can be a useful tool to recruit new teachers and staff.

Government Employment Regulations

Several major federal laws will affect hiring practices. When advertising for open positions, you must follow federal laws prohibiting employment discrimination.

Director's Showcase

Loren

Loren set up a meeting with the university ECE program director to discuss ways to streamline hiring students. They were able to add opportunities for overlap of care and transition from the outgoing student to the next student taking the position. They were also able to identify a process for students to apply for a permanent position and transition from the ECE program to Loren's center after graduation. Loren added a section to the organizational chart with clearly defined roles and expectations for the student teachers. Reading the updated chart and descriptions, the permanent staff better understood their own roles and responsibilities.

Kevin

Kevin needed to fill two positions: a support staff job and a lead teacher position. He posted a job opening with a detailed job description in the local newspaper and an online employment database, and he sent out a mass email to the parents at the center and his colleagues. Kevin was determined to find the right fit for the job openings and was willing to take time and explore all the applicants.

This requires specific efforts to attract job applicants from all minority groups. To better understand how your center fits into these requirements, visit the US Equal Employment Opportunity Commission's website (eeoc.gov). Equal opportunity employers must include an EEO statement on job descriptions, applications, and any recruitment statement. The *Civil Rights Act of 1964* and its amendments prohibit discrimination in hiring on the basis of race, color, sex, age, disability, or national origin. An EEO statement guarantees compliance with the 1964 Civil Rights Act.

Affirmative action plans designed to ensure recruitment strategies that will result in a diverse pool of applicants may also be required. Strategies include publishing ads in journals or newspapers with a large minority readership or contacting colleagues who might know qualified minority individuals in the field. With luck, job announcements will reach appropriate persons who will decide to submit applications for the position.

You must also comply with all applicable state and federal laws designed to ensure fair hiring practices in your employment practices (**Figure 5.9**). These laws are occasionally amended or changed, so check with your state's employment agency to determine the status of the legislation.

The Application

Once you have created a detailed job description and a recruitment plan, your next step is to develop or update your center's application or request for resumes, a formal document created by the applicant about their qualifications, to gather essential information about each applicant (**Figure 5.10**). As with your job listing, the application must comply with all applicable laws regarding nondiscrimination. Some information may be asked only if it relates clearly and directly to a candidate's ability to perform the specific job. For example, a person whose medical status includes a tendency to unexpectedly lose consciousness could not work safely in a classroom.

Funtap/iStock/Getty Images Plus

Figure 5.9 The government sets forth regulations to protect and provide equal employment opportunity for all. These regulations are intended to ensure fair hiring and employment practices.

Khanchit Khirisutchalual/iStock/Getty Images Plus

Figure 5.10 Submitting online applications allows early childhood programs to receive and review interested candidates' information in a timely and efficient manner.

The same person might, however, be a valuable employee in the type of position where constant alertness is not necessary.

It is best to take applications and resumes for one position at a time. Posting to your program website, sending out open position information to potential candidates, or using a job search website are all great ways to get a number of candidates. This avoids confusion for both the program and the applicant. If another position is open, have interested applicants fill out a second application for the specific position. After a position is filled, keep all the paperwork relating to top candidates. Keeping clear track of applicants for each specific position creates a paper trail that provides protection for the program in case of a legal challenge to hiring practices. Each new position that opens should result in a completely new search and pool of applicants.

The Hiring Process

While this can be a lengthy process, it is one that is very necessary when selecting the best candidate to fill a job opening. The application provides vital insights regarding the person, and the interview gives a chance to learn more while talking directly with the person. Questions must be developed before the interview process takes place so that appropriate information is gleaned from the candidate. Further, the determination of who and how questions will be asked must be determined. It is through this engaging opportunity that a possible "fit" is determined. Once the interview takes place and a certain candidate is selected, it is important to engage others within the teaching team to obtain their insights and do a thorough screening based on state regulatory requirements. Then, an offer can be extended.

5.5 Selecting the Best Applicant

Once you receive applications or resumes for a vacant position, you must screen them (**Figure 5.11**). The screening process is an initial sorting of the applications. Some candidates may clearly fit the qualifications identified in the job description while others may not. Divide the stack into each area, those who are qualified and those who are not. Then identify the number of candidates you wish to interview by narrowing down those who appear to fit the position you are looking for.

Carefully review each applicant's educational background but also the type and length of previous job experiences that the applicant has had. Make notes of possible items that you want to know more about. For example, one applicant might reflect taking a role planning a summer program for school-age children. In the interview process, it will be important to ask more about what the role entailed. Did they plan activities, were they responsible for guiding other staff members, or were they a lead teacher responsible for planning activities in the summer program? Asking questions gathers valuable information when it comes time to determine the best possible applicant.

Interviewing is a time-consuming process. Performing a thorough initial screening of applications assists with determining which candidates would best fit the job. Once you have screened the applications and have chosen the candidates who fit best, proceed to schedule interviews.

The Interview Process

The purpose of the interview is to give the applicant and the potential employer a chance to get to know each other better. As the program administrator, you are trying to find the person who will best match the role and demonstrate the characteristics desirable in a child care staff member. The interview provides another way for you to obtain information about the applicant.

Plan to have multiple people involved in the interview process, including the staff member who will supervise

Job Application
Child Care Program

Date ____________________

Name ____________________ Social Security Number ____________________

Present Address ____________________ Phone ____________________

____

I certify that I am 18 years of age or older, as required by (insert your state's licensing requirement if applicable).

Signature ____________________ Date ____________________

Position(s) applied for ____________________

What method of transportation will you use to get to work? ____________________

Would you work:

Full-time? ________ Part-time? ________

List days and hours available to work ____________________

____

List any friends or relatives working for us (names). ____________________

____

Please list all child care experience that can be documented (other than caring for your own children).

____

Are there any other experiences, licenses, certifications, or skills that you feel would especially qualify you for work with our organization? If so, describe.

____

____

Goodheart-Willcox Publisher

Figure 5.11 Job applications collect vital information from interested job applicants. It is important to collect the same information from all individuals no matter what level they will be working at within the early childhood program.

Hiraman/E+/Getty Images

Figure 5.12 Conducting job interviews allows for program leadership to understand more about the job candidate, and for the job candidate to learn more about the program and job expectations.

this person directly, someone in a similar role, someone else in the administrative team, and yourself. When interviewing for an assistant teacher's position, the lead teacher or program supervisor of that classroom should be a part of the interviewing team (**Figure 5.12**). If the position is a higher-level, managerial role, the other supervisors who will work with that individual should participate. For higher-level positions, you may ask a member of the personnel committee from the board of directors to participate in not-for-profit programs, since the actual recommendation to hire goes to the board for official approval. Directors or owners of small, for-profit programs with only a few employees may want to include a parent representative or local child development expert in the interview process. Very large programs may have a personnel specialist on staff who handles the hiring procedures.

Before interviewing applicants, develop a form to evaluate each candidate (**Figure 5.13**). To compare responses fairly, be sure the same questions are asked of each candidate. Having a standard set of interview questions and rating system can help compare candidates utilizing the same criteria. Avoid questions that can be answered with a simple yes or no. Avoid writing during the interview. Instead, complete your written evaluation of the candidate immediately following the interview.

Next, think about how the interview will be conducted. Plan and organize the interviews ahead of time to gather the most accurate information. The interview should be conducted in an atmosphere of respect for the candidate. Some candidates may bring a **portfolio**, which is a binder or electronic collection of samples of an individual's previous work or work completed within a teacher education program. Review this carefully as it can give clear examples of a person's competencies. Not

every person interviewed will be the right one for the job. However, each should be treated with the same consideration. Trick questions, high-pressure tactics, and condescension will not help find the best applicant.

Recognize that the interview is a stressful time for the applicant. Each one wants to make a good impression and is hopeful of being offered the job. As the program administrator, you have the responsibility to ensure the interview is conducted in a fair, considerate manner. You must ensure that those involved with the interview understand their role and are comfortable in their responsibilities. You may need to train your employees on how to conduct a proper, respectful interview. Your goals are to identify the person whose training, experience, and personality best match the responsibilities of the job and to have inspired them to want to work at your center.

Interview Questions to Consider

While there are many standard interview questions that are typically asked, consider questions to ask candidates specific to the position (**Figure 5.14**). When hiring a teacher for a specific age group, ask them to describe what issues they find most important about the age group. What do they like best about that age? What behaviors do they consider challenging or fun? How did they tackle problems with a co-teacher at the last job? Ask them to define the role of a classroom teacher, the director, and the support staff. How they answer more specific questions can help determine if they will be a good fit for the program.

Observation

One of the most difficult aspects of hiring staff for a child care center is trying to find individuals with caring and compassionate personalities. Working with children and their families requires special characteristics. Some of these qualities are very difficult to discern in an interview. Somehow, through the selection process, try to identify whether an individual has these characteristics. For any position that involves classroom work, consider requiring that a candidate spend time in the room with the children. Allow at least 45 minutes to an hour for this part of the interview. This will give the individual time to interact with the children and will allow the lead teacher time to assess the candidate's direct involvement.

Concluding the Interview

At the end of the interview, give candidates a chance to ask questions. Individuals applying for higher-level positions should have a basic knowledge about how child care programs operate and usually have several questions. These may include questions about services, clientele, sponsorship, and their role in the overall structure of the program. Most applicants want to know what the

Criteria for Ranking Interviewed Applicants for Teacher Position

Name of applicant _____

Date of interview _____

Criteria	**Score (1 = poor, 3 = adequate, 5 = excellent)**				
1. Education meets job criteria.	1	2	3	4	5
2. Experience meets job criteria.	1	2	3	4	5
3. Expressed attitudes about children are consistent with program philosophy.	1	2	3	4	5
4. Classroom observation indicates ease and warm rapport with children.	1	2	3	4	5
5. Comments and answers indicate knowledge of children's development.	1	2	3	4	5
6. Personality seems to include characteristics desirable in individuals working with children.	1	2	3	4	5
7. Ability to organize and implement a developmentally appropriate classroom.	1	2	3	4	5
8. References.	1	2	3	4	5

Total _____

Comments: _____

_____

_____

Signature of interviewer _____

_____

Goodheart-Willcox Publisher

Figure 5.13 All candidates for a position should be evaluated using the same criteria.

position will pay and what the benefits are. When all the candidate's questions have been answered, no matter how the interview went, thank the person warmly and politely for their interest in the program. Avoid making an immediate offer. Instead, advise the candidate of when a final selection for the position will be made and whether that will be conveyed by letter, email, or phone.

The Review Process

Once an interview is completed, the review process begins. First, take time to evaluate the individual in writing on the rating scale and consult with others who participated in the interview. Decide if the candidate is moving on in the process and check their references. Complete all the interviews and discuss with everyone

helping in the interview process before making a decision. Plan to complete the review process and inform all candidates of the decision no later than two weeks after the interview. This is courteous and allows those who were not selected to continue their job search. This also allows you to secure a preferred candidate before they accept another offer.

References

Another essential part of the employment process is checking the candidate's references. Reference checks often involve calling previous employers or coworkers and personal contacts of the candidate. Directors sometimes avoid this time-consuming task. However, you can learn valuable information about the potential employee

Typical Interview Questions for a Teacher Applicant
Why are you interested in working in the child care field?
How did you hear about the opening in our program?
What kinds of work have you done with children in the past?
What kinds of things do you like to plan and do with children?
What do you think a good center should do for children and families?
What special talents or abilities could you bring to the program?
How would you handle a situation like ...? (pose a discipline problem)
What kinds of things do you think young children need?
What do you think would be the "perfect" day for the group of children in your care?
What would you like to be doing five years from now?

Goodheart-Willcox Publisher

Figure 5.14 Questions like these give you more information about an applicant than simple yes or no questions.

from their references. Prepare a questionnaire with categories to check and a section for comments to complete as you speak with each reference. The form can be relatively simple, yet still cover the necessary information. Those responding can be as brief or lengthy as they prefer, but they will be more forthcoming if you show interest and engagement in the candidate and their experiences. A candidate may also supply written references, or letters of recommendation. Licensing requirements may mandate that letters of recommendation be on file for each employee.

Making a Final Selection

When making the final selection, use all the information available. This would include rankings of the candidates as well as the rankings from the other staff and board members who participated in the interviews. In private programs, this might have included other staff, parents, or a child development consultant. Discuss the reasons behind their rankings of candidates. As a group, talk about the candidates' references and everyone's reactions. If you all agree on the best candidate, the decision is made. If there is disagreement, continue to discuss the candidates and the best match for the job until the group can come to a consensus. Ultimately, the decision should be one that is consistent with the rankings and acceptable to yourself, the staff who will work with the individual, and the board.

Hiring a New Employee

Once you identify the right candidate, contact them with a job offer. You may choose to delay notifying the other potential candidates that the position went to someone else until the preferred candidate accepts. When you contact the successful candidate, provide the job offer,

including information about the potential start date and salary. They may have more questions or need time to consider before accepting. As soon as they accept the offer, set up an appointment to meet with them. State employment laws differ regarding the need for a **contract**, a legal agreement signed by the new employee and the program, that commits each to the terms specified in the agreement. These terms usually include starting salary, starting date, commitment to personnel policies, and an ending date when the contract expires.

Employment at will refers to hiring an employee without using a contract. This means the employee or the program can terminate employment at any time. No reason is needed. This type of employment condition exists in most states as long as the program does not use a contract or other personnel policies that state otherwise. It is a good idea to have personnel policies examined by an attorney or employment specialist to ensure that the employment situation is beneficial to the program and acceptable to the board of directors. Because of changing labor laws in many states, ensure that you have the necessary current information when hiring a new employee.

Compensation

Federal and state laws affect the wages and benefits that can be offered to a new employee (**Figure 5.15**). Minimum wage legislation mandates the minimum amount that an employee can earn on an hourly basis. If the minimum wage is raised by law, the program must increase wages. In turn, this will mean adjusting the budget and, possibly, the tuition charged to families. The salary offered to a new employee should be comparable to prevailing wages for similar positions in the area. It will also depend on what the program can afford to pay and the new employee's experience and education.

Figure 5.15 All earned wages are required to be reported to the government and taxes withheld as determined by federal and state laws.

As an employer, you must offer some required benefits. Both federal and state laws will affect what these benefits are and how much they will cost the program. Full-time employees may be entitled to more benefits than part-time employees. You may choose to offer additional benefits to attract and retain quality employees. Possible benefit considerations include health insurance, retirement, leave with pay, short- and long-term disability.

Criminal Background Check

Before hiring any new employee, be aware of the laws in your state. Concern about child abuse has led most states to enact laws designed to protect children in child care. Several well-publicized cases of reported sexual abuse in centers have resulted in the passage of child protective legislation. These laws ensure the safety of children in child care settings. Early childhood centers cannot hire anyone convicted of a crime against children or named as the perpetrator of a founded report of child abuse.

All selected candidates for any position in an early childhood center must pass a required criminal background check. In some states, this includes a fingerprint background check. The state police and/or the affiliated outlet of the Federal Bureau of Investigation (FBI) usually performs the background check. When a job applicant is from out of state or has moved around from job to job often, these clearances are particularly important. You may use a service to process the appropriate background checks.

Employers may also require an employee disclosure statement from applicants. This is a sworn statement signed by the applicant. It affirms the person has not been convicted of child sexual abuse-related crimes. It clearly states the employee will be dismissed if the criminal background check indicates a conviction. Some states

may require that provisional employees awaiting clearance must always work within eyesight of a permanent employee.

The potential occurrence of child sexual abuse in a center must be taken seriously. It is the early childhood program owner's or director's responsibility to ensure that the children in care are safe. Criminal background checks require additional paperwork. They take time, effort, and money. However, they help to protect children against someone who may be intent on harming them. Some states impose substantial fines or even criminal prosecution on programs that employ staff without adequate clearance.

Before a New Employee Can Begin

All new employees must complete the necessary paperwork before they can be officially hired. This ensures that the program has all the information needed for local, state, and federal records. It is easier to obtain this information from applicants before they are on staff. Once they are working on a daily basis, completing forms and acquiring required physicals or tests will be difficult to schedule. This information is essential for licensing purposes and must be on file. Whenever a job is offered to someone, make it clear that these forms must be completed before work can begin (**Figure 5.16**).

The US Department of Justice through the Immigration and Naturalization Service requires all employees to complete an I-9 form. This Employment Eligibility Verification Form verifies the employee's eligibility for employment in the United States. As an employer, you will examine the employee's evidence of identity and employment eligibility (for example, passport, birth certificate, or government-issued ID) and complete the employer portion of the I-9.

Information Needed from New Employees
• Completed application form
• Current health appraisal
• Proof of negative TB test
• Information in case of an emergency
• W-4 form for income tax purposes
• Criminal background clearance
• Proof of educational status
• Reference letters
• Form I-9

Figure 5.16 New employees should have all documentation on file and all paperwork completed before beginning employment.

Conditions of Employment

Certain conditions of employment must be met by new employees. State licensing regulations usually determine these conditions. Typically, employees must be free of contagious diseases or conditions that could threaten the children in their care. Their criminal background checks must be cleared. They must complete any required drug testing. Their claims of education and experience must be truthful. Employees should be aware that deceit in any of these areas is grounds for dismissal.

Probationary Period

As a protection for the program, establish a **probationary employment period**, which is a period of 90 to 180 days that gives an employer the chance to get to know the new employee before making a permanent commitment. New staff must demonstrate their ability to work within the philosophy of the program. A staff member who promises positive guidance yet uses harsh, humiliating discipline is not meeting this condition of employment. It could be a longer or shorter period if preferred. New staff who successfully complete the probationary period and are moved to permanent status are frequently rewarded with a slight raise in salary.

5.6 Staff Orientation

Starting a new job can be overwhelming. No matter how much advanced preparation a new employee does, it is hard to begin a new position. Program directors must find ways to help new employees become oriented to their jobs. Each staff member needs to feel welcomed as a valuable addition to the team.

Planning Orientation

Most people come into a new job wanting to do well. They want to be recognized as individuals, and they want to be viewed as competent. They need to feel that they are liked and that they belong. As each of these needs is met, the individual becomes more comfortable and confident, and their commitment to their new job grows. To welcome new employees and give them the information they need to succeed, establish an organized **orientation plan** that includes both formal and informal ways to help new staff become acquainted with the center and their role in it. The plan should include general information about the program and other information specific to the job or classroom to which the new person is assigned.

Introducing the New Employee

Help new staff members feel more comfortable in the center by making sure they have been introduced to the other staff who will be working near them (**Figure 5.17**). Help each new hire meet a core of acquaintances who know their way around the program. Introductions may be made at a staff meeting or training session, if convenient. Refreshments and a time for informal conversation can show the new person that the center staff are warm, caring, and interesting individuals.

Providing a Mentor

The new employee may find it helpful to have a more experienced staff person assigned as a **mentor**, or a person who serves as an advisor, role model, and friend. Success in a job requires that a new person develop a thorough understanding of the routines, personalities, and priorities within the work setting. The mentor can provide knowledge of "the way things work" that can smooth the way for a successful beginning for the new employee. Sometimes, this relationship simply develops on its own. However, it is a good idea to ask a specific staff member to take on this role. The mentor should be someone who can warmly welcome the new employee and possesses the qualities that contribute to success on the job and in interpersonal relationships. A troubled and unhappy staff member with a negative attitude is not an ideal choice for a mentor.

As the program administrator, try to avoid taking on the task of mentoring new staff. See the leader role as one that is responsible for hiring, monitoring, and evaluating a new employee. You will also have to terminate an employee if the person does not work out well in the job. These functions do not mesh well with the mentor's role as a listener, advisor, and friend.

SolStock/E+/Getty Images

Figure 5.17 To support new staff members in feeling comfortable with their job role, it is important to introduce them to everyone, provide an orientation process, and train them as needed.

Explaining Procedures and Goals

You should have briefly discussed the purpose and goals of the early childhood program as a part of the interview process. The new employee will, therefore, have a basic idea of the mission of the organization. At the beginning of employment, it is helpful to review both the goals and the basic philosophy of the center. Doing this personally with each employee ensures there are no misunderstandings. In a larger organization, delegate this duty to a staff person in charge of personnel.

Most programs also have various procedures regarding employment. The paperwork necessary to request a vacation day or the procedure for using a sick day must be explained (**Figure 15.18**). Each program will have unique information that must be given to the new employee. This may include

- the goals and philosophy of the program;
- a description of the agency;
- the organization of the center and the new employee's place in the organizational structure;
- the employee dress code;
- center safety and security protocols;
- a floor plan of the center, including exits;
- samples of forms used for various paperwork they will encounter;
- the center phone numbers;
- hours of operation and yearly calendar;
- procedures to follow in case of an emergency;

- student drop-off and pick-up procedures; and
- the names of authorized adults permitted to pick up each child.

Overall, selecting appropriate staff members takes time and attention. Having a thorough approach to the process with guidance from state and local employer guidance is important. In addition, professional organizations such as NAEYC provide excellent guidance when determining what qualifications are necessary for teaching staff at an early childhood program.

Director's Showcase

Loren

Loren solved many existing problems in her program with an updated organizational chart. All the teachers and staff were able to see and understand each other's clearly defined roles, which alleviated some arguing over job descriptions and roles. In meeting with the director of the university's ECE program, she was able to implement strategies to help smooth the transition between the end of the semester and the beginning of a new one. Loren designated some of the experienced teachers as mentors for new students and employees to provide support and help with guidance or learning the program.

Kevin

Kevin worked with his local resource and referral agency to develop a continuing education program for his staff. After meeting with his staff, he learned that many were interested in taking the next step in the educational process, such as pursuing their CDA or enrolling in a two- or four-year college program. Kevin filled his two open positions with qualified applicants. He completed employee orientation with them and provided guidance to help ease new hire anxieties. He built upon his new hiring practices and decreased the volume of staff turnover.

Reflect

Lorena and Kevin are experiencing what many early childhood leaders are experiencing across the nation. As you think about your role when recruiting and hiring staff, what concerns would you have with the process as a new leader?

KLH49/E+/Getty Images

Figure 5.18 Staff members will need a system of communication to complete when requesting days for vacation or sick leave.

Chapter 5 Review and Assessment

Summary

5.1 Define characteristics of quality early childhood teachers and staff.

- Teachers and staff members must understand the importance of children being nurtured and treated with kindness. This includes treating them gently, both physically and emotionally with an awareness of the need to maintain a tolerance of differences.
- Children must have adults who encourage and support their efforts using mature judgment and gentle humor. Teachers must have an education that provides a good working knowledge of children's development and be eager to learn more.
- The teaching role requires that the person be open to new ideas. All staff must be good and worthy individuals who are dependable, come to work on time, and complete required records carefully and honestly.

5.2 Develop an organizational structure.

- The number of staff you will need to hire will be determined by the size and nature of your program. A very large program will need classroom teachers, office personnel, and support staff such as janitors and cooks.
- Before hiring anyone, you must think through the organizational structure of your program. An organizational chart can be developed that shows lines of responsibility. It will help you determine what positions you will have to fill.

5.3 Prepare early childhood job descriptions.

- Job descriptions explain how the position fits into the organizational structure. This includes a clear explanation of job duties.
- Applicants need to know what their potential duties would be so that they can decide if the duties are a good fit for their skills, experience, and interests. It is always wise to include information about the center, its philosophy and mission, any employee benefits, and a salary range to attract suitable applicants.

5.4 Recruit qualified job applicants.

- A recruitment plan is the method you use to make sure potential employees know that your program has a job available.

- Your plan should consider potential locations for advertisements that are likely to be seen by those you want to attract. Your plan and hiring practices must be in compliance with state and federal anti-discrimination hiring legislation.

5.5 Interview and select qualified staff members.

- Potential employees must be carefully screened and interviewed before working with children. This will include checking references, health appraisals, and criminal background clearances.

5.6 Establish an employee orientation program to welcome new hires.

- New employees must complete all paperwork necessary for your program records.
- A probationary period gives you additional time to make sure the new employee will be able to carry out the job.
- An orientation plan can help a new employee get off to a good start. It should be planned carefully so the individual has all the information needed to function as a full member of the staff.

Review

1. Explain what is meant by the statement "Child care is a labor-intensive field." (5.1)
2. List the three categories under which program staff can be grouped. (5.2)
3. How is an organizational chart useful? (5.2)
4. What often determines an adult-to-child ratio in a classroom? (5.2)
5. What is the function of a job description? (5.3)
6. How does the Civil Rights Act of 1964 and its amendments affect hiring practices? (5.4)
7. What is the purpose of an employee disclosure statement? (5.4)
8. What is the purpose of a probationary employment period? (5.5)
9. What is the purpose of an orientation plan? (5.6)
10. How can a mentor be helpful to a new staff member? (5.6)

Showcase Your Skills

1. Look at the help-wanted classified section from the Sunday edition of a large metropolitan newspaper. Find ads that are for jobs in programs for children. You might find these listed under terms such as: child care, preschool teacher, child care aide, administrator, director, etc. Examine how each ad is written. What does each ad tell you about the job? In which of these jobs might you be interested? (5.3)

2. Invite a center director to speak to your class about the interviewing process. Find out what types of questions are asked. Is the applicant asked to spend time in a classroom? How is the interview for a teaching position different from that for a staff support position? Does the director conduct the interview alone or do others participate? What suggestions would the director have for other new directors regarding the hiring of staff? (5.5)

3. Role-play an interview situation to fill a teacher's aide position. Assign the following roles: the director, the classroom master teacher, a member of the personnel committee of the board, and the applicant. Demonstrate how the interview would proceed from greeting the candidate to saying good-bye. Continue the role-play to include the discussion of whether or not to hire the candidate. After the decision has been made, ask the rest of the class why they agreed or disagreed with it. (5.5)

Matching

Match the following terms with the correct definitions:

A. administrative staff
B. class size
C. classroom staff
D. employment at will
E. job description
F. orientation plan
G. organizational chart
H. portfolio
I. positive self-esteem
J. support personnel

1. Employee group that provides essential support to program activities, such as administrative assistants, cooks, and maintenance staff.
2. Those people who work directly with the children in a program.
3. All of the children assigned for the majority of the day to a specific teacher or group of teachers within an assigned classroom space.
4. Knowledge that a person is a good and worthy individual.
5. Plan with formal and informal ways to help new staff members become acquainted with the center and their role in it.
6. Those employees with organizational and planning skills who provide direction for the total program.
7. Spells out the duties, qualifications, and experience needed to perform a position successfully.
8. A visual image that indicates job titles and the lines of authority within the program.
9. Hiring an employee without using a contract.
10. Binder or electronic collection of samples of an individual's previous work or work completed within a teacher education program.

Yok_Piyapong/iStock/Getty Images Plus

6 CHAPTER

Budget and Finance

Learning Outcomes

After studying this chapter, you will be able to:

6.1 Analyze the similarities and differences between a proposal and a business plan.

6.2 Explain the differences between for-profit and not-for-profit programs.

6.3 Describe the types of expenses that are involved in operating a child care program.

6.4 Apply how to develop and analyze the program budget.

6.5 Discover financial strategies that create effective management of program funds.

6.6 Investigate necessary financial services that support a child care program.

6.7 Recognize considerations within program finances to make purchasing decisions.

Key Terms

audit
break-even point
budget
business plan
cash flow
cash lag
cash reserve
co-pay
cost coding
cost-per-child analysis
encumbered funds
fiscal year
fixed expenditures
for-profit programs
guarantee
in-kind support
line of credit
market rate
matching grants
not-for-profit programs
optional expenditures
petty cash
proposal
sponsor
start-up budget
tax-exempt
variable expenditures
vendor
vouchers
warranty

Introduction

Any successful program must be financially sound. The early childhood leader's job includes planning and monitoring the flow of money so bills and staff salaries can be paid (**Figure 6.1**). This includes identifying sources of income for the program. The development of a budget, or projected spending plan, provides the financial forecast for the program. Even the best program for children will not be able to survive if it cannot pay its bills. Since the budget is based on the income expected, it must be examined often to be sure that the income is not lagging. If income is less than expected, the budget must be adjusted to reflect the smaller income.

The National Association for the Education of Young Children (NAEYC) feels strongly in their *Advancing Equity in Early Childhood Education Position Statement,*

NAEYC/DAP standards

Standards covered in this chapter:

2c

2G

Drs Producoes/E+/Getty Images

Figure 6.1 Managing program finances is a key role of the early childhood program leader.

published in April of 2019, that leaders are responsible for providing high-quality programs that are committed to equitable outcomes for children. This means financially leading the program to plan and implement budgets that are equitable to meet the needs of the children and staff. Considerations must also be given to how the program will serve different settings that reflect the values, beliefs, and practices specific to the community served.

Keeping track of how money comes into and flows out of the program is an important part of managing the various financial aspects of the program (**Figure 6.2**). Based on a carefully prepared budget, careful financial monitoring and decisions can be made. This includes an awareness of the money that was planned but is not necessarily available when needed. Altering spending patterns of the program may need to take place and purchases or expenditures may have to be postponed until the expected income arrives. Each fiscal year provides necessary insights on the trends of income and expenditures that a program experienced. This assists with budget planning for the next fiscal year.

Ridofranz/iStock/Getty Images Plus

Figure 6.2 Tracking finances can be done several ways. Based on the size of the program, this can be a very simple system of tracking or a more comprehensive system for larger programs.

Director's Showcase

Salma

Salma was just named director of a church-based program licensed for 60 children in a rural area. While she has served the program for several years as assistant director, her work with the retiring director on financial planning for the program overall had been minimal.

Maria

Maria, a family child care home provider, is new to the industry. For years she has taken care of her own children and a few young family members. Now that her children are in school for a full day, she has decided that caring for outside children would provide her with the opportunity to work from home and the flexibility to care for her own children when they return home from school. While she worked from a family budget when caring for her children and those of her family members, she is now realizing the importance of planning for the financial success of her in-home child care program.

6.1 Financial Planning for a New Program

An early childhood program's proposal and business plan requirements will vary depending on the type of program, for example whether it is for profit or non-profit, and the type of financial support being sought. A new program might seek a loan from a bank, or it may

work with a large employer interested in providing child care for its employees. A program might look for grant opportunities from a government agency or foundation. Whether it is a person or agency, the goal is to obtain financial support for the early childhood program from an audience who may know nothing about child care. Their questions will focus on the early childhood leader's abilities to lead a program. To prepare for these situations, the program administrator will need a business plan or proposal.

A business plan is best suited for early childhood programs that have an owner (**Figure 6.3**). A **business plan** is required by banks or other lending agencies that require significant details about the program's financial planning and the owner's necessary skills to carry it out. Government agencies that lend money to small businesses, such as the Small Business Administration (SBA), and commercial loan agencies want assurance that whoever is requesting the money is familiar with the business aspects of child care. These lenders must be convinced that the owner will be successful and pay back the loan in a reasonable amount of time.

A proposal is often requested by grant sources such as government agencies or foundations. A large employer who will be investing in child care services for its employees will also need significant explanation since they are providing most of the capital. A **proposal** is a document explaining what the director wants to do, why there is a need to do it, why the director is qualified to do it, and what kind of help is necessary. It must give the audience confidence that the submitted plan can be fully implemented. A proposal provides the program administrator the opportunity to think through ideas or plans and realistically address their implementation. The administrator then writes these plans in a detailed

katleho Seisa/E+/Getty Images

Figure 6.3 Developing a business plan often requires assistance from a licensed accountant or other professional resource that best understands the needs of an early childhood program.

format often provided by the requesting grant funder or agency and explains them in a way that allows those unfamiliar with the early childhood field to understand them.

Grant Availability and Expectations

A variety of grant money sources may be available for early childhood programs, including government agencies, charities, local organizations, and foundations. Each funding source will have a particular focus for its grants. State and national government departments and agencies usually have a *Request for Proposal (RFP) process* (**Figure 6.4**). The process includes a formal document that outlines an organization's intent to purchase a good or service. A proposal is sent in response to the grant agency's RFP, by a certain deadline, with requested and detailed information. In the field of early childhood education, RFPs can typically be found on the US Department of Education or Administration for Children and Families websites. Programs can often find foundations supporting early childhood education online. A foundation will detail the grant's guidelines and requirements including deadlines on its website. Carefully read the mission and purpose for the foundation before writing for funding. Foundations look for programs that match their overall goals and objectives. Applications that characterize how the early childhood program significantly aligns with the foundation's goals and objectives will be most successful.

Mini-grants may be available from local sources. County and city governments may channel money to programs that will meet the needs of local citizens. During the COVID-19 pandemic, for example, state and local governments provided emergency funds to keep child care services open for essential workers. Community action agencies, human services offices, or United Way agencies may all support local programs. These types of organizations may advertise funding resources via electronic alerts, their websites, and other electronic means. Local service and professional organizations, such as Rotary Clubs, business and professional women's clubs, or Kiwanis, may also provide funds. Many professional organizations publish information on their websites or within e-newsletters about available grants or other sources of funding.

Funding Agency Expectations

Funding agencies have a reason for their existence and goals that they want to accomplish. The goal may be very broad, such as "to strengthen families" or "to improve society." Some goals may be more specific, yet still provide flexibility for a variety of projects. Reading all the agency's information, including explanatory materials and guidelines, will help a child care administrator to decide if their program is a good candidate for funding and develop an appropriate plan that demonstrates a match in priorities. The available information usually points out any changes in the funding agency's priorities from the previous year. Additional information often describes the purpose and reasons behind the availability of money. If there is no clear, logical link between the early childhood program's plans and the agency's goals and objectives, the administrator would be best served looking to other agencies for funding.

When the funding agency's expectations and the early childhood program match, the next step is to determine what funds would be available. Funding sources vary substantially in the amount of money they have to offer. A government agency or foundation may have hundreds of thousands of dollars to grant, whereas a local agency may have several hundred. In general, be aware of the typical size of grants provided by an agency or foundation, when available. Large foundations usually produce a year-end report in which the awarded grants are listed and can be accessed on their website. Funded projects are described along with the amount of money awarded. These reports are a good source of information regarding the types of projects the agency or foundation awarded. However, small, private sources of funding may not publish a report of their activities. Their funding information may be more difficult to access.

Within their guidelines, agencies and organizations identify the types of programs that are eligible for funding. Some grants are open to any type of agency. Others may be limited to not-for-profit agencies only. Some may

alvarez/E+/Getty Images

Figure 6.4 Writing a Request for Proposal (RFP) to acquire funding can come from a variety of grant resources to include government agencies, charities, local organizations, and foundations.

be limited to projects that are sponsored by secondary schools or government-sponsored programs, such as a county child care program. Careful reading of the guidelines will help to determine whether an early childhood program is eligible for funding.

Another important consideration is funding restrictions. For example, if an early childhood program receives no funding from outside sources except tuition, there may be few restrictions other than those required by licensing. If, however, the program receives money from government agencies, private foundations, or charitable organizations, there may be additional restrictions or guidelines to meet (**Figure 6.5**). These restrictions typically relate to areas of program participants' eligibility, use of money, and/or program philosophy or activities. Considerations must be made when any restrictions are tied to the receipt of money. As the early childhood program leader, it is important to realize that once the grant money is accepted with stated restrictions, the program is legally bound to honor those restrictions.

Business Plan Considerations

In many ways, a business plan is like a proposal. Both types of documents are meant for the purposes of convincing the recipient that the early childhood program administrator is knowledgeable about child care and demonstrates an accurate understanding of the costs involved in the project that is requesting funds. The business plan must be carefully prepared and consistent. The budget must reflect consistency and be supported by a narrative that explains the plan. The plan must have a professional appearance.

Using language that is familiar to the field of early childhood is probably less important in a business plan. The reader is typically familiar with terms used by professionals in the business world. For example, rather than demonstrating an understanding of "developmentally appropriate practice used by program staff to meet the needs of the target population," which would be more appropriate for a proposal, the business plan will be more interested in demonstrating "who exactly is the target population (meaning paying customers) that are seeking appropriate child care services." In a business plan, proving that there are enough people willing to pay for the service to support a profitable business assures the potential lender that the program will have the ability to repay the loan.

Identify your available resources in your business plan (**Figure 6.6**). For example, if you have found a suitable building that could easily meet licensing standards, include information about this location for the lender. Further, if you have contacted trained teachers who are accessible for immediate hiring purposes, mention this in your plan. If your program can purchase equipment inexpensively from a center or business that is closing, the potential lender will view this as part of your resources and positively recognize your planning. A business plan must demonstrate an accurate sense of what things cost. Banks and other lenders have access to information on the typical costs of child care services. Lenders will question a business plan if the projected costs and projected income are outside of the typical ranges. A successful plan is based on sound financial and resource planning and will explain any projected expenses or income that is outside of the norm.

Questions to Ask Yourself Before Accepting Money with "Strings Attached"
• How difficult will it be to meet these restrictions in my program?
• Are these restrictions consistent with the philosophy and goals of my program?
• Are these restrictions ones that I need to implement with or without the money?
• Will this additional money help to build a stronger program?
• Will money commit the program to something that cannot be continued over the long run?
• How much money will it cost to implement these restrictions?
• Is this money for one year only, or will it continue over several years?
• What will happen to the program when this money is no longer available?

Goodheart-Willcox Publisher

Figure 6.5 Asking yourself these questions assists with determining if the related restrictions provided by the grant opportunity are worth the investment of time.

shapecharge/E+/Getty Images

Figure 6.6 When developing the business plan, it will be important to research all available resources to assist with projecting costs.

Director's Showcase

Salma

When a new warehouse facility was being built in the community, Salma, still in her assistant director role, recognized that new young families were likely to move to the area and researched increasing the size of the program. She contacted the CPA that provides oversight for the program, who recommended that she explore what the program would require to increase capacity, such as necessary renovations or locating an additional facility close by. Salma knew her work was cut out for her!

Maria

Maria realized that putting together a business plan was the important next step in formalizing a business as a family child care home provider. She needed to talk with a local banker to ensure that she was financially stable enough to support the business and would have money available from the bank in case she needed it. After talking with the banker, he put her in contact with a local accountant to discuss how to best set up her new business venture.

Director's Showcase

Reflect

As Salma and Maria begin thinking about financial planning and creation of a budget, what considerations will each need to make?

6.2 For-Profit and Not-For-Profit Status

Child care programs can be divided into two main categories: for-profit and not-for-profit (**Figure 6.7**). **For-profit programs** are operated to make a profit for the owners. How the program is organized will impact the legal issues that must be addressed. For-profit programs are usually privately owned centers that may be owned by an individual or a group. Some owners may be actively involved in operating the center, while others may have provided money to help get the program started, but they do not help with the day-to-day work of the center. The tuition, budget, and operation of the center are coordinated to generate a profit for the owners. The program is expected to meet all state

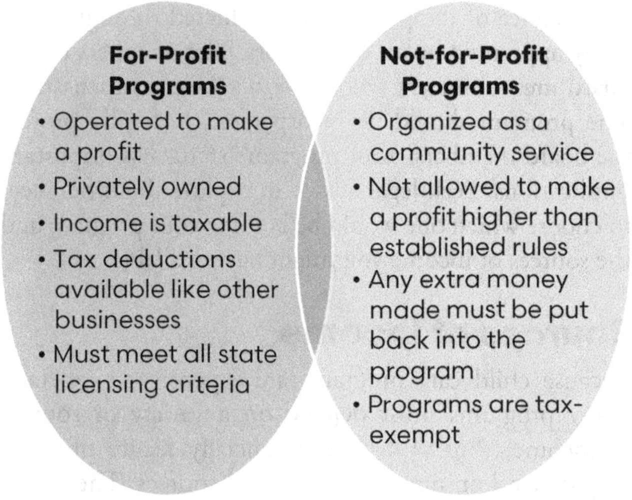

For-Profit Programs
- Operated to make a profit
- Privately owned
- Income is taxable
- Tax deductions available like other businesses
- Must meet all state licensing criteria

Not-for-Profit Programs
- Organized as a community service
- Not allowed to make a profit higher than established rules
- Any extra money made must be put back into the program
- Programs are tax-exempt

Goodheart-Willcox Publisher

Figure 6.7 Knowing the difference between for- and non-profit assists with choosing the best financial structure for the program.

licensing regulations and quality-rating system criteria, should the program participate. Legally, the programs are treated like any other profit-making business. The income is taxable, and the types of tax deductions available to any business apply to these programs.

The advantages and disadvantages of a for-profit program are similar to those of any business. Major advantages include making a profit and opportunities for independent decision making. Successful programs can result in substantial income. Owners can also feel the pride of operating a flourishing business. A major disadvantage is they are usually not eligible for government or foundation grants. Opportunities for grants are minimal, and for-profit programs cannot do **fundraising** activities. Also, people may be less likely to give gifts to these programs because such gifts are not tax deductible. The program's financial success depends on its ability to make a profit.

Not-for-profit programs are legally organized to operate without making a profit and may also be referred to as non-profit programs. They are usually organized as a community service. Legally, they are not allowed to earn a profit higher than a certain amount based on government established rules and regulations, which are readily available through the Internal Revenue Service (IRS). Any extra money earned after all expenses are paid must be put back into the program in some way. This may include purchasing needed equipment, giving staff bonuses, or improving the facility.

These programs are also **tax-exempt**, meaning they do not have to pay taxes on purchases for the program. They usually receive some support from outside sources and are often eligible for government and foundation grants.

Governance of the program is conducted through a formally appointed board of directors. The members of this board are volunteers who serve without compensation. The program should be incorporated to legally protect the board members. Your program's status has important implications. Seek legal advice to explore the differences to choose which one would be best for your program and the sources of income you might have available.

Sources of Income

Because child care programs are expensive to operate, many programs must depend on a variety of sources of income (**Figure 6.8**). A financially secure program may depend on money from several sources. These may include

- tuition;
- public funds;
- private funds;
- charitable organizations and foundations;
- fundraising activities; and
- in-kind support.

For-profit programs typically rely solely on tuition, whereas not-for-profit programs can access multiple sources of revenue streams.

Tuition

Tuition is the fee charged for child care services. Paid either weekly, bi-weekly, or monthly by enrolled families, the amount of tuition must be high enough to cover the program's expenses. However, this amount cannot be too high for families to discourage enrollment and is often referred to as the *trilemma of child care*. This trilemma is how the field strives to provide available and affordable quality care for the children and families served in an area. Because the cost of quality care is expensive, this continues to morally challenge program leaders when determining costs based on the needs of the program to operate on a daily basis.

barisonal/E+/Getty Images

Figure 6.8 Income can be generated from several different sources depending on the type of program.

While more will be discussed later in the chapter, another tuition determiner is to determine the market rate. The market rate is what the general population in the area, based on the type of child care services, is paying for their services either in a center or family child care home program. This information can be gathered by calling and inquiring about weekly tuition rates at early childhood programs in the area. Once the information is gathered, this process assists with setting tuition rates and serves as justification for raising rates in an established program. Discount considerations may also need to be considered for families with multiple children enrolled in the program.

Public Funds

Various government agencies provide funds to support child care programs. Major sources of public money for child care currently include the *Child and Adult Care Food Program (CACFP)* and the *Child Care and Development Fund (CCDF)*. Most of these are used to sponsor for-profit and not-for-profit programs that provide care for low- to moderate-income families. State and national agencies representing child welfare, education, labor and job training, public health, and human services often provide funds for child care services. When a family is determined to be financially eligible for support, the government agency pays a part of the cost of care. The family's **co-pay** is the amount still needed to pay for the tuition and is the family's responsibility. This remaining tuition amount is paid directly to the child care provider. The administration of these programs varies by individual state. The availability and determination of whether a program is eligible for funds depend on the political and economic situation in the state.

Private Funds

Some programs are supported financially by private individuals or private organizations. Churches are among the largest sponsors of child care programs in the United States and are not-for-profit programs. Resort areas, apartment complexes, and malls are examples of private organizations that sometimes provide money for the operation of children's programs, but they are typically for-profit entities that provide care.

Charitable Organizations and Foundations

Charitable organizations and private or community foundations, such as the United Way, and local service or fraternal organizations, may also provide funding to start or support a needed not-for-profit early childhood program. Many corporations, businesses, and individuals also establish charitable foundations. These are ideal considerations when pursuing the opening of a new facility. In addition, because they are non-profit, programs can write additional proposals to support the center. Some programs blend funding streams from several grants. These grants, along with tuition, can provide money needed to fully fund the programs.

Fundraising Activities

Many not-for-profit centers organize fundraising projects to provide extra funds for their programs. Most states require a special permit to do charitable fundraising. Fundraising activities usually will not result in enough money to keep a center in operation (**Figure 6.9**). However, the extra money raised may be enough to buy a new piece of playground equipment, or it may even provide a new addition to a building. Often, fundraising projects are used to obtain start-up money for a new program. A project, such as a car wash, fun fair, or spaghetti dinner, can be an opportunity for staff and parents to have fun working together on a project that will benefit the children. Fundraising events can be a way to build community even when they do not raise the expected amount of funds.

In-Kind Support and Matching Grants

In-kind support refers to items or services received from another source without having to pay for them. For example, if a religious organization allows use of its building for free or at a deeply reduced rate, this saves from paying the cost of rent and utilities. The in-kind contribution refers to the value of the donation. If the rental of the space would normally cost $500 per month, then over a 12-month period the savings would be $6,000. This represents an in-kind donation of $6,000. Thus, even though in-kind donations do not involve an

actual exchange of dollars, they do represent a monetary value to the program.

Some grants are called **matching grants**. This means for every dollar the early childhood program provides the granting agency will match it with additional money. Sometimes matching grants offer two or three times the basic amount. With some matching grants, the value of an in-kind donation can be counted toward the request for matching funds.

Sponsored Early Childhood Programs

Many organizations care about children. Although they do not operate child care programs themselves, they may be able to help maintain a non-profit program. The National Association for the Education of Young Children (NAEYC) advises, in its Code of Ethical Conduct updated in May 2011, that a program leader's ethical duty is to follow sound fiscal practices when these groups are willing to **sponsor** a program by making a commitment to provide ongoing support. This support may be through donations of money, space, equipment, or supplies. Some support may be in the form of services. Groups of medical, legal, or educational professionals may be willing to provide help in their areas of expertise. In return for the commitment, the organizations usually receive positive publicity for their effort. The group also gains satisfaction from helping to meet the child care needs of the community. Various agencies of the state or federal government may also provide sponsorship.

Community Groups

Many programs receive support from groups within the community. The United Way has a long history of helping to raise funds for local child care. The YMCA/YWCA and Jewish Community Centers have also become active sponsors of child care, half-day programs, and school-age care. Programs sponsored by religious congregations provide a large part of the child care in the United States. Churches, synagogues, and other religious facilities often have available space that meets state licensing standards. These spaces may be offered rent-free or for a reduced rental as part of a commitment to the community.

Other local groups that may sponsor child care include

- community recreation departments;
- health or fitness clubs;
- service clubs or organizations;
- apartment complexes; and
- shopping malls.

With community sponsorship, additional spaces for children become available through local support (**Figure 6.10**).

CatLane/iStock/Getty Images Plus

Figure 6.9 Simple fundraising events such as a bake sale can help to raise funds to purchase necessary equipment for use in the classrooms.

SDI Productions/E+/Getty Images

Figure 6.10 Sponsorship by community members can be as simple as local high school students doing a car wash to raise proceeds to support a local early childhood program.

Government Departments

Specific departments of both the state and federal government may sponsor child care services for their employees. Anywhere there is a large state or federal office building, there may be a need for child care. This not only includes the state and federal capitols, but also cities where there are regional offices. Branches of the military also sponsor child care for their personnel. The *Military Child Care Act of 1989* provided funding for child care centers and family child care homes. This act recognized the need for adequately paid, well-trained personnel as an important component of a quality, accredited child care program.

Colleges and Universities

It is common to find child care programs on college or university campuses. Offering quality child care helps the institutions attract faculty and staff who might otherwise accept jobs elsewhere. Students attending higher education programs may also have children. Child care may be an important factor in their decision to attend a school. Often these colleges and universities offer educational programs in Child Development and/or Early Childhood Education. An on-campus child care program can provide students with opportunities to work with children. These centers are often referred to as "laboratory center programs," because they give students direct experiences with a variety of children. These centers can provide the highest quality of care since they are a teaching location for majors in the field of early childhood.

Public Schools

Public schools may also sponsor child care for several different reasons. An on-site child care program helps teen parents continue their education. These schools may offer parenting classes as well. This arrangement allows young parents to be with their children during parts of the day, develop parenting skills, and complete their high school education.

A child care program may exist to care for the young children of the teachers and staff of the school district. If lack of available child care has been a problem for district employees, a district-sponsored center may help solve the problem. In addition, vocational child care programs may also sponsor full- or half-day programs that serve as laboratory programs. Students who are pursuing education in these areas usually have one or more courses where they must work directly with children.

Another area that has become quite common is partnerships between early childhood programs and a local school (**Figure 6.11**). With the wide sweeping Pre-K movement across the nation, federal dollars have been allocated to state education systems to assist with the implementation of these programs. Because of this, many schools have reached out to the child care community for access to classroom space. Oftentimes schools will provide the licensed teacher, assistants, and funding for equipment and supplies. The early childhood program provides the space, some equipment, and staffing to support before- and after-school care. This partnership creates a win-win situation for the children and the community.

Employers and Company Foundations

Employers are discovering that the lack of quality child care is a significant issue for their employees. There are growing numbers of employers who financially support child care programs for their workers. Many employers are discovering the advantages to offering child care as a benefit to their employees, such as lower absenteeism,

kali9/E+/Getty Images

Figure 6.11 School programming requires many budget considerations due to the unique needs of a program operating for designated months in the year.

less turnover in staff, and a more productive workforce. Some companies provide only partial support, with the employee paying part of the tuition. Others pick up the full cost of the care. Employer-sponsored care is found frequently in the healthcare industry, but other businesses are also beginning to offer it. The employer may sponsor the child care assistance directly or through a foundation supported by the company.

Employer assistance to families with child care needs can take many forms. Some employers have a child care center at the employment site. Parents can visit their children during lunchtime or breaks. Sometimes, a group of employers will work together to provide a child care center at a site that is convenient for all employees. Nursing homes and hospitals often work cooperatively because their employees have similar schedules. Employers may provide money to support an already existing community facility. They may also support child care through the provision of **vouchers**, which represent money that employees can use to help pay for care in a program of their choice. Employers may also provide assistance in finding available child care and parent education programs. Government tax incentives have encouraged the growth of employer-sponsored child care.

Director's Showcase

Salma

As Salma researched the cost of increasing the program's capacity, she recognized that it was going to be expensive. She proposed approaching the new warehouse leadership to ask for their financial support. With very limited child care in the area, she decided that with a well-written proposal the company may decide that supporting their expansion could be mutually beneficial. The program's banker supported this plan and offered to go with her to the meeting. Their CPA was also supportive and mentioned how important it would be to emphasize their not-for-profit status.

Maria

Maria's development of a business plan allowed her to secure a $2,000 line of credit with her bank. Her new accountant then began talking with her about developing a budget. While it would not be extensive, having this as a guide was important. Maria began looking into all the costs of running a home child care program and formulating her budget plan.

Director's Showcase

Reflect

Which type of early childhood program would you be interested in administering? For-profit or non-profit? Based on your choice, list each consideration based on what you have learned and why it will be important.

6.3 Developing a Budget

When leading a successful program, it is necessary to figure out how much the program is going to cost to operate. This, in turn, assists with understanding how much income will be needed. It is easy to understand that if there is not going to be enough income to cover expenses, the program will not thrive. The program administrator must figure out how to increase income or cut expenses. This process of balancing income and expenditures requires the use of a budget. A **budget** is a plan for the coordination of income and expenditures (**Figure 6.12**). It is a plan for understanding what money is available over an established period.

Start-Up Budget

When planning for a new early childhood program, the owner must create a **start-up budget** to cover several months of preparation. The budget will apply to expenses incurred before the center opens and income is received. These funds are necessary to support the planning and preparation of the new center (**Figure 6.13**).

SARINYAPINNGAM/iStock/Getty Images Plus

Figure 6.12 Creating a start-up budget, or continuing to develop an existing one, is time-consuming and requires lots of thought.

Expenses That Must Be Incurred Before the Center Opens
Director hired (if not yourself)
Attorney fees
Rent/deposit paid
Facility cleaned, renovated, decorated
Equipment and supplies purchased
Utilities turned on
Expenses incurred in recruitment and hiring of staff
Expenses incurred in recruitment and enrollment of children

Goodheart-Willcox Publisher

Figure 6.13 These are expenses to cover before the program actually opens.

The start-up budget is separate from the main budget. Typical start-up costs include

- rent or purchase of a facility;
- necessary classroom equipment and supplies;
- food service equipment and supplies;
- playground equipment and installation;
- vans or buses for transportation purposes;
- insurance costs;
- housekeeping supplies;
- office equipment and supplies;
- marketing campaigns; and
- utilities costs.

A new center owner has several venues for financing and raising funds for their start-up expenses. They may seek a bank loan. They may also contact established government programs, such as the Small Business Administration (SBA), for financial support, grant funds, or business guidance. If the center owners identify the need for child care within the community, they may approach local service clubs, employers, or religious groups to seek start-up capital. Owners may look for private investors as a source of funds. If the proposed center is a not-for-profit, the new owner may research grant funds available from community-sponsored organizations or agencies that promote community development, human services, or the creation of new jobs. If the program complements an organization's mission and goals, it may be willing to help fund the costs of getting started.

Be careful not to underestimate the costs of getting started. Setting up a new program for young children is expensive. Often it takes time for new centers to reach full capacity. Expect reduced tuition income until enrollment is full. Your start-up funds must include enough money to keep the program going until full tuition is being received on a regular basis.

Fiscal Year Budget

A budget guides spending for the first year of operation and all successive years. Typically, this determines a set period during which a particular budget or source of grant money is in effect. This is called a **fiscal year**. A fiscal year may or may not be the same as a January-to-December calendar year. For example, if grant money from the state or another organization begins on July 1, then the fiscal year concludes on June 30 of the next year. At the end of the fiscal year, reporting takes place to account for the program's use of the money. Depending on the nature of the grant, a loss of unspent money must take place. Hence, the importance of tracking this revenue for expenditure before the fiscal year ends.

Keeping track of a fiscal year is easier for smaller programs. Larger programs may have several grants for special projects and the fiscal years for each of these grants could potentially be different. Tracking this money may become more complicated. For example, federal government grant money has a fiscal year that runs from October 1 to September 30, whereas local government fiscal years may be different. This will all need to be considered when applying for and receiving these funds. Many sophisticated accounting software programs are available to assist with monitoring these funds. Doing the research to find out the best solution for the program is part of the process when budgeting for an early childhood program. Keep in mind, when accepting public money, audits are a natural part of the process. An **audit** is done to examine the accuracy of records and to verify expenses. Business professionals recommend an audit for all programs to close out the fiscal year.

Identifying Expenses

Developing a workable budget requires a careful analysis of projected expenses. The more accurate the budget is the better able the administrator will be to make wise financial decisions. Many programs with directors who love to work with children flounder because those same directors do not have a finance background or do not understand or feel comfortable handling "money matters." However, administrators influence the financial well-being of their programs. Their decisions involving money can affect staff morale, and the director often must make financial decisions among several equally valuable options. For example, a director with multiple locations may choose to purchase a climber for the playground of one center, but not for another. The staff at both centers may recognize the obvious need for the climber to replace an aging, unsafe piece of equipment and accept this decision. However, if the staff feels that one site is favored over others, the decision could cause problems. A decision to lower the quality of the food provided may save money but may also cause families to leave the program. Choosing a cheaper grade of paper products may be a more acceptable way to save money. The purchase of a computer and administrative software may seem like an expensive idea. However, if it increases the efficiency of the office staff, it may save the cost of hiring additional personnel. A deliberate program leader must be aware of the impact of budget decisions on the quality and stability of the program.

When planning a budget for the upcoming year, estimate program expenses as accurately as possible. If the program has been in operation for a while, utilize information from past budgets. When preparing a budget for a new program, consider each category of expense in the budget. While some budgets are more extensive than others, four general areas of expenditures with subcategories cover a variety of program sizes. Those areas include

- personnel;
- facilities;
- programming; and
- equipment.

Preparing a budget always involves some educated guesses. It is challenging to predict how much the prices for supplies or food will increase during the next year. In addition, predicting things like extreme weather conditions that require additional heating or air conditioning costs are difficult to plan for. Therefore, plan for these occurrences as closely as possible. Within any budget there are three different types of expenditures, including fixed, variable, and optional (**Figure 6.14**).

Goodheart-Willcox Publisher

Figure 6.14 When creating a budget it is important to categorize expenditures to assist with the tracking process.

Fixed Expenditures

Fixed expenditures are those expenses to which the program is committed. Fixed expenses are predictable and do not vary significantly throughout the year. For example, once a lease is signed, the program has a commitment to pay a certain dollar amount for rent.

Variable Expenditures

Variable expenditures are costs that are paid on a regular basis, but the amount may vary. Utilities, such as electricity, water, and gas, are variable expenses that must be paid each month. While the amount of these payments may vary from month to month, a program can predict how much they will be for the year fairly accurately.

If a program does not have as much income as expected, examining variable expenditures may be a way to save money. Likewise, if there is more money coming in than expected, costs in the variable category may increase without significant impact to the budget. Some variable costs change throughout the year due to fluctuations in enrollment, such as classroom supplies or food expenses.

Optional Expenditures

Optional expenditures represent the wish list. These are expenditures for nonessential items or services. Only when there is extra money toward the end of the fiscal year will the program consider using some of that money for optional items. Possible expenditures could include new software, additional playground equipment, or hiring a consultant for additional staff training.

Anticipating Income

Anticipating income involves some thoughtful guesswork. If a program has been in operation for multiple years, past income data is available for review that gives information regarding enrollment fluctuation. This is valuable information as it portrays what percentage of the center has been full. When calculating income from tuition, it is important to remember that center enrollment will fluctuate. Operating at 100 percent capacity, 52 weeks a year is not possible. As the child care administrator, you will need to have a grasp of your community's needs and the current economic direction to predict their impact on your center's enrollment. As discussed earlier, an awareness of the **market rate**, or typical cost of child care in the area, determines next steps when considering tuition increases.

With new programs, projecting income will be difficult. Budget preparation must assume that a new program will not have full enrollment immediately. It may take several years for a program to reach that goal. Therefore, when anticipating income, be cautious. Base income projections on less than full enrollment tuition.

If the program will have other sources of income, such as government or foundation grants or fundraising activities, consider the impact of when and how much it will receive. Grants may provide specific amounts, but fundraising may be unpredictable. It is usually more prudent to underestimate income for the program rather than to overestimate it. Increasing a budget is easier than decreasing it.

Budget Formatting

A useful framework to create a program budget is to identify four general categories of expenditures—personnel, facilities, programming, and equipment—and then identify subcategories for each. Create subcategories that best fit your organizational purposes. For example, in the area of personnel, subcategories typically include salary and wage costs, federal and state taxes, Social Security taxes, and Medicare taxes. The size of the program often dictates how an administrator determines the categories and subcategories. Other subcategories within personnel might include

- payroll;
- unemployment insurance;
- worker's compensation;
- employee professional development;
- personnel incentives;
- child care employee discounts;
- health insurance; and
- retirement plans.

When working with a complicated budget, many businesses use **cost coding**. This means identifying each major budget category with a number code (**Figure 6.15**).

For example, the personnel general category is given the number 200. Then, the subcategories would be further identified by 200-level numbers, such as 201 for payroll and 202 for unemployment insurance. When using a system such as this, it is feasible to then subdivide the subcategory into additional, more specific items (for example, 200 for personnel; 210 for payroll, 211 for teacher salaries, and 212 for office staff salaries). This allows for ideal tracking and access to budget information. This information could be helpful in making decisions for the next year.

6.4 Budget Analyzing

The budget is a plan based on the projected amount of income expected. If throughout the year income is less than expected, the budget will need to be revised. When creating a budget at the beginning of the year, it should be flexible. Actual spending patterns must be modified to reflect any change in the amount of income predicted. For example, delaying purchase of some new riding toys in June may be necessary if income is less than what was noted in the budget. However, if income is greater than expected, you may have the ability to purchase additional items even though these costs were not originally in the budget plan. Analyzing the program budget on a regular basis allows for the administrator to have a better understanding of the program's financial state (**Figure 6.16**).

A Budget Format Organized Around Program Categories

Budget Category	Budget Item	Amount
100	**Administrative and general costs**	
	Salaries and fringe benefits (Director, secretary, bookkeeper, etc.)	$ _____
	Audit and legal costs	$ _____
	Office equipment and furniture	$ _____
	Office supplies	$ _____
	Postage	$ _____
	Phone	$ _____
	Insurance	$ _____
	Travel	$ _____
	Advertising	$ _____
200	**Physical plant and maintenance**	
	Rental or mortgage	$ _____
	Utilities	$ _____
	Custodial salaries and fringe benefits	$ _____
	Custodial supplies	$ _____
	Maintenance on building/grounds	$ _____
300	**Classroom/educational costs**	
	Salaries and fringe benefits Teachers, aides, substitutes	$ _____
	In-service training	$ _____
	Classroom supplies	$ _____
	Classroom equipment	$ _____
	Field trips	$ _____
400	**Food and nutrition**	
	Salaries and fringe benefits Cooks, aides	$ _____
	Food supplies	$ _____
	Kitchen equipment	$ _____
	Food service supplies	$ _____
500	**Admissions and parent services**	
	Newsletters, parent handbook	$ _____
	Parent education classes/meetings	$ _____
600	**Transportation**	
	Salaries and fringe benefits Driver	$ _____
	Vehicle rental or purchase	$ _____
	Maintenance	$ _____
	Operation (fuel, oil)	$ _____
700	**Health care**	
	Health supplies First-aid kit, bandages, toothbrushes, disposable gloves, antiseptic	$ _____
	Contracted health services	$ _____
800	**Other**	
	Miscellaneous	$ _____

Figure 6.15 The budget categories for larger early childhood programs can be complex.

shapecharge/E+/Getty Images

Figure 6.16 Monitoring the program budget on a regular basis guides the early childhood leader in better understanding the financial health of the program.

Cost-per-Child Analysis

Doing a cost-per-child analysis provides a clearer view of an early childhood program's financial health. Perform a **cost-per-child analysis** by looking at each main age group within the program. Next, identify the costs of providing service to each group on a monthly or daily basis. Then, divide this total by the number of children enrolled. This will provide a number that reflects the costs provided for each age group. Be sure to include staff wages and benefits, rent, classroom supplies, utilities, etc.

Doing a cost-per-child analysis will likely show that the cost to provide care for infants or toddlers is higher than the cost of care provided to school-age children. This cost is largely because of the additional adults hired to meet the necessary adult-to-child ratios. School-age children will need more art and project supplies than toddlers, but the overall cost will be higher for the younger groups. Preschool groups will usually have longer hours in the center than will school-age groups, so the cost of the service will reflect that additional time.

With a completed cost-per-child analysis, the administrator has identified the cost for each part of the program. Then, the administrator can compare the program's tuition rates to the cost-per-child rates and consider if tuition rates need to be adjusted and how much. For example, one flat tuition rate for all age groups would not suit the financial needs of a program or of the families enrolled. A higher tuition for infants and toddlers is normal in comparison to school-age children. However, a program may find that charging the entire cost-per-child rate for infants to be too much for families to afford. It might charge a bit more than the calculated cost-per-child for school-age children in order to balance the expenses and

better serve the financial needs of families. A program should perform a cost-per-child analysis regularly to track that tuition income and expenses remain relatively balanced.

Calculating the Break-Even Point

Once a program determines its budget estimate of income and expenses, the next step is to check if there will be enough money to pay the costs of program operation. This means reaching the **break-even point**, the place within the budget that enough money is available to cover basic expenses. Financial management is like juggling. If income is not sufficient to meet expenses, the program administrator will have to figure out some way to increase income or cut expenses. These choices will have either a positive or negative impact on the program finances. As an administrator, the more experience you have, the greater your ability will be to recognize which risks are worth taking and which choices are best for your program. For example, a program leader is thinking about raising tuition, which may cause some families to leave the program. If so, the empty spaces would need to be refilled quickly at the increased tuition rate. If there is a delay in replacing the children that have left the program, this might be more of a risk to the program overall and the leader may need to reexamine the decision to raise tuition. The break-even point represents the calculation of the number of children who must be enrolled to meet the program's expenses. If the number of children decreases, or expenses increase, then the administrator is forced to adjust tuition or find other sources of income. However, if the administrator has a good sense that the families enrolled in the program could withstand an increase in tuition, the increase may be worth the risk.

6.5 Financial Management

Program administrators make financial decisions throughout the year. They can utilize a variety of resources, such as financial information from reliable websites, public library materials, and a certified public accountant (CPA), small business financial advisor, or other business professional, to help guide these decisions. As a child care administrator, you will need to recognize that when financial decisions are made, you must consider certain economic realities. Promised money may not come through and enrollment is not constant—families move, work schedules change, and parents' employment changes. Occasionally, there are instances when money may even become available that was not anticipated.

katleho Seisa/E+/Getty Images

Figure 6.17 Making financial decisions requires on-going thought, access to financial information, and outside expertise such as a CPA to help guide decisions.

Your decision-making process should always weigh the positive and negative influences on the program's incoming money (**Figure 6.17**). Understanding basic financial management terms and financial realities will help you when making these decisions.

Cash Flow

Cash flow is a term that refers to the movement of money into and out of a program's bank account. Early childhood programs can receive money through tuition, subsidy money, fundraisers, and grants, depending on the status of the program. When planning your program budget, consider the total amount of income from all sources. Then map out a spending plan that is in line with expected income. Keep in mind that throughout the fiscal year, certain payments will be required. Staff salaries, utilities, and insurance are among the items that must be paid on time. However, money can only be paid out if the expected income has been coming into the program. Closely monitor receipts to ensure they are in on time and send reminders when incoming payments are tardy. Ideally, money flows into the program and, in turn, obligations are paid out all in a timely manner.

Cash Lag

Cash lag refers to situations when money is owed to the early childhood program but has not been received yet. This impacts the program's cash flow. Cash lag can be a major problem for a small program due to the limited amount of money being generated each week. A program may not have enough money in its bank account to cover bills if money due is not coming in on time. An example of this can be a program that relies heavily on state subsidy reimbursements. Due to state

rules and regulations, a cash lag typically occurs at the beginning of each new fiscal year. A significant time gap may also occur between receiving approval for a special grant and receiving the actual funds. Administrators must plan and diligently track not only their forecasted budgets, but also the actual money coming in. They must ensure the program has enough money to cover all its debts.

Cash Reserve

To address cash lag issues, administrators should build a **cash reserve**. The program administrator sets aside money each year, or whenever possible, to cover times when money is not flowing into the program. For example, if state subsidy checks are always late in the summer months due to the new fiscal year, the cash reserve is available to pay expenditures such as staff salaries. Once the subsidy money comes in, they replace what was accessed within the reserve fund.

Bad Debts

Unfortunately, every program, sooner or later, has some experience with bad debts. These occur when someone simply cannot pay the program for services already received. In a child care program, bad debts typically originate from unpaid tuition. Families have numerous reasons for not paying tuition—from employment difficulties to health issues to divorce or separation. Divorced or separated parents may disagree about the obligation to pay child care costs and neglect to pay the child care program until they resolve this dispute in court.

Bad debt may also occur if a state subsidy program determines that a child is not eligible or no longer eligible for a subsidy and refuses to pay. The parent of the child may not have filed the correct paperwork, met with their caseworker, or now be earning too much money to qualify to cause the disqualification. However, the child care program has provided services in good faith, because the subsidy is paid after the services have been completed.

The director's role is to stay on top of these issues and to navigate a resolution when they arise. You may feel sympathy for a parent who has just left an abusive spouse and has no money or the family who is ineligible for a subsidy. However, as with electric or cell phone services, if payment is not received, then the service should be cut off. A program that allows bad debts to accumulate is damaging itself and its reputation.

There is no sure way to prevent an occasional bad debt from occurring. One helpful policy is to require payment from all families in advance. Some centers assess late payment fees to discourage missed deadlines. At some point, if fees are not paid, the family will have to be discharged from the program. Detail your program payment policies within your parent handbook. Have parents sign acknowledgement that the policies have been read and understood as part of your enrollment and orientation process. If a parent misses a payment or begins to fall behind, send reminder notices quickly. The further a parent falls behind, the harder it is to catch up. The larger the amount owed, the more likely it is that the early childhood program will lose the money.

While there are ways to pursue an overdue account such as taking a family to small claims court or hiring a collection agency, these options cost money and neither approach offers any guarantee that the program will collect the bill. If a parent has moved away, lost a job, or undergone a severe financial crisis, it may not be reasonable to pursue the payment. Unpleasant though it may be, bad debt is a reality, and the program administrator must plan for it.

Encumbered Funds

When reviewing the amount of money available for use at any given time, you must consider **encumbered funds**. This is money for which the program has made a commitment but has not yet paid out. For example, if several pieces of new equipment have been ordered, there is a commitment to pay for those items. While there is time between when the order was placed and when it arrives, the seller expects the program to pay the bill within a certain allotted time, such as 30 days, after delivery. You must carefully track how much money has been committed or encumbered to pay for these items. This is money already spent by the program. If you forget encumbered funds are due, the program may overspend and not have enough money to pay for them when the bill arrives.

6.6 Needed Financial Services

Not all banks and financial services are equal. Banks offer a variety of accounts and options beyond simply a business checking or savings account. Research several banks and the option they offer a small business before deciding. Some banks charge a service fee for each check a small business writes. Others only charge a fee if the balance in the checking account drops below a certain amount. Some banks pay interest on certain checking accounts. Other banks offer higher interest rates on savings accounts. Some banks may give better

kate_sept2004/E+/Getty Images

Figure 6.18 Checking with a variety of financial institutions concerning rates and fees is important before making a decision.

rates on loans to established customers. As a program leader, shop around to find the bank or financial institution that offers the best deal for your program (**Figure 6.18**). As the program grows and large sums of money are involved, the interest that is accumulated on program accounts can be substantial. A CPA or other financial advisor can offer advice on the types of accounts or other forms of savings to pursue to best suit your program's needs.

Line of Credit

If your program does not have accumulated money saved in a reserve account, consider securing a **line of credit** through a lending institution. This short-term loan extends a preapproved amount of money. Once repaid, the amount becomes available to be borrowed again, like a credit card but with lower interest rates. You may not want or even plan to borrow funds and pay interest to pay bills. However, a line of credit can be a quick solution when you experience a cash lag. Negotiating the terms and interest rate with the lending institution ahead of time allows for an understanding, up front, when it comes time to repay the money, so the costs to the program are limited.

Credit and Debit Cards

Credit cards can serve two purposes in the child care setting. First, credit cards enable the program to receive payments from parents who wish to charge the cost of their child care. Once the parent pays by credit card, the program will receive its money. This is true even if the parent does not pay the credit card company. To have this guarantee of payment, the center will pay a fee for the use of the credit card company's service. These fees vary widely by credit card processing service and can be quite

Figure 6.19 Many parents utilize bank and credit cards to pay the cost of their child's tuition.

substantial. Before deciding to use a credit card service, consider the following.

- What are the fees to the program associated with the credit card service?
- Will the credit card portal work with the program's website?
- Does the credit card company provide processing equipment that is compatible with the program's current technology and is that equipment free of charge?
- Will the service attract more families?

Many parents like the convenience of being able to pay by credit card (**Figure 6.19**). It can be quicker and more convenient than other forms of payment. The center can also benefit from the guaranteed payment of bills placed on the card. This can help to reduce amounts lost through bad debts.

The program will need a credit and debit card set up in the program's business name. The debit card is a card linked directly to the program's bank account. When the program makes purchases, the funds are withdrawn immediately. For credit cards, more time is available to repay the cost of the purchase. Depending on the type of credit card and its terms, the program may need to pay the amount within 30 days. Others will carry a balance but charge high interest rates. Be careful! Prudently plan the payment schedule to minimize high interest charges.

The convenience provided by either type of card assists with making purchases online or in person. Also, credit or debit cards have become the most common way to purchase items. Monitor credit and debit purchases carefully. Authorize only specific staff members to make debit and credit purchases, and keep cards in a safe place where they will not be stolen or misused. In addition, collect credit card monthly statements to reconcile purchases each month and for annual tax preparation.

Director's Showcase
Salma

As Salma and the program's CPA pulled together the budget, they started to have ideas about not only suggesting a company foundation to help support the program's growth but also the possibility of doing a community fundraising event. As Salma presented the proposed budget, the warehouse company's board expressed interest in becoming involved in the local community and supporting local businesses within the surrounding communities. They offered to have their marketing department help with the planning of the fundraising event and absorb all costs associated with the event. Salma was thrilled! She could now share the news with the center staff. This opportunity was going to go forward and they could begin making purchasing decisions for the new program.

Maria

After Maria configured everything within the budget, she began to feel much more confident about how this would help to support her family's income. She and her husband discussed how this would provide their family flexibility by staying at home and being available to care for their own children during school breaks. Having time off for family vacations and during holidays also seemed possible based on her budget projections. Maria's next step was to determine what equipment and materials were necessary to meet state licensing standards as well as the costs associated with what she needed.

Director's Showcase
Reflect

When analyzing a budget, why is a cost-per-child analysis important? What are critical considerations when managing finances? What financial services would you consider working with and why?

6.7 Purchasing Decisions

A center must have the necessities for proper operation, including equipment, materials, and supplies, available as needed. The administration must ensure that these items are not only budgeted for but purchased and on hand. The array of program essentials include

- classroom supplies and materials;
- office supplies and equipment;
- indoor and outdoor play equipment;
- cleaning supplies and equipment;
- kitchen supplies and equipment;
- paper products;
- repair and maintenance items; and
- food.

Managing inventory and the purchasing responsibility includes making sure that items are available as they are needed to keep the center functioning. As the director, you may choose to delegate this, in part, to other staff members. It makes sense, for instance, for the cook to develop the list of needed groceries. An office assistant is the logical person to inventory and order office supplies. A larger program might have an administrative staff member, responsible for purchasing, who coordinates orders and checks for the best deals. Corporate-owned programs typically have an entire department that purchases in bulk to reduce expenses. The program leader coordinates with these individuals and departments to ensure that the program has what it needs to operate smoothly.

Bulk purchasing may save the program money, but only if there is enough storage space to handle the large quantities being ordered to avoid issues (**Figure 6.20**). For example, one center purchased a bulk amount of construction paper at a discounted price. The paper was stored in the center's basement. Unfortunately, during the rainy season, the basement flooded, and the paper was ruined. The administrator had to buy more paper and ended up spending more money than if they had bought several smaller orders of paper throughout the year. Another program declined a local grocery store's offer of sale-priced frozen turkeys because the center did not have enough freezer space. While bulk purchasing saves money, it is important to buy items that the program will use.

Teachers and other staff who work regularly in the classroom should have input in choosing materials for their classrooms. Oftentimes if each classroom has its own budget, then the teachers help to coordinate purchasing and closely manage the use of classroom supplies. Empowering teachers to manage their own classroom budgets assists them in better understanding financial constraints, planning and managing their classroom materials, and setting priorities to purchase more expensive items.

Seasonal Discounts

Sometimes your program can save money by paying attention to the time of the year when it purchases items. The geographic location of your program will have some effect on whether it can benefit from the changing of the seasons. Locally grown products will cost less. Fresh fruits, vegetables, and other produce are least expensive to buy during harvest season. Purchasing the same items out-of-season will be more expensive and either shipped from another country or in canned, frozen, or dried forms. Be aware of seasonal buying and the patterns established by the retail world. For example, stores put seasonal items on sale at the beginning of the season and provide deep discounts at the end of the season. Sales on towels and linens usually take place at the beginning of a new year. Planning purchases around seasonal availability and discounts will help you save your program money on essentials.

Vendor Relations

As director, you will review all orders to ensure that the program has what it needs and is staying on budget (**Figure 6.21**). While the office may need a new copier, you may need to postpone or deny this purchase if the funds are not available for its purchase. Your constant

Trong Nguyen/Shutterstock.com

Figure 6.20 Purchasing in bulk oftentimes saves money and can be done by the program leader or another designated staff member.

vm/iStock/Getty Images Plus

Figure 6.21 Delivery of fresh produce assists the program with providing the best product to the children with cost in mind.

awareness of the program's financial status and purchases will support you in making smart purchasing decisions. **Vendors** are the sellers of the various supplies and equipment that the program needs. Your program's vendors will vary from small specialty stores to large discount chains to department stores and online educational retailers depending on the items you need. Comparison shopping can reveal price differences from one vendor to another. You may also establish relationships with each of your vendors to better understand what they offer and how they can best support your program. You may find that they will offer price discounts if you ask for them. Some retailers offer special deals to not-for-profit programs. Others will not. A loyal sales representative may alert you to when the retailer has an upcoming sale. Your vendor relationships can save the program money and establish a good reputation in your community.

Bids

Another way to save money on expensive items, such as carpeting or new furnaces, is to obtain bids from several vendors who sell equivalent items. Many programs have a policy regarding major purchases. Any time the program needs an item that is more than a preset limit, such as $500, the director must obtain bids from several vendors. When seeking bids, provide potential vendors with all the information on the equipment being purchased, including any installation fees, service contracts, and accessories, to avoid price increases. When planning to buy an appliance or other major purchase, compare several different brands by looking closely at the features and compare in pricing.

Petty Cash

Petty cash is cash on hand for small, unexpected expenditures. The director or other authorized staff members pay for small items, such as extra stamps or a delivery person's tip either with their own money or funds directly taken from the petty cash. Staff members then submit their receipt for the items to the director who saves all the receipts as part of their expenditures journal and reimburses the staff members from the petty cash if they used their own money.

Procedures for the use of petty cash should be established, including designating which staff members are authorized to use it. All use of petty cash should be documented by receipts from purchases. Any item over a preset limit, such as $5, should have to go through regular purchasing procedures. While these procedures may seem elaborate, they can discourage casual, unnecessary use of the fund. The director usually designates only a small amount of money for petty cash expenditures, but it can be quickly squandered. Because a program can spend a substantial amount of money without adequate monitoring, a system for tracking petty cash expenses is important.

Other Purchasing Considerations

Cost is not the only factor to consider when making purchasing decisions. Although the price of an item is important, there are other hidden costs that must be kept in mind. The terms **warranty** and **guarantee** mean the same thing when purchasing items. They mean that the item purchased is backed by the manufacturer and is expected to last for at least a certain period. Warranties and guarantees typically cover repairs if the product is defective or if it breaks under normal use. They may also provide a replacement if the item breaks within the specified time frame. When considering the purchase of an expensive item, be sure to check the warranty or guarantee. Repair bills on an inferior product can be costly.

Vendors may differ in their return policies. Some vendors have generous return policies. If the program is dissatisfied with the purchase for any reason, the vendor will take it back. Other vendors refuse to handle returns, so the decision to purchase is a final one. Some will allow exchanges for other merchandise but will not give money back. Other items might initially come with a free or minimal cost trial offer period. The program can test the item and return it without payment if it is unsatisfactory for the intended use. These offers are very helpful when considering the purchase of an expensive item such as accounting software that will be utilized by the program. Tricycles, indoor climbers, and office copiers are examples of equipment that can often be obtained on a trial basis. After using an item during the trial period, the staff may agree that they want to purchase it or determine that it has not been useful.

Delivery and Service

The ease or difficulty of having an item delivered or repaired can represent a cost to the early childhood program. Every day that the center needs an item but cannot use or access it can be costly in labor, money, or reputation. For example, the refrigerator used in the infant classroom is broken and irreparable. An additional staff member has to be brought in to shuttle between the classroom and kitchen to prepare and obtain bottles and baby food throughout the day. Several days of this could be costly. Weighing whether to pay the delivery fee of $150 or waiting until a truck is available from a friend to go pick it up could potentially be more costly. In addition, the program leader may also need to be present when the item is picked up so that it is signed for, which takes away from other duties. Vendors may also provide service for the items they sell. Inquiring before entering into any business agreement with a vendor is important to avoid hidden costs.

Support for Local Businesses

If a program is based in a smaller community, local merchants may expect the program to purchase goods from them rather than online merchants or those from farther communities. With so many online options to buy from when living in an area with limited options, sometimes purchasing needs can be met locally at almost the same cost as from a distant supplier. Contacting local vendors before an online purchase is made allows for cost pricing and shows a willingness to support the local community. The decision to buy locally may be seen as support for the hometown. This positive public relations decision can strengthen the program's position within the community.

Government Program Assistance

While some food reimbursement funds are provided through the US Department of Agriculture's Child Care and Adult Food Program (CACFP), they only cover part of the costs involved in early childhood programs. Frequently, you must maintain a great deal of paperwork when participating in government food programs. Only certain types of food are eligible for reimbursement, and you must keep careful inventories. Local authorities who oversee the program will conduct food audits often. Auditors will track and match

- the amount of food purchased;
- the type of food purchased;
- daily menus;
- the number of eligible children in each classroom;
- the attendance days of eligible children;
- the amount of food portions served each day; and
- the amount of food left over and still on the shelves.

In some states, programs cannot serve food from the food reimbursement programs to ineligible children. The program must typically pass the cost of the unsubsidized food on to parents in the form of higher tuition fees.

Transportation Service

Some programs offer transportation services to get children to and from the program. This may include picking children up at home and returning them there at the end of the day. Some centers limit this service to only one part of the center's enrollment (**Figure 6.22**). For example, transportation may be provided for school-age children only. It brings children from school to the after-school program. Most parents cannot leave work in the middle of the day to drive their children from school to the center. This service is necessary to support enrollment in the school-age program.

Providing transportation can be costly for the program. Administration must conduct a careful analysis to ensure it is a necessary expense. Most programs will have to charge extra for this if it involves door-to-door service. If parents are unable or unwilling to pay for the

Hispanolistic/E+/Getty Images

Figure 6.22 Transportation services to local schools and homes assist parents but costs must also be considered and charged appropriately.

Director's Showcase

Salma

After three months of preparation and community fundraising, in addition to a hefty investment by the warehouse company's newly established foundation, the new facility was opened just down the street from the original location. To assist with the company's employee needs, Salma switched the original location to housing infants, toddlers, and twos while the new facility location cared for preschool and school-age children. In total, they were able to care for 60 additional children. Salma was able to purchase from local stores, which extended goodwill into the business community,

and the employees of the new warehouse location were happy to have quality child care for their children. Salma and her staff were excited to expand and better serve the community.

Maria

Maria was able to officially open her licensed family child care home within three months. The credit line offered to her by the bank helped to cover the purchase of necessary equipment and supplies. She was also able to do some local advertisement and set up a social media page to recruit families to her care. Within one month, Maria had a waiting list and was happily caring for the children in her care and being available to her own children after school and on school breaks.

convenience, the program will not be able to afford to provide it. If arrangements can be made for children to ride their regular school buses from school to the after-school program, there may be no extra cost. Head Start and other special purpose programs may receive money to support transportation services, including home pickup and return. Child care programs rarely receive any support or reimbursement money for transportation services.

Overall, any successful program must be financially sound. The early childhood leader's role is to plan, monitor, and oversee all expenditures of the program. Based on the type of program, identifying sources of income while developing a budget is key to managing a

Director's Showcase
Reflect
As you do cost comparisons, what types of considerations would you make to get the best price?

financially stable organization. Working with and holding to a reasonable budget, including implementing consistent buying habits while tracking procedures, allows for a program leader to feel confident as they oversee the ongoing financial picture of the program.

Chapter 6 Review and Assessment

Summary

6.1 Analyze the similarities and differences between a proposal and a business plan.

- Finding financial support for a child care program of any size requires effort and hard work. Most individuals are not wealthy enough to have all of the money necessary to start and operate a program. Seeking outside sources for support will be required. Presenting a clear, thoughtful proposal or business plan may make it possible to receive additional money.
- Proposal writing requires the identification of a particular need while the business plan is written for the purpose of securing a loan from a bank or other lending institution. Both provide critical information that convinces either an agency or lender of the intent to implement a plan related to opening a child care program. Through these processes, real costs and responsibilities are determined and explained when operating an early childhood program. This plan of action involves including a budget and plan that support the narrative provided in either document.

6.2 Explain the differences between for-profit and not-for-profit programs.

- For-profit programs cover expenses and make a profit based on the income generated by the child care program. Example programs would be those owned by an individual or corporate company. Non-profit, on the other hand, are typically subsidized and the goal is to generate enough money to cover expenses of the program. An example might be a program sponsored by a religious organization or a foundation.

6.3 Describe the types of expenses that are involved in operating a child care program.

- There are typically four main areas within a child care budget. Those areas include personnel, facilities, programming, and equipment. Based on these four areas, subcategories are created to reflect expenses and will vary based on the size and type of early childhood program.

6.4 Apply how to develop and analyze the program budget.

- The budget is a plan based on the projected amount of income expected. If throughout the year income is less than expected, the budget will need to be revised. When creating a budget at the beginning of the year, it should be flexible. Actual spending patterns must be modified to reflect any change in the amount of income predicted. Two strategies are very helpful when developing and analyzing a budget to include a cost-per-child analysis and break-even point. Analyzing the program budget on a regular basis allows for the administrator to have a better understanding of the program's financial state.

6.5 Discover financial strategies that create effective management of program funds.

- Creating a budget provides an opportunity to see the reality of how money flows into and out of the program. Then, financial resources can be managed more carefully. This includes staying current with money owed by families so that when purchasing decisions are made, they are based on current cash flow. In addition, taking time to research and secure appropriate banking options that support the projected financial needs of the early childhood program is important.

6.6 Investigate necessary financial services that support a child care program.

- Depending on the type of program, for- or non-profit, this serves as a guide when determining options that might be available. While for-profit programs are limited to revenue-generating options to help support the program budget such as fundraisers and sales of extra services such as a dance classes, non-profit programs can write for many grant opportunities and qualify for foundation funds. Successful financial management is crucial to the success of any child care program. Program leaders are responsible to non-profit boards, owners, and corporate leadership. The "buck stops here" is the overall expectation for directors of any size program. Being knowledgeable by seeking out financial expertise and resources is highly advised and expected.

6.7 Recognize considerations within program finances to make purchasing decisions.

- Many purchasing strategies stretch available money. This includes bulk purchasing, and an awareness of warranties included with the purchase of large items. These help to save the program money. Purchasing decisions must also take into account storage capacity, delivery charges, and ease of service, if needed. For example, food service requires space for storage and preparation. In addition, there are many food items that must be fresh which can impact the frequency of serving due to the food expiration date. Whether food is prepared on site or by contracting with a food service, the benefits and drawbacks of each should be analyzed.

Review

1. Explain how a proposal and business plan are different. (6.1)
2. Explain why it is important not to use familiar terms in the field when writing a proposal. (6.1)
3. Identify the reasons why a funding agency needs to understand the population being targeted for services. (6.1)
4. Explain the difference between a for-profit and non-profit program. (6.2)
5. What should a start-up budget reflect? (6.3)
6. When figuring a cost-per-child-analysis, what is the process? (6.4)
7. Why is it a good idea to build a cash reserve? (6.5)
8. What does it mean when a program has encumbered funds? (6.5)
9. Why is it important to obtain bids from various vendors? (6.6)
10. Give two examples of bulk purchasing and explain the advantages and disadvantages. (6.6)
11. What strategies assist with saving money on expensive items such as the replacement of carpet or a furnace? (6.7)

Showcase Your Skills

As discussed in this chapter, Salma and Maria are beginning new businesses. Salma is increasing the capacity of her program to meet the needs of a local employer moving into the area. Maria is opening a business in her home to provide care for children in the community. Both need to check the costs, services, and convenience of doing business with the local banks in their area.

Based on the information shared in the chapter and by doing an internet search of three reputable financial institutions in your area, answer the following questions.

1. Does the institution pay interest on business checking accounts?
2. Does the institution offer lines of credit? If so, what are the interest rates?
3. Are there penalties if the checking account falls below a certain limit?
4. Does the institution offer incentives for business savings accounts? If so, what are they?
5. Using the gathered information, write a one-page narrative that provides insights into which financial institution you would consider doing business with and why.

Matching

Match the following terms with the correct definitions:

A. cash flow
B. cash reserve
C. encumbered funds
D. for-profit program
E. market rate
F. not-for-profit programs
G. petty cash
H. sponsor
I. vendors
J. vouchers

1. Representation of money provided by companies that their employees can use to help pay for care in a program of their choice.
2. Cash on hand for small, unexpected expenditures.
3. Money for which the program has made a commitment but has not yet paid out.
4. Person, group, or organization that makes a commitment to provide ongoing support to a program.
5. Typical cost of child care in the area.
6. Money set aside to cover times when money is not flowing into the program.
7. Movement of money into and out of a program's bank account.
8. Business legally organized to operate without making a profit, often as a community service.
9. Sellers of the various supplies and equipment that the program needs.
10. Businesses operated to make a profit for the owners.

Rawpixel/iStock/Getty Images Plus

7 CHAPTER

Marketing and Planning for Enrollment

Learning Outcomes

After studying this chapter, you will be able to:

7.1 Examine the differences between public relations and marketing.

7.2 Discover strategies when welcoming parents and children to the early childhood program.

7.3 Investigate best practices as children and families transition to the early childhood program environment.

7.4 Establish procedures that will assist teachers and parents as children adjust to the early childhood program environment.

Key Terms

home visits
marketing
orientation meeting
public relations
separation anxiety
social media savvy

Introduction

As you begin a new program, consideration must be given to how you will let people know of the new addition to the community. You must think about ways to attract families who will enroll their children. How do you want your community to view your program? How do you create interest in your program throughout your community? How would you manage classroom placements and enrollment to meet your budget commitments? How can you support teachers and parents as children adjust to the early childhood program environment?

The choices you make regarding each of these areas influence the way people view your program and determine their interest. It is important to establish a reputation for knowledgeable programming, fair policies and procedures, and sensitive care for children. It is the program's reputation that will affect the support, or lack of, by your community.

7.1 Public Relations and Marketing

The term **public relations** refers to an awareness of and a positive attitude toward a business. We often refer to this as the image of the business. **Marketing** is the promotion of your business, which includes many potential activities that create awareness. Public relations is based upon the promotion of the business's values and mission, which creates positive feelings about what the business has to offer to the general community. Second, it is how individuals who work for the business embrace and help to support the business. Before we look more closely at the application of public relations and marketing to an early childhood program, let's think about this in the broader context of a highly successful company—Walmart (**Figure 7.1**).

From an early childhood program perspective, there are many ways to consider building a program's reputation in a community. Public relations efforts should support the idea that a program is an asset to the community. As was previously discussed in an earlier chapter, the director is the leader who works with the support of

NAEYC/DAP standards

Standards covered in this chapter:

NAEYC

2a, 2b, 2c, 6a, 6c

DAP

2B

Director Showcase

Taisha

Taisha is excited to be opening a new program in the town where she was born and raised. She opened a small program licensed for 30 children. Her goal is to eventually increase the licensed capacity to meet the growing needs of her town that has just received news that a large company will be relocating in their area and will be hiring 300 people in the next six months.

Meredith

Meredith, on the other hand, accepted the role as director of a large family-owned program that had been serving the community for 25 years. Licensed for 150 children, the program is located in a major metropolitan area and has access to working families that support local and major businesses in the area. Because the area has grown so much, there are two other corporate-owned centers that have opened in the past year to accommodate all of the growth in the area.

the staff to establish and maintain the values and mission of the early childhood program. This should radiate throughout the program each day by the interactions that you experience and observe within the program and, most importantly, between the children and parents. If the internal organization is healthy, then the next step is to invest time in the community by participating in activities to help local residents get to know more about the program. When you or other representatives of your center participate in community activities, you help local residents get to know your program. They see you as an active contributor to the well-being of the area.

There are many ideas to contribute to the community. This includes sharing relevant information that supports

Walmart: Implementing a Company's Mission and Vision

As one of the world's largest retailers, Walmart emphasizes its customers. Walmart exists to offer quality merchandise at the lowest prices and to do it with the best customer service possible. They place high value on serving their customers by respecting the individual, striving for excellence, serving the customer, and acting with integrity.

The greeter who typically meets customers at the front door is one of their most notable customer service strategies, which is based on Walmart's core values. This foundation is the focus of television commercials, social media, and other forms of advertising. These values began back in the founder's days. Employees observed his work ethic and decided it was necessary to match the company culture with the founder's values. To this day the company still embraces these values and continues to shape their culture. The company uses its strengths to support communities by investing money in initiatives such as education, disaster relief and preparedness, and environmental sustainability. From a public relations and marketing perspective, Walmart has been successful at creating a powerful image in the communities where they are built.

Goodheart-Willcox Publisher

Figure 7.1 Based on the actions of top leadership, Walmart has worked to implement a vision and mission within their company culture that has resulted in a public image that supports local communities.

SDI Productions/E+/Getty Images

Figure 7.2 Early childhood leaders engage in their communities by speaking at local service clubs to spread the word about the program and its services to children and families.

children's development, such as best practices in the area of health and safety, and quality parenting resources. This can be done by sharing on a website, social media platform, and even working with local newspapers in smaller communities. The local human services and health departments hold local fairs, which would allow opportunities to host your own booth to distribute information about your program and parent education materials. When helpful information is made available to all parents, those parents who need child care will become familiar with your program.

Effective directors try to expand their influence in the community. Here are some public relations examples of what you might do as a director. Volunteering to be a guest speaker at a local service club can help community leaders learn more about quality child care (**Figure 7.2**). Getting to know other human service agency directors can help you to keep them up-to-date about your program. It also reflects a commitment to communication and cooperation with heads of agencies that regulate child care. Joining local business and economic development groups raises awareness in the community. Organizations such as the Chamber of Commerce like

to feature new community services by providing public relations support and may feature your program in one of their community communications. Groups such as these often develop marketing materials to encourage new businesses to move into the area and assist newly establishing companies in caring for their employees. More than ever, companies are realizing that access to quality child care is a need of working parents.

From a marketing perspective, becoming **social media savvy**, or a user who is familiar with websites and applications that share content or provide social networking, is necessary to be successful. Parents' lives revolve around technology, including using their phones and other devices to access social media. One way to use social media for the program is to obtain written permission from parents to share pictures of their children engaging in program activity, which can increase the visibility of your program. Other suggestions include collaborating with businesses and the local paper to share pictures on social media pages to attract attention to the program. Annual events such as the National Association for the Education (NAEYC) of the Young Child Week, provide suggested marketing content to utilize on websites and social media pages as opportunities to engage with the community (**Figure 7.3**). From a marketing perspective, all of these activities are human-interest stories that feature your center and its investment in the community.

Your personal reputation in the community reflects on your program and public relations effectiveness. Are you viewed as an honest, mature, hardworking, and compassionate person? Are you and your staff seen as individuals who can be counted on to work for the good of the community? Is your staff aware that their public behavior reflects on your program's reputation? Simple things like

Methods for Engaging with the Community

Visits from community helpers

- Police department
- Fire department
- Local business leaders

Community events

- Parades
- Outdoor activities at a park
- Community fundraisers

Engaging with citizens

- Students visit a nursing home to sing
- Open house for community members
- Special board meeting honoring community members

Goodheart-Willcox Publisher

Figure 7.3 Engaging with the community in person can lead to social media and website engagement, as well.

answering the phone with courtesy can be important. Greeting visitors, answering questions, and helping parents find services they need can all affect the image of your program. Each of these qualities radiate the foundation of the values and mission set forth by your program and are part of your marketing strategy.

One essential part of building your program from a public relations perspective is to be sure you are meeting the needs of community families. For example, operating a quality infant program is not profitable on its own. However, if parents are satisfied with their child's care, the likelihood is greater that they will stay with your program as their child gets older. While there are many public prekindergarten programs, your community might be one that relies heavily on partnerships. If you are one of those programs, you can maintain the child's enrollment by providing the space and equipment, while the local school provides the teacher and supporting materials. The continued enrollment supports your financial forecast and the program receives publicity for having a partnership with the local school. A full enrollment in your preschool class can lead to offering out-of-school-time care, which can help to balance the cost of providing quality infant and toddler care. Ultimately, families want to stay with centers that their children are happy attending and are working well to meet their needs.

Many parents-to-be do not give much thought to the idea that they may need quality child care options. Many are surprised when they start looking for care and recognize the cost. It can be difficult for parents to cope with the reality of needing to return to the workforce

and having to leave their child in the care of others. Part of the marketing strategy should be to speak to prenatal groups to provide information about your program; include information to local birthing centers to help parents become aware of your program. Helping to educate your community about this issue is necessary and should be a part of your public relations and marketing strategy.

It is important to understand that when parents first approach your center, they may have mixed feelings about leaving their child in the care of someone else. They want good quality care, but they also want it to be convenient and inexpensive. A helpful marketing strategy is to give parents information about the cost of quality child care that includes the qualifications of you and your staff, the program's licensure, and your program's participation in your state's quality rating system. Providing information and displaying all of these aspects educates and assures parents as they begin to explore various child care options (**Figure 7.4**). Seeing the efforts made by your program may assist in their realization that they have found the right place for their child and family needs. As your program continues to grow, there are so many public relations and marketing considerations to be made when establishing a new program or operating one that has been serving the local community.

Public Relations and Marketing Strategies

The priority for a new program is to build enrollment quickly so it can become financially stable. When either operating or buying an established program, the goal is to maintain and grow enrollment so that the program remains financially stable. Let's take a look at how two

Ijubaphoto/iStock/Getty Images Plus

Figure 7.4 Parents often go to the internet to research a program's staff qualifications, the program's license, and participation in a state quality rating system before ever calling to set up an appointment to see the program.

different early childhood program directors embraced public relations and marketing to support the communities in which they lived.

Keep in mind two goals when planning public relations and marketing strategies. One goal is to market programs to people who may be interested in enrolling their children. The second goal is to create a positive image of the program within the community. As discussed at the beginning of the chapter as well as within earlier chapters, the promotion of the program's values and mission serves as the foundation to create positive feelings about the program within the community. It is this foundation that sets a program apart and establishes the intent and desire to provide quality early childhood program services.

A goal of every child care center director should be to personally establish and maintain a reputation that reflects a commitment to leading a quality early childhood program. This can be achieved through a good reputation within a town where care will be provided. Leading a program that has an established reputation in the community is ideal. Doing your homework by checking around to see what that reputation is helps when there are established expectations and relationships. Ultimately, a good reputation helps to ensure that a program will continue to attract new families and is an asset to the community. A good "word-of-mouth" reputation can ensure community support when times are tough.

In order to build enrollment, make sure that the people who need an early childhood program know about it. Established programs are known within communities but will still need to reach out to potential customers such as new businesses in the area, keeping in mind new competition in the area. Successful marketing strategies will support efforts when reaching out to the community to market an early childhood program.

Marketing Considerations

No matter the type or size of the early childhood program, it is imperative to focus on the importance of strong partnerships with families. They are the best advertisement and your customer! Collecting information from families on a regular basis allows you to determine your program's unique features. With a little investigative work of your own you can communicate your program's unique offerings compared to those of your competition. This ability to "stand out from the competition" is not unique to early childhood—all industries have to do this.

To begin this section, let's consider the strategies done by a very large company. Amazon has a carefully crafted message to consumers that early childhood program leaders can learn from (**Figure 7.5**).

Amazon: Iconic Branding

In the mid-1990s, a little-known company began selling books online. In a relatively short period of time, the company went from selling books to being the "go to" e-commerce giant that has an expansive product line, exceptional delivery, and customer service. Think about the presence that Amazon has today through branding and advertising. The choice of "Amazon" came from the idea that the Amazon River was the biggest river in the world, and the owner's goal was to be the biggest online store in the world. In addition, "A" was at the beginning of the alphabet and "Z" at the end. Hence, the logo that we all know very well, the arrow in the shape of a smile that points from the "A" to the "Z," is the one that we, as customers, receive satisfaction from because they carry everything from A to Z.

Amazon found a unique way to brand themselves as a household name for essentials and nonessentials alike. Now, think about how this applies to the market of early childhood program services. What do you uniquely offer that families with young children want? How can you position your "brand" in your community?

Goodheart-Willcox Publisher

Figure 7.5 Establishing a brand within a community will need thoughtful consideration when communicating the unique differences the program will offer to families and their children.

Use of Advertising

There are many different types of advertising. These include websites, social media platforms, online ads, brochures and flyers, newspaper ads, and informational meetings, to name a few. Each of these has specific advantages, target populations to consider, and other benefits. Most also may have a cost that had to be investigated before making a commitment. Another caution that has to be considered is the importance of keeping legalities in mind when utilizing staff, children and family pictures, statements, or opinions of the program within printed materials, a website, or within any social media postings. Many resources, including hiring a local advertisement company or graphic designer, can assist with developing an advertising plan.

Writing and Matching Advertising to the Market

Smaller programs often choose to use written materials. These could be left at the local grocery store; pinned up on bulletin boards at the library, elementary school, and the community center; and also included within established businesses in the area. These materials need to be easy to understand and clearly explain information about the early childhood program. They should include a description of the age range of children served, location and phone number, statement of program philosophy and goals, special services or programs offered, and insights regarding the staff's educational backgrounds.

When researching cost, printing materials can be expensive. For information that may change, such as tuition costs or hours of operation, it is more cost-effective to display this information on a website, or other social media outlet, for easy adjustment. Ultimately, most interested families are going to contact the program directly for current prices, hours, and availability.

Be careful that materials reflect the community, its diversity, and is respectful of the children and families that will be served. Craft a message that avoids providing "cute" advertising. For example, while it might be cute to have a cartoon of a frazzled teacher with an "out-of-control" child, in retrospect this does not present an image of a competent, quality early childhood program. It is important to have materials that are professional in appearance and content.

When determining how to spend advertising dollars, it is wise to figure out how to best reach families. If a program is located in a larger metropolitan area, advertising in a newspaper could be very expensive. Although it might be seen by many people, it would also cover a broad geographic area and some potential families who read the ad might live too far away to have any real interest in enrollment. For smaller areas, it might be best to target an ad in a small, regional paper or put up banners that serve nearby neighborhoods (**Figure 7.6**). Both would potentially be a more cost-effective choice.

Program directors need to include the services they plan to offer. For example, if a program wants to continue an expansive school-age program, the target population to reach out to would be families with older

children enrolled in the local elementary school. Options could include sending home information with school communications and connecting with the principal to post program information on the school website. Other resources that are helpful in getting out the word about a program include pediatrician offices, pharmacies, and grocery stores—all places that families frequent. There are also other strategies to consider, including the internet and other forms of "old-style" advertising that still continue to be effective today.

Website

Having a website is valuable because many of today's parents grew up with the internet and go to it first to find options for child care (along with so many other things). A website that contains reviews and postings from currently enrolled families can be very attractive. Many programs post video tours of their programs, as well as pertinent documents such as the state license and biographies about themselves and their staff. This information is helpful for perspective parents to review before deciding on a program.

Any videos or pictures need to include the classrooms, playgrounds, kitchen area, and transportation. While posting information regarding the program's mission, vision, and overall philosophy is important for prospective families, the ability for them to see happy children, caring staff, and clean and healthy spaces for children to spend their day can be even more crucial. A strong child care website should also include contact information (digital and phone) for the center, hours of operation, location, and ages of children served.

It is also helpful to link the website to other sites where parents of young children are likely to see it. Besides sharing information with local businesses, a child care program should connect with human resources departments. This makes local businesses aware of available child care and they may include this information on their employee website. When posting to other websites, always be sure to list an email address where prospective clients can get additional information about your program.

Social Media Platforms

There are many social media platforms to use with a variety of permissions to consider. Social media allows the opportunity to immediately share the exciting, developmentally appropriate activity taking place at a program. From children engaged in a cooking or art activity, to large groups of children playing with a large parachute outside or tending to the program's garden—all are powerful and engaging images. However, they also have to be monitored closely and permission must be obtained from legal guardians to include images of children enrolled in the program.

Kristen Alexandria

Figure 7.6 Programs serving smaller areas can utilize banners to advertise what is taking place to encourage interest and inquiry into their program services.

towfiqu ahamed/iStock/Getty Images Plus

Figure 7.7 When deciding to use social media, program leaders must obtain permission from legal guardians, monitor posted images, and respond to comments in a timely manner.

There are many considerations when trying to gain permission to post images to social media (**Figure 7.7**). For example, most states have regulations around not posting pictures or videos of children in foster care to social media to protect the child's privacy. In addition, a parent might work in law enforcement and may not want their child featured for safety reasons. It is important to be aware that once these social platforms are utilized, they must have constant and competent oversight to monitor what and how information is shared and to protect the image of the early childhood program.

Brochures and Flyers

Brochures and flyers are ideal for smaller programs and can get out target information about specific programming for larger ones. Both provide printed information, can be produced in large quantities, and given to interested individuals. Brochures usually have several pages, while flyers are more likely to be a flat piece of paper, folded or unfolded. Typically, due to the use of color, pictures, and need to be tri-folded, brochures are more expensive to produce. Flyers are simpler to prepare and less costly. Either way, desktop publishing capabilities and copy centers make it relatively easy to produce professional-looking brochures and flyers. Just like with social media, permission must be obtained from legal guardians before any images are printed for use.

Newspaper Advertisements

Utilizing a local newspaper ad can be a cost-effective way to advertise the opening of a program. Many programs utilize this resource to share information about informational meetings, open houses, and presentations by special guest speakers to keep their community aware of their programs. The cost of an ad is usually determined by the amount of space needed, assistance provided by the newspaper staff when preparing the ad for publication, and the length of time the ad appears.

Informational Meetings

Scheduling meetings of interest on a variety of parenting topics typically piques a parent's interest and they share with their friends and coworkers (**Figure 7.8**). This includes engaging local child development experts to do live or virtual sessions of interest. Reaching out to local companies encourages them to invite their employees, major apartment complexes can share with their residents that have young children, and local churches and social clubs are great populations to target when providing informational meetings. Topics such as behavior and guidance of young children typically engage a large attendance and follow-up interest in a program.

Community Resources

In many areas there are local Child Care Resource & Referral Agencies. It is here that parents can contact a hotline or send an email to gain insights on locations of quality child care sites in their area. Using the Child Care

Director's Showcase

Reflect

As you think about your area and opening a new program, what public relations and marketing strategies would you engage? Who could you target in the business community? What types of advertising options would you consider?

izusek/E+/Getty Images

Figure 7.8 Bringing in local experts to speak on a variety of parenting topics allows for parents to ask questions and gain insight about their child's development.

Resource & Referral Agency is a very valuable strategy to help with advertising to the community and getting the word out about local child care options. Part of their mission is to reach out to the local business community to share the value of quality child care programming. Now, more than ever, employers want their employees to have quality care for their young children so that they are more productive in the workplace. Overall, once a successful public relations and marketing strategy is engaged, enrollment begins, and the next step is to welcome children and their parents.

7.2 Making the Program a Welcome Place for Parents

Entering child care can be an exciting adventure for children and their parents. It is a milestone in growing up. As with any major life change, the emotions felt by parents and children are likely to be both positive and negative. For children, there is the pleasure of finding new friends and toys. At the same time, children usually experience separation anxiety and fears about being away from a parent (**Figure 7.9**). Depending on their age, they may also

jacoblund/iStock/Getty Images Plus

Figure 7.9 Some children are anxious and experience separation anxiety when being left by their parent at an early childhood program.

have doubts about finding friends, and a general anxiety about their ability to cope with this new experience.

For parents, there is the joy of seeing their child take a major step toward independence. When parents are happy with their choice of program, they are usually pleased at the opportunities for play and learning their child will have. Yet, for parents, this is a difficult time also. They often feel guilty for leaving the child. If the child has not been in child care before, the caregiving parent may feel a great sense of loss at not being with the child all the time.

While these are two different issues to contend with, meeting caregivers where they are in the process of bringing their child to the program must be addressed. Think about a time when you did not experience the best first impression. An example would be walking into a restaurant, looking around, and all you see is a dining area that needs cleaning and a few bugs scramble across the floor in front of you. Would you stay and eat a meal there? Now, think about being a parent that is leaving their child for the first time at a place that was dirty, unwelcoming, and in complete disarray. From the parents' perspectives, not only are they having to pay a considerable amount of money for their child to be cared for, they are going to be extra aware of the overall look of the facility. Your other customer, the child, reaches out to play with a bunch of broken toys. Is that fun? Is it engaging? The look, the feel, the smells, the entire atmosphere must "feel" comfortable and safe. From initial contact to on-site tours that result in enrollment, all are opportunities to welcome families into the early childhood program.

Telephone and Email Inquiries

Most parents will make their initial contacts with a center either by phone or email. The attitude, helpfulness,

Director's Showcase

Taisha

Since Taisha's program was much smaller, she was able to do more of a "first come, first serve" system. This allowed her to use simpler enrollment processes and as openings, became available, she could quickly help parents to make a commitment to her program and the child began attending. Due to this, welcoming both the child and family to the program was often a quick process. This resulted in lots of considerations to be in place to support the child as they began attending the program.

Meredith

Since Meredith had a much larger program the process of enrollment management had several more steps to consider and a greater length of time. Her first priority was to develop smooth procedures for registration as well as a written waiting list and tracking processes. This provided a formal system for Meredith to provide for interested parents who were serious about having their child attend her program. This resulted in an enrollment process that provided more time to support the new family and their child.

Kristen Alexandria

Figure 7.10 Larger programs typically have office staff to assist with answering the phone and emails, and greeting families as they arrive.

and timely response of the person who answers the phone or email will make an initial impression on the family. In a very small center, where you are the director-teacher-assistant, you might need voicemail to handle routine calls. A pleasant message promising to call back later in the day when you are not with the children will reassure parents of your priorities. You can also leave pertinent information such as your operating days and hours within this message and even direct the caller to your website for more information or email contact.

Larger programs may have an assistant who can answer the phone or reply to emails (**Figure 7.10**). You must be sure that whoever answers the phone or answers emails is knowledgeable about the program, friendly in tone when speaking, and when writing correspondence. The phone should be answered with a pleasant greeting, the name of the center and, "May I help you?" An email needs to attend to the question being posed using correct spelling and grammar when responding. By having several people within the program trained to handle routine calls and emails saves the director time and empowers staff to support interested families.

One way to keep track of calls is to develop a log sheet that is kept by the phone. It should be divided into columns so that basic information about the call can be quickly recorded. Information to be kept should include

- the date and time of call;
- the name and number of caller;
- the nature of call;
- any further action to be taken regarding the call; and
- any action completed (**Figure 7.11**).

A log like this can help to ensure that if a caller has been promised a program flyer, that it has actually been sent.

🕐 PHONE CALL MESSAGE LOG 🕐

DATE:	☐ TELEPHONED
TIME:	☐ RETURNED CALL
CALLER:	☐ PLEASE CALL
FOR:	☐ WILL CALL AGAIN
CONTACT INFO:	☐ CAME TO SEE YOU
MESSAGE/NOTES:	

DATE:	☐ TELEPHONED
TIME:	☐ RETURNED CALL
CALLER:	☐ PLEASE CALL
FOR:	☐ WILL CALL AGAIN
CONTACT INFO:	☐ CAME TO SEE YOU
MESSAGE/NOTES:	

DATE:	☐ TELEPHONED
TIME:	☐ RETURNED CALL
CALLER:	☐ PLEASE CALL
FOR:	☐ WILL CALL AGAIN
CONTACT INFO:	☐ CAME TO SEE YOU
MESSAGE/NOTES:	

Graphics Studio Zone/Shutterstock.com

Figure 7.11 Tracking calls is necessary to collect valuable information that keeps the program leader in contact with potential families interested in enrolling.

Sometimes promises made over the phone are forgotten. This causes ill will and leads callers to think you don't care about them. With a written log, you can be sure to return calls, look up answers to questions, or send out information.

There should also be either a log sheet or appointments within the center's electronic calendar that reflects up-to-date appointment times. If a parent wants to come in to discuss enrollment, an appointment should be set up as quickly as possible with the appropriate staff member.

Above all, whoever the parent meets first either through phone or email, that person should speak and write clearly and be courteous. Parents may be reluctant to make that first call when exploring child care options, especially if their child has special needs.

Children with Disabilities

When a parent of a child with a disability is considering enrollment, they will need assurances that communication will be essential. While the parent will be sharing specific information regarding their child, the staff need to be prepared to ask questions, request clarifications, and be informed about care and safety procedures. Parents often have the special equipment their child needs during the day. Should they not have it, program staff may be able to help arrange for needed items or purchase using center funds that are often reimbursed by state programs. In addition, many state-funded early intervention programs, educational, and charitable organizations exist to help meet children's needs and will coordinate services with early childhood programs. This may include special training, educational materials, or additional equipment items.

As the program director, you must be sure that your staff has access to information, equipment, and support. Every child needs to participate in all activities as fully as possible and this comes from establishing procedures to ensure children's safety and to help provide them with successful experiences. In addition, specific training or continuing education will need to be provided to you and your staff to help them become familiar and comfortable with certain disabilities (**Figure 7.12**). This results in sensitive staff who are well-trained and eager to welcome all children by providing a positive experience in a group-care environment.

First Visits Leave Lasting Impressions

There are many ways to leave a lasting impression. The first place to start is to have numerous signs of welcome to the program space while balancing a look and feel that maintains program safety and security of the children in their care (**Figure 7.13**). One of the easiest ways to minimize confusion is to have simple, clear directional signs, to help parents know where to go and

andreswd/E+/Getty Images
Figure 7.12 Staff must have access to regular continuing education opportunities in order to ensure children's safety and happiness.

Kristen Alexandria
Figure 7.13 Programs should offer a welcoming space that also provides a feeling of safety and security.

how to gain entrance through established security. As we have all experienced, entering a strange building with no directory can be overwhelming. Standing in the middle of a hallway, helplessly looking around and not understanding how to gain access, is not a positive experience. Signage and arrows with posted instructions on how to contact the program for entrance throughout the building assist with finding the correct areas upon gaining entry into the building. For programs in a neighborhood area, make sure that the physical address can be found in the latest navigational apps that many people utilize as well as provide electronic instructions that can be easily transmitted either by email or text to an enrolled parent.

Provide bright bulletin boards placed by the entrance of the programs to serve as a warm greeting. This includes information about program leadership and staff members. In addition, train staff to make friendly impressions by using appropriate eye contact, positive tones of voice, and smiling. It is important that the environment have a cheerful hum of busy activity, children's songs playing, smells of cookies baking, and children's art displayed. This assures parents that their choice of early childhood program is a happy place for their child to be.

Considerations When Registering and Enrolling Children

Directors must determine the appropriate group placement for new child enrollments. As we discussed in the budgeting chapter, children are often placed in groups based on their ages. In most cases the director must consider several classrooms of the same age group and identify the group where the child and parent will feel most comfortable.

As families exit your program, it is important to establish a process to track the reasons families left the program. This provides valuable information and can make changes to the program based on the feedback. An example would be if a family withdrew because of inconvenient center hours or a concern about their child's experience. Gathering information from your customers, parents and children, give insights that allow for ongoing development of resources to assist the families attending the early childhood program.

7.3 Helping Parents Help Their Children

Sometimes, parents don't know how to help their children get started in the center. Some parents might tell their children, "If you're not good, the teacher won't like you!", or "Just be quiet and don't cause any trouble." These kinds of comments frighten children. Rather than help, they make the child's adjustment to the center more difficult.

Center staff can help by preparing a list of suggestions that will help parents know what to say and do to help their children. They can encourage parents to understand that this new transition can be stressful for the child. Modeling appropriate behavior and words can go a long way to help the parent and the child. They can assure

Ridofranz/iStock/Getty Images Plus

Figure 7.14 Often, parents have mixed feelings about having their child attend an early childhood program due to a sense of loss or guilt over leaving their child with someone else.

parents that the staff will have concern and compassion for their child.

Teachers can also help parents understand their own feelings about child care. Most parents have mixed feelings about leaving their child at a child care center (**Figure 7.14**). There is relief at having a few hours without the responsibility of caring for the child. However, there is also a sense of loss and guilt over leaving the child with someone else. For some parents, this can be quite overwhelming. A caring teacher can help to reassure the parent that these feelings are normal. Staff are also important in helping the parents see clearly that their children are being cared for well. If the parent is comfortable with the situation, the child's adjustment to the center may be easier.

Most children experience **separation anxiety**, or fears about being away from their parents or caregivers. A sensitive, well-trained teacher can help children handle this new situation. Families approach the start of child care with mixed feelings. There is relief that a good child care program has been found. However, there is also the realization that their child is taking a significant step away from the family and into the larger world. Most parents view a good preschool setting as a positive experience for children. Yet, parents often feel guilty about leaving their child in the care of others.

The family may also be experiencing other major changes. Child care is often needed because a parent is starting a new job or job training. This also can be a cause of stress and worry for the parent. Following a divorce, the single parent may seek child care. The child will already be facing dramatic changes in his or her family structure. The staff of your program should be prepared to accept the concerns of parents and children. Sensitive help and understanding can ease the separation anxiety that both

Director Showcase

Taisha

As her program enrollment began to grow, Taisha realized that children were entering her program often within a day or two of their enrollment. While some children and their parents seemed to do well with a quick transition, others did not. One of her staff members asked if they could potentially talk with her about this issue to address the needs of children who were having difficulty.

Meredith

Because her program was larger and the wait time for enrollment was longer, Meredith realized that she needed to keep communications active with the family. She also noticed that she and her office staff were spending a great deal of time talking with parents and answering the same questions. She realized this was not a good use of their time and decided to implement strategies that provided necessary information but did not take up so much of her and her staff's time.

parents and children may experience. Smooth entrance of children into the program helps to build a program's reputation. Parents talk to other parents. When a family feels good about the child care decision they have made, they will tell others. When a teacher compassionately helps children adjust, the parents become supporters of the center.

Develop procedures that support and enhance children's adjustment to child care. Compassionate entrance procedures into the program can result in happier, more comfortable children. It can be the best advertisement for your program. These entrance procedures should include parent orientation, a home visit (if possible), a gradual entrance for the child into the classroom, and ongoing reassurance and communication between staff and parents.

Parent Orientation

New families should be reassured that they have made a wise decision in choosing your program. They need to know that the program has a well-trained staff. They should feel that their children will be nurtured and kept safe. This may be done through an individual home visit, group meeting, or virtually.

Home Visits

It is often a good idea for teachers to visit with parents and children in their own home. These are referred to as **home visits**. This allows the family to get to know the teacher within a familiar environment. Meeting the teacher in the center can be intimidating to parents and children. For parents, meeting the teacher as a visitor to their home may be more comfortable. Parents can be given needed information about the classroom and center operation as well as see that the teacher is a kind and caring individual.

The child is aware that the teacher and parents are getting to know each other. Children also like to show teachers their room, pets, special toys, or a favorite play area. When entering the classroom, the child will see the teacher as a familiar face and a friend. Children are likely to feel more secure because they have already met the teacher.

For the teacher, home visits can give greater insight into the child's home and family life. The teacher can help the child by mentioning information related to the home visit, such as "How is your bunny today?" or "I liked the pretty blue color of your room." The teacher can also be more aware of the lifestyle and concerns that parents may have.

Home visits are a valuable way to get to know parents and children (**Figure 7.15**). They can also be costly in

Abdullah Durmaz/E+/Getty Images

Figure 7.15 Home visits allow staff members to meet children, their families, and answer any questions that parents have.

staff time. If there is any concern about the safety of a staff member during a home visit, it is essential that at least two staff members make the visit together. It may also not be feasible to make a home visit because of time, safety, travel distance, extended bad weather, or parent unwillingness.

Group Meetings

If several families enroll at the center at the same time, a group meeting may be appropriate. This **orientation meeting** gives new parents in the program a chance to learn more about the center. They also have a chance to meet other new parents and to get to know the staff. Orientation meetings are usually held in the fall, but they may be held anytime a new group of children have started at the center. You may plan only one meeting, or several as the year progresses. Orientation meetings often form the beginning of a series of parent education programs.

Any orientation meeting needs to focus on helping parents feel comfortable with the center, the staff, and each other. Refreshments are important in setting a relaxed tone. Name tags help people get to know each other. Slides of center activities, or a brief video showing quality child care, can also be useful in holding parents' interest. If information must be presented in lecture form, keep it brief. Use handouts or posters to emphasize your points. It is important that this first meeting be relaxed, fun, and interesting. If it is not, parents will be reluctant to return to other meetings.

The parent orientation meeting serves several purposes. It should

- introduce parents to their child's teacher and classroom;
- help parents understand the program philosophy;
- give parents the daily schedule and examples of typical activities;
- explain basic procedures and policies regarding attendance and health;

Kristen Alexandria

Figure 7.16 Providing reading materials on child development and other topics can help parents understand their child better.

- describe fee and payment policies;
- identify additional services that may be available through your program;
- help parents understand changes they may see in their child's behavior;
- give parents information on how to help their child cope with separation anxiety; and
- reassure parents and answer questions they may have.

Programs can do other things to support parents. Some centers have developed a parent handbook that answers many questions. A lending library of books on child development and parenting can be helpful (**Figure 7.16**). Other centers plan ongoing meetings for parents. Help in arranging carpools or finding additional needed services can create the sense that the center is a place for parents as well as children.

Director's Showcase

Reflect

There are so many things to consider when enrolling and welcoming families into your program. What would be your top ten list of considerations as you developed your plan?

7.4 Helping Children and Families Adjust

There is more to enrolling children than just getting parents to "sign on the dotted line." You must also develop procedures for helping children enter and adjust to the center. For some children this will be an easy process. For others, it will be more difficult.

Director Showcase

Taisha

As Taisha and staff members continued to refine the transition plan for new families, it became apparent that many of the children who were struggling were children who had parents that were experiencing breakups and other family issues. While they were committed to work with these families, they also realized how quickly they could get caught up in custody issues. Gaining more information was important as they established relationships with the family.

Meredith

One of the strategies that Meredith was able to convince the program owners to buy was the use of a software program that provided ongoing communication to parents. After shopping around, she was able to purchase a software system that provided an app for parents to download on their phones. Through this app, newly enrolled families were receiving ongoing communication from the child's teacher and talk with the child about what had taken place during the child's day. Many parents commented on how this helped them to better understand what their child was doing throughout the program day.

Child development experts recommend a gradual entrance into the center program. Children need a chance to visit the classroom with parents before being expected to stay (**Figure 7.17**). During this short visit, they can look around and meet the teacher. They can discover the locations of toys, bathrooms, and cubbies. Children should be reassured that the staff of the center is kind and caring. They should also see that parents and staff respect each other.

Whenever possible, plan another short visit or keep the first day of attendance brief. Allow the child to bring a security object such as a stuffed toy, pillow, or blanket to help with the transition from home to center. Be sure your staff is trained to provide sensitive support for each new child. Even though your center is a wonderful place, new children and their parents may feel some separation anxiety.

Children's feelings of nervousness, fear, loneliness and even sadness must be respected. It is unrealistic to think that new children will walk right in the first day without a twinge of concern. Children deserve to be treated as you would want to be treated in a new situation. Gentle support and encouragement provided by well-trained staff can help children adjust to the center.

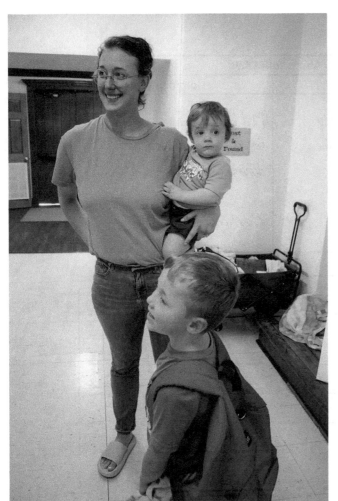

Kristen Alexandria

Figure 7.17 Scheduling a tour to meet the teacher and visit the classroom helps the parent and children transition to a new early childhood program environment.

Happy, well-adjusted children are your best advertisement. When children like the center, parents tell other parents. They are also likely to keep their child in your program for as long as the child needs care. A poor center is often like a revolving door. Children may be enrolled and withdrawn from the program quickly as parents discover the program is not what they want.

Parent Reassurances and Communication

Part of helping parents feel comfortable with your center is maintaining communication with them. When parents feel at ease in talking with the center staff, important information can more easily be passed back and forth.

Parents must be kept informed about how their children are doing. Parents who feel guilty or anxious about leaving their children need to know that the teachers understand their concern. Normalizing these feelings can go far in

building relationships with parents. When the staff can share interesting parts of a child's day, the parent knows that the child has been carefully supervised. Parents may also often feel that they are missing significant milestones in a child's development. Communication between staff and parents can help minimize some of that feeling of loss (**Figure 7.18**).

Communication works positively in both directions. Staff shares information with parents. Parents share information with staff. Much of what happens at home affects children's behavior in the center. Ideally, parents will inform the staff when something significant has occurred in their children's lives. Likewise, staff should share significant classroom events with parents.

Supporting Children and Families with Difficult Circumstances

In cases of divorce or separation, noncustodial parents may feel uninvolved with the center. Even though they may be actively involved at other times with their children, they are usually not included on the center's mailing list, or they may not see invitations, notices, or newsletters sent home with the children. Many centers ask the custodial parent for permission to include the noncustodial parent and grandparents in center communications and activities. Of course, this decision is made by the custodial parent and must be respected. When approved, however, it gives the noncustodial parent a better understanding of the child's daily life in child care.

Children who are receiving care from a foster parent also have difficulty with transition into child care. Due to the many transitions they have experienced and a lack of consistency with where they might be staying or who is caring for them, acting out is a strong possibility. Some foster care children do the opposite and will not participate and verbal communication with them is difficult. It will be important that the program director obtains as much information as possible regarding what the foster parent knows about the child. This includes acquiring the name of the child's case and/or social worker. These individuals often check on the children while in your care and, due to litigation, may want a statement about the children's welfare in your care. Recognizing that these children come with these extra expectations allows for the program leader and staff members to embrace these families with open arms.

Communication Options

Communication between parents and staff is particularly important when the children are young. Information is needed on naps, bowel movements, formula or food

Good Things to Know About Your Child			
Setting	**Date/Time**	**Event**	**Comments**
Play area	9/25 11:15 a.m.	Kasey pulled herself into a standing position in the play gym.	First time we have seen this at the center. Has she done this at home? Way to go, Kasey!

How the Day Went
Child:
Feeding: _____
Sleeping: _____
Toileting: _____
Self-care: _____
Caregiver/Date: _____

Goodheart-Willcox Publisher

Figure 7.18 Many programs utilize daily written forms to communicate child activity with parents.

intake, and general mood. Young children cannot use words to describe how they feel. Caregivers and parents often have to be detectives to determine whether a child is ill or simply tired. Many centers develop a simple form for communication with parents. Teachers then simply check off information that parents need to know on a daily basis. Handwritten daily sheets give the parent information typically at the end of the day. However, the use of parent communication apps have become quite popular. These features provide immediate communication, and many are a part of the complex software

systems discussed in the budget and finance chapter. Communication through technology is many times an expectation of today's parent (**Figure 7.19**). Utilization of this feature is a wise investment.

You should also consider other forms of communication with parents. When you have a variety of contacts with parents, each can find what is most useful. Many families like to receive the following:

- newsletters and parent handbook;
- monthly menus;
- a schedule of classroom activities;

Kristen Alexandria

Figure 7.19 The use of technology to communicate is often the expectation of parents.

- a notice of special events for children and families;
- information on center open houses; and
- invitations to parent-teacher conferences.

Again, many of the complex software systems provide all of these features. Once they are activated within the system, information can flow quickly and efficiently to keep parents and caregivers informed. When planning events, make sure to meet the needs of all of the family types within your program. Whether it is a single parent, grandparent, family member, foster parent, or lesbian or gay family, all family units should be respected. Respect and consideration can be shown through the center's efforts to make them feel welcome and transition a child to program care. Everything you do to help parents, or those serving in that role, feel comfortable with your program will build their commitment to your center. It is key for program leadership and staff to compassionately help a child and parent adjust to child care so that the program gains a satisfied family.

Chapter 7 Review and Assessment

Summary

7.1 Examine the differences between public relations and marketing.

- Marketing allows your program to successfully know that it exists using several outlets and strategies shared. You must determine ways to advertise your program to the families who are most likely to enroll. From a public relations standpoint, you must always be concerned about the long-term reputation of your program within the community. Public relations engages the program director with the community by creating and sustaining public awareness that is both positive and collaborative.

7.2 Discover strategies when welcoming parents and children to the early childhood program.

- Registration and enrollment procedures should be developed that support the smooth entrance of children into the center. These procedures must be clear and easy to explain. They must also take into account the priorities of funding sources and group limitations imposed by licensing.
- The size, age range, hours of needed care, and number of adult staff needed can all vary. These factors also can determine how expensive a group is to operate. Decisions regarding placement of children in groups are important. They can affect the ease with which a child adjusts to the center. They can also affect the cost of operating the classroom.

7.3 Investigate best practices as children and families transition to the early childhood program environment.

- Establishing communication and extending considerations to newly enrolling families allows for a smooth transition to the early childhood program. This is often when parents are at a heightened state of concern regarding their child's ability to adjust to new caretakers. This includes parents of children with special care needs. Multiple communication avenues must be available to assist with this process. This includes face-to-face and electronic options that are all available to the early childhood program leader and staff members.

7.4 Establish procedures that will assist teachers and parents as children adjust to the early childhood program environment.

- Strategies assisting both children and adults to adapt to child care should be carefully considered. Sensitive handling of separation anxiety can help ease adjustment. Ongoing communication with parents and a gradual entrance for children are essential components of a good beginning. Helping families adjust positively to child care helps build their long-term commitment to your program.

Review

1. Explain what public relations is and why it is important to an early childhood program. (7.1)
2. Explain what marketing is and why it is important to an early childhood program. (7.1)
3. List four types of advertising that could be used to let people know about your program. (7.2)
4. What are the benefits of using social media and what legality considerations must be made when using them? (7.2)
5. Describe some ways early childhood leaders of either a center or home program could expand their influence in the community. (7.2)
6. What considerations would a center-based program need to make to welcome visitors and potential clients? (7.3)
7. What considerations would a home-based program need to make to welcome visitors and potential clients? (7.3)
8. Care for special needs children or those coming from difficult circumstances have extra considerations that a program leader and staff members must prepare for. What are some examples of those considerations? (7.3)
9. Give an example of a gradual beginning for a child entering the center as a new enrollee. (7.4)
10. Name four types of communication that can be used with parents. (7.4)

Showcase Your Skills

1. Design an advertising flyer to interest potential students in this class. Briefly identify the goals of the course. Include a description of the class and the main areas that you study. Include all the necessary information an individual would need to know to enroll in this class. (7.1)

2. Plan and staff an informational booth with your classmates at your local county fair, shopping mall, or other locations where young families might be. Prepare posters, banners, etc., that will attract young families to your booth. Obtain brochures and articles from professional organizations, or prepare your own, that describe what to look for in quality child care. Also prepare or obtain printed materials on how to help children adjust to child care. Distribute these to interested families. Be ready to explain the information and its importance to anyone who might stop to collect materials on these topics. (7.1)

3. Obtain permission to attend a parent orientation meeting at a program for children. Observe the process of the meeting. Write your reactions to the following questions after the meeting. Discuss your reactions with your class. Were any special measures taken to help parents feel welcome and at ease at the meeting? What topics were discussed? Were parents helped to get to know each other? Was the meeting a pleasant experience for the parents? If you were a parent, would you want to go to another meeting? (7.3)

Matching

Match the following terms with the correct definitions:

A. home visits
B. marketing
C. orientation meeting
D. public relations
E. separation anxiety
F. social media savvy

1. Promotion of your business, including many potential activities that create awareness.
2. Activities that create an awareness of and a positive attitude toward a business.
3. User who is familiar with websites and applications that share content or provide social networking.
4. Fears about being away from parents or caregivers.
5. Meeting that gives new parents in a program a chance to learn more about the center.
6. Occurs when teachers visit parents and children in their own homes before the children start in a program.

Administering a Quality Child Care Program

Chapter 8   Educational Programming

Chapter 9   Maintaining a Safe and Healthy Program

Chapter 10   Engaging and Supporting Families

Chapter 11   The Complex Role of Leading Others

Chapter 12   Supervising and Supporting Program Staff

Chapter 13   Managing People and Setting Expectations

Chapter 14   Supports for Director Success

Chapter 15   Program Evaluation to Support Quality Improvement

8 CHAPTER

Educational Programming

Learning Outcomes

After studying this chapter, you will be able to:

8.1 Review programming strategies supporting the implementation of developmentally appropriate curriculum.

8.2 Examine the role of play as learning for infants and toddlers and preschool- and school-age children.

8.3 Discuss decisions necessary when planning a daily schedule for varying ages of children served in an early childhood program environment.

8.4 Distinguish between the different types of guidance strategies for infants and toddlers, preschoolers, and school-age children that contribute to each child's emotional support and well-being.

Key Terms

associate play
attachment theory
atypical development
behaviorist theory
cognitive development
cognitive theory
cooperative play
emotional development
family style
free play
group time
pedagogical lens
physical development
play
positive guidance
psychosocial development
psychosexual development
relationship-focused program environment
social development
social learning theory
sociocultural theory
supervision
theoretical perspectives
typical development

NAEYC/DAP standards

Standards covered in this chapter:

1a, 1b, 1c, 1d, 4a, 4b

1C, 1D, 4D, 4E, 4G, 5D

Kristen Alexandria

Figure 8.1 Early childhood leaders support teaching staff to provide enriched learning environments.

Introduction

In educational programming, early childhood leaders must be aware of two NAEYC Program Standards in particular that support staff with appropriate implementation of appropriate practices in the classroom. Standard 1, *Relationships,* emphasizes the importance of establishing warm, responsive relationships between teachers and children and creating a predictable, consistent, and harmonious classroom while also addressing challenging behaviors (NAEYC, 2021). Program leaders provide oversight and guidance to support the interactions taking place in the classroom between teaching staff and children. In implementing Standard 3, *Teaching,* an early childhood leader must support teaching staff so that they are designing enriched learning environments (**Figure 8.1**) and creating caring communities for learning (NAEYC, 2021). Further, program leaders should encourage teaching staff to supervise children appropriately and respond to children's interests and needs while making learning meaningful through play. The program leader is the person who supports staff as they provide quality educational programming for the young children in their care.

As previously discussed, a program's philosophy and mission are the cornerstones used to determine the curriculum and its implementation. Using the **pedagogical lens**, which means understanding best practices for teaching and setting up classroom environments, directors uphold the importance of using developmentally appropriate practices when implementing educational programming. This includes having play as the foundation for learning by all ages of children that attend the program. Early education experts have long recognized that play is how children learn in the early years. Each age during a child's development provides wonderful opportunities for play.

Guidelines help teachers match the classroom environment, schedule, and activities to the children's readiness and needs. These guidelines inform teachers in identifying objectives or goals for what they want the children to gain from their experiences. Teachers think about planning activities that assist children in reaching these objectives. By focusing on children's needs, likes, and abilities, teachers design an environment to meet these needs and provide support for children in accomplishing the developmental tasks of early childhood. Using this approach, based on developmental appropriateness, teachers avoid activities that are too easy and boring for the children. This also helps prevent a teacher from planning activities that are too challenging and frustrating.

Finally, the program leader provides support to teachers when children are demonstrating behaviors that are inappropriate. This includes observing the teacher's supervision of children, providing consultation when teachers are frustrated with a child's behaviors, and encouraging and interceding when necessary. It is through the leader's guidance that the teaching staff better understands age-related characteristics and can identify the best ways to guide and support children.

8.1 Program Strategies Supporting Developmentally Appropriate Curriculum

NAEYC's 10 Program Standards achieved a collective understanding among early childhood professionals regarding appropriate expectations when caring for children and their families. Numerous theories have

Director Showcase

Davey

Davey provides in-home child care and has three new infants and a toddler enrolled in her program. Davey has been working in child care for five years, and this is her second year running her own in-home program. With the addition of the new children, she is now at capacity for her program. She will hold a meeting for the children's parents and caregivers soon to address her philosophy on play, expectations of children and families, and daily schedules.

Roxie

Roxie is new to her role as a child care director. In the past, she served as a toddler teacher and loved having her own classroom in the large child care program where she recently started working. She has noticed that her replacement, Lonna, is struggling with program planning for the toddlers. Roxie realized that she would need to meet with her to provide guidance in program planning and learning objectives. After they met together, Lonna seemed happy with her classroom arrangement and was working on getting a daily routine and schedule set up to coordinate with the other classroom teachers. The two also discussed an implementation strategy and decided to include observation times, by Roxie, to continue discussing the impact of the changes made.

contributed to the overall understanding of children's development. The field of child development emerged in the early 20th century. The effort initially began by looking at **atypical development**, or abnormal behaviors. Then, researchers realized a need to understand **typical development**, or normal behaviors. Research began to focus on a child's overall development in four domains and has been studied based on designated time frames, or stages, as a child grows from infancy to childhood.

- **Cognitive development** refers to a child's brain growth and overall functioning.
- **Social development** is a child's interactions with significant adults in their lives, peers, and the community in which they live.
- **Emotional development** is how a child learns to recognize their own feelings while also interacting with significant adults and peers.
- **Physical development** refers to the coordination of small and large muscles to support the child's movement and coordination abilities within the environment.

Each one of these areas are supported by many different **theoretical perspectives**. These are ideas that have come from a structural framework, explanation, or tool that has been tested and evaluated. This multitude of perspectives, developed over decades of time, provides greater insight into children's growth and development. In addition, varying theories provide different and sometimes conflicting recommendations when understanding young children. As in any field related to human development, this continues to provide a healthy debate in regards to children's overall development.

Reviewing the Theory

As part of an early childhood leadership role, it is important to be aware of some of the major child development theories. The following is a brief overview of the major theorists and their contributions to the foundation of child development.

- **Psychosexual development.** This theory of development was pioneered by Sigmund Freud, who believed that children's development occurs in a series of stages based on pleasure areas of the body. Freud believed that these stages created conflict within the child and how this was resolved for the child influenced overall adult behavior.
- **Psychosocial development.** Expanding on the work of Freud, Erik Erikson identified developmental stages throughout the life span and believed that social interactions and experiences created points of conflict during identified stages in a child's life that contributed to the child's overall social-emotional development (**Figure 8.2**).

Erikson's Psychosocial Developmental Stages		
Stage/Age	Task	Description
Infancy (Birth to 1 year)	Trust versus mistrust	Babies learn about trust from their caregivers who meet their needs, including food, attention, physical contact, interaction, and safety. When needs are not met, they perceive the world as an unpredictable place.
Toddler (1 to 3 years)	Autonomy versus shame and doubt	Toddlers learn self-help skills, such as feeding, toileting, dressing, and undressing and, as a result, increase confidence. Toddlers who lack control or independence may experience shame and doubt. Some caregivers punish toddlers for not doing things "right" while they are still learning new skills. This can undermine confidence.
Early childhood (3 to 6 years)	Initiative versus guilt	Through discovery and exploration, young children learn about the world and their place in it. They learn what is real and what is imaginary. They learn to take initiative to claim their place in the world. Too much criticism and punishment can result in feelings of guilt and shame.
Middle childhood (6 to 12 years)	Industry versus inferiority	Children develop competency both at school and at home. They develop a sense of self and confidence from becoming competent in the outside world. If they or others consistently compare them negatively against others, feelings of inferiority can surface.
Adolescence (13 to 18 years or older)	Identity versus role confusion	Preteens and teens begin to understand and experiment with a number of different roles. A task during this stage is to integrate multiple roles such as sister, daughter, student, athlete, friend, and employee. If a central, or core, identity is not established, role confusion exists.
Young adulthood (18 to 40 years or older)	Intimacy versus isolation	During later adolescence and early adulthood, close relationships form. These relationships should involve sharing oneself emotionally. Success in this stage depends on success in earlier stages. Failure to establish intimacy results in emotional or psychological isolation.
Middle adulthood (40 to 65 years)	Generativity versus self-absorption	Adults in middle adulthood begin to place emphasis on assisting others and improving the next generation. This can be done in many ways, including parenting, teaching or training others, or passing on cultural values. Failure to do so leads to self-absorption.
Older adulthood (65 years and older)	Integrity versus despair	In the last stage of life, adults review their life and reflect on its meaning. If people are satisfied with their life, there is a sense of integrity. Without it, despair may emerge as the end of life approaches.

Goodheart-Willcox Publisher

Figure 8.2 Erikson's stages of psychosocial development from childhood to adulthood.

Piaget's Stages of Cognitive Development

Stage	Age	Description
Sensorimotor	Birth to 2 years	Babies begin to learn about the world through their senses. At first, learning relies on reflexes but more purposeful movement later enhances learning.
Preoperational	2 to 7 years	Toddlers and young children communicate through language. They recognize symbols and learn concepts. Both hands-on experiences and imaginative play are keys to learning.
Concrete operational	7 to 11 years	Children in this stage learn to think logically. They can make generalizations, understand cause and effect, group and classify items, and suggest solutions to problems.
Formal operational	11 years and older	Children master both logical and abstract thinking during this stage. This includes making predictions and considering "what if" questions.

Goodheart-Willcox Publisher

Figure 8.3   Piaget's stages of cognitive development reflect the growing abilities of children's thinking.

- **Behaviorist theory**. In this theory, John Watson and B.F. Skinner believed that children's development was based on either positively or negatively reinforced behaviors that a child displays and an adult controls. Simply put, the theory promoted rewards for good behaviors and punishments for undesired behaviors.
- **Cognitive theory**. Jean Piaget and Lev Vygotsky proposed in their theory of development a set of stages with the assistance of an adult that contributed to a child's overall intellectual growth. While both were able to differentiate children's thinking from adults by identifying age ranges in which certain elements of cognitive development were taking place, they also recognized that the adult's interactions assisted with cognitive functioning due to a child's social and cultural upbringing (**Figure 8.3**).
- **Attachment theory**. John Bowlby believed, from a social perspective, children are born with an internal need to form attachments with the significant adults in their lives. If these attachments are secure, children will thrive. If they are less secure, the development of the child can be significantly impacted.
- **Social learning theory**. In this theory, Albert Bandura felt that social engagement with others was key to development. Children's environmental interactions, parents and peers included, help children develop new skills and acquire new information to further develop their skillsets. One additional theorist, Urie Bronfennbrenner, expanded this theoretical lens by identifying ecological systems that include the immediate individuals in a child's life, neighbors, teachers,

peers, community, societal functioning, and even major events. His view was that the environment was a significant contributor to the child's overall development.

- **Sociocultural theory**. Lev Vygotsky, mentioned earlier, expanded his theory by agreeing that learning comes from interacting with supportive adults with two additional areas of emphasis (**Figure 8.4**). The first area was actively learning through supported hands-on experiences, and the second area was the child's cultural interactions with parents, caregivers, and peers.

While these varying theories are studied, merged in some instances, and highly debated, looking at aspects of each shows the importance of implementing developmentally appropriate curriculum. Leadership and teaching staff sharing an understanding of child development

Kristen Alexandria

Figure 8.4   Vygotsky believed that children learned by interacting with supportive adults who provided hands-on experiences and positive interactions.

theory strengthens the mission and goals of the program. They are able to align regarding important aspects of classroom programming, such as

- the value of serving diverse groups of children;
- the role of the teacher in the classroom;
- the choice of equipment and activities;
- the daily schedule;
- the expected behaviors of the children; and
- the interactions between staff and children.

The director and staff must have a collective understanding of children's development for a program to operate smoothly. Adults who are familiar and practice aspects of these theories find it impossible to work in a program where there is conflict surrounding differing opinions and beliefs. A collective approach provides a shared satisfaction in working with children and an overall comfort level when implementing developmentally appropriate practices.

Developmentally Appropriate Practices

Developmentally appropriate practices (DAP) utilize methods that promote optimal development and learning through a strengths- and play-based approach to engage learning (NAEYC, 2020). While constantly evolving, DAP views children as unique individuals who engage in designed learning environments across all domains of learning—physical, cognitive, social, and emotional—to include practices that are culturally, linguistically, and ability appropriate for each child (**Figure 8.5**).

Planning developmentally appropriate activities for young children requires that a teacher ...
• knows age characteristics of the children in the group;
• knows the types of equipment and activities preferred by the age group;
• knows how to prepare the classroom and activities for optimum use;
• knows how to plan concrete, "hands-on" experiences;
• understands the progression of development, so activities can be matched to children's developmental readiness;
• knows each child's unique characteristics;
• knows where to go to get new ideas;
• understands how to create a positive, supportive learning environment; and
• is sensitive to the social and cultural context in which each child lives.

Goodheart-Willcox Publisher

Figure 8.5 Teachers must consider many different aspects when planning developmentally appropriate activities for young children.

A program that has a quality daily program of developmentally appropriate activities requires careful planning. It does not just happen. There must be a match between what the children are ready for and the activities available to them. Teachers need to plan the room arrangement, select appropriate equipment, plan the daily schedule, and include special and group activities. A quality program will fascinate and challenge young children. It will not bore or frustrate them. When children are involved in quality program practices, they look forward to daily programming and feel successful and good about themselves.

What Needs Must Be Met Through Daily Program Planning?

Since the early childhood leader is responsible for all staff, this includes making sure that they are participating in quality, ongoing professional development, and are aware of the age-related characteristics and needs of their classroom group. Teaching staff must understand that it is through their careful observation and conversation with parents that they develop a knowledge of each child's individual needs. Directors must also support teachers in understanding the patterns of growth in the physical, social, emotional, cognitive, and language areas of a child's development. This includes being sensitive to the social and cultural context in which children live.

Directors should have set expectations for supervision and be aware of the teacher's plans for daily programming. **Supervision** is oversight by teaching staff that includes monitoring the environment and activity to keep all children safe throughout the day. Upon review of lesson plans, directors should clearly understand listed activities that will support the development of the children in each of these areas. For example, an obstacle course might be set up to help children develop better large muscle coordination. Buttoning a doll's dress aids small muscle coordination. Playing with dolls while involved in socio-dramatic play contributes to the children's social skills and helps children explore new ideas and relate play to real-life experiences. Planning for all areas of development is not difficult when the room is well equipped for the class age group and when the teacher understands the needs of the children. However, it does take deliberate care and effort to ensure that all areas of development are included.

Quality programs for children require careful planning and administrative oversight. This includes a well-thought-out daily plan that has appropriate daily programming. It should provide a social context in which children feel comfortable and secure. The time given for each activity

Kristen Alexandria

Figure 8.6   Daily programming should include activities that allow children to engage and create without being hurried.

should allow children to begin the activity, engage in it, and complete it without hurry or interruptions. It should also include the following scheduling elements:

- free play (**Figure 8.6**);
- group times;
- music and movement;
- snack and meal times;
- nap time;
- outdoor time; and
- diapering or restroom time.

Each one of these elements should be available to all ages of children and adapted to the age of children in the classroom. It must be flexible and serve as the consistent framework of the activity each day. Within these periods is when additional planning takes place. Well-trained teachers understand the importance of the daily program by providing a successful and satisfying experience for each child in the classroom. Let us explore more to include some suggested developmentally appropriate activities.

Free Play

Directors should support play as it is the heart of the day, but is also frequently the most misunderstood. Referred to as **free play**, this is where teachers plan opportunities for children to enhance their creativity, use their imagination, problem-solve age-appropriate tasks, and use their social skills with peers. Young children are bombarded with sights, sounds, and experiences all the time. Play activities, particularly dramatic or pretend play, give children the opportunity to make sense out of all their varied experiences. This time allows children to make choices about the things they want to do. It is a time when they can work on those things that have meaning to them.

Children can master new skills and integrate new information with previously known ideas through play. Those who are tense or experiencing stress can choose soothing activities. Others who have had an emotionally upsetting experience may choose to use the dramatic play props to recreate the experience in a safe, controllable setting. Generous time to play allows for child-initiated activity where children have the opportunity to decide what they want to do and to control the amount of time they spend with it. Child-driven playtime promotes initiative, autonomy, responsibility, and self-direction.

Group Time

Whether an administrator is responsible for a small or large early childhood program, they must ensure that all children have the opportunity to learn what it is like to be a part of a group. Most classrooms have several times during the day when the children come together for large or small group activities. The very nature of group activities tends to make them "teacher-directed" times. Teachers must be encouraged by their administrator to be mindful that group times do not stretch longer than their children's attention can handle. Smaller groups are usually easier for toddlers and two-year-olds. Typically, preschool-age children have learned the basics of how to be members of a group. If the activities are lively, children may be able to stick with them longer. If there is little waiting time for a turn, there will be less frustration. When teachers carefully plan group activities to be developmentally appropriate, children will find them more interesting.

One of the most wonderful benefits of **group time**, or spending time together as a class, is allowing children to enjoy listening to books. Many outstanding children's books are multicultural, depict a wide variety of family structures, and focus on special topics such as understanding feelings. Books help children understand themselves and others better. They can aid children in making sense out of the complex adult world. They can also provide sheer pleasure. Many classrooms have several different story times throughout the day. Full-day programs may have a story time in both the morning and afternoon. Books should also be available for informal reading times during free play or quiet times as well (**Figure 8.7**). Some teachers have story time for their entire group. Other teachers have found that breaking into two or three smaller story groups is more successful. With the smaller group format, teachers can choose stories with the interests and abilities of that particular group in mind.

The amount of time devoted to story time will vary. Older children like more complicated stories and can

Kristen Alexandria

Figure 8.7   Books help children understand themselves and others better, which is why they must be available for free play and quiet times.

sit and listen for longer periods. Younger children, whose books are mostly pictures, will enjoy the experience more if it is kept shorter. All young children are beginners at the skills of listening to stories and enjoying books. A story time that is too long or a book that is too complicated will frustrate and bore them. This can lead children to avoid stories later on. In general, early childhood leaders should be aware that any group time should not be longer than 10 to 15 minutes and based on the age and abilities of the class. For example, children who are three years old should start with 3 to 5 minutes at a time. The only way to determine what is right for a group is to try out the schedule and see how it works (**Figure 8.8**).

Group times should be scheduled so that children feel successful when participating. If the times are too long, children will act up, and the teacher will feel frustrated. When children are engaged in the group time activities and feel good about them, they will want to come back for more.

These will influence the appropriate length for a group time list
• ages of the children in the group
• nature of the group activities
• temperament and attention span of the children
• other elements of the schedule around the group time
• the teacher's skill in keeping children actively participating

Goodheart-Willcox Publisher

Figure 8.8   Several considerations are necessary as teachers plan developmentally appropriate group times for the young children in their care.

Music and Movement

Music with movement can also be planned for an entire group of children. As with story time, many teachers prefer to break the large group into several smaller groups. This makes the activities less intimidating for cautious children. Music helps children become familiar with another aspect of the world by singing, experimenting with rhythm and beat (**Figure 8.9**), and moving to music (Andress, 1998). Music provides another form of communication. It can convey feelings and emotion that are difficult to express in words. Music can be relaxing for a tense child and can stimulate the interest of a bored child. Using music to soothe children who are ready for a nap is also a helpful technique. Through music, children learn songs of their culture as well as basic elements of tone and rhythm.

With the uptick in childhood obesity and the increase in children's time spent outside of the classroom taken up by screen time, many national efforts are working to get young children moving. Local health departments and library systems often work in conjunction to encourage movement by young children. Whether children are acting out a story or listening to music where children can follow directions, teachers should be incorporating music and movement activities throughout the day. For example, singing a song while pushing a child on the swings can be a delight for teacher and child alike. Movement activities help children become more confident with their bodies. They learn how their bodies move and what they can do. Confidence and coordination can improve through lively opportunities for movement. Movement activities done outside can provide greater freedom for the children to investigate how their bodies move.

Kristen Alexandria

Figure 8.9   Access to musical instruments allows children to experiment with rhythm and beat.

Snack and Meal Times

Snacks and meal times are an essential part of the day. A busy schedule at the center will expend a lot of the children's energy. When children are hungry, they are more likely to become irritable and difficult. One of the more popular ways of handling snack and meal times is referred to as **family style**. This style is used during times when there are no mandated precautions due to a local, state, or national health crisis as it encourages children and teachers to sit together at tables. Serving takes place from child-size platters and a fashion that is age-appropriate. While two-year-olds might have their first portion pre-plated and then an opportunity to practice spooning out a second portion of fruit mix, children three and up typically serve themselves out of bowls with serving spoons and use small pitchers to pour their own milk. Children of all ages should be allowed to talk together, sharing thoughts and experiences as they eat. This opportunity deepens relationships and friendships while also allowing children to be together in a relaxed setting.

Another benefit of family-style meals is the use of language, math, and social skills. Being together at meal times allows multiple opportunities to not only engage in conversations but to also share about the activities in the classroom that day. Eating together enhances social skills (**Figure 8.10**). Children practice sharing, public speaking, taking turns, waiting, and using manners. Many times, children will share home events, discuss storylines of favorite programs, explain a new skill they learned or sport they are playing, or even make up stories. Children can also apply emerging skills. The more the teacher involves students in the essential tasks of meal times, the greater the applied learning. Having children set tables for meals provides opportunities to sort and count napkins and spoons. Pouring water or milk exercises hand-eye coordination. Washing plates and cups

requires dexterity. Even wiping tables can provide teachable moments. These language, math, and social skills are foundational to ongoing learning in the early childhood program environment.

Nap Time

Children who attend full-day programs need a nap or rest time in the afternoon. Many children arrive at the center early in the morning and feel exhausted by early afternoon. The teacher should determine the length of the nap time by the needs of the children in the group. Toddlers and two-year-olds may need two hours of sleep to feel refreshed. Older children may only need 60 to 90 minutes of rest time. However, napping needs are individual. Some children will require more and some much less than their peers will. Some teachers may allow soundly sleeping children to wake up naturally even if the length of time extends into afternoon activities. They ensure that the sleeping child or children are in a safe spot and conduct normal activities within the room with the other children. Other teachers will wake all of the children up at the same time so that everyone can participate equally.

Because of this, nap time may be a time when teachers' and children's needs conflict. After a busy morning, teachers may be anxious to get children to sleep so that they can get a quiet break and work on upcoming classroom activities. However, some children may not be able to sleep or may not need as long a nap as their teachers would like. Early childhood leaders should encourage their staff to have quiet activities planned for those who do not nap. Quiet reading or working on puzzles are ideal suggestions that individual children can do on their cot or mat while others are resting. Teachers should never, ever sleep when their children are napping. This is unsafe for the children and in direct conflict with state and licensing regulations. As the director, you should monitor classrooms during nap times and work with your teachers to ensure that the choices made about nap time are child-centered decisions.

Outdoor Time

All children need time to play outdoors. Sunshine and fresh air help to give them a feeling of well-being. Typical childhood activities that can be disruptive indoors are acceptable outdoors. Running, jumping, and yelling are all part of normal outside fun. Outside play provides natural opportunities for large muscles to be used and for the physical activities of childhood (**Figure 8.11**). The teacher should make a deliberate effort to incorporate outside time into the daily schedule.

The outdoor schedule will depend on the climate and weather patterns of your center's geographic location. Where seasonal weather patterns vary a great deal, the

Hero Images/iStock/Getty Images Plus

Figure 8.10   Children should have opportunities to talk together, share thoughts, and experience family-style meals together.

The outdoors allows children to connect to the many qualities of nature ...

- Nature is universal and timeless, it is present in our history, stories, myths and dreams.

- Nature is unpredictable, due to the ever-changing contrasts of life in the outdoors.

- Nature is bountiful, with so many shapes, sizes, colors, textures, smells, and tastes.

- Nature is beautiful, with so many things to touch and see.

- Nature is alive with sounds created by wind, rain, birds, and crickets.

- Nature creates a multitude of places due to the many landscapes that are available.

- Nature is real, due to its circle of life.

- Nature nourishes and heals and gives our bodies opportunities for sunlight and fresh air.

Goodheart-Willcox Publisher

Figure 8.11 Experiencing nature is crucial for children's growth and development.

amount of time spent outside will have to be adjusted as the weather gets colder. The center may request that children have appropriate snow or rain gear on hand for outside activities. Providing a list of appropriate items helps caregivers know what is expected for particular weather. In climates where the weather is consistent, the amount of time scheduled for outside may be similar year-round.

There may be several outdoor times in a day, or one longer time. The decision about how much outdoor time to schedule may depend on the

- weather;
- age of the children;
- location and ease of accessibility to outdoor play space;
- availability of a protected, shaded space;
- ability to make a variety of interesting play activities available outdoors; and
- accessibility to restrooms and a water supply.

If the outdoor play area is nearby, it may be easy to go out in the morning and afternoon. When the playground opens right off the classroom, children may be free to choose indoor or outdoor activities during free play. If reaching the outdoor area requires a substantial walk, scheduling of outdoor time may not be as flexible. If the center's outdoor area is small, teachers may need to schedule time in advance to avoid overcrowding with other groups. Teachers may also find additional ways to

provide outdoor experiences. Walks, hikes, field trips to parks, or community recreation areas help to meet the need for more vigorous activities.

Diapering or Restroom Time

State regulations determine which sinks are designated exclusively for handwashing, the size and location of the diaper-changing table within a given space, and the location and number of the bathrooms for children who are toilet learning or fully utilizing these facilities. State and local regulations for diapering areas and restrooms are typically set forth by either the state licensing agency and/or health department. The number of toilets and sinks within the designated program space determines the license capacity, or number of children permitted to utilize the space. Potential locations for diapering and restroom areas fluctuate across state standards and close attentiveness to these regulations will be necessary.

Children must always have access to a toilet when they need it (**Figure 8.12**). Younger children may need more frequent bathroom times than older children. On warm

Kristen Alexandria

Figure 8.12 Bathrooms should be easily accessible for all children in the classroom.

days, when children drink more liquids, additional trips to the bathroom will be required. Bathroom time before nap time is also important to prevent embarrassing accidents while children are sleeping.

The need for children to wash their hands on a regular basis is also a priority. Sinks should be accessible and include all of the appropriate items within a child's reach. Handwashing after toileting, messy play activities, or nose blowing, and before eating takes up a big part of the day. The classroom schedule must have flexibility to incorporate proper hygiene.

Supervision of sink, bathroom, and diapering areas is necessary. For example, when playing outdoors, there will always be children who will need to go to the restroom. Staff will need to accompany younger children or be within close proximity when older children are utilizing

Director's Showcase

Reflect

Based on the information shared in this section, what elements of daily programming do you believe are the most difficult for teaching staff to implement?

the facilities. An adult must be available to accompany children to the bathroom areas and ensure that young children are safe and do not get lost or wander off.

8.2 Learning for All Ages Through Play

Play allows children to engage in activities with other children, adults, toys, equipment, materials, and is essential for learning. Wittmer and Petersen (2006) found that beginning in infancy, children have interest in and enjoyment with others. Play evolves and changes at each stage

Director's Showcase

Davey

During the caregiver meeting, Davey was able to go through her daily routine and expectations of children. Some caregivers at the meeting expressed interest in how Davey would meet the learning needs of all of the children with a wide variety of ages and abilities. Using information she had gained at a local early childhood workshop she attended, she shared the importance of developmentally appropriate practices. As the group continued to discuss the topic, one caregiver shared that she had initial concern that her child would not be challenged enough. However, now that she better understood the purpose of developmentally appropriate practices, she was going to continue with her daily planning and routines. In addition, she and several others at the meeting stated that sharing this information with parents was also going to be very helpful.

Roxie

After implementation of their agreed-upon plan and follow-up meeting together, Lonna has had to adjust her daily schedule and routine frequently. Initially, her expectations were to follow the daily schedule to the minute every day. Roxie was able to help Lonna realize through the regular observations that flexibility and being able to change activities is appropriate and will happen frequently. Roxie was also able to set up a mentor/mentee relationship with one of her veteran teachers in the classroom next door to Lonna's classroom to help her learn more about developmental appropriateness when working with toddlers.

Director's Showcase

Davey

While Davey addressed concerns at the caregiver meeting that was held, she was also experiencing more frequent questions from parents about how she is meeting the needs for the multiple ages of children in her care. After some thought, Davey decided to pull together information for a parent meeting. One parent voiced concern over the amount of time spent playing and not in structured learning. She asked Davey, "How are the children learning if all they do is play all day?"

Roxie

Roxie was thrilled to see that over time Lonna was able to follow her daily schedule consistently and the mentor/mentee opportunity was really allowing her to learn more. With ongoing growth of the program, a new room was opened with new teaching staff. With both classrooms at capacity, Lonna and the other teachers began to discuss their frustrations with behavior issues during group time, which included biting and hitting. Parents were also starting to complain and the teachers were worried that they might lose children due to their parents' unhappiness with the behaviors taking place in the classrooms.

of development allowing children to flourish. Figuring out how things work, how others play with or around them, and what is acceptable and not acceptable when playing with peers provides essential social and emotional skill building within the classroom. Each of these elements allows for a day of routine and sets a comfortable pace for the group as they are together. It also plans opportunities to engage with each other, the teaching staff, and the materials provided within the classroom environment. Most importantly, these elements serve as the foundation in which children are allowed to play. Play is the fundamental means by which children gather and process information, learn new skills, and practice old skills (Fromberg, 2002). The opportunities are endless and provide opportunities to understand, create, manipulate, and transform. As an early childhood leader, it will be important to understand the importance of play, support teachers to provide environments full of play opportunities, and educate parents on its developmental benefits for young children.

Infants and Toddlers: Play Utilizing Their Senses

It is in infancy and toddlerhood that play begins and it all starts with the people that surround the child. If adults are warm, receptive, and engaging, the baby grows into a toddler who trusts and engages in interactions that are more complex. While these interactions are not as recognizable as say, when a preschooler is pretending to be a firefighter, the effort of engagement, inquiry, and learning cause and effect allows the child to learn through their senses. They select toys and other materials by making their own choices and then figuring things out through touch, taste, smell, sound, sight, and movement. Through this exploration, discovery becomes the foundation for knowing and understanding (**Figure 8.13**).

Kristen Alexandria

Figure 8.13 Infants and toddlers should have opportunities to explore indoors and outdoors throughout the day.

Common types of play that infants and toddlers engage in (Yogman et al., 2018) include:

- *Interpersonal play*—engagements between infants and peers or teachers in which social and emotional exchanges take place (e.g., peek-a-boo)
- *Exploratory or sensorimotor play*—exploring items to understand what they are (e.g., banging, mouthing)
- *Relational play*—toddlers begin imitating the use of objects (e.g., using a pitcher to pour juice)
- *Constructive play*—using open-ended materials to create something (e.g., stacking several blocks)
- *Symbolic play*—using one object as another object, idea, or action (e.g., using sand as food to cook in pots and pans)
- *Rough-and-tumble play*—engaging in physical actions (e.g., crawling over other infants)

For infants and toddlers to benefit from play and interactions with peers, the teaching staff must provide a sense of security, the right kind of stimulation, support throughout the play process, and a relaxed and playful interaction that meets each child's individual needs (Luckenbill, Subramaniam, & Thompson, 2019).

Play happens throughout the day, and the daily schedule for infants and toddlers must be flexible and reflect their needs. While there should be some general pattern and sequence to the day, teachers should adjust the schedule as needed. Rather than following a rigid, minute-by-minute, preplanned routine, caregivers must be sensitive to the individual needs of each child in their care. If one child gets hungry early, they should be fed. If a child is not quite sleepy at the usual time, they should be rocked and quietly helped to relax. Teaching staff need to be actively and emotionally involved with the infants and toddlers in their care. Every interaction is important as the infant and toddler begin to recognize the warm, caring faces of the staff members and the predictability of their behaviors. These interactions, whether they take place during routines such as diapering, or during floor time, are an important part of the play provided in a quality program.

Preschoolers: Pretend Play to Understand the Real World

Play blossoms in the preschool years. Pretend and make-believe play extends from toddlerhood as children try out new ideas and skills. Communication and the types of activities guide the interactions between participants. This includes the levels of involvement in small and large groupings who participate together. They show a level of cooperation. Storylines become more complex, incorporating series of steps, combinations of actions, in-depth interactions, and a variety of roles for children to assume. For example, playing house allows children to take on roles of parent, grandparent, sister, or brother. Family pets are typically included in the role-playing fun as well. Children act out their roles in variety of activities, such as eating a family meal, going on a picnic, attending a special occasion, or participating in a family outing. The complexity of the play provides opportunities to improvise and create dialogue with each other, practice taking turns, role-play, share, and empathize with one another.

Play is brain building. According to Berk (2019), the significant differences in unstructured and structured play benefits the preschool-age child.

- **Associate play** occurs between the ages of three to four years. It involves interacting with others with limited cooperation necessary. This could be children playing on a playground, but all doing different things in the same area.
- **Cooperative play** occurs in children ages four years and older. It involves interacting with others due to similar interests in both the activity and the children involved in the playing.

As the Academy of Pediatrics has encouraged, play is foundational to the development of the brain, its structure, and overall functioning. For the preschool-age child, linking a developmentally appropriate curriculum with a multitude of materials and equipment enhances the overall process of learning.

School-Age Children: Play as Social Interaction and Relaxation

The school-age child does indeed still need to play. This play, while much more formal in nature and complexity, allows opportunities for friendships to evolve. In the preschool years, play was mostly centered on the activity that was taking place. However, beginning in the early school years, friendships are supported by children interested in the same type of play but these friendships may not be long and enduring. For example, if an argument stems from the play, then it could be that children determine quickly that they are "no longer best friends." At about eight years of age, children begin to like each other's personal qualities and respond to each other's needs and desires.

Due to the ongoing development of play, teachers of school-age children need to plan a variety of interaction opportunities. Outdoor play may result in friendly games of chase, wrestling, rolling, and even hitting. In out-of-school time programs, it will be important more now than ever to allow children to play together and choose their own activities. Children require a break from the structured academic school day (**Figure 8.14**). Free play allows conversations with friends and opportunities to practice cooperation, leadership, following others, and ways to manage aggression. Whether it is playing board

Director's Showcase

Davey

When she prepared for the parent meeting, Davey had developed talking points and gathered resources to hand out to parents. As she talked with the parents on the scheduled afternoon, she explained how she adapted different pieces of curricula to fit the needs of the children in her care. She also spent time discussing how important it was to meet children where they are and build upon existing skills and knowledge. Throughout the presentation, she continually emphasized how play was essential when meeting children's needs to learn and she shared parenting information found on the CDC's website.

Roxie

To address the biting and hitting behaviors displayed by the toddlers, Roxie thought it would be important for her to first observe the classrooms. She also encouraged the teachers to record the times of day when biting and hitting was taking

place and what was leading up to the encounters. After a couple of days of observation and gathering information, they all met again. Based on the information, Lonna and her co-teacher decided to split some of the group activities into two separate times right before snack since that seemed to be a high time for the disruptive behaviors. This turned out to be a great first step! She and her co-teacher found the children to be more engaged and the negative behavior issues decreased. The other classroom teachers decided that they would encourage the use of outdoor play and large motor movement to help with children who were struggling with behavior issues. They, too, found that when the toddlers in their room were able to run and climb, the release of pent-up energy throughout the day helped to lessen the hitting and biting behaviors. By engaging the teaching staff in conversations, discussing strategies together, and empowering the staff to make needed change, Roxie observed the behaviors decreasing significantly in both classrooms.

Kristen Alexandria

Figure 8.14 Children attending out-of-school-time programs should take a break from the academic school day and participate in a variety of interactive opportunities.

games or outdoor group activities, the opportunity to play together allows children to learn the skills to support their in-school time by transferring abilities to discuss, work together, and follow rules.

Child care administrators need to support and help their teaching staff to structure their curricula with an emphasis on play for all age groups. While the play activities change based on the age, interests, and needs of the group, all children need time to explore and play as a key way to learn and grow, and play must be a planned and incorporated part of the child care day.

Director's Showcase

Reflect

What are your thoughts regarding Jean Piaget's statement: "Play is a child's work"?

8.3 General Principles When Planning Daily Schedules

Time in classrooms for all ages of children served needs to be organized. Children thrive with daily schedules and depend upon those caring for them to have routine and consistent schedules. These schedules are generally divided into long blocks with children moving throughout the classroom. The purpose is to not only meet children's needs, such as diapering and bathroom

Director's Showcase

Davey

As Davey started making adaptations to her daily planning based on the information she had learned by preparing the parenting workshop, she found that due to the variety of ages of children in her care, the use of just one daily schedule was difficult. She had two mobile infants, one toddler, and four preschool age children in her care. While the older children could manage restroom breaks, infants and toddlers could be tricky to take care of due to their diapering needs. While she wanted to provide consistency in her daily program, Davey was struggling with how to balance all of the children's needs and keep parents informed concerning their child's day.

Roxie

During a recent staff meeting, Roxie encouraged the toddler teachers to share the success that they had in dealing with the hitting and biting issues within their classrooms. One of the ideas that the staff implemented was an interactive daily schedule for use in the classroom. Using actual pictures of the children going outdoors, coming in from outdoor play, participating in lunch and group times, she offered this idea as something that might be helpful for the teachers and children. Roxie emphasized the possibility of success by sharing her own observations when assisting in the toddler classroom. The three teachers in the four-year-old classroom seemed interested. However, one of the three was very skeptical if this would be helpful, especially with some of the more rough-and-tumble boys in the classroom. Roxie encouraged the staff to think about it and offered to purchase a tablet for the classroom to take pictures to create an interactive daily schedule.

times, but also to provide organizational activities that stimulate children physically, cognitively, socially, and emotionally. These opportunities enhance learning and growth and foster meaningful interactions between the children and teachers. In addition, with careful observation, teachers can fine-tune their program planning to address the needs of individual children in their care. The basic principles of planning a daily schedule include predictability, flexibility, variety, and balance. These principles can serve as guidelines in helping teachers to plan interesting days in the early childhood classroom.

Predictability

Young children respond to predictability. In fact, they depend upon it. A daily schedule that provides the same structure from day to day provides security for them. They like to know what is coming next. They also use the schedule as a way of telling time. It is not unusual to hear a teacher say, "Your mom will be coming right after nap time." Children who are familiar with the order of the schedule usually have an easier time of moving through the transitions of the day.

Flexibility

An early childhood classroom schedule or plan should not be rigid. Trying to make the minutes of every day work out like every other day is unrealistic. Each day is unique. Some days, the children will be deeply absorbed in activities just when the schedule calls for change. On other days, the children will be ready for a change long before the schedule calls for one. Teaching staff that utilize flexibility within their daily plan have the advantage of unexpected opportunities. For example, a group of children may have an exciting day when a giant crane is brought nearby to raise the beams for a new building. Teachers should be encouraged to tap into these unexpected learning events to stimulate interest in a variety of building- and construction-related activities. A teacher who ignores this surprise learning opportunity misses the opportunity to connect their children and their education to real-world situations and the larger community. Children engage more and learn more fully when their teachers can adjust and take advantage of not just their classroom's resources but the world around them.

Variety

A number of activities should be available in some form every day within an early childhood program. Water play, easel painting, block building, and dramatic play should be available on an ongoing basis. While these activities might look different in an infant room from those in a preschool-age classroom, teaching staff should make ongoing adjustments. For example, while a sensory table with water and accessories may be readily available to preschool-age children during center time, infants and toddlers might have a scaled-down experience with individual dishpans in a teacher-led small group activity (**Figure 8.15**). As children are participating in activities, teaching staff should constantly monitor times when children become bored or unengaged. Signs of boredom may include children avoiding the activity or performing it inappropriately. A teacher may renew interest by adjusting certain elements, including

- the setup location within the room;
- the props for the activity;

Kristen Alexandria

Figure 8.15   Children should have access to multiple sensory activities each day.

- the basic arrangement or setup of the activity; and
- the related activities.

Children like to repeat their favorite activities, and they learn from repetition. Adding different elements that are new and different can stimulate children's interest and creative use of materials.

Balance

Planning a daylong program can be a challenge for new or inexperienced staff. A schedule that works well for a half-day program cannot simply be stretched out for a full day. An hour-long free play period cannot become three hours of free play. Both children and teachers become bored if the schedule is not balanced. Think of riding on a swing when looking at your schedule. The schedule should move back and forth between different types of activities. These activity segments should provide a balance for each other that keeps the day engaging and enriching for both children and adults.

When planning the daily schedule with new or inexperienced staff, the early childhood program leader must emphasize the importance of the appropriate balance among the following types of activities:

- active times versus calm times;
- time for individual activities varied with time for group activities;
- child-initiated activities balanced with time when the teacher plans and directs the activity;
- rest times balanced with lively times; and
- indoor times varied with outdoor times.

A good program is never boring. When activities go on too long or are too similar, children may become bored or restless and display negative behaviors. An intentional, engaging program complemented by a carefully planned daily schedule can eliminate many potential discipline problems.

How Does a Daily Schedule Look?

A daily schedule shows the sequence of activities that the staff will follow throughout the day. It should incorporate the elements of good planning. Teachers can develop meaningful schedules for both half-day and full-day programs (**Figure 8.16**). While most schedules have times included on them, teachers should view these times as tentative. For example, if the story time is scheduled for 20 minutes, but children are restless, a wise teacher shortens the story and moves on to a lively activity. It is a good idea to follow the same sequence every day so that children learn to predict what is next. However, it is also necessary to adapt the actual amount of time devoted to a program element to meet the needs of the children.

Children should have the opportunity to explore (**Figure 8.17**). Self-directed, or minimally directed, exploration allows children to acquire skills, gain information about the environment around them, and practice emerging skills. Katz (1987) felt that a rule of thumb is to have children engaged in large-group activities for one-third of the time, in small-group activities

Rawpixel/iStock/Getty Images Plus

Figure 8.17   All children should have the opportunity to explore in self-directed, minimally directed, and teacher-directed activity to gain more information and practice emerging skills.

for one-third of the time, and in individual activities for the remaining one-third of the time. When thinking about the program day from a broad perspective, this is attainable for all ages. For example, an infant is engaged in the activity happening around them. If they are held in the arms of a teacher during a story time that includes others, listening to music as the group claps and sings together, and naps similar to others in the room, they have met the large-group threshold. Then, an infant can participate with others close in age as the teacher introduces things that are soft. The teacher can have a blanket, teddy bear, and other materials for a small group of children to experience. Finally, one-on-one time with their teacher can include being rocked to sleep or fed, swaddled, and held during a difficult time, or reaching and swatting at things attached to an activity chair. These are all examples of how even the youngest children begin to form some sort of a schedule in their daily life.

Teachers must adjust schedules for children according to the ages within the group. Infants and toddlers require a more individualized classroom schedule designed for their age-related characteristics. Infants need a setting where the schedule fits their patterns. Toddlers, however, may enjoy slightly more routine, but periods need to be shorter than those for preschoolers are. Three-year-olds may become disorganized and frustrated after a free play-time of 45 minutes and a story time of 10 minutes. Five-year-olds enjoy a longer free playtime and may also be ready for longer group and story times. Ultimately, the teacher must stay in tune with the group of children in their care to make necessary adjustments, including recognizing the clues of when and why inappropriate behaviors are taking place.

Half-Day Program
9:00 Arrival and free play activities
10:00 Cleanup, bathroom, handwashing
10:10 Snack, roll call
10:30 Story time
10:45 Outdoor free play
11:25 Music/movement
11:40 Finger plays, quiet activity
11:55 Preparation to go home

Full-Day Program
7:30 Quiet activities for early arrivals
8:30-9:15 Breakfast available
9:20 Group story and welcome
9:35 Free play activities
10:35 Cleanup
10:45 Music/movement
11:00 Outdoor free play
11:45 Bathroom, handwashing
12:00 Lunch
12:25 Story time, small group quiet activities
12:50 Bathroom, handwashing, preparation for nap
1:00 Nap
3:00 Wake-up, bathroom, handwashing
3:10 Snack
3:25 Story, music
3:35 Free play and preparation to go home

Goodheart-Willcox Publisher

Figure 8.16   Suggested class schedules for half- and full-day programs serving preschool children.

Director's Showcase

Davey

Throughout the week, Davey started to slowly make adaptations to her daily planning. When she was able to reflect back on her day in the evening time, she started to realize that this might not be as hard as she once thought. Rather than thinking of her schedule in 5- to 10-minute intervals, she started planning in 30-minute time blocks. That way she could best address the needs of the two mobile infants and the toddler. Since the preschool-age children were more flexible and their attention spans longer, she could plan for activities that kept them learning and playing. In addition, their bathroom needs were easily supervised since the restroom was located right across the hall from the area used in her home. She found that by doing this type of strategy, she was able to provide consistency in her daily program and balance the children's needs. Her information sharing with parents also became more efficient.

Roxie

While one of her teachers struggled with the thought of "one more thing to manage" in the classroom, she and the other teachers soon found that the children were delighted to see the visual pictures created by the use of the tablet. By showing mini-albums of pictures set up for basic routines like going outside, coming indoors, washing hands, and eating lunch, the staff noticed that the children were understanding what was coming next throughout the day. During her observations, Roxie was also seeing less frustration as teachers were meeting children's needs. In fact, the small group of "rough-and-tumble" boys were observed serving in the "helper" role by taking turns moving the pictures on the interactive visual schedule.

Director's Showcase

Reflect

What do you see as the benefits for classroom schedules for each age group served by an early childhood program?

8.4 Appropriate Guidance Strategies for Young Children

The general atmosphere or tone of the center tells a great deal about whether this is a good place for children to be. A visitor's first impressions of a classroom should be positive. Rooms that convey a feeling of harshness and stress send a message that something is wrong. Intentional teachers know how to create a climate that is warm and supportive for children. Staff members who lack training or commitment often resort to guidance methods that are not based in sound child development practices. It is on the early childhood program leaders to support teachers with this necessary training by providing ongoing professional development opportunities. In addition, program leaders must continually learn more ways to implement appropriate guidance techniques to include classroom appropriateness for all ages.

Director's Showcase

Davey

Davey has a well-behaved group of children in her program. As is typical, though, the children do experience difficult days, during which they express their emotions in negative ways. Some children have a tough time during transitions when they have to wait for meal time or for the next activity. One child in particular has been biting whoever is near her when they are transitioning between activities. It has become more frequent, happening almost daily. Davey is concerned that parents will start getting upset and question her ability to supervise the children.

Roxie

Lonna, the toddler teacher, once again sought out Roxie's help with the high-energy children in her classroom. All of the children are very inquisitive and sometimes struggle with transitions. During the transition from active outdoor play to lining up and quietly walking back to the classroom, Lonna commented that she has noticed a number of negative behaviors among the children. One child often refuses to come inside and will hide in the play structure and refuse to come out. Roxie offered to observe and then they could meet as a teaching team to determine next steps.

Teachers who are successful in using developmentally appropriate guidance methods pay attention to a number of key characteristics, including

- typical characteristics of the age group with which they are working;
- the individual needs of each child within the group;
- what the theories say about common developmental tasks and patterns;
- the appropriate expectations of children's behavior;
- any specific situations that occur on any given day; and
- providing a range of interesting experiences each day.

Intentional teachers behave in ways that are predictable to children. However, the behavior should never be rigid nor unfeeling. Effective teachers realize that what is fair to each child is measured by what each child needs and not necessarily by similarity. Well-trained staff use a variety of positive guidance strategies that are aimed at helping children learn to think about and control their behavior.

Teacher Behaviors That Minimize Problems

Many potential negative behaviors can be avoided through careful planning. Daily programs that are developmentally appropriate match the interests and abilities of young children. A balanced schedule, a variety of activities, and opportunities for child-initiated activities will appeal to virtually all children. A safe atmosphere where children feel secure to explore and express thoughts and ideas will stimulate their willingness to cooperate. A **relationship-focused program environment** is one in which adults are caring, warm, and respectful and will nurture children's self-concept and confidence. The emotional tone of the center should be a positive one (**Figure 8.18**). In a relationship-focused program environment, teachers create and support a climate that is warm and supportive for children. The techniques the teachers utilize guide children's behaviors and are appropriate to the children's ages and the individual differences displayed. Most importantly, teaching staff realize the importance of having many approaches to children's behavior (**Figure 8.19**). An early childhood

Decreasing Behavior Problems in the Classroom
• Review the daily schedule to see if there are persistent "trouble spots" that can be eliminated by schedule rearrangement. Allow enough time for children to become deeply absorbed in their activities, but not so much time as to become bored. • Review the activities to determine they are developmentally appropriate and there are a variety of things to do. • Provide many opportunities throughout the day for children to make choices. • Make sure there are sufficient opportunities for active play. • Plan activities that will allow each child to experience success in numerous ways. • Get to know children as individuals and build a personal relationship with each one. • Examine the room arrangement for areas that are not used much or where trouble frequently occurs. Rearrange the room to make it more usable by the children. • Always give children advance warning before expecting cleanup or switching to a new activity. • Anticipate particular combinations of children that lead to behavior problems. • Assign a staff member to "stay close" to help the children find compatible ways of resolving disagreements. • Take the time to talk to children about why they must do or not do certain things. • Children need to be helped to see the logic behind adult decisions and behaviors. • Help children to become aware of the feelings of others and the impact of their behavior on others. • Remember that behavior has two parts: actions and feelings. Teachers must be sensitive to the feelings behind behaviors although, at times, they may have to stop behaviors. • Start the group (or enroll a new child) gradually at the beginning of the year. • Avoid having a whole classroom full of new children arrive at once for a full day. • Give each child a chance to get to know the teachers and the routine in a small, more easily controlled group. • Be careful about your own tone of voice, body posture, and general health status. • Teachers who feel and look cranky usually convey that attitude to children. • Set few limits, but be clear and firm about those that are important to maintain the safety and well-being of the group.

Goodheart-Willcox Publisher

Figure 8.18 Teachers are responsible for setting up and maintaining an environment where children experience positive guidance strategies.

Kristen Alexandria

Figure 8.19 Teaching staff should utilize many approaches to helping children learn and express their emotions.

program leader not only observes these interactions but also serves as a sounding board when behaviors become difficult. The utilization of positive guidance techniques helps children grow in self-control.

When children grow in commitment to a relationship, their willingness to "work at it" also grows. When they feel good about themselves and positive about their teachers, they are less likely to engage in disruptive and destructive behaviors. Teachers' actions and attitudes influence children's behaviors. Intentional teachers minimize the likelihood of negative behaviors in the classroom.

Using Positive Guidance

Many experts have written about the value of using *positive guidance* in the classroom. For most teachers, this skill must be learned. Like learning a new language, it is mastered through deliberate practice and a belief in the value of its usage. **Positive guidance** is based on the idea that children are more likely to listen if direction is given in an affirmative way. Adults stress what children are allowed to do rather than what they are not allowed to do. Children are guided to understand what behaviors are acceptable instead of being faced with an endless string of "do nots." Teachers carefully avoid interacting with children in ways that create power struggles.

Young children are beginners at understanding rules. They are unfamiliar with the reasons adults think some behaviors are acceptable and others are not. They are trying to get a sense of their own independence at the same time when their behavior often brings them into conflict with others. As they are growing, they get tired of being "little" and being "bossed around" all the time. When directions are stated positively, children are less likely to feel their control of their own behavior is being threatened or challenged. Positive guidance is an effective strategy in the classroom for the following reasons:

- Children are less likely to be resistant to teacher directions.
- Children feel they are retaining control of their behavior.
- It is usually more precise and gives children clearer instructions.
- It is respectful of children's feelings and is less "bossy."
- It provides a model of effective communication among adults.
- It helps children to know what they are allowed to do.

Other components of positive guidance are important to understand when working with children. These include the following:

- Avoid the use of embarrassment or humiliation of children to control their behavior.
- Respect the misbehaving child even though the behavior must stop or change.
- Avoid the use of value-laden labels like *brat, little doll, babyish, selfish, bully*, etc.
- When talking or referring to children, avoid ridicule and sarcasm.
- Always refer to families and other staff members with respect.
- Never use physical punishment or techniques that hurt the child physically or emotionally.
- Avoid the use of "star charts" or other methods that compare one child with others.
- Recognize each child's efforts, not just individual successes.
- Consider the use of redirection. For example, if a child throws sand in the sandbox, remind them with the statement, "Mansur, if you throw sand again, you are telling me that you need to throw the sponge balls and leave the sandbox."
- Opportunities for use of choices are effective. "Marisol, we are going outside. Will you be wearing your sweater or your jacket?"

Positive behavior and guidance strategies vary depending on the age and development of the children.

Infants and Toddlers: Addressing Needs

Teaching staff who work with infants and toddlers recognize this is a period of quick growth and development. Infants and toddlers communicate their feelings and intentions through behaviors, and staff must be keenly aware of children's development (**Figure 8.20**). While a young infant's distressing cry is indicating a need, a mobile infant's cry might be one of frustration, and a toddler's cry is one of establishing a sense of self. All of these behaviors need adults who will understand, label, and direct the behavior to appropriate outlets. It is crucial for teachers to understand that when a child is exhibiting demanding behaviors, this could be a sign that no one is meeting their needs for protection, boundaries, love, affection, and kindness. With so many developmental stages taking place in a short time, teaching staff need to be prepared for

- separation anxiety;
- stranger anxiety;
- tantrums;
- biting;
- fearful, cautious, and withdrawal behaviors; and
- hurting others by hitting, pinching, and scratching.

While each one of these behaviors can be alarming, it is also important that these behaviors be addressed by adults who

- observe and determine what the child is trying to communicate.
- work closely with the child's family to plan strategies for reducing these behaviors.

Kristen Alexandria

Figure 8.20 Teaching staff working with infants must be keenly aware of the varying types of behaviors displayed and respond appropriately according to those needs.

- provide one-on-one attention to the child.
- shadow the child to watch for environmental triggers that might be instigating the unwanted behaviors.
- give positive attention to appropriate behaviors.
- adapt the environment to engage and calm behaviors.

Each of these strategies, used by infant and toddler teaching staff in partnership with the child's parents, allows opportunities for all involved to work together to better understand what the child needs.

Preschoolers: Redirection and Modeling

Preschoolers are learning so much about the environment around them. Adults working with them need to provide consistent schedules, routines, and developmentally appropriate expectations for the children in their care. One of the key strategies to use is emphasizing what you want the children to do, rather than not to do. For example, instead of saying "stop running," say, "walking feet." When children are having difficulty with others, labeling what is taking place and how to manage it is much better than saying things like "stop playing together." Take the time to stop hurtful behaviors and model ways of resolving issues. Children will learn from your modeling the strategies necessary to play well with others. Let us look at an example together.

> Two children in the block area are fighting over the use of the handheld cars. There are four cars and two children. The teacher redirects the interaction by saying, "I see the two of you are upset over who should play with the cars," and waits for children to respond. As the children explain, the teacher asks leading questions like, "How could both of you play with the cars? Let's see. How many cars are available to play with. Hmm … there are two of you, let's count the cars together. One, two, three, four … and there are two of you. Shall I pick the two cars that each of you will play with, or do you want to take turns choosing? It looks like there are enough cars for both of you to choose one for each hand."

Positive guidance strategies allow children to manage their emotions, learn to think of strategies to work out issues, and continue the play relationship with another peer. All are essential skills as a preschool-age child continues to grow and develop.

School-Age Children: Positive Behavior and Guidance Strategies

Because school-age children have the ability to consider another person's perspective and intent, guidance strategies are more focused in nature. Rather than redirect an issue, which was a highly successful strategy for a preschool-age child, the school-age child wants to know all the reasons why they should or should not have a choice in almost any situation (**Figure 8.21**). For example, a school-age child might argue that they were the first one to use the electronic gaming system and they should be allowed to stay on it as long as they want. However, the time limit set by the program is 15 minutes. The constant questioning of each decision may lead to an exhausted adult providing a snap response such as, "Because I said so." While some adults may feel this is an answer that children should accept, the child is left feeling as if they have no voice or an ability to sort things out on their own. Nor do they get the opportunity to practice thinking on their own to determine their preference or make their own decision. To alleviate a situation such as this, the adult should maintain a time limit. However, with the small group of children that it pertains to, the teacher could offer an extra 5 minutes that the children could collectively decide upon. If the extra time is agreed upon by the group, then offering a strategy for monitoring the time by the use of a timer or on the teacher's stopwatch feature on a phone would be a good decision. This strategy allows for choice, dialogue, ongoing solutions, and adult assistance to help keep track of the time constraint.

Having the ability to make a choice supports learning how to use strategy. For example, if the adult continuously makes choices for the child, the child does not learn to weigh choices nor fully understand consequences. The child will push the limits, no matter how safe or dangerous those limits might be. Why? Because they are expecting an adult to keep them safe and make

Kristen Alexandria

Figure 8.21 Because school-age children need to understand the reasons why they should or should not have a choice, teachers must be prepared to discuss options and provide appropriate guidance in the decision-making process.

Director's Showcase

Davey

Davey decided that she needed to start having the older children help her with routines such as meal and snack times. Because of this, the children had roles that they assumed. For the child that was biting, she gave her a spray bottle and sponge to help clean the table off for meal and snack times and any other areas to keep this child focused and doing large-body movement. Since some of the others wanted to do the same, Davey invested in a few more small spray bottles, put a little water in them, and had sponges on hand. Interestingly, within a short time those children were not so eager to help. However, her biter was! She decided to think of more transition activities to help this child because focus and movement was important to meet their needs and redirect the behaviors to something positive.

Roxie

As Roxie observed in the classroom, it became apparent that "quiet" meant one thing to Lonna, and something very different to the high-energy children. Lining up and quietly walking back to the classroom was a disaster! After asking Lonna if she could utilize a new strategy with the children, Roxie led the children indoors and gave them the choice of being slinky snakes or tiptoe mice. To Lonna's surprise, the group assumed a role and into the building they came with an appropriate noise level. Seeing that the use of choice with the children was effective, Lonna began the same strategy and found it to be successful. Again, by partnering with the teaching staff, solutions were discovered, and Roxie was able to coach and support her teaching staff.

Director's Showcase

Reflect

Of the many positive guidance ideas and strategies shared in this section, which ideas were new to you?

the decision for them. The child becomes indecisive and even paralyzed by any decision. As the child gets older, they learn to seek out an authority figure among their peers to follow, which can lead to blindly trusting and following peers or other adults and can lead to risky behaviors and activities. Teaching staff can help children develop their ability to make good choices by role-modeling conflict resolution and talking through the decision-making process. This takes time and energy, but the investment provides opportunities for children to learn how to work things out together and become decision-makers.

Ideally, your new hires and your current teaching staff will be familiar with and committed to the use of positive guidance. If not, you will need to make it clear that you expect this type of guidance in the classroom. You might consider providing access to training sessions or leading a training session if your staff is not familiar with or is not applying positive guidance successfully.

Chapter 8 Review and Assessment

Summary

8.1 Review programming strategies supporting the implementation of developmentally appropriate curriculum.

- Developmentally appropriate practices view children as unique individuals who engage in specifically developed environments that support each child's physical, cognitive, social, and emotional learning.
- These practices must be culturally, linguistically, and ability appropriate for each child. Activities that are planned by teachers must keep in mind the children in the group and provide equipment appropriate for the age group.
- Children must have "hands-on" experiences with activities that are matched to children's developmental readiness and unique characteristics. Teaching staff must know where to go to get new ideas; provide positive, supportive learning environments; and be sensitive to the social and cultural context in which each child lives.
- A program that has a quality daily program of developmentally appropriate activities requires careful planning.

8.2 Examine the role of play as learning for infants and toddlers, preschool-, and school-age children.

- Play in infancy and toddlerhood begins with the people who surround the child. Adults are warm, receptive, and engaging, which supports the baby to grow as a trusting and engaged toddler who enjoys selecting toys and other materials by making their own choices and then figuring things out through touch, taste, smell, sound, sight, and movement. Through this exploration, discovery becomes the foundation for knowing and understanding.
- Play blooms from just playing alone, to playing alongside each other. In the preschool years, children begin engaging in more cooperative and role-playing opportunities. Preschoolers begin to show a level of complexity in their play as it provides opportunities to improvise and create dialogue with each other, practice taking turns, role-play, share, and empathize with one another.
- Play, for school-age children, is an important opportunity to learn how to have the ability to make a choice to support learning and use

of strategy. The investment in play by this age child is to have opportunities to learn how to work things out, become decision-makers, and collectively work to solve issues when they arise.
- Teaching staff can help children develop their ability to make good choices by role-modeling conflict resolution and talking through the decision-making process.

8.3 Discuss decisions necessary when planning a daily schedule for varying ages of children served in an early childhood program environment.

- The basic principles of planning a daily schedule for varying ages of children includes predictability, flexibility, variety, and balance. These principles can serve as guidelines in helping teachers to plan interesting days in the early childhood classroom.
- While an infant's schedule is often based on their needs, initially, as they grow to a toddler, the importance of routine is a factor. They need lots of flexibility and variety, along with a balance of rest because their bodies are so active.
- The daily schedule for preschool- and school-age children provides large gaps of scheduled time for all of the wonder and opportunities to explore and play. Schedules with consistency are important to young children.

8.4 Distinguish between the different types of guidance strategies for infants and toddlers, preschoolers, and school-age children that contribute to each child's emotional support and well-being.

- Positive behavior and guidance strategies vary depending on the age and development of the children. Teachers carefully avoid interacting with children in ways that create power struggles.
- Infants and toddlers communicate their feelings and intentions through behaviors, and staff must be keenly aware of children's development.
- Preschoolers are learning so much about the environment around them. Adults working with them need to provide consistent schedules, routines, and developmentally appropriate expectations for the children in their care.
- While redirection is a highly successful strategy for a preschool-age child, the school-age child wants to know all the reasons why they should or should not have a choice in almost any situation. They respond to strategies that include choice, dialogue, ongoing solutions, and adult assistance to help keep track of time constraints.

Review and Assessment

1. How do the guidelines of developmentally appropriate practices influence the daily program for children? (8.1)
2. Identify the areas of development that should be addressed in planning daily activities. (8.1)
3. How can you vary story time for the children? (8.1)
4. What factors should determine how much outdoor time to schedule? (8.1)
5. Why is play an important component of the daily program? (8.2)
6. Identify four general principles to follow when planning a daily schedule. (8.3)
7. Describe a well-balanced daily schedule. (8.3)
8. What are the differences between planning for a half-day program and planning for a full-day program? (8.3)
9. What is meant by engaging in *relationship-focused care* with children? (8.4)
10. Explain the concept of positive guidance. (8.4)

Showcase Your Skills

1. Visit several programs serving preschool children in your community. Observe which activities the children seem to enjoy. How does the teacher prepare and set them up? Does the teacher add special materials or props? Make a notebook of activity ideas that were successful with the children. In class or within the online discussion board, discuss the activities and why you think they are developmentally appropriate for preschool children. (8.1)
2. Develop two daily classroom schedules for full-day programs. For one schedule, assume that all of the children arrive at the same time on a bus. For the other, assume that the children arrive at various times between 7 a.m. and 9 a.m. In class or within the online discussion board, discuss how these differences affect the elements of the schedule. (8.2)
3. Choose one classroom to observe that is for either toddlers, preschoolers, or school-age children. Write down 7 to 10 instances of typical behaviors children display. (Do not use names; rather use nicknames, such as Boy A and Girl C.) Document

which strategies the teacher(s) use to guide the children. After the observation is complete, take time to write a summary of what took place within the classroom. Identify the guidance strategies you observed. Demonstrate how the teacher's timely use of positive guidance kept the problems from getting out of hand. (8.4)

Matching

Match the following terms with the correct definitions:

A. atypical development
B. cognitive development
C. cooperative play
D. emotional development
E. free play
F. pedagogical lens
G. physical development
H. positive guidance
I. relationship-focused program environment
J. supervision

1. Refers to a child's brain growth and overall functioning.
2. Involves interacting with others due to similar interests in both the activity and the children involved in the playing.
3. How a child learns to recognize their own feelings while also interacting with significant adults and peers.
4. Abnormal behaviors.
5. Based on the idea that children are more likely to listen if direction is given in an affirmative way.
6. Environment in which adults are caring, warm, and respectful and will nurture children's self-concept and confidence.
7. Oversight by teaching staff that includes monitoring the environment and activity to keep all children safe throughout the day.
8. Occurs when teachers plan opportunities for children to enhance their creativity, use their imagination, problem-solve age-appropriate tasks, and use their social skills with peers.
9. Understanding best practices for teaching and setting up classroom environments.
10. Refers to the coordination of small and large muscles to support the child's movement and coordination abilities within the environment.

FatCamera/E+/Getty Images

9 CHAPTER

Maintaining a Safe and Healthy Program

Learning Outcomes

After studying this chapter, you will be able to:

9.1 Plan a safe and healthy environment for children and staff.

9.2 Establish and implement policies concerning health issues in an early childhood program.

9.3 Follow proper food safety policies and practices to support proper nutrition.

9.4 Meet special health needs of children and staff.

9.5 Create emergency policies and procedures.

9.6 Recognize issues related to child endangerment and the importance of reporting possible child abuse.

9.7 Discuss the importance of working with a health and safety committee.

Key Terms

ad hoc committee
Early Intervention Program (EI)
health
mandated reporters
pedophiles
protective factors
safety hazards
toxic stress
universal precautions

NAEYC/DAP standards

Standards covered in this chapter:

2c

1D, 1E, 2B, 3G

Introduction

Many possible sources of danger for young children are covered by licensing regulations. While states vary in their requirements, all states make an effort to ensure that the physical surroundings are safe for children. As a program director, you are responsible for making sure that the program complies with all licensing regulations. This includes compliance whether inspectors and regulators are present or not.

Some programs are careful to meet all standards when an inspection is scheduled but become less careful at other times. Practices such as keeping medicines in a locked cabinet or taking care to make sure all unused outlets have outlet covers, can seem less important when inspectors are gone. However, the program leader must demonstrate support for maintaining these licensing regulations. They have been established to help keep children safe. Staff will be more careful themselves if they sense your commitment. Everyone must understand that if a child is harmed because the program does not comply with safety regulations, resulting lawsuits could destroy the program. Depending on the issue, this could even mean personal liability for those who were responsible.

The impact of a worldwide COVID-19 pandemic has reshaped how we think about health and safety in our child care programs. Programs, now more than ever, are faced with serious concerns regarding the health and safety of children. The number of children entering child care grows each year. Likewise, the number of adults working in child care jobs continues to grow. Health, safety, and social issues that had little impact on child care a decade ago have become major factors in the establishment of center policies and procedures.

Concerns over health and safety issues and their resulting legal implications have made this area of administration more difficult. Continually changing advice can create new and increasing challenges for early childhood leaders, for example the ever-changing policies and procedures related to COVID-19. There is a need for a program to develop clear policies that can guide staff and parents through difficult decisions. Administrators must design policies to protect both children and staff. If not, mistakes in judgment or behavior in this area can have serious consequences. Plans for ongoing policy revision and staff education are essential.

NAEYC Standard 5 regarding health and safety states that "to benefit from education and optimize quality of life, children need to be as healthy as possible" (NAEYC, 2021). **Health** is a state of complete physical, oral, mental, and social well-being and not merely the absence of disease or infirmity (World Health Organization, 1948).

Director's Showcase

Elena

Elena is the director of a large child care center affiliated with a major metropolitan hospital. Her child care center population has many children of hospital workers including doctors, nurses, and support staff. Child care centers in Elena's area have been shutting down or closing due to low attendance and staff shortages during the pandemic. Because her clientele are frontline healthcare workers, the center has remained full, and she has even extended hours in the morning and evening. However, Elena has struggled to keep healthy teachers in classrooms.

JaNya

JaNya is a home child care provider. She has a waiting list for enrollment in her program and has had to turn many families away. JaNya is trying to find a way to accommodate more children while still keeping a germ-free and safe program for the existing families in her care. JaNya is concerned about what will happen to her business if her community goes into quarantine as cases of COVID-19 variants continue to rise.

The early childhood program space must be a safe place for children and staff. The program leader must ensure that policies reflect appropriate health and safety practices. In an effort to ensure safety, proper supervision is necessary for many of the risks that help children grow in their own confidence. For instance, while exploring children may enjoy having a tree to climb, a creek to jump across, and a gate to swing upon, the program must limit or decrease the risks of some typical childhood pleasures. Staff may struggle with judging how to let children be children while also minimizing the risk of injury. Children need the excitement of exploring, the joy of running free, and the exhilaration of climbing. At the same time, those in charge of children's care must supervise and make decisions about what they can and cannot allow.

9.1 Planning for a Healthy and Safe Environment

Children and staff will be spending a large portion of their day inside the center. The center must take care to make the environment a safe, secure place. This includes maintaining required health records for staff and children. Careful planning for eliminating possible hazards requires attention to room arrangement, furniture, and objects that are in the classroom as well as in public areas of a program environment. Involving staff to assist with these areas is a significant consideration. This includes their assistance when educating parents on the importance of recommended immunizations to utilizing developed safety checklists for classroom and common areas. Taking note of areas of concern and problem solving to eliminate current and possible hazards and threats to health and safety are of utmost importance.

To maintain health records, *NAEYC Standard 5* provides specific guidance.

> "The program maintains current health records for each child: within six weeks of a child beginning the program, and as age appropriate thereafter, health records document the dates of services to show that the child is current for routine screening tests and immunizations according to the schedule recommended, published in print, and posted on the websites of the American Academy of Pediatrics, the Centers for Disease Control and Prevention (CDC), and the Academy of Family Practice". (NAEYC, 2021)

Since so many children, parents, and staff come together daily in a family child care home or child care center, everyone is exposed to multiple individuals every day. Careless health practices can result in the spread of disease at the center.

Figure 9.1 The utilization of software programs and apps assist program leaders as they document and monitor a variety of required recordkeeping to remain in state compliance.

Many child care programs utilize specific software or apps that assist with the documentation and monitoring of immunization records (**Figure 9.1**). In addition, these systems can assist with monitoring the cleanliness of classrooms, tracking supply needs to keep a facility clean, and maintenance and repair needs and records. Many times, state licensing requirements will require a review of enrolled children's immunization records and expect an overview of how administration tracks the health and safety of an early childhood program. Utilization of today's technological resources is highly recommended.

Keep the Center Clean

Recommended best practices from NAEYC (2021) states:

> Ventilation and cleaning are used, rather than sprays, air freshening chemicals, or deodorizers, to disperse odors in inhabited areas of the facility and in custodial closets. Scented or unscented candles and air fresheners such as potpourri, plug-ins, essential oils, incense, sprays, diffusers, and mists are not used, and use of personal fragrances are discouraged.

When cleaning, use fragrance-free, third-party certified, least-toxic products (**Figure 9.2**). When disinfecting or sanitizing, use EPA-registered chlorine bleach and other disinfecting and sanitizing products for their intended purpose and in strict accordance with all label instructions. Mix fresh chlorine bleach solution daily. Post the proper concentration and bleach/water solution ratios.

Directors must make arrangements for the regular cleaning of the center. They consider the size and complexity of the center when planning the schedule for custodial care. Some centers need full-time custodial help.

Organization	Website	Description
EcoLogo	ecologo.org	• Originally founded by the Canadian government in 1988, EcoLogo is now recognized worldwide as a reputable third-party certifier for environmentally preferable products. • They have 122 standards categories. • Companies can apply for certification of their products and then go through a review and audit before being approved.
United States Environmental Protection Agency (EPA)	www.epa.gov/saferchoice	• Created by President Richard Nixon in 1970 to protect human health and the environment. • The EPA does more than certify products. They also develop and enforce regulations, give grants, and study environmental issues, among other things.
Green Seal	www.greenseal.org	• A non-profit organization founded in 1989 as the first non-profit environmental certification program in the United States. • Their mission is to protect human health and the environment by "accelerating the adoption of products that are safer and more sustainable." • Green Seal follows the EPA's requirements for third-party certification.

Goodheart-Willcox Publisher

Figure 9.2 These agencies provide excellent information for program leaders to consider when making decisions related to environmental issues and concerns.

Others are able to hire part-time custodians or contract with a cleaning service. All staff and administration must focus on decreasing the spread of germs, cleaning high-traffic areas more frequently, and keeping children safe by keeping classrooms clean.

Some elements of maintenance, such as garbage removal and bathroom cleaning, must be completed throughout every day. Other tasks, such as dusting, may be done every other day. Carpet cleaning may need to be done only every six months depending on the age of children served in a classroom. The administration should develop a checklist to ensure that elements of cleaning are not missed. They can schedule tasks on the list and check them off when completed. Checklists are also very beneficial when identifying hazards throughout the early childhood program space.

Avoiding Safety Hazards

Infants and toddlers have no judgment concerning what is safe and what is not. Their care is fully in the hands of the adults in the early childhood program. The director and teaching staff must consider how best to keep them safe. Eliminating safety hazards daily helps keep children and staff safe. A **safety hazard** is a potential source of harm or injury to a person (NAEYC, 2021). Young children have a developmental need to explore

their environment, but this also means that staff must be vigilant. There must be constant awareness of what each child is doing. Staff must make sure there are no objects on or near the floor that could be dangerous to crawling infants or pushing, pulling, and climbing toddlers. The following general guidelines taken from the AAP in 2016 on *Promoting Safety and Injury Prevention* suggest the following to prevent accidents:

• No toys smaller than one inch in diameter should be available for play. If an item fits into a 35-millimeter film container, it is too small for children under age three.
• Toys should be checked for small parts that could be pulled off and swallowed.
• Large motor toys should be checked to ensure that small fingers cannot be pinched in moving parts.
• Dolls and other play objects should be checked to ensure that eyes are not attached with pointed parts that could be pulled out.
• Bulletin boards that are placed low should not have items attached by thumbtacks.
• Shelves should be balanced or anchored so that they cannot be pulled over by a climbing child.
• Low-level storage areas should be locked.
• No child should go into the bathroom unsupervised or left unaccompanied in a diaper-changing area.

- Evacuation plans should include the use of wheeled cribs where several infants and toddlers could be placed and wheeled out to safety quickly. This avoids the situation of one caregiver trying to carry several children.
- Blinds with cords that are accessible to children must be adjusted and out of the reach of any child to prevent accidental choking hazards.

Potentially hazardous objects and materials are present in any child care home or center. It is the responsibility of all staff members to protect children from these hazards and continually look for possible dangers.

All state and local regulations will have safety hazard rules and administrators and staff must follow regulations to maintain licensure. While there is no complete list to avoid all possible hazards in the program environment, careful thought and alertness are necessary to spot potential hazards. Becoming aware of potential hazards specific to the early childhood program area is necessary for the health and safety of children in your immediate care. For example, a center located on a second floor will need to consider safety hazards related to stairs and windows; a center located in an old building not designed for child care may have additional potential hazards to identify such as lead in pipes or chipping paint on the walls that contain lead.

Check for Outdoor Safety Hazards

The child care administrator should assign a staff member to perform playground safety inspections on a regular basis. This staff member should be trained to carefully inspect equipment for

- rotting wood or splinters;
- weakened S hooks or fasteners on climbers or swings (**Figure 9.3**);
- bolts with protective covers missing from the exposed ends;
- rusted parts;
- vandalism;
- the temperature of play surface; and
- accurate depth of impact absorbing material underneath climbing structures and swings.

Staff should examine the outdoor areas for wasp nests, dead tree limbs, animal burrows, or holes in the ground. They should check for insect-infested areas, animal remains or deposits, standing water where insects could breed, and uncovered manholes or wells. Remove or correct any hazards that are found. As with the indoor environment, the outdoor area should always be kept in compliance with state and local licensing regulations.

Young children sunburn easily. In March 2011, the American Academy of Pediatrics (AAP) issued guidelines

kate_sept2004/E+/Getty Images

Figure 9.3 Staff members are the first line of defense when monitoring the playground areas for any safety hazards.

on limiting and protecting children from sun exposure. This included policies for wearing sunscreen or protective clothing to be safe. This further included regular training for staff and caregivers to raise sun exposure awareness. Children should not be exposed to the sun for long play periods during the late morning and early afternoon. Other forms of protection such as hats with brims, unbreakable sunglasses, T-shirts, umbrellas, awnings, and tops for strollers provide protection from the sun. If the program does not have a shaded place to play, consider how you can add some shade (**Figure 9.4**). Picnic

eggeeggjiew/iStock/Getty Images Plus

Figure 9.4 Children should have many forms of protection from the sun, including T-shirts, hats, sunglasses, and sunscreen.

shelters, fast-growing shade trees, party tents, and covered porches can all make it possible for children to play safely outside.

Some early childhood programs may have issues with insect-borne diseases. While local authorities can provide insights, there are many products available for use to control issues such as this. Any chemicals utilized must be safe for use around children. In addition, if an insect repellent is deemed useful to avoid bites from insects such as mosquitos, use of these products must first be discussed with parents.

Facility Maintenance

Early childhood program space either in a home or center environment is heavily used each day by the many individuals that occupy the space. When monitoring these spaces, checklists are often utilized to assist with recognizing indoor and outdoor hazards. Whether it is areas that could contain potential pinch hazards, safety locks on child-accessible cabinets or doors, cribs or cots that could have broken mechanisms, inappropriate spacing on crib slats, or rips on materials used, all of these concerns must be monitored and repaired immediately.

Other custodial and maintenance needs may involve more specific requirements. For example, some programs may have aquatic features such as splash pads, water fountains, and even swimming pools that must have provisions for maintenance. All state requirements specify the need for impact-absorbing materials under climbing structures. Whether this is sand, wood chips, or rubberized materials, all must have constant attention to depth and durability of the impact choice being utilized. Facilities will require yard work that includes keeping grass mowed, leaves raked in the fall, and snow and ice removed during the winter months. Due to the continued use of the facility, ongoing maintenance help includes having someone who can fix loose doorknobs, oil squeaky hinges, and take care of basic maintenance of equipment.

Health and Safety in Family Child Care

When children are cared for in a private home, it is important that the family child care home provider think about the liability and the need to have business policies in place. While larger center-based programs have systems that are more complex in place, a provider who is on their own needs to have policies and procedures in place to include the following:

- Locked storage cabinet to store a licensing compliance file, children's records, child abuse and reporting, and all other important documents

CasarsaGuru/E+/Getty Images

Figure 9.5 Keeping the environment clean is a constant task throughout the day in many areas of the child care program.

necessary to support the operations of the family child care home.
- Higher liability levels for homeowner's insurance and automobile insurance when transporting children.
- Policies outlining the days and hours of operations to include days that the program will be closed and how families will be notified if the provider is sick and cannot provide care.
- Procedures for entry and exit of children from care, verifying who can or cannot pick up a child, notifying parents if a concern exists, how illness and injuries are handled, storing and administering medications, transporting children, etc.
- Care of ill children to include how the provider will inform parents of the child's physical and emotional well-being.
- Constant monitoring of the environment and checking to see that all materials and equipment are in good working condition and are clean, safe, and free from any hazards (**Figure 9.5**).

While not an exhaustive list, there are many health and safety considerations when providing care in the home. This includes the provider's home being open to parents and any other regulatory monitoring agencies.

Director's Showcase
Reflect
Either as a program director or family child care home provider, what would be specific concerns that you would have if faced with another pandemic or emergency response to a sickness outbreak in your area?

While most homes have a designated area for their children to be throughout the day, it is important to childproof the entire home. Parents have a right to see all areas of the home. While this may feel invasive, it is a reality when providing care in a private home.

9.2 Establishing and Following Child Care Health Policies and Practices

Many programs are open for twelve hours each day and have many people involved in working within the same space. Because of this, it will be crucial to establish and follow practices that support a safe and healthy place. This includes being aware of the many state and local regulations while also involving the staff and children in following these practices. This takes not only careful planning but continuous communication and monitoring by the early childhood program leader.

Director's Showcase

Elena

Elena has struggled to keep her staff healthy. The center follows CDC guidelines and has implemented more frequent handwashing, requires staff members to wear masks, and performs temperature checks for everyone who enters the center including all staff and children. She has also designated a space in the center, separate from the rest of the center, for children who feel sick during the day and are awaiting pickup to go home. Elena has printed the center's policy on illness and the precautions everyone is taking and then posted them prominently for families and employees. She has also started a text alert system to communicate with families and employees about center news and any situations as they arise.

JaNya

JaNya has remained at capacity since the beginning of the pandemic. She follows health department protocols and has taken safety precautions seriously. She requires a daily temperature check for everyone who enters her home, frequent handwashing, spreading out of the cots at nap time, and mask wearing. She has also had to cancel the local librarian who comes to read to the children weekly as well as other educational guests who visit to share activities with the children.

Practices to Prevent the Spread of Disease

The Centers for Disease Control (CDC) has developed a set of health practices called **universal precautions**. These practices require that all staff treat every situation as having the potential to spread disease. Uniform sanitation and protective behaviors have been identified. Because of the seriousness associated with bloodborne diseases, these precautions are primarily focused on situations that might involve the handling of bodily fluids, such as vomit, diarrhea, blood, or mucus. All are potential hazards when working with small children, and staff must be trained to manage these serious health-related issues.

Air Quality

Living during a pandemic has brought air quality issues to the forefront. Caregivers and children have learned to live and play while wearing a mask to decrease the spread of viruses. Children are more vulnerable than adults are to the effects of unhealthy substances in the air they breathe. They are easily susceptible to respiratory diseases. To protect the health of everyone in the center, policies regarding air quality should be developed. Staying up to date on public health recommendations and the ever-changing landscape of daily life during a pandemic is vital to keeping children and staff healthy.

It is important that children have opportunities to play in the fresh air (**Figure 9.6**). Many newer buildings have windows that do not open. The ventilation systems may be inadequate to provide sufficient airflow. This condition can increase the potential for respiratory diseases. Disease breeds in dark, damp, warm, unventilated areas. Children need the opportunity to play outside in the fresh air every day, as the weather permits. Rooms should be aired out on a regular basis.

andreswd/E+/Getty Images

Figure 9.6 Playing outdoors each day is important for children's development, health, and wellness.

Activities such as pesticide applications and painting should be scheduled for evenings or weekends when the center is empty. Efforts should be made to plan construction or renovation for off-hours or days when the center is closed. If this is not possible, the construction area should be sealed off so that any dust and other construction-related air pollution are confined to the workspace.

Handwashing

Careful handwashing is the best and most effective protection against the spread of germs and disease. The hands of children and staff should be washed upon arrival at the center and when coming in from outside. Hands should always be washed after diapering, toileting, and wiping noses. Additional need for handwashing includes before and after cooking activities and snack or mealtimes. Staff should also wash before administering medication or first aid. Adding more frequent handwashing times

and opportunities are encouraged for the prevention of the spread of viruses and germs.

Based on guidelines provided by the CDC (2021), follow this handwashing procedure (**Figure 9.7**):

1. Wet hands with clear, running water (warm or cold), turn off the faucet, and apply soap.
2. Rub hands together to create a lather on the back of your hands, between your fingers, and under nails.
3. Scrub hands for at least 20 seconds.
4. Turn on the faucet, rinse hands well under clean running water.
5. Dry hands using a clean towel or air-dry them.
6. Use a towel to turn off the faucet to prevent re-contaminating hands.

Using Disposable Gloves

Disposable gloves should be available in every room of the center. Staff should use gloves when changing diapers

HOW TO WASH YOUR HANDS PROPERLY

WET HANDS

USE SOAP

RUB HANDS PALM TO PALM

LATHER THE BACKS OF YOUR HANDS

SCRUB BETWEEN YOUR FINGERS

RUB THE BACKS OF FINGERS ON THE OPPOSING PALMS

CLEAN THUMBS

WASH FINGERNAILS AND FINGERTIPS

RINSE HANDS

DRY WITH A SINGLE USE TOWEL

YOUR HANDS ARE CLEAN

Hoi Sook Ying/iStock/Getty Images Plus

Figure 9.7 While state regulations vary in regards to handwashing expectations, washing hands thoroughly is important.

bernie_photo/E+/Getty Images

Figure 9.8 There are many surfaces that need constant disinfection including table tops, food service areas, changing tables, contaminated toys, and other areas that may become soiled throughout the day.

and cleaning up bodily fluids such as vomit, diarrhea, blood, or mucus. After use, staff should throw away the gloves in a waste receptacle and wash their hands.

Disinfecting

Like handwashing, disinfecting is an essential part of maintaining a healthy, safe environment (**Figure 9.8**). It is not expensive, but it does take a little extra time. A sanitary disinfected facility is required for a quality childcare program. A bleach solution should be used to disinfect

- tables, before and after eating or an activity;
- changing tables, after each diaper change; and
- toys that children have mouthed or otherwise contaminated.

Based on guidelines provided by the CDC (2009), a standard bleach solution should be made fresh daily and kept in every room, out of reach of the children. A large amount can be made at one time and divided into quart-size spray bottles for individual rooms. The standard bleach solution is 1/4-cup bleach to a gallon of water. If made in quart containers, the amounts are 1 tablespoon of bleach to 1 quart of water. A stronger solution of 1-part bleach to 10-parts water may be used for more heavily contaminated areas.

Diapering

Changing diapers requires a safe and appropriate place. An easily accessible area that can be kept clean should be designated as the diapering area, and all diapering should occur in this area. It is essential that food handling areas and diapering areas be kept separate. The surface of the diapering area should have some type of disposable pad or leak-proof paper placed on top. A plastic bag or plastic-lined container should be available for disposal of

diapers. Follow CDC guidance (2016) when providing a safe and healthy diapering procedure to reduce the spread of germs when changing diapers.

1. Put on disposable gloves, if used. Cover diaper-changing surface with disposable liner. If using a diaper cream, dispense it onto a tissue now. Be sure to have all supplies (e.g., clean diaper, wipes, diaper cream, plastic or waterproof bag for soiled clothing, extra clothes) accessible.
2. Place child on changing surface and unfasten diaper. Clean the child's diaper area with disposable wipes and always wipe front to back.
3. Place used wipes in the soiled diaper, discard the soiled diaper and wipes in the trash can. Remove and discard gloves, if used.
4. Slide a fresh diaper under the child. Apply diaper cream, if needed, with a tissue or freshly gloved hand. Fasten the diaper and dress the child.
5. Wash the child's hands with soap and water and place child in a safe, supervised area.
6. Remove liner from the changing surface and discard in the trash. Wipe up any visible soil with paper towels or a baby wipe. Spray the entire surface with bleach solution.
7. Thoroughly wash hands with soap and water.

Tooth Brushing

Each child should have an individual, labeled toothbrush. Children should brush their teeth each day after mealtime. The American Academy of Pediatrics recommends brushing with a fluoride toothpaste twice a day as soon as teeth erupt (AAP, 2016). A very small smear of toothpaste is needed for infants and toddlers; more toothpaste can be added as children get older. After use, toothbrushes must be stored upright and exposed to the air so they can dry. There must be sufficient space between toothbrushes so they are not touching each other. A separate, inverted, disposable cup with a hole in the bottom for each toothbrush is a good way to store the brushes between uses.

Napping

Children should have their own mats and blankets with their names on them. Most state regulations require that mats or cots should be placed head to toe and with at least three feet of open space between each mat. The position of the cots or mats should include enough space to prevent children from coughing and breathing on each other. Linens should be washed each week or more frequently as needed (**Figure 9.9**). Cots or mats should be stored so the sleeping surfaces used by different children do not touch each other. Certain cots stack without allowing any surface areas to touch. Racks on which

nito100/iStock/Getty Images Plus

Figure 9.9 All bedding materials should be washed weekly for older children and changed daily for infant sleeping areas.

mats can be hung also can provide suitable storage. Wiping cots or mats regularly, using the recommended bleach-water disinfecting solution, helps to mitigate the spread of germs.

Policies Concerning Illnesses

In today's world, focus and attention on individual health to stop the spread of COVID-19 and other illnesses is extremely important. No matter how careful child care providers are and how diligently protocols are followed, children will still get sick. Caregivers need to be informed about exposure to illness, and specific policies and procedures to follow. The staff must have clear procedures to follow in case of illness and to communicate with parents and caregivers. In addition, all local health departments' regulations and reporting processes must be followed. The guidance can always be found within the state regulations or by calling the local health department location or state licensing agency.

Signs of Illness

All staff should know the typical signs of illness as children can become seriously ill very quickly. Each staff member should take responsibility for alerting the responsible teacher or senior staff if a child appears to be ill. Fever, vomiting, rash, and/or diarrhea are relatively easy to spot. Changes in behavior, internal injuries, or a sore throat might not be as obvious. Often children who are becoming ill show few symptoms other than unusual irritability. Once you have determined that a child is sick enough to be sent home, a parent should be called. The center should have an isolation area where the child can rest comfortably until the parent arrives while also being supervised at all times.

Policies About Administering Medications

Parents may request that center personnel administer medication to their children. This is a serious responsibility. Care must be taken that the right dosage is given on time. The Administration for Children and Families, US Department of Health and Human Services (2015), provides guidance on medication distribution and includes the following:

- All medication, over-the-counter and prescription, must be in the original, labeled container.
- Medication must be in a locked first-aid kit in the classroom or the refrigerator.
- Staff must wash their hands before and after giving medicine.
- All necessary information, such as times for dosage, should be given to the staff in writing by the parent.
- Staff members should record the time when medication is given and sign initials.
- No medication should be given without parental consent.
- Permission from the prescribing physician is sometimes required by licensing regulations.
- Staff should notify parents if the child has refused to take the medicine or has gotten only part of the dose.
- The medicine must be kept at the appropriate temperature.

Great care and attention should be given when managing any medication distribution. There is a variety of government resources available that you can utilize to educate your employees on proper medication administration. State and local regulating authorities offer guidelines for education and child care settings. In addition, the National Capital Poison Control Center is available 24 hours a day to assist with any questions (**Figure 9.10**). Provide your teachers and staff with the proper training and resources to ensure their safety as well as the health and safety of the children within your care.

National Capital Poison Control Center

1-800-222-1222
poison.org

Available 24 hours a day to answer questions.

Goodheart-Willcox Publisher

Figure 9.10 The National Poison Control Center is the best resource to access when questions need to be answered concerning substances that might be ingested by children.

9.3 Food Safety and Proper Nutrition

NAEYC (2021) has said that "nutritional well-being is fundamental to children's development and learning. Nutrition practices must be embodied in written program policies that are shared with staff and families and implemented consistently through well-developed procedures."

Food will always be located within an early childhood program environment. Meals that are provided for children or those that are brought from home must all be managed appropriately. Snacks, beverages, and bag lunches hold the potential for food contamination. Sanitary conditions and proper storage of food items are essential to minimize any danger of foodborne illnesses.

Safe Food Handling

The CDC (2021) recommends the following food safety precautions regarding food storage:

- Keep refrigerated items at 40°F or less. Keep frozen foods at 0°F or less (**Figure 9.11**).

vgajic/E+/Getty Images

Figure 9.11 It is important that refrigerated foods be stored at 40°F to support food safety precautions.

- Do not allow refrigerated foods to sit out. Place leftovers in the refrigerator promptly and label with the current day's date.
- Be sure all meats and eggs are thoroughly cooked.
- All unrefrigerated foods should be stored at least six inches off the floor. Use containers that will prevent contamination by insects or rodents.
- Keep counter areas and utensils washed. Do not allow contamination from one food to spread to another.
- Wash surfaces with soap and hot water and sanitize with a universal bleach solution.
- Do not use food from dented, leaking, rusted, or bulging cans. Avoid using home-canned foods.
- Cover or wrap refrigerated foods to prevent contamination and label with the current day's date.

- Place tight-fitting lids on garbage containers. Keep containers with food waste separate from those used for soiled diapers. Diaper containers should be clearly labeled, out of the reach of children, and emptied throughout the day.
- When washing dishes by hand, use a three-compartment sink. Follow these steps:
  1. Wash thoroughly in hot water containing detergent solution.
  2. Rinse.
  3. Sanitize by immersing dishes in lukewarm bleach solution (1 1/2 teaspoons bleach per gallon of water) for at least two minutes.
  4. Air-dry. Air-drying dishes that have been sanitized using bleach leaves no residue because the chlorine evaporates as the solution dries.
- Keep all food preparation areas clean. These are never shared spaces with diaper-changing stations.

Be sure food for children is cut into small bites to minimize choking hazards. Infants and toddlers are particularly vulnerable to choking. Their food should be cut into 1/4-inch pieces. Thick peanut butter, round slices of hot dog, nuts, grapes, popcorn, hard candy, and string cheese are potential hazards for young children. These foods should not be served. Safe food practices are essential in the center. Food poisoning caused by contamination at the center is a serious health threat. An outbreak of food poisoning would also be a major threat to the reputation of the center. Your local cooperative extension agent or the Centers for Disease Control (CDC) website can help with food preparation concerns.

Nutritional Requirements for Infants and Toddlers

Nutritional requirements and guidance for infants and toddlers comes directly from the *U.S. Department of Agriculture (USDA) Food and Nutrition Service*. One program in particular, *Child and Adult Care Food Program (CACFP)*, not only provides potential funding for the program overall in the meals that it provides to enrolled children, but also insights when introducing infants and children to healthy eating habits. This includes healthy meal planning and a multitude of resources that support best feeding practices for babies and toddlers when using a bottle or cup, serving solid foods, buying and preparing foods, choking prevention, information on food allergies and intolerances, and partnering with families. From menus and meal patterns to advice on breakfast cereals, yogurts low in sugars, and food lists for infants and toddlers, this program offers a wealth of nutritional insights.

Nutritional Requirements for Preschool Children

Nutritional requirements and guidance for preschool-age children also comes directly from the *USDA* and participation in the *CACFP* program, which continues to build upon the healthy eating habits established when children were infants and toddlers. This program provides early childhood programs with healthy meal planning based on a multitude of resources that support best feeding practices for preschool-age children, buying and preparing foods, choking prevention, information on food allergies and intolerances, and partnering with families. Menu and meal patterns provide advice for nutritious breakfasts, snacks, lunches, and dinners for programs that are open for extended hours. This program offers a wealth of nutritional insights and is a proponent of family-style meals. This type of meal structure encourages children to sit together, serve their own portion size on their plate, and interact together at all meals. Teaching staff are expected to sit at the tables with the children and participate. All of these efforts establish age-appropriate nutritional and eating-habit expectations for preschool-age children.

Nutritional Requirements for School-Age Children

The school-age child can have quite the appetite. Programs with before- and after-school care typically provide breakfast and an afternoon snack. Children who are out of school and at the center for a full day will also require lunch and even dinner for programs open after 6 p.m. The CACFP program continues to build upon healthy eating habits by providing healthy meal planning based on nutrition resources. The program provides established menu and meal patterns and advice for nutritious breakfasts, snacks, lunches, and dinners for centers that are open for extended hours. The school-age section offers a wealth of nutritional insights and encourages family-style meals. Children are encouraged to sit together, serve their own portion size, and interact together at all meals to include the staff. All of these efforts establish age-appropriate nutritional and eating-habit expectations for children participating in out-of-school-time programming.

Overall, mealtimes are opportunities for children to serve themselves while also assisting with the younger children (**Figure 9.12**). The CACFP program provides supports to centers and family child-care homes. As discussed in future chapters related to budget and finance, providers may be eligible for partial reimbursement of the cost of the food that they serve to the children. While there are necessary records to claim the money,

Figure 9.12 Opportunities to serve themselves allow children to explore and enjoy mealtimes together.

these forms and processes can be obtained from the child care agency in the area. Child Care Resource & Referral Agencies may have professional staff that work directly with providers in the area to not only participate in the program but they also provide technical assistance to come out to the program location to help with setting up and completing the monthly requirements to receive these funds. While the reimbursement is not a lot of money, it can amount to several dollars a day. Over a year's time, this can represent a nice sum of money and needed additional income. Most providers who participate have found that it is worth the effort.

Health and Safety Considerations

Considerations by age-group for children's health and safety are often based on their developmental abilities. For example, an infant's mobility is limited. However, a toddler and preschool-age child move about the space with little understanding of what is a safe choice. Child care administrators and staff must consider the equipment choices and setup of classrooms to best meet the needs of the varying ages of children serviced in an early childhood program.

Health and Safety Concerns for Infants

Meeting the health and safety concerns of infants is an ongoing task for program leaders to monitor to include their staff members. From the type of cribs that are purchased, the thickness of the mattresses, type of diaper-changing area, steps to change diapers, storage of breast milk, bottles, baby foods, and medications—all are time-intensive tasks that are ongoing and expected each day. All items used for one infant must be marked and kept separate from the others. Whether it is trays to store bottles or bins that hold the necessary needs of the

baby being cared for, it is a lot to manage day in and day out. Program leaders must continually observe the interactions taking place in the classroom as well as the ongoing cleaning routines expected of the staff. Equipment includes the use of high chairs, rockers, floor toys, structures to pull up on, and soft materials to crawl and roll upon. Cribs, as mentioned earlier, are constant upkeep with most states regulating slat width use on the bed railings to avoid any chance of a child becoming trapped. Staff in this area must have immediate access to sinks and running water. In addition, routines that include wiping down the multitude of areas that must be sprayed with designated cleaning agents demands that policies are in place and staff are trained to implement these procedures each day to provide consistent health and safety assurances for the infant program.

Health and Safety Concerns for Toddlers and Preschool Children

Children in the toddler and preschool classroom areas have differing concerns. Children of this age are walking, talking, and caring for their own personal needs, therefore the health and safety aspects shift. Program classrooms and playground areas must be constantly monitored for equipment that may be broken or unusable and be clean for use inside and outside. Electrical plugs must be covered (**Figure 9.13**). This age of children

Figure 9.13 Electrical plugs must be covered to protect children and provide safety from possible electrical shock.

needs lots of initial supervision and role-modeling of appropriate health and safety aspects. From routines that include handwashing on a regular basis, to assisting with and monitoring any toileting issues, to pointing out and having discussions about "safe decisions" versus "not-safe decisions," children need adults who will surround them with this constant yet nurturing reminder and role-modeling. For example, a child may want to jump from the top of the slide on the playground. The teacher needs to immediately recognize and label for the child this as a "not-safe decision" then talk-through what the child can jump off on outside. This comes from engaging the child in the conversation and role-modeling the decision-making process.

Children of this age also need lots of assistance with managing their own bodily fluids and the importance of handwashing. Directors need staff members who are willing to help with and guide children of this age to learn how to do this. While some preschool-age children catch on quickly, others do not. Teachers must prepare for just about anything, and directors need to provide those supports. Illnesses are certainly transmissible in this age group, and classrooms need to be constantly cleaned throughout the day as well as in the evening time. This includes bathroom areas, toys, shelving, equipment, and other items that support meal service. Teachers must constantly be on the lookout for choking hazards, unsafe behaviors between children where someone can get hurt, and participation in monthly routines where children practice fire and tornado drills, strangers in the building drills, and other necessary procedures to keep children safe.

Health and Safety Concerns for School-Age Children

Unlike the infant, toddler, and preschool years when children's growth is fast and very sensory in nature, school-age children's growth begins to steady. Their immunity has strengthened and the likelihood of more frequent illness begins to decline. A child in this age group may get the latest stomach or respiratory flu bugs that are going around and should be encouraged to use ongoing handwashing as well as healthy personal hygiene routines as much as possible.

Finding a location or facility appropriate for proper school-age care may be difficult. The facility must have accessible water; larger bathrooms; a small kitchen area for fixing snacks; access to a large, age-appropriate outdoor play space; and ideally, a gym for active indoor games. Many elementary schools or school districts are reluctant to have these programs in their buildings due to the state licensing requirements for school-age child care programs, which can be in conflict with the school's procedures and safety regulations. Overall, having appropriate space to accommodate school-age children is a necessity. Larger bodies like to move and play group games, which requires adequate indoor and outdoor space and equipment. As mentioned in other age groups, careful supervision of play spaces is essential. In addition, because this age group can be hard on equipment, staff must stay aware and monitor equipment on a daily basis. Gated areas need to be monitored, and playgrounds must have equipment that is appropriate for the size and skill of school-age children. Having spaces separate from the young children provides appropriate facilities for out-of-school-time programs.

Special Health Concerns

Child care programs must meet the special health needs of the children in their care. They must understand and take seriously allergies, disabilities, chronic diseases, and compromised immune systems. It is necessary to develop an individual care plan and provide for the education of staff who will care for each child with special health needs. One area in particular, dietary restrictions and allergies, are common among children and should be taken seriously. Training with certain medications for all staff within the program if a child has a reaction to a known food allergy requires priority care. Staff members should work with parents to learn as much as possible about a child's particular condition and needs. The child's doctor may recommend books or materials that could be helpful. Sometimes it is necessary to assign additional staff to classrooms with children who have special health concerns (**Figure 9.14**). An extra adult may be necessary to ensure that the needs of all the children are met.

Alerting Parents to Contagious Diseases

During non-pandemic times, other contagious diseases and viruses affect daily life in an early childhood program.

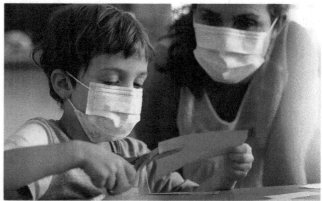

Juanmonino/E+/Getty Images

Figure 9.14 When serving children who have special health concerns, it will be necessary to assign additional staff to help care for the child's needs.

Chickenpox, fifth disease, cytomegalovirus (CMV), and other typical childhood diseases may cause serious complications. They could also be dangerous for parents who may be pregnant or have weakened immune systems themselves. Whenever children in the center have been exposed to these highly contagious diseases, parents should be alerted by letter or email. Typical symptoms of the disease should be described. Local health department authorities or licensing regulators may provide useful prewritten templates with critical information for you to share.

When Children Must Isolate from the Center

Knowing when to exclude children from the program for health reasons is not always easy. Many children are contagious with a disease before they show any symptoms. For example, by the time the chickenpox rash breaks out, the child has already been contagious for several days (**Figure 9.15**). In general, the following conditions make it necessary to exclude children from the program:

- open, oozing sores that cannot be covered;
- diarrhea;
- high fever;
- unidentified rash;
- untreated lice; and
- forceful vomiting.

These are usually signs of contagious conditions that cannot be ignored. Children may be able to come back to the program before all signs of the condition have gone away. A doctor's written release should be obtained and is often required by local regulatory authorities before a child re-enters a program. Often, a public health nurse or clinic can be consulted by both parents and staff to provide information and advice.

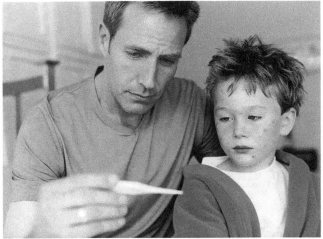

Digital Vision./Getty Images

Figure 9.15 Parents must monitor a child's illness and keep them at home to prevent the spread of contagious disease.

Confidentiality

Many aspects of work in early childhood education require a commitment to confidentiality. Even with the struggle of contact tracing that became part of the routine to manage during the pandemic, all staff were still expected to maintain confidentiality. The health status of children, families, and staff are among those topics that must not be discussed by anyone who is not directly involved. Only those who must know in order to do their jobs should be communicating about the health status of anyone affiliated with the program. Policies should be clear to all staff. Confidentiality is an area of employee conduct that is taken seriously. Consequences for breaching confidentiality should be included in the program's personnel policies and addressed immediately if confidentiality is broken.

9.4 Meeting the Special Health Needs of Children and Staff

Caring for the special needs of children can be a time-intensive task for a leader of an early childhood program. Between securing staff and providing them with ongoing professional development to providing program space that supports the health, safety and nutritional needs for the child being served, know that families may not be receptive to hearing your concerns about their child. They may resist following through with a referral for services. Other suggestions are to patiently urge family members to speak with their child's primary healthcare provider who might be better received in such circumstances. Keep in mind that the relationship with the child and family may only be an investment in planting a seed for the family to think about the development of their child who will eventually access services later.

Including Infants and Toddlers with Disabilities

Those working closely with children are often the first to identify a child's unique needs. A teacher may notice that an infant is not achieving the developmental

Director's Showcase

Elena

Elena has children enrolled in her program who have disabilities. The children are of varying ages and have different disabilities. One of the children in the program was diagnosed with trisomy 21 or Down Syndrome shortly after birth. She is now two and is thriving in the toddler classroom. Her parents have expressed concern about the health of their child during the pandemic due to a fragile immune system. The child had open heart surgery in infancy to correct a heart defect due to her diagnosis. Elena and the classroom teachers began by meeting with her parents to discuss protocols to ensure health and safety and to problem solve issues that may arise. However, they are thinking that they need to continue planning for the needs of this child.

JaNya

JaNya has one child in her care with severe allergies, both environmental and food allergies. JaNya follows a strict diet protocol for the child, paying attention to cross contamination of foods that may cause an allergic reaction. She and the parents of the child developed a nutrition plan together with the help of a nutritionist and JaNya is able to communicate with the parents as well as the nutritionist as needed or as issues or questions arise. This has really impacted how she has had to prepare food and care for this child and wonders what else she might need to be planning for.

milestones as quickly as their same-aged peers are. Early identification of a developmental delay or concern can be vital to long-term outcomes for children. As a program leader, supporting the staff who are voicing concerns about development to parents can be a difficult but important discussion. Conversations can begin with "Have you noticed your child has not yet learned to pull up?" or "I have noticed that your child is not making sounds like the other children; is this the same behavior you see at home?" Recognize that parents might be frightened or even angered by the notion that something might be "wrong" with their child. When working with infants and toddlers, teachers and staff can help parents begin the process of determining a special need or concern.

Every state has a federally mandated **Early Intervention Program (EI)** that provides specialty services for infants and toddlers with developmental delays. As a center director, you need to become familiar with the early intervention services available in your area. EI programs are often a part of the state department of education or the state department of health. Becoming a referral source for your local EI program could be beneficial to your program. Services provided by the EI team can include occupational therapy, physical therapy, speech language pathology, child development, behavioral health, and nursing. Providing information and access to these services for families helps children get the early services they need. Early intervention services may be provided in the child care setting as well as in the home. Many providers will give ideas and activities to help support the child while in your care.

Including Preschoolers with Disabilities

Many times, if preschool-age children are enrolled in early intervention, their services may take place within the classroom (**Figure 9.16**). Having access to therapists and specialists can be beneficial for staff to learn about the specific needs of the child. EI providers often give suggestions and activities to help aid in the development of the child but can also answer questions and concerns that caregivers and staff may have. Communication with service providers is key in the developmental health of the child. When children age out of the EI program,

kali9/E+/Getty Images

Figure 9.16 Children who participate in early intervention programs often receive visits from various therapists at the early childhood program site.

typically at the age of three years, if the child is still in need of services, the public school system in the district the child lives in will continue services. This transition process can be a stressful time for the child, parents, and other caregivers. Leaders of early childhood programs along with their staff need to communicate with and provide input to the local school providers to facilitate a smooth transition in services.

Including School-Age Children with Disabilities

School-age children with disabilities may require some additional supports during the time they are in group care. It may be necessary to have additional staff in the classroom for a child who needs extra help during the transition from school to child care. Other children may require specific supports used during the school day to continue into after school care. These items may include visual schedules and/or supports, extra time during transitions, sensory activities and products, or physical supports. Having continuous communication with caregivers and school service providers and teachers is extremely beneficial in helping children with disabilities in out-of-school-time settings.

9.5 Preparing for Emergencies

No matter how careful an individual is to maintain a safe, healthful environment, an unexpected emergency will probably occur at some time. The best way to handle an emergency is to anticipate it. Plan for what you and staff members would need to know and do if an emergency would arise and how to care for those who might be injured (**Figure 9.17**). Communicate frequently with staff, caregivers, and children about safety plans, who is in charge, and detailed instructions for what to do. That way, staff can handle an event or situation immediately by utilizing the plans put in place.

Emergencies can arise that require actions on the part of staff members to keep children safe. Child care workers

must protect the children in their care from potential child abuse. Programs that design security to prevent entrance of unauthorized individuals enhance the physical and emotional well-being of those inside the facilities. A well-implemented security system contributes to the caring and nurturing atmosphere a program provides for both children and adults.

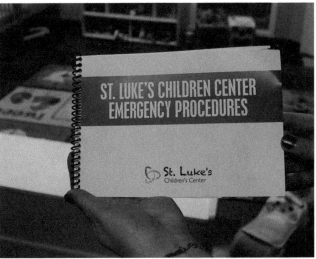

Kristen Alexandria

Figure 9.17 Written plans should be constantly reviewed with staff so that they know what to do if an emergency arises and how to care for any injured children or adults.

Keep Emergency Numbers Posted

Besides 911, non-emergency numbers for fire, ambulance, police, and the nearest poison control center should be posted beside each phone and in each classroom, office space, kitchen, and other public areas. Emergency numbers and email addresses for parents should also be easily accessible and portable in case of emergency. All classroom staff should know emergency procedures and have assigned roles in carrying out emergency plans. Keep in mind that emergencies may occur when a substitute teacher is in charge of the classroom. Make sure substitutes are aware of the emergency procedures.

Administering First Aid

Many states have requirements regarding first aid training for child care providers. Even if training is not required, it makes good common sense to have several staff members trained to provide first aid quickly and effectively, if needed. Having a certified person on staff also reassures parents that their child will be well cared for if an accident were to occur (**Figure 9.18**). It may also reduce the center's risk of charges of negligence and potential lawsuits.

A first aid kit should be available and easily accessible to staff in each classroom while being out of reach of children. The American Red Cross recommends the following items be contained within a kit:

- compress dressings;
- variety of adhesive bandages;
- adhesive cloth tape;
- antibiotic ointment;
- antiseptic wipes;
- emergency blanket;
- breathing barrier (with one-way valve/adult and child-sized);
- instant cold or hot compress;
- non-latex gloves;
- three- and four-inch rolling gauze;
- three-inch by three-inch sterile gauze pads;
- oral thermometer;
- triangular bandages;
- tweezers; and
- Emergency First Aid Guide.

First aid kits should be checked on a regular basis to be sure that they are fully stocked. Items inside with expiration dates should be checked regularly to determine that they are not out of date.

Alerting Staff

A procedure should be established for alerting additional adults in the center if an emergency is occurring. It may require several adults to care for and possibly evacuate the non-involved children, provide first aid, make emergency phone calls, use a fire extinguisher, sound an emergency signal to either alert or provide an "all clear," or guide emergency medical personnel to the location of the emergency. If anyone must be taken to the hospital, at least one familiar adult should go along to stay with the child until a parent arrives.

There may be times when it is necessary to get everyone out of the center quickly. Fires, floods, tornadoes, power outages, chemical spills, intruders, bomb scares, and other emergencies may require immediate evacuation of the building. These typically involve some sort of a signal that all staff must understand and be prepared to immediately do the steps necessary to protect the children and themselves. Each of these types of emergencies generally have very specific steps to follow, which points out the necessity for regular training of staff and practice drills.

Evacuation Plans

Emergency exit plans should be worked out carefully before any need arises. This includes considerations for infants, toddlers, preschoolers, and school-age children. Each has mobility issues to consider as well as the amount of required staff available in which to mobilize the different age groups of children. Regular practice drills should be held on a monthly basis. Staff in each room should know which exit to use and an alternate route if necessary. Diagrams of exit routes should be posted in every room and in the hallways (**Figure 9.19**). One staff member should be designated to check the building quickly to make sure that all children are out. Once outside, one staff member from each classroom should be responsible for taking attendance. Plans should be made in case children need to be transported

RossHelen/iStock/Getty Images Plus

Figure 9.18 Staff members should be trained regularly on how to provide first aid quickly and effectively.

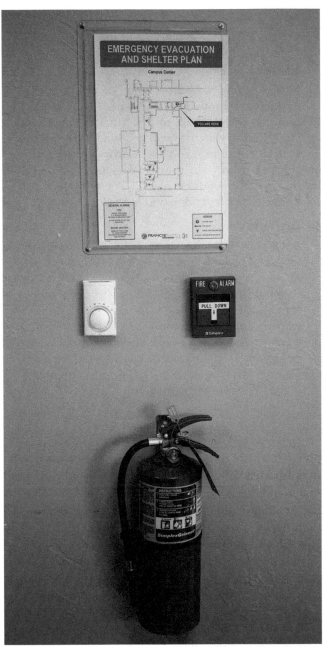

Kristen Alexandria

Figure 9.19 Evacuation plans should be prominently posted using diagrams for staff members to follow in case of an emergency.

to another location. Communicating with other child care programs or child care homes in case of a natural disaster or emergency when developing an emergency plan can be helpful.

Family Notification

Plans should include steps to notify families, if necessary. Local radio stations can broadcast messages. Specific staff can be designated to call parents according to an organized phone list or phone tree. Some of the software purchased for use to manage a program's finances and data can create "a push," which

is an electronic message to parents with emergency information. Each state's emergency planning agency develops guidelines to assist various program personnel in preparing for unexpected emergencies. Be sure to check your own state's requirements.

Severe Weather Preparedness

All states tackle various types of weather issues. From severe thunderstorms to winter weather, all of these weather-related events can potentially have dangerous outcomes. Hence, early childhood programs must be prepared. This can include regular monitoring of the national weather center bulletins and local media stations, to other times when drills allow children to practice places to go and ways to position their bodies for protection. Evacuation from a facility that has been damaged must include preplanned locations where parents can pick up children from another planned for and disclosed location. Extra blankets, first aid, and the ability to mobilize a small group of infants in one crib with wheels are all considerations (**Figure 9.20**). These drills must have plans and times during the year that they are practiced so that the staff are aware of the procedures any time of day.

Lockouts and Lockdowns

Procedures should also be developed to secure the center in the event of an outside threat. The procedures should be practiced. How will staff be notified that the center must be secured? Who will lock the doors? Who will contact the emergency services with the information regarding what is happening? How will parents be notified to stay away from the area around the center until emergency personnel have resolved the problem?

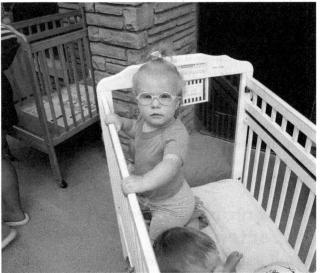

Kristen Alexandria

Figure 9.20 Use of cribs assist when moving several infants and toddlers during evacuation procedures.

Director's Showcase

Reflect

Moving children from one location to another location takes lots of planning. What plan would you suggest to either Elena or JaNya?

Lockdown drills are a source of particular anxiety for staff, children, and families. Staff may need guidelines and training on barricading doors, deciding to escape if possible, and calming panicked children. It is vital that all staff be trained in these emergency procedures, and that someone be clearly in charge if the program leader is unavailable. When drills occur, the administration should document the drill (for example, when it occurred, how long it lasted, etc.) and any feedback or suggestions from staff members. The administration may also decide to notify parents either before or after drills and provide guidance on how to discuss them with their young child.

9.6 Policies Concerning Child Endangerment and Abuse

The *Federal Child Abuse Prevention and Treatment Act (CAPTA)* requires each state to have provisions or procedures for requiring certain individuals to report known or suspected instances of child abuse and neglect. For this publication, information regarding mandatory reporting laws was collected for all states. Statutes in all 50 states as well as the District of Columbia, American Samoa, Guam, the Northern Mariana Islands, Puerto Rico, and the US Virgin Islands identify the professionals and other persons who are required to report instances of suspected child maltreatment. These statutes also address reporting by other persons, the responsibilities of institutions in making reports, standards for making a report, and confidentiality of the reporter's identity (Children's Bureau, 2022). Child abuse can occur in any family or neighborhood; at some point, most programs will have to deal with this situation. Staff training and center policies regarding suspected child abuse are essential in order to take appropriate action.

Recognizing and Reporting Suspected Cases

All staff should be trained to recognize signs of possible child abuse (**Figure 9.21**). As children arrive and throughout the day, staff should note any unusual bruises or other injuries. Children's comments should also be

Director's Showcase

Elena

In the large child care center, Elena maintains policies and procedures to address child endangerment and child abuse. She regularly schedules staff training with the local child welfare program staff to keep current on rules and regulations. The trainings also help the staff become informed and more confident in their knowledge about child abuse prevention and reporting.

JaNya

JaNya has developed a solid relationship with her local child care licensing staff. Through that connection, she was able to establish a relationship with the staff in the local child welfare office. Her former licensing worker became a child welfare worker, and they maintained their relationship. Because JaNya is alone in her program, she can access information and ask questions of her child welfare staff. She also finds support in an online home childcare provider group.

noted. It is important for staff to listen to the child reporting suspected child abuse situations but avoid asking too many questions and making them repeat themselves. If the situation requires a forensic interview, questions and inquiries are better left to professionals specializing in child abuse intervention.

All individuals that work within early childhood programs are classified as **mandated reporters**, or people who work with children and are required to report suspected child abuse to the proper authorities. The program must have specific procedures in place to support staff in meeting this obligation. As a program leader or a person designated to serve in some type of supervisor or coordinator role, this includes being alerted to staff concerns. One person on the supervisory staff should be designated to evaluate the situation and make the report. When one person has responsibility to make the report calls, that individual will become familiar with the questions that will be asked. That staff member can also help classroom staff understand what investigative procedures will occur and what will be expected of them. A written report should contain the following information:

- the date and time of the observation
- the observed injuries;
- any comments made by the child or parent;
- the staff consultation with the program's designated reporter; and
- the time the report was made.

Signs of Physical Abuse	Signs of Neglect	Signs of Sexual Abuse	Signs of Emotional Maltreatment
• Has unexplained burns, bites, bruises, broken bones, or black eyes • Has fading bruises or other marks noticeable after an absence from school • Seems frightened of the parents and protests or cries when it is time to go home • Shrinks at the approach of adults • Reports injury by a parent or another adult caregiver	• Frequently absent from school • Begs or steals food or money • Lacks needed medical or dental care, immunizations, or glasses • Consistently dirty and has severe body odor • Lacks sufficient clothing for the weather • States that there is no one at home to provide care	• Difficulty walking or sitting • Suddenly refuses to change for gym or to participate in physical activities • Sudden change in appetite • Demonstrates bizarre, sophisticated, or unusual sexual knowledge or behavior • Reports sexual abuse by a parent or another adult caregiver	• Shows extremes in behavior, such as overly compliant or demanding behavior, extreme passivity, or aggression • Inappropriately adult (parenting other children, for example) or inappropriately infantile (frequently rocking or head-banging, for example) behavior • Delayed in physical or emotional development • Reports a lack of attachment to the parent
Consider the possibility of physical abuse when the parent or other adult caregiver:	Consider the possibility of neglect when the parent or other adult caregiver:	Consider the possibility of sexual abuse when the parent or other adult caregiver:	Consider the possibility of emotional maltreatment when the parent or other adult caregiver:
• Offers conflicting, unconvincing, or no explanation for the child's injury • Describes the child as "evil," or in some other very negative way • Uses harsh physical discipline with the child • Has a history of abuse as a child	• Appears to be indifferent to the child • Seems apathetic or depressed • Behaves irrationally or in a bizarre manner • Is abusing alcohol or other drugs	• Is unduly protective of the child or severely limits the child's contact with other children, especially of the opposite sex • Is secretive and isolated • Is jealous or controlling with family members	• Constantly blames, belittles, or berates the child • Is unconcerned about the child and refuses to consider offers of help for the child's problems • Overtly rejects the child

Courtesy of US Department of Health & Human Services Child Welfare Information Gateway

Figure 9.21 Program leaders and staff members should be aware of the signs of abuse and neglect.

Parents should be aware of the center's obligations and policies regarding reporting suspected abuse. They must also understand that telling the classroom staff that they "lost it last night" does not release the staff from their obligation to report abuse. It is best to include information on this policy in the parent handbook, post it in visible areas, and mention it during the enrollment orientation.

Identifying a Child Predator

Both parents and directors alike fear the possibility that someone who wants to deliberately hurt children could begin working with young children. **Pedophiles**, better known as *sexual predators*, are individuals who are intent on making inappropriate sexual advances on children and are known to seek employment in jobs or activities that bring them into daily contact with children. With 24-hour access to news, publicity for alleged abuse in early childhood programs can have a serious effect of frightening both parents and center staff. Program leaders must have built-in safeguards to minimize the possibility of hiring a staff member whose intentions are to harm rather than to help children. Applications for employment must be reviewed carefully. This includes looking for unexplained gaps in employment history or a pattern of brief employment in several different places. Take the necessary time to obtain original copies of all state-required clearances and criminal background checks. Be particularly cautious about individuals who seem to appear in your community "out-of-the-blue" or who have relocated from other states. Also keep in mind that criminal background checks will not reveal anything about abuse crimes an individual may have committed while still a juvenile (**Figure 9.22**). Use the technology available to research possible hires. Social media can provide a plethora of information about the types of people who will seek employment.

Due to widely publicized situations involving allegations of child sexual abuse in programs, parents may look upon staff with suspicion. This can result in staff members feeling untrusted and uncomfortable when providing the basic comfort and care that young children need. Program policies must include procedures designed to protect both children and staff. Suggested policies include:

- Two staff members should handle the supervision of nap and bathroom areas.
- Two staff members should be present whenever a child has to change clothes for any reason.
- No child should be taken alone to an isolated area of the center. The isolation area designed for sick children should be observable and supervised at all times.
- No child should ever be left unattended.

The best way to ensure the safety of both children and staff is to be extremely careful in staff hiring procedures. Parents should be allowed to visit the center at any time. An open-door policy for parents helps to reassure them that the staff has nothing to hide and there is nothing

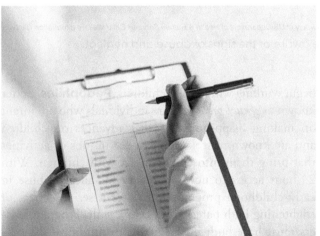

Hiraman/E+/Getty Images

Figure 9.22 Applicants will need to complete criminal background checks and other necessary documents to secure employment in an early childhood program.

secretive going on behind closed doors. Many centers and child care homes have incorporated the use of video cameras in classrooms. Using a safe and secure site for parents to check in on their children provides another layer of protection for both children and staff. This can also ease anxiety that some parents experience when leaving their child in the care of someone else.

Knowing Who Should Be Picking Up a Child

During the enrollment process, parents should identify those adults who are authorized to pick up children from the center. A form should be developed where a parent can identify by name, phone number, and address those authorized persons. The parent should be informed that the child will not be allowed to leave the program with any person who is not on that authorized list. In case of unforeseen circumstances, verbal permission from the parent by phone, along with positive identification of the person trying to pick up the child, will be acceptable. In many centers, adults who bring children to and from the center accompany them to their classroom door. Sign-in sheets and/or electronic check-in and checkout procedures should be posted so that everyone is aware of when children come and go from the program each day. Other programs have staff meet children at the entrance and take them to their classrooms to minimize the number of adults in the building. All programs must have in place security precautions in order to prevent entry by unauthorized adults. This may include the use of automatic locks on main doors with pass codes, a card entry system, camera and voice recognition system, or other major security process to keep children safely behind locked doors after they have arrived. Keep in mind that additional security measures may be necessary in some areas.

Suspecting an Adult of Intoxication or Impairment

When an intoxicated parent (or one who appears to be under the influence of drugs or may be suffering from some sort of a health issue) arrives to pick up a child, these steps should be followed:

- The teacher should confront the parent with the concern while another staff member alerts the program director.
- The parent should be asked to leave. Before they exit, another authorized adult to pick up the child should be contacted for child pickup.
- If the parent insists, there are no laws allowing the program or staff to detain the child. Advise the parent before they leave with the child that the

police will be called immediately to report a suspected drunk or impaired driver. Be prepared to describe the car, license plate, home address, and probable route home.

- Contact the parent the next day, when they are most likely sober. Arrange a conference to discuss the incident.

It is always better to err on the side of caution when it is suspected that a child may be in a potentially dangerous position. As noted before, those who work in the field of early childhood are mandated reporters and concerns such as this fall within that expectation.

Trauma-Sensitive Classrooms Supporting Young Children

For many children, attending child care programs is a part of a consistent social and emotional healthy childhood. For some children, it is the only consistent social and emotional healthy part of childhood. Children experiencing trauma are enrolled in every program across our country.

Childhood trauma affects all areas of child development. It can affect the way a child interacts with the world and others around them. **Toxic stress**, or lasting serious stress experienced by a child without support from a caregiver, can impact brain development, immune system responses, and cause lifelong health problems (Shonkoff 2012).

Child care providers can be the **protective factor**, or an attribute in an individual or family that promotes the health and well-being of a child, in the life of a child in their care. By being a consistent presence and providing a safe and healthy environment, child care providers can help alleviate the effects of toxic stress (childwelfare.gov).

During times of community and national crises, such as a global pandemic, all children will experience some form of stress. Building a trauma-sensitive classroom and program will only serve to enhance the development and social and emotional health of young children.

In *A Framework for Trauma-Sensitive Schools* McConnico et al. discuss common themes among successful trauma sensitive classrooms (**Figure 9.23**). Those common themes are programs that build a sense of community, provide social and emotional connectedness, knowledge of impact of trauma, building capacity of educators and caregivers, building resiliency, mindset change, and social justice (McConnico, 2016).

It is important for all caregivers working with children to be trauma informed. The amount of information and resources for caregivers to learn more about childhood trauma is readily available and further education is strongly encouraged.

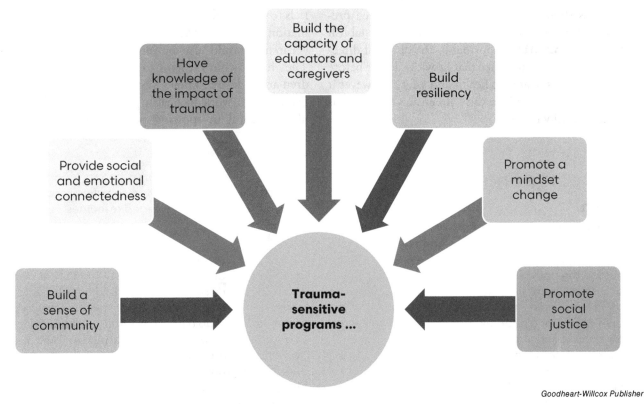

Figure 9.23 Providing a trauma-sensitive program is a commitment to do the hard work to connect with and support the child and their family.

9.7 Why Does the Program Need a Health and Safety Committee?

Because centers are faced with an array of both legal and ethical concerns, the center's health and safety practices must be taken seriously. Genuine thought and effort must be put into making the center as safe as possible for all those who spend their days there. As the program leader, the role is to independently try to figure out every possible hazard in the environment in which the children stay each day. Oftentimes, health and safety policies are developed based on these regular environment assessments combined with state and local regulations. Since this area has rapidly changing knowledge about disease, safety precautions, and increasingly complex legal issues, many programs have established special committees focused on health and safety.

Programs should consider having an established preventive health and safety committee. They may establish an **ad hoc committee** reporting to the board of directors as an advisory committee that provides advice before making decisions related to health and safety. However it is organized, the committee can help ensure the center is a safe and healthy place.

Who Should Be on This Committee?

Membership on this committee should include individuals who are in a position to provide helpful information to the group. Ideally, this committee should include both a doctor and a lawyer. Many concerns involving contagious diseases and the legal impact of the *Americans with Disabilities Act* must be constantly monitored. As program leader, having help to remain up-to-date on judicial decisions, changing interpretations of the law, and medical practices relating to bloodborne pathogens and contagious diseases would be very beneficial.

It is also advisable to include two to three full-time staff members on the committee. These individuals represent staff concerns and should also be able to communicate clearly with the staff regarding the concerns and recommendations of the committee. Membership on this committee, while somewhat time-consuming, should be a part of a master or lead teacher position (**Figure 9.24**). Ideally, these staff members work at the program the majority of the day, and in certain areas throughout the program. These individuals should have assistant teachers that assist them with any added job responsibilities and duties. Depending on the issues at hand related to health and safety, this staff member must have the time to serve as a resource person for the committee and staff members that they represent. These staff members may also assist with developing training programs and materials to educate the entire staff in new or changing information and procedures.

Parents should also be included on the committee. They have a commitment to quality care for their children and a desire to make sure the center is a safe place. Parents who work in health professions can be particularly helpful in spotting potential trouble spots. A

SDI Productions/E+/Getty Images

Figure 9.24 Allow opportunities for staff members to be engaged in committees that support the ongoing programming taking place.

representative from the board of directors should also sit on the committee. It may be possible to request that members of the board who fit into the categories needed also serve on this committee. For example, parents on the board may also be nurses or lawyers. They may be more willing to put in the time and effort needed than someone else who has no direct involvement with the program.

Responsibilities

The committee should be charged with several specific responsibilities. This will help to keep it from getting off track. These responsibilities should include

- periodically inspecting the center to look for potential hazards;
- identifying and categorizing infectious diseases;
- advising on procedures to minimize the risk of spreading contagious diseases;
- identifying and addressing educational needs of staff and families in regard to contagious disease;

- advising the director regarding center compliance with state and federal laws; and
- identifying an official agency spokesperson to represent the program to the news media.

The committee should try to anticipate as many potential health problems as possible that may occur within the early childhood program environment.

Different categories of health concerns should be established. Guidelines can be set for dealing with these different categories. For example, all centers will eventually have to deal with an episode of impetigo, lice, or pinworms. These are unpleasant health issues, but common ones when caring for young children. They can be dealt with in a routine manner. Centers may also have to deal with Hepatitis B, AIDS, or other more serious diseases. Obviously, policies and staff training for these two types of contagious illnesses will be different. A health and safety committee can be established in every size program including a family child care home. Although the amount of people involved might be smaller, it is a great way to problem solve health and safety issues and deal with areas of concern or need.

Director's Showcase
Elena and JaNya

Both Elena and JaNya will have daily struggles to keep their staff and children healthy. As we read in the chapter, the many guidelines and recommendations can be overwhelming. However, both have striven to think about better systems to manage issues as well as contacting the correct resources to assist when questions have arisen. In addition, receiving regular training and education for themselves, staff, and parents has approached this important issue in a very holistic and positive way.

Chapter 9 Review and Assessment

Summary

9.1 Plan a safe and healthy environment for children and staff.

- A center must be a safe, healthy place for children to explore and learn.
- Adults caring for the children are responsible for following licensing standards. They must regularly inspect equipment to ensure that it is safe.

9.2 Establish and implement policies concerning health issues in an early childhood program.

- Child care directors must also consider the health and safety of the staff. This includes providing all of the resources necessary as well as policies and procedures to follow.
- Child care administrators must establish policies to ensure children's safety while they are at the center. These include the use of universal precautions to prevent the spread of disease.
- Guidelines regarding other health-related aspects of the center must also be established. Parents need to be informed of these policies when they enroll their children at the center. Appropriate training to help staff in dealing with health and safety issues is mandatory. Many times this is set forth by local and state regulatory agencies.

9.3 Follow proper food safety policies and practices to support proper nutrition.

- When food is prepared and served, practices are established to minimize the risks of choking and/or food contamination and must be followed carefully.
- State and local regulators often monitor these practices. Foodborne illnesses can wreak havoc on an early childhood program, which is why close monitoring and food practices are implemented.

9.4 Meet special health needs of children and staff.

- An awareness of the special health needs of children is important. This includes having open and honest communication with a family.
- Early childhood leaders and staff members must be patient with families coming to terms with the need to reach out to referral services.
- States provide early intervention services to support these families.

9.5 Create emergency policies and procedures.

- All staff must practice emergency procedures. Either natural or man-made events can create situations where children and staff are in danger.
- Program directors must have very detailed plans in place that include regular drills and communication with the staff. Parents are also important components to that communication as they need to be aware of drills and plans should the need arise.

9.6 Recognize issues related to child endangerment and the importance of reporting possible child abuse.

- All individuals working within an early childhood program are considered "mandated reporters." They must report any suspicion of child abuse based on observed situations with children to the proper authorities.
- Those working with young children each day are the front line to watch for these issues and advocate for the child whose voice may or may not be heard.

9.7 Discuss the importance of working with a health and safety committee.

- A health and safety committee should be established to assist in the development of center policies. Issues related to both wellness and liability must be considered.
- The importance of handwashing should be stressed. NAEYC has detailed guidelines for programs, both large and small, to follow.
- When adults in charge of the care of children follow best practices and licensing recommendations, children will be safer and healthier.

Review

1. How do centers balance risk with appropriate childhood activities? (9.1)
2. What is the best defense against the spread of disease and illness? (9.2)
3. Why is polluted air more of a problem for young children than for adults? (9.2)
4. For what kinds of problems should outdoor equipment be inspected? (9.1)
5. What types of foods present potential choking hazards for young children? (9.3)

6. Explain what is meant by the term *universal precautions*. (9.2)
7. Identify three actions that can minimize the safety hazards in the classroom. (9.1)
8. When must children be excluded from the center due to illness? (9.4)
9. Why is it important to plan and hold practice evacuation and severe weather drills? (9.5)
10. How can a director minimize the possibility of hiring a staff member whose intentions are to harm rather than to help children? (9.6)

Showcase Your Skills

As part of the daily struggles to keep staff and children healthy, there were many areas reviewed that had guidelines and recommendations. It is important to have systems in place to manage issues. This includes knowing who the correct resources are to include local authorities. In addition, there might be specific training and education opportunities to access. It's your turn to be the expert in this area.

Based on the information shared in each section of this chapter, it is now your turn to serve in the role of consultant. Choose one of the following areas to further develop.

1. Develop a written plan to conduct an evacuation drill for either a family child care home or center classroom environment. Consider the areas where signs would need to be made showing appropriate exits, assign any tasks that must be done to specific individuals, and suggest the amount of time it might take to empty the program environment to the outside of the building. Include factors that might cause confusion or delays in evacuating a child care facility. (9.5)
2. As a small group of three classmates, role-play a situation where a parent arrives intoxicated to an early childhood program. Assign the roles as either family child care home provider and parent or role of director, parent, teacher, and child. Develop a written plan of how this would be managed to include those authorities that would be contacted. (9.6)
3. Develop a plan to have an ad hoc health and safety committee for a local child care center. Include specific items that the committee would share knowledge and develop recommendations. Prepare policies that the committee would need to follow to best support the early childhood programs. (9.7)

Matching

Match the following terms with the correct definitions:

A. ad hoc committee
B. Early Intervention Program (EI)
C. health
D. mandated reporters
E. pedophiles
F. protective factors
G. safety hazards
H. toxic stress
I. universal precautions

1. People who work with children and are required to report suspected child abuse to the proper authorities.
2. Attribute in an individual or family that promotes the health and well-being of a child.
3. Potential source of harm or injury to a person.
4. Federally mandated program that provides specialty services for infants and toddlers with developmental delays.
5. Committee that reports to the board of directors as an advisory committee that provides advice before making decisions related to health and safety.
6. Individuals who are intent on making inappropriate sexual advances on children.
7. State of complete physical, oral, mental, and social well-being, not simply the absence of disease or infirmity.
8. Lasting serious stress experienced by a child without support from a caregiver that can impact brain development.
9. Practices developed by the CDC that require all staff treat every situation as having the potential to spread disease.

skynesher/E+/Getty Images

10 CHAPTER

Engaging and Supporting Families

Learning Outcomes

After studying this chapter, you will be able to:

10.1 Understand the connection between effective communication and family engagement.

10.2 Identify strategies to facilitate communication between families and staff.

10.3 Describe ways of providing understanding and support for families.

10.4 Identify ways to engage families and encourage involvement in program activities.

Key Terms

conference
family engagement
parent handbook
support system
workshop

Introduction

Children succeed in their child care experience when the center staff and their families or caregivers are comfortable with each other. This success is directly related to the type and quality of communication you have with caregivers. Ideally, the program staff works in partnership with and provides support to caregivers and families. As with other aspects of the atmosphere in the center, you, as the director, set the tone. Your warm, respectful greetings and responses to caregivers are noticed by

Kristen Alexandria

Figure 10.1 The goal for every program leader is to hire caring and compassionate staff members.

NAEYC/DAP standards

Standards covered in this chapter:

2b, 2c, 4a, 6c

2A, 2B, 2C, 2D, 2E, 2F, 2G, 4B, 5D

all. Staff orientation and training should stress the need for respect for families. Ideally, if you have been able to hire caring and compassionate staff members, respect for caregivers will come easily (**Figure 10.1**). Consideration for families and caregivers is an extension of your care for their children.

Not all the caregivers in the child's life will be pleasant and polite to you and the staff. This can make your job harder. It is important to try to treat even these caregivers politely. You do not have to give in to their demands. You do not have to give them special favors. However, you must maintain a respectful demeanor. This is where it helps to have an official center policy on which to rely. If someone wants a special discount or favor, you can easily say, "I'm sorry, but our center policy is…. We feel it is a fair policy for all." Few people are willing to argue that center policy should be broken just for them, even though they might like it to be.

10.1 The Communication-Engagement Connection

The Head Start program has developed a research-based, well-designed framework for *family engagement*. **Family engagement**, developing a relationship with and supporting caregivers, is essential to a successful early childhood program. What this framework stresses is that family engagement is a collaborative process to build positive relationships between early childhood educators and families and caregivers. The Head Start *Parent, Family, and Community Engagement (PFCE) Framework* focuses on building relationships with key adults in the lives of children through culturally and linguistically responsive communication. The ultimate goal of the framework is to build relationships with caregivers to promote positive child outcomes and ultimately success in later years. The Head Start PFCE Framework can be helpful in engaging families. Hallmarks of this framework are listening and accepting, learning and finding mutual understanding, and reaching an agreement on

Director's Showcase

Betsy

Betsy has a small child care business in her home. She has been struggling to find ways to engage and involve families in activities and participate in aftercare events she plans. She planned a fall festival for the children in her care as well as their families. Betsy decorated her home and planned fun games for all ages. There were only two families that attended, and Betsy is looking for other ways to help build a sense of community with the children and their families.

James

James is the director at a small center. Recently, the center's teachers and staff have been experiencing difficulties in communicating with parents and caregivers during drop-off and pick-up. James has noted the teachers' frustration. They also observed a teacher trying to engage a caregiver about their child at pick-up time while the caregiver was on her phone. The caregiver ignored the teacher's request and continued to talk on their phone. James has had conversations with the center's teachers and staff and have had many ask for support and help in more effectively communicating with parents and caregivers. James is brainstorming ways to assist them in engaging families and caregivers.

plans and next steps (**Figure 10.2**). These are basic steps in relationship building, but imperative to helping and supporting family engagement. Foundational for these steps is effective communication. It is through communication that you and your staff will establish, learn about, understand, and begin a relationship with your center's families.

Inclusivity and diversity of children and families need to be considered in all areas of program development, particularly communication and family engagement (**Figure 10.3**). The Zero to Three program encourages program administrators to consider the following to engage families:

- Reaching out to diverse populations when recruiting for enrollment.
- Providing training to all staff members about diversity and how to welcome and include all populations.
- Mindfully recruiting a diverse population of program administration, staff, and children.
- Providing inclusive enrollment and program paperwork, including electronic forms that can be

Hallmarks of the Head Start Parent, Family, and Community Engagement (PFCE) Framework

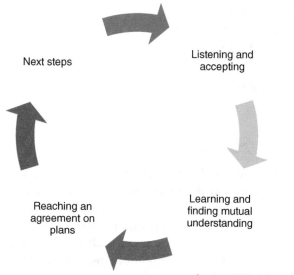

Next steps

Listening and accepting

Learning and finding mutual understanding

Reaching an agreement on plans

Goodheart-Willcox Publisher

Figure 10.2 The Head Start Parent, Family, and Community Engagement (PFCE) Framework focuses on building relationships with key adults in the lives of children through culturally and linguistically responsive communication.

completed using voice software or paperwork in caregivers' native languages.
- Engaging nontraditional families in leadership roles and inclusion in program planning.

Making connections with your families' cultures and backgrounds will enhance the early childhood program and classroom. Consider areas of the program and how to include a variety of family structures; add books to story time that reflect the population of the classroom; develop inclusive curriculum in every classroom; and ensure that all your children, families, and staff are well

AleksandarGeorgiev/E+/Getty Images

Figure 10.3 Today's families are diverse and require opportunities to engage in the early childhood program in many ways.

represented in your program. Diverse populations of caregivers and families deserve to be a part of a warm and welcoming environment. When you understand and welcome the diversity of your families, you are better able to communicate and connect with them. Families who feel understood and connected with your program are more likely to engage in all your program has to offer.

10.2 Strategies for Effective Communication

Communication between child care staff and caregivers can come in a variety of ways. Most caregivers are eager to learn more and know about their children and how they are doing. Some parents may exhibit behaviors that make you question their concern about their child. You and your staff must refrain from judgment and make every effort to connect and build relationships with these parents and caregivers. Making these connections will only benefit the development of the child and make daily care run smoothly.

Parent Handbook

A handbook explaining basic center procedures, policies, and philosophy is important in helping parents understand how the center works. Any program working for NAEYC center accreditation must have a **parent handbook**, which is a basic tool of written communication to which parents can refer (**Figure 10.4**). Among topics you might want to include in your center's parent handbook are

- the types of programs offered by your program;
- a statement of nondiscrimination policies;
- any admissions policies and procedures;
- fee policies;
- arrival and departure policies;
- general procedural policies;
- health policies and concerns;
- program history, philosophy, objectives, and governance;
- an event calendar;
- general staff qualifications and training;
- program address, phone numbers, and center address;

Ivan Pantic/E+/Getty Images

Figure 10.4 Parent handbooks are key to providing an overview of basic center procedures and policies and explaining the program's philosophy.

- a typical full-day schedule and summer school-age schedule; and
- a statement informing parents that the center is a mandated reporter for any incident of suspected child abuse.

The parent handbook is a useful reference for caregivers. It helps them to know that they have entered into an agreement with a well-organized and stable program. A handbook enhances the image and professionalism of your program.

Home Visits

Home visits used to be routinely done by teachers. Home visits give teachers a chance to meet with families in a setting where they feel more comfortable. Teachers are also more easily able to recognize important elements of the family's cultural, religious, and ethnic heritage and lifestyle by visiting the home (**Figure 10.5**). They can

Ridofranz/iStock/Getty Images Plus

Figure 10.5 When teachers make home visits they can recognize and become better acquainted with the family's cultural, religious, and ethnic heritage and lifestyle.

get a sense of the reading materials in the home as well as the types of entertainment the family enjoys. The better the teachers know the families of the children, the more likely they are to feel comfortable with each other. When teachers know the families, they also gain a better understanding of the children.

Unfortunately, teachers in many centers no longer make home visits. Working parents may not have the time or energy to welcome visitors. Teachers have more paperwork and responsibilities than they did when most programs were half-day nursery schools. Some programs, such as Head Start, continue to have home visits as a part of their program. Head Start programs usually have specific staff members designated as home visitors. These staff members not only serve as a link to the program, but they also play a role in supporting families and creating learning opportunities that help them build routines and assist their child's development.

In the busy world we live and work in, home visiting has become difficult for many. Taking advantage of technology can help in the place of home visits (**Figure 10.6**). The use of video calls via a computer or phone can greatly improve and build relationships between staff and caregivers. Children can show their favorite toys, pets, or books and where they eat meals. Caregivers are given the opportunity to speak one on one with teachers and staff about their child. This is a cost-effective, safe, and less time-consuming way to connect with caregivers and families.

Teachers may also visit a child's home, if the child and family have become friends with the teacher. The teacher may be invited to a birthday party, summer picnic, or special dinner. These can be pleasant occasions. The teacher must be careful, however, that a special friendship with a family does not lead to favoritism of that child in the classroom.

Figure 10.6 Communicating virtually allows for flexibility between teaching staff and parents in place of home visits.

A home visit may be especially helpful when a child is having difficulty adjusting to the center. A chance to show off meaningful things from home life can help a child feel more comfortable with the teacher. Children seem to adjust to the center more easily when they feel that they have a special, one-to-one relationship with the teacher. The teacher may better understand the child's home life and be able to bring elements of it into the classroom to enhance the child's comfort level. While home visits are no longer considered necessary in most programs, they can be helpful in supporting that special relationship between child, family, and teacher.

Visits to the Center

Caregivers should feel welcome at the center any time. This is important in reassuring them that their original impressions of the center are correct. It confirms that the center is a safe place for their children and can alleviate anxiety and stress. Many centers try to have an area that serves as a parent reception room. It can be an informal meeting place, a waiting area, or just a place to sit and have a cup of coffee. It is the ideal place to set up a lending library of books, magazines, or pamphlets that may be of interest to caregivers. Some centers also organize clothing or coupon exchanges. Parents can exchange clothing or coupons they do not need for others that they can use. Some centers will add a swap and shop page to their social media or even hold a yard sale at the center.

Caregivers may drop in at inconvenient times for your staff. When the children have settled down for a nap, or in the middle of cleanup time, a parent may arrive. As caregivers become more familiar with the schedule and secure with the center, they become more sensitive about the best times to visit.

The center can also plan special events to encourage caregivers and even extended family to visit. Events such as a Thanksgiving dinner each year on a day in late November, a spring play day with special outdoor games and activities, a planting day where families can help plant seeds in a vegetable garden or flowers and bulbs around the center, or a summer water play day can be ways to involve the entire family (**Figure 10.7**). Children love to show off their classrooms and work. These events serve as a great community-building opportunity as well as a time to connect with individual caregivers and families.

Parent Conferences

Some centers make it a regular practice to schedule a **conference**, or a meeting between teacher and caregivers, at some point during the year with each parent. Licensing requirements in some states call for parent

Director's Showcase

Betsy

Betsy has decided to add home visits to her program. Since she has fewer children than a child care center, she is able to schedule home visits with each family twice a year. The caregivers seem to be on board with the visits, and the children are excited to show off their homes. Betsy has clearly defined the expectations and reasons behind the home visits for her families. She emailed information to each family with things she wants to discuss as well as a projected beginning and ending time for the visit. Because she is beginning the NAEYC accreditation process, she can emphasize the need for participation in home visits. She is also careful to relieve the stress around home visits by assuring the families that their homes do not need to be spotless nor do they need to stress about how it looks. She has scheduled visits on the weekends so she can visit during the best time for the families and so they do not feel pressure to provide a meal.

James

James previously worked as a teacher in another large child care center before they became the director at their current center. During their time as a teacher, they participated in home visits with each child in their classroom. They remember spending a number of days making home visits and that some of those visits were spent waiting for the family to come home and often ending in a no-show. James has implemented a home-visiting program for all new children enrolled in the center. Since they have been struggling with ways to help teachers and staff engage with families, they have decided to try to add a home visit for each child in the center. Because of the size and number in their center, James is spending some time working on logistics and started with a parent survey email. From the survey, they were able to learn that about half of the families and caregivers preferred an in-home visit, while the other half preferred a video call.

conferences. Parents are aware that this is a routine conference and are usually not too concerned about it.

Some new teachers may be very comfortable working with young children but may feel uncomfortable having conferences with parents. It is usually helpful to provide some training for them. Giving teachers guidance in structuring a parent conference can help the meeting go more smoothly. A leading expert has developed a pattern for teachers to follow when meeting with parents and recommends the following:

- Prepare an agenda for the meeting ahead of time for the caregiver to see.
- Have all materials, records, and examples of the child's work ready and organized for review.

AzmanL/E+/Getty Images

Figure 10.8 A meeting space that is comfortable and pleasant provides necessary support for both the teacher and the child's caregiver.

- Organize the meeting place so it is comfortable and pleasant (**Figure 10.8**). It is best for the teacher to sit beside or at an angle from the caregiver. Sitting across a desk or table can be intimidating. Using first names also helps keep the conference more informal.
- Consider the caregiver as a partner in the work of helping the child. Provide positive suggestions in a tone that is respectful. Use clear language and avoid jargon.
- Listen carefully to concerns and suggestions. Rephrase what the caregiver has said for clarification.
- Evaluate how the conference is going as it proceeds.
- Respond to the caregiver by summarizing the conference, preparing an educational plan, and planning for follow-up.

kali9/E+/Getty Images

Figure 10.7 Special events where family members are invited to participate can allow children to share in the many outdoor activities that a program provides.

Director's Showcase

Betsy

Betsy recently enrolled a six-week-old infant. The infant is the first child in the family and was conceived after years of infertility. The parents visited and observed Betsy's program numerous times before the baby was born and appear to be anxious about returning to work. Betsy has reassured the parents but is keenly aware of their stress and anxiety every day at drop-off time. Both parents call frequently throughout the day to check on their baby. Betsy understands their anxiety and always answers their calls and questions. She has been brainstorming to find solutions to ease this couple's worries as well as add ways to update and communicate with all her caregivers during the day.

James

James added a new infant classroom to their program a few months ago. There are now two infant rooms, and both are at capacity. The addition of an entire classroom has added unforeseen issues, and James is finding ways to rework daily routines and how their staff communicates with caregivers of infants and toddlers. Drop-off and pick-up times are chaotic and stressful for caregivers, children, and staff. James has found that caregivers want to communicate with them and the teachers at these times. While they understand the need for information exchange, this adds to the chaos and confusion. They have recently strategized with the infant staff and are working toward resolutions.

Occasionally, additional conferences must be scheduled. Perhaps the caregiver or teacher has some special concerns about a child. Often these conferences are related to behavior problems, possible developmental delays, or special concerns about vision, hearing, or speech. In many cases, it is the child care teacher who first notices that a child may have a problem. Caregivers who are used to their child's mannerisms or who may be unaware of normal developmental patterns may not notice that their child needs special screening.

A teacher who is working closely with a family or caregiver may be aware of very personal information about the family and child. Parents should be assured that their conferences and their child's records are confidential. This confidentiality is a legal requirement under the *Family Educational Rights and Privacy Act of 1974*.

Communicating with Caregivers of Infants and Toddlers

As a director, you will see the differences in caregivers of infants and toddlers and caregivers of older children. Caring for younger children is often cause for more communication with parents and caregivers. During the course of an average day in child care, there are numerous events that need to be communicated to caregivers. Caregivers like to know about feeding amounts and schedules, diaper changes, progress on developmental milestones as well as social interactions. Finding ways to communicate daily events with caregivers is often challenging and can prove difficult if a routine is not established with child care staff (**Figure 10.9**).

Communicating with caregivers of infants and toddlers may be different from communicating with caregivers of older children. Caregivers of infants and toddlers may need more frequent and detailed updates and information daily. Caregivers are often a diverse group and in order to reach them, it is wise to have several different forms of communication (**Figure 10.10**).

These items are in addition to regular center- or program-wide communications. Some centers are now adding surveillance cameras to each classroom so parents can watch their child's room online. This can be a valuable tool in helping parents feel confident that their child is happy and receiving quality care. As a director, your best strategy is to use a combination of communication methods and stick primarily to the ones that work best with your families.

oatawa/iStock/Getty Images Plus

Figure 10.9 One of the major ways early childhood programs are communicating with parents and caregivers is through text communication, often supported by commercial apps.

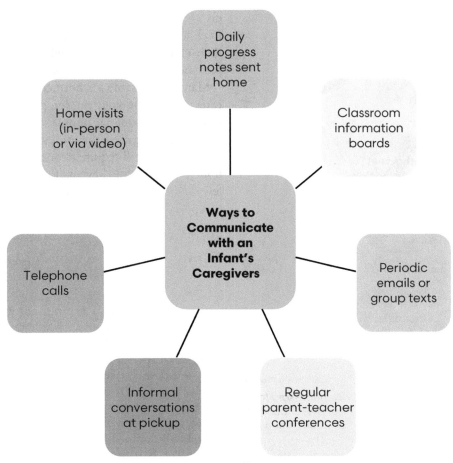

Daily progress notes sent home

Home visits (in-person or via video)

Classroom information boards

Ways to Communicate with an Infant's Caregivers

Telephone calls

Periodic emails or group texts

Informal conversations at pickup

Regular parent-teacher conferences

Goodheart-Willcox Publisher

Figure 10.10 To support the parent-teacher relationship, teaching staff working with infants and toddlers will need to communicate more frequently with specific detail to support quality communications.

Communicating with Caregivers of Preschool-Age Children

Communicating with caregivers of preschoolers can be similar to communicating with those of infants. They will need more information than caregivers of older children but may not require as much as with infants. Children of this age are busy and exploring their environment. There may be times when a caregiver needs to be informed about an accident or minor injury. Caregivers also need to be informed of daily routines and events that happen throughout the day.

Director's Showcase

Betsy

Betsy has been able to implement frequent communication with caregivers throughout the day. She texts a picture along with an update of events or any other information to parents individually three times a day. Because her enrollment is limited, she is able to do this in a short amount of time. She has scheduled these texts into her daily routine and has given caregivers a range of time to expect a text. This has eased many worries of her new parents and provided them with numerous pictures of their child thriving in child care.

James

James has been able to add another staff member at pick-up time to give teachers the ability to communicate with caregivers. They have also adapted a checklist with pertinent information that teachers can complete throughout the day to send home with the infants. This allows for caregivers and staff to communicate about other issues during pick-up time and not on daily routines. James is present in the classroom during the chaotic times and can model effective communication with caregivers for the staff as well as answer questions and ease everyone into a new routine. The additional staff member eases the burden of the classroom teachers in caretaking tasks and frees up time for quality communication.

Goodheart-Willcox Publisher

Figure 10.11 While not as detailed as was necessary for the care of infants and toddlers, parents of preschool-age children will need many forms of daily communication.

Many of the same forms of communication discussed previously with caregivers of infants apply to the preschool population (**Figure 10.11**).

Communicating with Caregivers of School-Age Children

Older children receiving after-school or out-of-school care are able to communicate about daily events and routines directly to their caregivers. This does not mean that information should not be shared between teachers and caregivers. Children enrolled in after-school care often

ipuwadol/iStock/Getty Images Plus

Figure 10.12 One of the ideal communications for parents with school-age children is weekly newsletters sent by email or posted to social media pages.

do homework or work on school projects in their time in child care. It is important for caregivers to know what their child worked on and what they have left to complete before the next school day.

Many of the same forms of communication used with caregivers of the younger age groups can be used with those of the school-age population. Caregivers of this age group may not need the same detailed account of daily activities, but still require frequent updates and information about scheduled events (**Figure 10.12**). There are a few methods of communication to use that are specific to this population (**Figure 10.13**).

Director's Showcase

Betsy

One of the children that attends Betsy's program is part of a family who are Indigenous Americans. Betsy has cared for two other siblings in this family and has developed a good relationship with the parents and grandparents. The family is delighted when invited to share the culture of their Indigenous tribe. With the help of family members, Betsy has been able to share their tribal alphabet with the other children in her care. The grandmother is a fantastic storyteller, and Betsy has invited her to come in each month for a story time. Through the years, Betsy has coordinated with the family to invite other child care families to cultural community events such as annual Pow Wows and Tribal Dances. Betsy also hosts a tribal feast at her home during her fall festival. She has found the children love learning about the Indigenous culture, and the families have made connections with each other through these events.

James

James has many new families and some first-time parents after the addition of the second infant classroom. The teachers have reported higher stress levels among the caregivers of children in this room. They also have been receiving phone calls from the new caregivers throughout the week about their children or with questions or concerns. James has decided to start a group for all caregivers of infants and schedule monthly speakers and professionals to advise and support the new families. They have also started a social media group for the caregivers to communicate with each other about questions or provide reassurance about their children. James asked two veteran teachers and a parent of school-age children to join the group to provide information and answers from their own experiences.

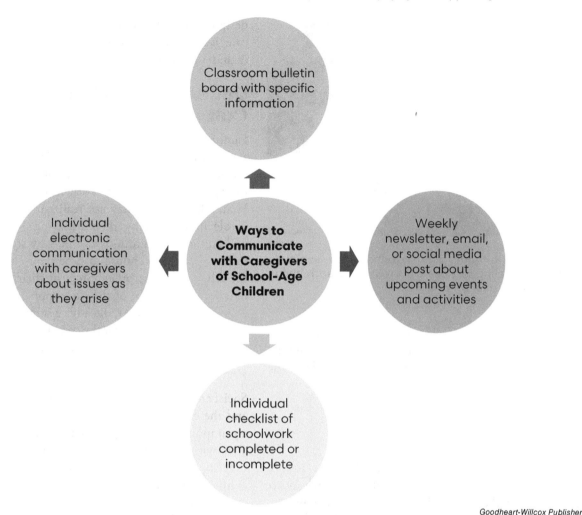

Figure 10.13 Communication with school-age parents is essential and can utilize a variety of effective strategies.

Director's Showcase
Reflect
Communication is essential within the early childhood program environment. What specific strategies would you implement to best support the infant and toddler classrooms, preschool, and school-age classrooms? What resources would you need to implement each?

10.3 Supporting Your Families and Caregivers

Your center may play an additional role in the lives of families and caregivers beyond providing child care. As your staff and caregivers and families get to know each other, they naturally begin to communicate more freely. Those caregivers who have few resources and no **support system**, or people to help them, may begin to share their problems with the staff. Staff members, as sensitive human beings, will vary in terms of how well they can cope with sharing in someone else's troubles. Though most of your staff will not have training in social work or counseling, they may want to help these families.

As the director, you will probably have contact with other human service agencies in your area (**Figure 10.14**). You should be familiar with the types of services they provide and the needs of the people they serve. Be prepared to advise your staff about services they can recommend to families. It is sometimes necessary to remind caring staff that they cannot solve everyone's problems, no matter how much they want to help. Point out that the best support may be to help the family find the right agency or service to meet their needs.

When your program is not in a large metropolitan area, families may depend on your program to help them get in touch with needed services. Your center, working together with local medical or educational personnel, can help families find the more sophisticated services that

Mikolette/E+/Getty Images

Figure 10.14 Referring a family for necessary social work or counseling services is the role of the early childhood program director and staff.

are available in a city. Children's medical centers, family guidance clinics, and rehabilitation agencies are examples of services that may be available but are outside of the local area.

Understanding Caregivers' Perspectives

Caregivers and teachers do not play the same role in children's lives. Ideally, they complement each other and work together for the best interests of the children. Problems sometimes arise when parents and teachers do not understand each other. Some caregivers may have little understanding of child development or developmentally appropriate programming. They may not understand why the teachers allow children to play with messy activities. They may be concerned when boys and girls both play with dolls and trucks. They may expect workbook sheets and strict discipline. It may be a surprise for them to see children freely moving around the room in busy activity. Teachers, on the other hand, may not have considered the factors that influence parental attitudes and behavior. They may assume that all caregivers trust them and understand the classroom activities.

Caregivers may not have the same level of energy. A parent with a chronic illness, a recent surgery, or a disability may be willing to get involved with center activities, but may be limited in the scope of that involvement. Some may be both mentally and physically tired after long and demanding workdays. Others work long days and still have energy to jump into evening activities. They volunteer to help with flea markets, center picnics, and fix-up projects.

Teachers can be more supportive when they understand some of the factors that influence caregiver behavior. You may find it useful to schedule some staff training

designed to help your staff become more sensitive to caregivers. Part of working effectively with caregivers includes getting to know them as individuals.

Understanding Social and Cultural Influences

Families usually do not live in total isolation. They interact with neighbors, belong to religious groups, and join social clubs. They identify with a particular ethnic or cultural group and are a part of other informal social groups. While they may or may not realize it, these groups play a role in influencing their behavior. Religious, social, and cultural backgrounds can be very strong influences in how caregivers choose to raise their children. Ideally, the advice of these other forces in their life are consistent with the advice of the professional child care staff. In some cases, however, the advice is not consistent. This can create added stress for the caregiver, confusion for the child, and discouragement for the staff.

Family Values

Social and religious group membership, past experiences, and the caregivers' own beliefs influence the values that are important to them. Sometimes these values closely align with the teacher's own values and the developmentally appropriate philosophy. Other times, there may be conflict between the values of the home and the center. For instance, caregivers who expect their children to be quiet and obedient and who consider play a frivolous activity may not appreciate an active, play-based curriculum.

Sometimes the value conflict can be easily resolved. A caregiver may take great pride in sending her daughter in an expensive "best" dress to the center. She may not understand that the child may not participate freely in the many activities if she is worried about messing up the prized dress. The caregiver may need to be reassured that she will not be negatively judged if her child comes to the center in old clothes. On the other hand, if a caregiver feels strongly that their children should be dressed in their best clothes for the center as a matter of respect or pride, the teacher may have to find a thoughtful solution (**Figure 10.15**). For example, special care might be taken with smocks and shoe coverings to allow the child to participate in messy activities.

A special effort must be made to ensure that value differences of this type do not become battlegrounds between families and the center. As caregivers and teachers get to know each other, areas of disagreement are more easily resolved. Sometimes the caregivers' values or expectations of the center are impossible to accommodate. For example, a caregiver who feels that a child should be denied lunch for misbehaving must be clearly told that

ferrantraite/E+/Getty Images

Figure 10.15 It is important to respect caregivers' dress expectations for their child based on their family values and culture.

the center cannot do that. When a request by a caregiver is in violation of licensing regulations or in opposition to the standards of appropriate and ethical care identified by the profession, the center must maintain its obligations to the child's welfare. The caregiver must be told this in a respectful, but firm, manner. Ideally, as caregivers and families become familiar with the philosophy of the center, and as teachers come to understand the values and concerns of caregivers, reasonable agreements can be reached.

Past Experiences

Previous experiences may influence how families and caregivers view the center and its staff. When earlier experiences with child care have been positive, they are likely to approach your program with a receptive and positive attitude. If earlier experiences were not good, they may be suspicious, angry, and quick to criticize. On the other hand, they may be thrilled to find a center that exceeds their expectations and surpasses their previous experience in positive ways.

Caregiver behavior is also influenced by childhood experiences. For instance, a caregiver who, as a child, was severely punished for lying, might become extremely agitated at the normal exaggerations and wishful stories of a child. Caregivers often react negatively to those children who behave in ways that were forbidden to them. These negative feelings may be in response to their own children or another in the center.

An additional influence on caregiver behavior is their experiences with other social services or schools. Those who did not have a positive school experience may look on child care as "another school." Some who have had experience with government bureaucracies may see the required paperwork for enrollment as just another intrusion into their lives. Caregivers bring both their positive

Director's Showcase

Reflect

As you work to lead others, how will you best model and support the social and cultural differences between your staff and the families in your program?

and negative attitudes and experiences with them as they enroll their child at your center. The center staff may have to go more than halfway to establish open communication with these families. Resistance by parents to volunteer or participate in center activities can stem from parents and caregivers not feeling comfortable, being self-conscious, or not knowing what to expect or what their role will be in their child's education. Directors and administrators can help alleviate these feelings of doubt or anxiety in parents by providing consistent opportunities for involvement, giving detailed expectations for the event, and continuing to invite and encourage parents to attend. Introducing caregivers to other caregivers with children in the same class or around the same age and fostering relationships can also aid in increasing parent involvement.

10.4 Engaging Families and Caregivers

Information bulletin boards, classroom newsletters, and group emails are all great ways to communicate with families and caregivers (**Figure 10.16**). The following section will discuss ways to involve caregivers in center activities.

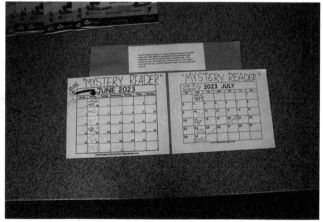

Kristen Alexandria

Figure 10.16 There are many ways to engage parents in program opportunities, such as signing up to be a "Mystery Reader" in their child's classroom.

Centers have hosted open-house night to exhibit artwork, learning center family night is great for parents to see what their children do during the day and for staff and parents to talk about different activities. There are a variety of ways to get families involved.

What Kinds of Parent Education Would Be Helpful?

Parent meetings and **workshops**, where speakers or educators can share information with caregivers, are a valuable addition to any children's program. Planning and organizing these meetings can be a time-consuming job, but they add an important dimension to the care you are providing. You may need to try several different meeting times or formats to identify what works best for your caregivers. Planning programs for caregivers is not the same as teaching children. Attendance will increase if they believe that what you have to offer may be helpful to them.

Many caregivers are eager to get all the help they can to become better. Most parents who grew up in the United States have little formal preparation for parenthood beyond a family and consumer course in middle or high school, such as family living or child and family development. When they are faced with making the decisions that parenting demands, they often feel unsure of themselves. Part of the value of workshops or classes is the opportunity for families to meet others with children of similar ages. They may not realize that many of their concerns are shared by other families. Caregivers often can relax when they discover that their child's "difficult" behavior is perfectly normal. Opportunities for parent education and the chance to be in a community with other parents are usually welcomed (**Figure 10.17**).

Adult learners are interested in topics that are immediately relevant to their needs (**Figure 10.18**). If they have an infant who won't eat, they are looking for advice on feeding. If they have a toddler who has grown increasingly

Topics for Educational Parent Meetings

Developmental ages and stages	Signs of developmental delays or problems	Activities to interest different age groups
Guidance and discipline	Gifts and toys that parents can create	How to childproof a home
Nutritious snacks and meals	How to encourage a picky eater	Rainy day activities
Preparing a child to enter school	How to choose appropriate toys	How to create a positive home environment
	How to deal with the stresses of parenting	

Goodheart-Willcox Publisher

Figure 10.17 Offering opportunities on popular topics in parent education should be provided on a regular basis.

Figure 10.18 Opportunities to learn more about parenting and meeting others establishes a supportive community.

negative and independent, they want information that assures them this is normal behavior. Caregivers who choose to participate in educational meetings are giving up precious free time. They are not as interested in abstract theories as they are in suggested solutions for current problems.

Don't be discouraged if attendance at initial meetings is low. Sometimes it takes a while for an idea to catch on. As the word gets out that the meetings are interesting and worthwhile, attendance will increase as will the sense of community among your caregivers. As you and your staff interact with the caregivers at these meetings, you will also become more attuned to their challenges and concerns and be able to support them through additional educational programs.

Involving Caregivers and Families in Center Activities

Research indicates that children are likely to gain the most benefit from the center if their caregivers are also involved with the program. Children profit more from their child care experience when the center staff and their families are comfortable with each other. Ideally, the center works in partnership with caregivers and provides support to the whole family.

In Head Start programs or parent cooperatives, each caregiver usually spends time in the classroom helping or observing. In child care programs, this is rarely possible because of work schedules. Caregivers are often at work during the time their children are at the child care center. Caregivers may have little enthusiasm for helping with center-based activities after working a full shift. Because of these conflicting schedules, it is often a challenge to get families involved with center activities and a continuing challenge to keep them involved.

However, the center should plan opportunities for family involvement with options for varying schedules. Chaperoning a single field trip day may be an easier commitment than coming in once a week or once a month for a story time. Participating in a weekend activity may be more acceptable to a caregiver who works full-time Monday through Friday. A caregiver may also be able to help outside of the center, such as preparing a newsletter or art project from their home. A staff member can coordinate activities and help match them to suggestions and requests from caregivers. Have a staff member keep track of family involvement in program activities. You may want to write a note to thank them for their time and participation or have a class create cards in gratitude for volunteering. Head Start programs and many grant-funded projects also require documentation of the numbers of people participating in various activities. Other programs have also found that keeping a record of participation is useful. It helps to identify those activities that caregivers prefer and those who want to be more involved.

Family-Centered Activities for Families

Most families are looking for activities they can enjoy with their children. The center has staff with the expertise to plan family activities that will be successful. They can plan simple outings or events that will not take a lot of energy, money, or time commitment from the parents. Examples include

- swimming parties at a local pool;
- potluck picnics at a nearby park;
- spaghetti dinners where the school-age children help;
- organized group trips to a children's play or child-oriented amusement park;
- children's fun fair or carnival; and
- creation of a "Me Book" after helping children collect family pictures and inexpensive memorabilia.

Often, group rates can be arranged if the activity involves an entrance fee. Amusement park or theater tickets might be very expensive for an individual family when added to the cost of parking, gas, and meals. The center might be able to arrange a cheaper package by coordinating group ticket sales, chartering a bus, and making box lunches for the trip. With this help, families who would not go on their own could participate.

Sharing in Center Activities

Caregivers have a variety of talents, hobbies, and backgrounds. There is much that they can share with the center. Children are elated when their family members

kali9/E+/Getty Images

Figure 10.19 Inviting parents to share a special talent in the classroom provides opportunities for learning and engagement.

come to the classroom with some special experience their friends can all enjoy (**Figure 10.19**). It helps to build pride and self-esteem for both children and caregivers alike. It also helps the children to see collaboration between center staff and their caregivers. There are many ways for caregivers to bring their interests into the classroom (**Figure 10.20**).

Volunteer Opportunities

In addition to providing special activities, there are many important volunteer jobs with which caregivers may be willing to help. Most directors try to make sure they never turn down an offer to help. Most are usually delighted to get some extra workers for special projects. For example, there may be opportunities to have information booths at a nearby mall, library, or community center to promote early childhood care in the community. Staff may not be available to spend their evenings or Saturdays handling the booth. However, a caregiver may be willing to help.

Extra help is always needed on field trips and to supervise any transportation. Repair or "fix-up" activities at the center may also be handled by volunteers. Volunteers can help to organize the workroom or center library. If you operate a lending library of books, magazines, and videos for caregivers or children, a volunteer may be willing to handle the checkout process.

Keep in mind that most caregivers are employed. Most may not be available for projects that occur during the day. Some who can volunteer for limited projects cannot commit themselves to long-term or time-consuming activities. Some may need child care or transportation if they are requested to help on weekends or evenings. Above all, be gracious if the caregiver must say "no" to a request and express appreciation in ways that sincerely let volunteers know you appreciate their help.

Fundraising

Families are a major force in any of the program's fundraising activities. Candy sales, car washes, flea markets, and raffle sales all depend on the participation of parents. This is another aspect of the program where a good relationship with families plays an important role. Offering a variety of fundraising events gives them choices about how they want to participate. Someone who might

Ways for Caregivers to Engage in the Classroom

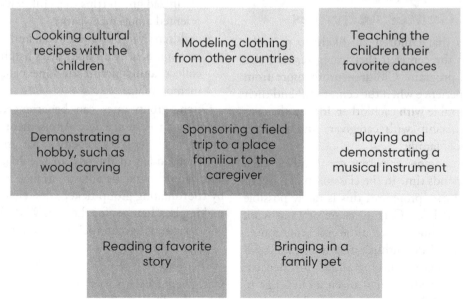

Goodheart-Willcox Publisher

Figure 10.20 Encouraging caregivers to share talents and hobbies are enriching experiences for children.

Director's Showcase
Betsy

Betsy has successfully integrated a new family into her program by providing them with frequent daily updates and reassurances. She has also been able to involve caregivers in cultural exploration of the local Indigenous tribe in their community events and activities. Betsy wants to have more caregivers involved in her program. She has had one family do a cooking demonstration of Vietnamese food for the children, while another caregiver works as a firefighter and took the children on a tour of his fire house during a field trip. Caregivers have been invited to chaperone field trips, like the one to the fire house. During these times, caregivers have connected with each other and with Betsy and built relationships with those in their community.

James

James has been able to address many of the staff's concerns about chaotic pick-up times in the infant classrooms. They have implemented new strategies to communicate effectively with caregivers as well as offered opportunities for their staff to observe communication techniques through their behavior modeling. They will continue to address the communication needs that come with a large child care center. James is also working on fundraising opportunities for families to participate in and to raise money to purchase new outdoor play equipment for the program. Involving those people who are part of the lives of the children cared for at their center is a tenet of high-quality child care, and James is striving to make that happen.

not be willing to sell raffle tickets might be happy to donate items to a flea market. A caregiver who might be delighted to participate in a sponsored golf outing might dislike the idea of selling candy bars.

Sometimes, caregivers need an evening away from their children to relax and have fun. One successful activity has been to raffle tickets for a "Night on the Town." The winners are treated to an evening of child care, dinner, and a movie.

Director's Showcase
Reflect

Based on the multiple opportunities to engage parents in the early childhood program, what would be your top 10 choices to implement and why?

Chapter 10 Review and Assessment

Summary

10.1 Understand the connection between effective communication and family engagement.

- Understanding caregivers and successful communication with caregivers are hallmarks of a quality child care program. Providing a warm and welcoming environment that values and includes all families is important for all early childhood programs.

10.2 Identify strategies to facilitate communication between families and staff.

- Family orientation programs, handbooks, and other forms of communication help parents feel more involved and comfortable with the center. Implementing strategies to help parents feel valued and heard leads to success in the classroom.

10.3 Describe ways of providing understanding and support for families.

- Caregivers are the primary influence in their children's lives. Child care center staff play an important role in providing support to families. This support can take on different forms. Some caregivers need help figuring out what type of care will best meet their needs. Others need help filling out paperwork or helping their children get a successful start in the center.
- Caregiver education, support programs, and referral to other family service agencies may be helpful to many families in the program. It takes coordination and effort on the part of staff to help families find the support they need and the level of involvement that is right for them.

10.4 Identify ways to engage families and encourage involvement in program activities.

- Caregiver involvement can take on many forms. Some like to volunteer to help in the center. Others have good ideas for fundraising activities. Those with a deeper level of commitment to the program may want to serve on the board of directors or participate in the accreditation process. Caregivers who are happy and satisfied with the program can be effective advocates for child care.

Review

1. Why is a parent handbook a valuable communication tool? (10.2)
2. What are some advantages of having teachers do home visits? (10.2)
3. What are some opportunities to provide for caregivers to visit the center? (10.2)
4. List at least three ways to communicate with caregivers. (10.2)
5. List differences in communicating with caregivers of infants and those of school-age children. (10.2)
6. What are adult learners most interested in when they come to an educational meeting? (10.4)
7. Why is it better to have a caregiver meeting that is made up of several short segments as opposed to a meeting with one long presentation? (10.4)
8. Why is it useful to keep a record of participation in the various activities offered to caregivers by the center? (10.4)
9. What are some ways to involve caregivers in fundraising activities? (10.4)
10. How can the use of technology help with communication between caregivers and child care staff? (10.2)

Showcase Your Skills

1. Plan a caregiver meeting to role-play in class. Consider how you would rearrange your classroom to make it more comfortable. Create an invitation that could be sent to caregivers and plan the content of the meeting. Determine your method of presentation, such as discussion, workshop, etc., and plan snacks. Identify other things that could be done at this meeting to help families feel welcome and relaxed. (10.2)
2. Prepare a classroom newsletter for the center you would like to have someday. Include articles that you have written, a heading, and information about one of your classrooms. Make the newsletter professional and attractive in appearance. (10.2)
3. Develop a list that includes the names, addresses, and phone numbers of human services agencies or organizations in your area. Identify the types of services provided by each group. Discuss in class situations where you might need to refer a caregiver to one of these groups. (10.4)

Matching

Match the following terms with the correct definitions:

A. conference

B. family
   engagement

C. parent handbook

D. support system

E. workshop

1. Developing a relationship with and supporting caregivers.
2. People in a person's life when support is needed.
3. Basic tool of written communication to which parents can refer with program questions.
4. Meeting between teacher and caregivers.
5. Event where speakers or educators can share information with caregivers.

11 CHAPTER

The Complex Role of Leading Others

Learning Outcomes

After studying this chapter, you will be able to:

11.1 Describe early childhood program leadership skills and characteristics necessary to support a quality organization.

11.2 Distinguish between healthy organizational elements necessary to build a solid climate in which teachers and enrolled families thrive.

11.3 Identify roles and responsibilities of the program leader that are unique to the early childhood program environment.

11.4 Utilize the NAEYC Professional Code of Ethics to provide guidance when leading an early childhood program.

Key Terms

advocates
code of ethics
climate
controlling
culture
directing
empathy
external roles and responsibilities
internal roles and responsibilities
interpersonal skills
networking
organizing
planning
reflective listening
staffing
Theory X
Theory Y

Introduction

Serving in the role of leader within any organization can be daunting, regardless of the size. The director's responsibilities are different from everyone else's in the program. While others will have a definite work schedule, a director's hours may change according to the work that must be done. While the teaching staff may worry about having the right colors of construction paper for a project, the program leader may be making decisions that could affect the ability of the program to pay the staff salaries.

Not everyone can or wants to lead others. To assume responsibility for a child care program requires leadership skills and characteristics that will motivate others to do the work necessary to care for children of all ages. A program administrator must build and maintain an organization that is healthy and thriving. Caring for children, their families, and the staff requires that an early childhood leader be in tune with the different needs of each. The roles and responsibilities, while often consistent, are ever-changing due to the variety of staff, family members, and children whom the leader must interact with and guide each day.

With constant interactions between people, many issues can and will arise. This often puts the director in a compromising position. Like other professionals, such as lawyers, doctors, and architects, child care workers follow a code of ethics (**Figure 11.1**). This guidance allows for the professionals in these fields to have guidelines to consider when determining the right decision based on the circumstances. While difficult at times, the code provides guidance and valuable insights useful to an early childhood program leader.

NAEYC/DAP standards

Standards covered in this chapter:

2c, 4a, 6a, 6b, 6c, 6d, 6e

1D, 1E, 2A, 2B, 2G

SinArtCreative/iStock/Getty Images Plus

Figure 11.1   A code of ethics is guidance for many professionals in a variety of fields.

Director's Showcase

Taisha

What an exciting time for Taisha! Interviewing and selecting staff has allowed her to identify people that she felt would mix well and come together collectively as a group. She has now determined the teaching teams, the assignments to age groups, and the classroom responsibilities that will be delegated. Taisha is hopeful that she has what it takes to lead a quality organization.

Meredith

Taking over an existing program has allowed Meredith to be shielded from making many initial decisions. However, she is following in the footsteps of a director that had been in the role for over 15 years. The staff has expressed to her that the program was functioning well and she should "leave things as is." However, within weeks, parents are starting to share their complaints about certain classrooms, and some of the staff have asked to talk with her privately about their concerns.

11.1 Leadership Skills and Characteristics

The person "in charge" of an early childhood program may have many titles such as director, administrator, owner, principal, or head of school. Whether within a center-based or home-provider program, this person is the early childhood program leader. It is their vision and problem-solving skills that will determine the future direction of the program. While efforts of other staff members will support necessary areas to support the program, the director must be knowledgeable and concerned about all aspects of the program. The director also must be aware of societal issues and influences that will impact the program.

The director of an early childhood program must be able to

- have a broad overview of the entire scope of the program;
- understand how decisions in one part of the program may impact other parts;
- make unpopular decisions when necessary;
- work whatever hours are required to get the job done;
- keep in mind the long-term goals of the program;
- create an environment where all feel respected and appreciated;
- stay up-to-date on new ideas and information relating to child care and early childhood education;
- be aware of the strengths of the program and areas that need to be improved; and
- direct others on the staff so they are helped to do their work effectively.

Success depends on the director's abilities. These abilities include solving problems, supporting a quality daily program, long-range planning, managing others, and paying the bills.

Management Responsibilities

Business experts, such as the highly published Stephen Covey, have identified basic tasks that must be performed by those in administrative positions. These essential system-building skills include the ability to plan, control, organize, staff, and direct (**Figure 11.2**). These fundamental skills are a part of the job of any early childhood program leader.

Planning

Planning for an early childhood director involves setting goals for the program and identifying methods or strategies for reaching those goals. It involves considering what

malerapaso/E+/Getty Images

Figure 11.2 Systems building within an early childhood program is like completing a puzzle by working to find the right pieces to connect together to provide quality programming.

the priorities of the program should be. This includes identifying a direction, determining community needs and ages of children to serve, utilization of space, and staffing needs. The task of planning also involves figuring out ways to meet goals. Some can be easily achievable while others take time. Planning requires bringing knowledge of future trends together with an understanding of the capabilities of the program.

Controlling

The function of **controlling** as an administrator includes regularly monitoring and evaluating the program as well as taking action, when necessary, to maintain and improve its quality (**Figure 11.3**). The director must know what is going on throughout the program. Accurate and up-to-date information assists them in making wise decisions.

This information can then assist in adjusting or changing the program. For example, if a classroom has lower attendance than others, the director will want to determine the factors that might be causing this issue. Based on the information gathered, the director might adjust the enrollment in the classroom and in turn modify staffing and work schedules, food inventory, and materials for the classroom. When problem solving, a director must consider many factors. Each factor is part of the controlling function of a director.

Organizing

Organizing for a child care administrator is determining an appropriate arrangement of time, people, and space. The organizing function results in a plan that will support the achievement of goals and the efficient operation of a quality program. The director is responsible for determining how to carry out the work of the program in the most advantageous way. The director determines the staffing

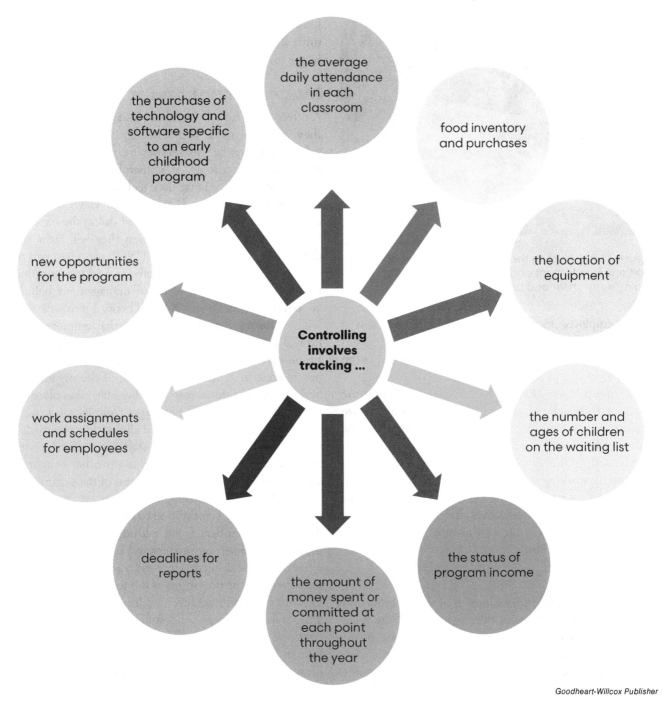

the average daily attendance in each classroom

the purchase of technology and software specific to an early childhood program

food inventory and purchases

new opportunities for the program

the location of equipment

Controlling involves tracking ...

work assignments and schedules for employees

the number and ages of children on the waiting list

deadlines for reports

the status of program income

the amount of money spent or committed at each point throughout the year

Goodheart-Willcox Publisher

Figure 11.3   Making decisions requires gathering information to take the best action for the program.

needs throughout the program, including the office area, the classrooms, and food and transportation services.

In addition, the director assigns job duties to staff members and holds them responsible for fulfilling their roles. The program leader must keep the program functioning smoothly by organizing staff into work groups, identifying work functions, and delegating duties. While there is no single "right" way to organize a child care program, the size of the program, the ages of children being served, the level of training of the staff, the additional services provided, and state licensing regulations will all affect the administrator's decisions. The director must design a clear organizational structure that works well and establishes and maintains multiple systems at a time.

Staffing

The **staffing** function refers to the recruiting, hiring, and retention of skilled individuals needed to operate a quality program (**Figure 11.4**). The director must create well-defined job categories as they prepare to recruit new employees. They must then recruit, identify, and hire appropriate staff for the program. The leader must also plan and

Figure 11.4 Finding the right candidate for open positions is important and supports the operation of a quality early childhood program.

provide employee orientation and ongoing training as well as develop clear, thoughtful personnel policies. These policies will guide decisions that define the relationship between the employer (the program) and the employee.

The interpersonal skills of the director are vital in the area of staffing. The program leader must communicate consistent expectations to new employees that can be evaluated fairly and dismiss those who cannot perform their responsibilities in a satisfactory manner. Developing appropriate working relationships among staff that help to support a cooperative work environment can be challenging. Many directors discover that the staffing component of their job is one of the most demanding in terms of time and effort.

Directing

Directing is the leadership function of the program and how the director influences others to successfully meet their responsibilities. The director may educate board members who have limited training in the child care field or keep the program on track toward long-range goals. Identifying problems, motivating personnel, and determining policies are all parts of the directing function. Clear and careful communication is necessary for successful leadership and should include

- clearly worded policies and procedures that minimize problems;
- acknowledgment and recognition for those who put forth special effort;
- thoughtful, concise communications;
- a willingness to listen to concerns without becoming defensive; and
- an openness to new ideas.

The program director must consider ways to make things happen. The program will not meet its goals and plans without specific strategies for reaching them. The

leader may find defining deliberate steps to achieve goals difficult, but this effort supports a healthy organization in the long run.

Management Styles

A director's personal management style is evident in how they view and treat their staff members. If the director values staff members as competent individuals, they will treat them accordingly. Staff members in response will likely work hard because they feel appreciated and their contribution is valued. If the director views staff members as lacking in commitment and doing the bare minimum within the classroom, then they will treat them differently. Douglas McGregor (1960) proposed two theories by which managers perceive and address employee motivation. These two styles of management behavior are referred to as Theory X and Theory Y (**Figure 11.5**).

The **Theory X** manager believes that employees have no real commitment to their jobs and cannot be trusted. Employees work only for money and have no loyalty nor interest in supporting the goals of the organization. Seeking out additional responsibility only takes place with more pay or rewards. The manager typically must oversee employees on a regular basis and all decisions are made by the administration. Ultimately, staff are expected to do as they are directed. Employee input is neither sought nor valued in the decision-making process of the organization.

The **Theory Y** manager believes that staff are self-motivated and committed to the organization's goals. These staff members enjoy adding their thoughts and ideas in a goal-setting process and feel valued. Feeling a sense of personal satisfaction and a sense of accomplishment becomes as important as money in motivating staff to work hard and achieve developed goals. Even when a supervisor is not present, staff can be trusted and will continue to function effectively. This perspective on human behavior results in a management style that seeks ideas and suggestions from staff. Employee input on goals and strategies is sought and valued. Staff are treated with respect and encouraged to work independently. Creative ideas are encouraged.

In general, it seems that the Theory Y style of management is more compatible with the values and humanistic nature of working with young children in a program environment. In quality child care, the director strives to create a place where children feel valued, respected, and nurtured. It makes sense that the program staff should be treated in a manner that reflects those same values.

Leadership Skills

Many of the skills associated with being an effective leader come naturally for some, while others may need to learn them. A leader needs interpersonal skills and the ability

Theory X

- Employees have no real commitment to a job
- Employees only work for money
- Employees have no loyalty or interest in supporting the goals of the organization
- They will only seek out more responsibility if more pay or rewards are offered
- Manager must oversee staff closely
- All decisions are made by management
- Employee input is not sought or valued

Theory Y

- Employees are self-motivated and committed to the organization's goals
- Employees enjoy adding their thoughts and ideas in meetings
- Employees feel valued
- Employees are motivated by a feeling of personal satisfaction and accomplishment, not just money
- Even when a manager is not present, employees will continue to function effectively
- Management seeks out employee input on goals and strategies
- Employees are treated with respect

Goodheart-Willcox Publisher

Figure 11.5   There are two styles of management behavior. Theory Y is more compatible with those who lead early childhood programs.

to communicate clearly. These skills help a group function effectively. A good leader provides recognition for the concerns and efforts of staff. Ultimately, the leader has a foundational value of relationships. An early childhood program must support children. It must also support adults in achieving their full potential in relationships that are based on trust, respect, and positive regard (Biddle, 2012). Some of the key abilities are interpersonal skills, communication, conflict resolution, group and individual decision making, and appropriate time-management skills.

Interpersonal Skills

Interpersonal skills are the qualities and abilities to get along with others and to help them feel at ease. They are essential for strong leadership. Many business leaders identify good interpersonal skills as one of the most important characteristics they desire when hiring new employees. Among the essential interpersonal skills for leaders are helping others feel at ease, listening, and empathy.

A good leader helps other people feel at ease, even in situations where they might not feel comfortable themselves. An early childhood program leader should smile, greet others warmly, and show confidence in social situations. They need to listen closely as others are speaking, including getting down to eye level for conversations with children (**Figure 11.6**). When talking with others, they must pay attention to their body posture, displayed emotions, and the words they are using while talking. Being an active listener in a conversation will alert them to potential problems that must be solved. Finding out details opens doors to innovative ideas about how to solve problems. Active listening provides a more accurate understanding of the situation.

Sometimes individuals simply need to express their feelings about a situation. An understanding leader can utilize **reflective listening**, repeating the other person's main point using slightly different words to ensure they heard and understood. This signals to the other person that they have been heard and provides an objective

kali9/E+/Getty Images

Figure 11.6 Early childhood leaders not only engage warmly with adults, they also do the same for children by getting down on eye level for conversations.

response that helps clarify situations where they might have mixed or confusing feelings. For example, if a teacher complains that a parent is always late picking up her child, a reflective listening response might be, "You sound upset that Mrs. Smith is often late." Teachers usually understand parents' problems but are appreciative if there is recognition of how these situations frustrate them. A child might come crying because another child grabbed a toy. The reflective listening response could be, "It makes you angry when someone grabs a toy away." By doing this, the child is heard and often is willing to discuss possible responses to the problem.

Empathy is the ability to understand how others feel and to recognize their point of view. A program leader should recognize staff members' feelings, attitudes, or concerns. Being empathetic toward someone with patience and sensitivity helps the other person feel understood and provides space for more positive outcomes. However, empathy does not mean that conflict will not occur. Leaders must make objective decisions regarding the program that may conflict with the requests or feelings of others. When this happens, acknowledging the other person's disappointment or anger and offering reasons behind a decision can deescalate a conflict. Staff feel more accepting of decisions when the program leader recognizes their feelings and thoughts even when they do not get their desired outcome. Effective leaders have a keen sense of identification with the concerns of others and a caring attitude.

Communication Skills

The leader's ability to communicate clearly with staff, families, children, vendors, and the community is vital. A leader should never assume that any individual understands an issue, task, or decision. They should provide thoughtful, clear instruction or explanation and answer questions thoroughly.

The program leader must make many decisions with advice and information from others. A group consensus may be useful in making some decisions, such as which night to hold a community open house. An example would be the purchase of new carpet for a classroom. This decision is made by the program leader but is based on bids or previous experience with a vendor. The choice of carpet color to purchase may be a decision that includes input from the teaching staff. Other decisions will require group input. For example, the purchase of new playground equipment requires input from teachers. The leader should collect their thoughts and ideas regarding which equipment would be appropriate for the groups of children that they work with. If a decision relates to a change in program operating hours, the leader might need insights from parents as well as members of the staff.

A leader makes some decisions alone. Due to the nature of an issue, confidentiality may be an issue to consider. For example, whether to terminate an employee for not following the program's policies is a decision for the program leader. What took place, when, and how are all issues that must be documented to include the conversations with the staff member (**Figure 11.7**). Discussing specifics with other teaching staff members is inappropriate. Gathering insights from others in managerial positions or other staff members to document an issue and make a final decision may be necessary. However, the ultimate decision is that of the program director.

One way to enhance communication in the center is to be open about the decision-making process. Not every decision will please everyone. Administrators who are effective communicators do not give in when tough decisions must be made. However, they are willing to share the overall scope of the decision with those who are affected by it. They seek input from those who work

acilo/E+/Getty Images

Figure 11.7 Program leaders must also work to keep certain issues confidential related to staff, children, or family issues.

directly in the decision area. They consider the pros and cons of different strategies. They also explain the rationale of the decision to those affected. In that way, staff understand the factors involved in making the decision, even when they may not agree with the outcome.

Effective leaders understand how to focus their communications based on the appropriate audience and what the message is. Complicated communications should be carefully written out. Some information, such as a change in policy or the date of a center event, must be shared with the entire staff. Other information, like a personnel evaluation, is confidential and should not be generally available. Some issues should be discussed directly with a staff member or parent as well as documented.

Body posture and expression also convey information to others. A director who rolls their eyes at the mention of a particularly difficult parent is quite clearly indicating a certain attitude toward that person. Anyone around will be aware of that attitude. Program leaders should be careful of their body language because they serve as a role model for positive, respectful attitude in all forms of communication.

Conflict Resolution

The early childhood education leader is a mediator and peacemaker in the center. Sometimes staff members simply need a way to express their feelings, and then they can return to their jobs. Others need to feel their presence makes a difference in the center and that things would not go quite as well if they were not there. Occasionally misunderstandings need to be cleared up, situations clarified, or conflicting points of view examined objectively (**Figure 11.8**). For example, a staff member who counted on using a particular piece of equipment for a project may be angry at another teacher for using it without

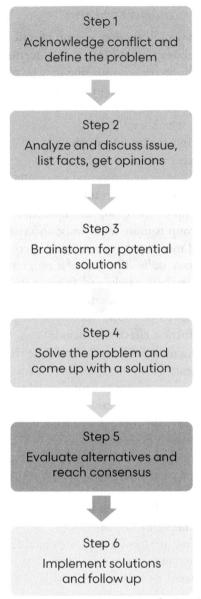

Step 1
Acknowledge conflict and define the problem

Step 2
Analyze and discuss issue, list facts, get opinions

Step 3
Brainstorm for potential solutions

Step 4
Solve the problem and come up with a solution

Step 5
Evaluate alternatives and reach consensus

Step 6
Implement solutions and follow up

Goodheart-Willcox Publisher

Figure 11.9   Following a sequence of steps when resolving issues supports better overall communications.

Iaflor/iStock/Getty Images Plus

Figure 11.8   Due to the work done together each day, misunderstanding and conflicting points of view can potentially cause conflict between teaching staff. The early childhood leader is the mediator and peacemaker in the center.

signing it out. The program leader helps resolve the situation while at the same time keeping it from becoming a major dispute between staff members. When using a conflict-resolution approach, steps include

- clarifying the situation
- expressing feelings verbally
- exploring viable solutions
- considering ways that the problem can be avoided in the future (**Figure 11.9**)

Occasional conflict cannot be avoided. It is bound to occur in situations where people spend time together. The program director's role is to stay out of the middle of such conflicts while also trying to help resolve them. One way to do that is by utilizing small groups to assist with decision making.

Group Decision Making

A director may pull together a group of staff with various points of view, expertise, ideas, and concerns to mediate a conflict. Group decision making may be effective in

- choosing or developing curriculum;
- rotating equipment;
- creating schedules;
- identifying playground needs;
- recognizing teachers;
- offering parenting topics and ideas; and
- planning fundraising events.

The makeup of the group can influence its effectiveness. The group is more likely to be successful in reaching its goal if members have compatible personalities and complementary skills. The role of a program director is to choose members wisely and support the group as it works together to include setting a timeline of when a decision needs to be made. Specific strategies that help the group function effectively include

- arranging for a meeting site and time that is convenient;
- creating a room arrangement that allows all group members to see and hear each other;
- making sure the room is well-lit and the temperature is comfortable;
- educating group members about the responsibilities of being a participant in the decision-making process;
- providing background information on the issue and an agenda prior to the meeting;
- organizing the agenda so group members have a chance to get to know each other (**Figure 11.10**);
- having some refreshments available;
- helping the group to clarify its goals;

Petegar/E+/Getty Images

Figure 11.10 Creating an agenda for a meeting clarifies the points of discussion in a meeting to include planning a little time for group members to get to know each other.

- providing resources that will help the group have the information it needs;
- clarifying or summarizing various points of view;
- helping the group form an action plan to achieve group goals;
- obtaining a commitment from group members regarding who will complete work that needs to be done before the next meeting; and
- providing child care or transportation for group members if needed.

A leader who organizes and supports staff by forming a productive group environment cultivates opportunities for success. Adults in the group can then work cooperatively on a particular problem or task and then make recommendations to the program leader. While collective decision making is an option that leaders can utilize to balance their administrative duties, the leader must make the final decision in most cases. This means the final responsibility for the results of that decision is on the program leader.

Individual Decision-Making Skills

Independent decisions may be simple or complicated. Simple decisions have fairly obvious answers. There is little at stake, and there will be few negative outcomes if the decision is wrong. For example, a decision on what color of construction paper to order might stimulate some interesting conversation. Overall, however, it is not a particularly important decision. A decision regarding whether to open an additional classroom could be very costly. If you do not open the new classroom, another program might meet that need in the community, which may result in the possible loss of enrollment to the competing center. On the other hand, opening the new classroom will take a commitment of money, time, and effort to get it started. If enrollment is too low to keep the classroom open, the decision will have been a costly one.

Successful decision makers usually follow a specific set of steps when making a complicated decision (**Figure 11.11**). First, they clearly identify the decision to be made. In the case of adding the classroom, focus on the demand for more child care spaces rather than a single aspect of the decision, "Where will we locate the classroom in our existing program?" Second, reexamine the established goals for the program. Ask, "Do the long-range goals of the program include expansion to meet all the child care needs of the area?" Third, consider if the program values the decision. Program values represent the common beliefs held by the program leader, board members, and staff regarding what is significant as the center accomplishes its goals and mission.

Once the broader questions are determined, the next step is to consider all the possible options that relate to the decision. This often includes the process of

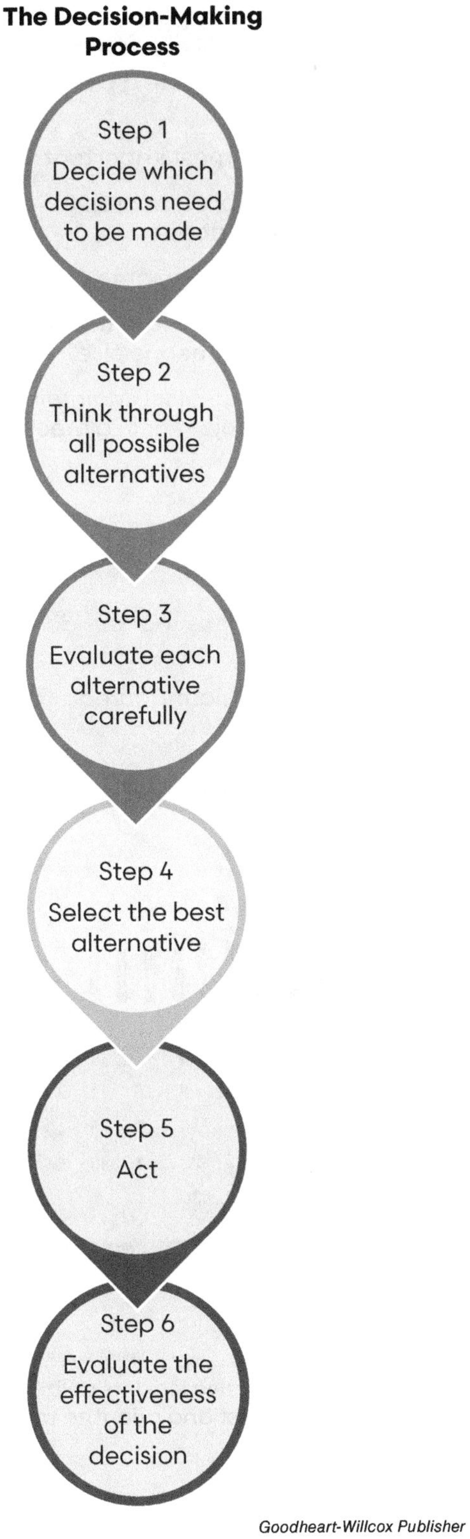

**The Decision-Making
Process**

Step 1
Decide which
decisions need
to be made

Step 2
Think through
all possible
alternatives

Step 3
Evaluate each
alternative
carefully

Step 4
Select the best
alternative

Step 5
Act

Step 6
Evaluate the
effectiveness
of the
decision

Goodheart-Willcox Publisher

Figure 11.11   The decision-making process is used to find the best solution.

brainstorming with others who help identify various possibilities. For example, the decision regarding the creation of additional spaces for children might be determined by identifying a workable strategy for providing those spaces. Establishing a new classroom may be a possibility, but repurposing space for additional classrooms in the

current space may also be a consideration. Next, examine the pros and cons of each option. Every considered option will have benefits and drawbacks. For example, a decision to expand the program will involve significant costs. Obtaining cost estimates of establishing a new classroom space or increasing space in certain classrooms would need to be investigated. When matched against the financial resources of your program, these costs give a more accurate picture of the impact of your decision.

After determining costs, the next step is identifying the worst possible outcome if a poor choice is made. Prompt questions to consider include:

- What is the risk to the program if everything goes wrong?
- Will the program be able to recover or survive?
- What could be done to minimize risks?
- What are the long- and short-term impacts?

While a harsh reality when making a major decision, this thought process is a necessary step in the decision-making process. Before spending program funds or borrowing money to enhance space, appraise the impact of the decision on the well-being of the existing program. If it is determined that the program can survive the worst possible outcome of a decision, then the option of going ahead becomes more reasonable.

After considering which option will result in the greatest possible outcome with the least amount of risk, the decision can be made. This decision can determine that a small amount of risk is worthwhile to move the program toward its goals. Or, based on the information gathered, the option to move forward is too risky for further consideration. Sometimes, even after much deliberation, there is still an element of uncertainty. This is where a program leader's knowledge, understanding of the program's history, and analysis of future trends can have great influence. Ultimately, a program leader is expected to decide.

Time-Management Skills

Most administrators find that there are always more things to do in a day than there is time to do them. Some directors shut themselves in their offices to work on paperwork all day. They may be surprised to discover that their staff members feel unappreciated and unsupported. Others may spend a great deal of time talking with personnel and maintaining an open-door policy. As a result, they may not complete reports, proposals, and records by their deadlines. A director who is unavailable to talk to parents may miss the warning signs that programmatic changes need to be made.

Time management is a necessary skill for any early childhood program leader (**Figure 11.12**). Programs have many moving parts. Staff, children, families, and vendors come and go throughout the day. Daily programming needs

Helpful Ideas for Managing Your Time

- Organize your tasks so all of the papers and information you need to complete a particular job are together.

- Prioritize your responsibilities so you clearly identify which tasks are the most important.

- Maintain a calendar that covers several months. Mark due dates for important projects or reports. Mark a reminder a week or so in advance of the due date so you won't forget about it.

- Handle each piece of paper once. As you review mail, decide immediately what to do with it.

- Decide which responsibilities should be delegated to other staff. Which tasks are the ones that only you can do? Which are the ones that could more efficiently be handled by someone else?

- Organize phone calls by using a duplicate message book so calls don't get lost. Maintain a record of what action is taken regarding calls. If you are working on a detailed project or in a meeting, have a message taken for you and call back later.

- Keep a list of things that need to be done, so you don't forget.

- Plan time each day when you can be available to talk to parents and/or staff. Organize time so that it occurs when staff and parents are free to talk.

- Identify those tasks that must be done on a regular or daily basis and those that are done on other regular patterns.

- Save time for your own professional growth and renewal. Read a professional journal, go to a conference, or even visit with another director to share ideas.

Goodheart-Willcox Publisher

Figure 11.12 Excellent time-management skills are crucial for effective early childhood leaders.

require attention, including food service, transportation for school-age children, and unannounced visits by regulatory agencies. Interested parents may drop in for tours of the facility, and deliveries arrive to support food service and classroom supply needs. The program leader may be responsible for making major purchases, visiting stores, and talking to vendors to obtain the most appropriate product. An early childhood director manages a great many tasks throughout the day. Effective leaders should have some core strategies to organize their tasks and obligations.

- Delegate to others that have appropriate training or are best resourced to assist with daily activity.
- Prioritize more important issues first when determining a starting place to deal with day-to-day issues.
- Set realistic deadlines to support success.
- Avoid procrastination. Putting things off typically makes issues harder to manage.
- Multi-task on easier process items. Focus solely on those items that will need more time.
- Utilize a daily planner, calendar, time-management app, or to-do list to prioritize tasks (**Figure 11.13**).
- Avoid distractions that detract from focused time, such as constantly checking email or scrolling through social media.

Early childhood program leaders must create strategies for organizing time. This supports effective day-to-day operations and creates satisfaction among the many program constituents who the leader works with each day.

Sviatlana Barchan/iStock/Getty Images Plus

Figure 11.13 Effective leaders utilize calendars and other strategies to list and prioritize tasks that must get completed.

Director's Showcase

Reflect

As you think about developing your own management style, what are areas that you need to be considering when managing others and dealing with conflict?

11.2 Building and Maintaining a Healthy Organizational Climate

A program's **climate** is the overall atmosphere and "feel" of the program (LeeKeenan & Ponte, 2018). Because an early childhood program environment can shift and change daily, some families and staff will handle that well, while others will not. All change becomes personal. As a program leader, managing change well builds and maintains a healthy organizational climate. But what if change is challenging for the leader? The leader must shift thinking from "what's in it for me" to "who is this for." If staff see a leader's distrust or lack of enthusiasm, change will not go well.

Anton Vierietin/iStock/Getty Images Plus

Figure 11.14   Program leaders must help staff understand that decisions are made for the greater good of the program and everyone involved.

Implementing Change

Staff need to understand that decisions are being made for the greater good of the program and everyone involved with it. A leader must identify the staff members for whom change is easy, those who will go along, others who take the "wait and see" approach but eventually will join in if they see things working, and those who "kick and scream" and point out every reason why the change will result in doom (**Figure 11.14**). Knowing which group each individual staff member represents helps a program leader plan how to share news of the change and the explanation of its necessity.

To avoid failure, approach the change opportunity with many modes of information. For example, a change in schedules may be needed and staff members' hours may need to shift 30 minutes later in the day. Rather than focusing only on the need to provide the correct staffing for state-licensing purposes, the director may speak broadly about how the change meets the needs of the children and the parents who must work to continue their enrollment. The families are the reason the program exists. In addition, there might be staff members who are willing to stay a little longer to assist the staff members who are impacted most. Thus, impacted staff can still get their own children to dance or baseball practices or scheduled appointments. Reminders of why a change is happening but also opportunities to brainstorm solutions together can assist staff members in accepting a change.

Change requires that programs be flexible. This takes courage, commitment, and a desire to make a difference for everyone involved. Program leaders may make a mistake by thinking that everyone will just agree or understand why something new must be implemented. Leaders must be prepared to embrace and be comfortable with the change. They must also be prepared that if the change does not go as planned, the goal is to be solutions-focused. Understanding more about change and its impact assists the program leader as they work to build a healthy organizational climate.

Building a Healthy Organizational Climate

Have you ever heard the saying "Rome wasn't built in a day"? The same can be said for a healthy workplace environment. How a new director joins a program has implications on the health of the organizational climate, whether establishing a new program, taking over from a retiring director who led the program for 25 years, or being promoted overnight due to the termination of an existing director.

Whether the child care center is new or one that is being taken over due to multiple circumstances, from that day forward the new director must establish themselves. To be effective, the director must strike a balance between having good management and good leadership skills (LeeKeenan & Ponte, 2018). When building a healthy organizational climate, staff need to see a program director encounter difficult and smooth situations. They also need to experience a leader who will do anything and everything that a staff member might be asked to do. Having a leader come alongside staff during a project like painting, moving furniture, or classroom setup, emphasizes that there is nothing their leader would not do. They need to see someone committed to doing the very same thing they should be committed to each and every day—meeting the needs of the children and their families.

Bloom (2010) identified 10 dimensions of organizational climate that program leaders must demonstrate (**Figure 11.15**).

Maintaining a Healthy Organizational Climate

An organization needs a delicate balance of the 10 dimensions. As a program leader, recognizing when to manage and when to lead takes time and attention from a personal growth perspective. Directors may want to do everything and take control. This mind-set, however, can appear as "my way is the only way," which can be a detractor for many program staff. Take a step back and think about how you want to be perceived. Do some

long-term planning and look beyond your own needs. Bloom's (2010) dimensions provide some ideas and strategies for maintaining a healthy organization.

Collegiality

Staff can be supported by daily interactions. Even the smallest greetings and farewells with a genuine voice and eye contact can be meaningful. Recognize if a teacher appears to be upset or distracted and reach out to them. Allow staff who attend workshops and other professional development opportunities to share what they learned at staff meetings or in newsletters. Value their support and create the expectation that they support each other every day.

Professional Development

Training has come a long way in the past two decades. There are a multitude of states that have invested in professional development systems including designated hubs where training can be located (**Figure 11.16**). These professional development centers typically have a registry system to join and is tied to state initiatives that may support the cost of training and development. A state licensing worker or the Child Care Resource and Referral agency can assist with identifying available professional development resources.

Director Support

Everyone needs a champion in their corner. As a program leader, you are that professional champion for each one of the staff. This means staying in tune with their professional growth, as well as finding a balance of building in supports that could assist with a personal issue that a staff member is experiencing. Showing care and concern is essential to maintaining a professional working relationship with each staff member.

Clarity

A center needs written policies and procedures that are easily accessible to all employees or families, as appropriate. In addition, these need to be reviewed on a regular basis, and staff should have input when this takes place. Some unpopular policies or procedures may remain due to licensing or accreditation requirements. Explain the reason for these policies to the staff and provide them with insights based on additional information. While the policies and procedures may still not be loved, a better understanding of the *why* will assist staff as they grow in their professional life.

Reward System

Not everything provided to the staff has to cost money. Leaving notes and other small gestures of appreciation

Dimensions for a Healthy Organizational Climate

Collegiality

The ability to be together, share information, and be emotional support for one another.

Professional development

Opportunities for staff to participate in ongoing educational opportunities to learn more about child development and education.

Director support

Providing quality feedback to teaching staff that gives the message that their work matters.

Clarity

Clear policies and procedures that support organizational functioning.

Reward system

Compensation and pay for early education professionals has been historically low; utilize other reward opportunities such as paid time off and model ongoing advocacy efforts to increase pay and benefits.

Decision making

Allow staff to make appropriate decisions by delegating and building leadership capacity within the teaching staff.

Goal consensus

Compromise when there are differing opinions regarding philosophies or work experiences.

Task orientation

Flexibility is allowed for tasks to be completed within a reasonable time frame.

Physical setting

Staff work in environments that are adequately filled with necessary materials, supplies, and equipment, and classrooms are well-maintained to be healthy and safe.

Innovativeness

Staff are allowed to use creative ideas to solve issues.

*Information based on research from Bloom, 2010.

Figure 11.15   In an early childhood program, finding a balance between leading and empowering others supports a healthy organizational climate where everyone benefits.

SC Endeavors - Creating a pathway to achieve success

Figure 11.16 Many states have online professional development systems where training can be located. They also usually include links to state initiatives that may support the cost of attending these trainings.

with the staff is a fun idea. Hosting lunch potlucks with themes allows for staff to show off their cooking skills. Talk with local businesses and see if gift cards or a coupon for a free cup of coffee or ice cream cone is a possibility. Parents can also be a great resource to help recognize staff. Working closely with a parent committee allows for parent involvement and sharing of creative ideas.

Decision Making

Not all decisions should be the sole responsibility of the program leader. Delegating to staff assists with the monumental task of day-to-day operations. This comes from the development of job descriptions that specify the expectations for teacher decision making. From an administrative perspective, mentoring staff interested in becoming a director someday allows them to contribute to the decision-making process. Ideas include being a part of the new employee hiring process or serving on a budget or fundraising committee.

Goal Consensus

There will be plenty of opportunities to work with the staff on areas of agreement and disagreement. The ability to come to a consensus may be complicated at times. With many ideas and perspectives, working to find a place where everyone feels comfortable is challenging. As a program leader, allow voices to be heard in a professional and respectful manner as well as role-model that this can be done in a positive way. While conflict management is covered in other chapters in greater detail, recognize that goal consensus is necessary to support the health of the organization (**Figure 11.17**).

Task Orientation

Early childhood directors can easily overload themselves when trying to get too many things completed in a day.

The early childhood environment is not the same from one day to the next. To organize your time and tasks, start by prioritizing the top five things to complete in a day. Completing these each day provides a sense of accomplishment, while also learning the delicate balance that is necessary to function effectively within the program environment.

Physical Setting

A safe and clean working environment in which to work is essential for all center staff members. In addition, the proper supplies and materials are necessary. Prioritize when teaching staff request classroom items. Task a staff member to assist with monitoring inventory levels and ordering replacements. Nothing is more frustrating to a teacher than paying out-of-pocket for supplies and materials that are necessary to do their job. When parents observe a consistently ill-equipped or chaotic classroom, loss of enrollment is highly probable.

Innovativeness

Everyone has good ideas. The leader's goal is to encourage the shared thinking and creativeness of staff members. Many resources are available to offer professional development opportunities for staff to share. A program that promotes creative thinking and acceptance of diverse ideas will thrive. Guide and nurture quality ideas and their implementation within your early childhood program environment.

Continual fostering is necessary to maintain a healthy organization. Expect different staff members to take the lead when improving the work space. Staff, children, and families should feel welcomed, cared for, and accepted when walking into the center each day.

Figure 11.17 Program leaders work to bring different ideas and perspectives into a place where everyone is comfortable and willing to work together.

Director's Showcase

Taisha

Once Taisha had some ideas regarding the organizational climate, she put together a plan. She was able to gain insights from the staff regarding their needs including a desire to learn more about how to effectively manage their classrooms and more about children's guidance to assist with the more challenging children. Taisha decided that she needed to reach out to the community and identify some professional development opportunities for her staff.

Meredith

Meredith realized that while the organizational climate would need her constant attention, she needed to look very closely at the personnel policies and teacher roles and responsibilities. To her astonishment, the program policies for staff and for families had not been updated in several years! There were misunderstandings about overall program policy, and parents had even reported that they had "heard" that some families received more vacation time at a reduced tuition cost than what they had been allowed. Meredith busied herself with revising the program policies.

Director's Showcase

Reflect

Think about workplace experiences you have had that were a result of either positive or negative organizational climates. What were the benefits or experiences that could have been better managed?

11.3 Roles and Responsibilities of the Early Childhood Leader

An early childhood leader has internal as well as external roles and responsibilities for small and large programs. The **internal roles and responsibilities** are all the duties the leader does inside the center on a day-to-day basis, such as staff scheduling and management, family meetings, tuition collection, and ordering curriculum supplies and food for meal times. A strong program with effective communication, a welcoming atmosphere, and a healthy organizational climate supports the director in these internal roles and responsibilities. The **external roles and responsibilities** of a director reach outward from the center and into the community. Early childhood leaders must engage with their surrounding community in a variety of ways to support and grow their program.

External Roles and Responsibilities

A stable program depends, in part, on the goodwill of others—other agencies, community leaders, government officials, and satisfied families. Activities that help people get to know the director and the early childhood program build support and interest. A director can utilize several strategies to establish the program as a valuable asset within the community. These strategies could include cooperating with other local agencies and organizations, serving as a community resource, networking with other programs and schools in the area, and advocating for the field.

Most communities have various agencies that are trying to provide services and help to families. Many human services agencies receive financial support from the same government program. Charitable organizations may be linked with national foundations and may have similar operational guidelines. These programs often have much in common. They need support from others in the community who share similar values and concerns. They require volunteers to serve on their board of directors. Also, they look for help and support with fundraising activities. Building these relationships is meaningful for the early childhood program. Familiarity with individuals and resources can be useful in referring children and their families with available community services.

Local groups often invite community resources to speak at their meetings. As a guest speaker, an early childhood leader has the opportunity to share more about the program and build community support (**Figure 11.18**). The service organization and the early childhood program both benefit from the positive publicity. While public speaking requires some evening and weekend hours, it is an effective way to build community awareness and support for the program. Any activity that builds your reputation as a good, decent, caring, trustworthy, hardworking leader of a quality early childhood program benefits the program. Impressions of the director or owner of a business strongly influence attitudes toward the business itself.

Figure 11.18   Sharing about the early childhood program with local groups is one of the many external roles for a program leader.

Networking is developing a group of professional colleagues to interact and communicate with. This requires keeping track of the people met in various situations. Networking takes place on many levels. Locally, you may get to know the directors of other programs who lead either proprietary or not-for-profit programs. They may connect you with directors they know from a broader geographic area, such as other parts of the state or country. You may attend early childhood conferences and meet other directors as well as influential leaders in the child care field to learn and share ideas. Networking does not mean using or manipulating people. It is creating a group of colleagues and friends who can share common concerns and, on occasion, help each other.

Advocates are people who speak out or act on behalf of their beliefs. Part of the early childhood leader role is supporting the importance of quality care for children, which often leads to voicing support of improvements in the laws, regulations, and decisions that affect child care programs (**Figure 11.19**). As a child advocate you might

- meet with legislators to discuss child care issues;
- write letters giving your opinion on pending legislation;
- send informational articles to legislators;
- attend town meetings sponsored by local legislators;
- encourage others to become more active in contacting legislators;
- invite representatives to visit your early childhood program for a tour; and
- work with local, state, and national elected representatives.

Legislators may not be well informed about the topic of early childhood care. Work to build a relationship with your legislators based on trust and respect, and then share quality information about the field and encourage them to reach out to you should they need further information.

Another strategy when working with legislation is trying to influence the passage of legislation or public policy. To do this, many people need to be on the same side of the issue. Legislators and public officials take notice when they get numerous emails, letters, social media contacts, or visits on the same topic. Many groups that work on behalf of children and families have found it necessary to work together to present strong support for a bill or program. Building coalitions with other groups can strengthen the position on the passage of legislation or public policy. Cooperative efforts to promote common interests can be surprisingly effective.

Internal Roles and Responsibilities

An early childhood leader has numerous internal roles and responsibilities when leading an early childhood program of any size. Areas covered in previous chapters include

- establishing and maintaining quality child care programs;
- identifying necessary facility equipment and supplies;
- budget and finance to include staffing costs and considerations;
- marketing and planning for enrollment;
- educational programming;
- maintaining a safe and healthy program; and
- engaging and supporting families.

These areas have been discussed at length to help you better understand the necessary systems and complexity of serving in the role of early childhood program leader. However, the key is knowing when to manage and when to lead. For example, the areas mentioned previously are focused on managing people, problems, and tasks.

Figure 11.19   Advocating for children, families, and the field of early childhood is key for program leaders.

A leader, on the other hand, navigates these issues within the context of the program's shared vision, mission, and goals. Hill and Lineback (2011) recommend the following to build leadership effectiveness:

- Model the kind of behavior expected.
- Stay informed regarding the needs and expectations of those working within the program environment.
- Provide an environment that empowers, inspires, and builds a team mentality.

These three essentials take time and ongoing attention to accomplish. In addition, the director must constantly learn more about themselves as a leader. Continuous professional development and access to resources are vital to a leader's learning and growth. When staff see program directors admitting that they may not know something or have made a poor decision, regularly seeking out resources and opportunities to learn more, and making decisions that are fair and equitable, the staff's respect and trust of those leaders increase. Establishing trust and respect takes time and will vary based on the ebb and flow of staff. While many teachers remain long-term employees in their programs, turnover is a reality in the field. Employee turnover results in different personalities, expectations, and overall experiences in the program. A director must be consistent in the support of the program's culture, communication strategies, and atmosphere when implementing internal day-to-day operations.

Program Culture

Program leaders shape the culture between the program's many constituents, including employees, children, and families. **Culture** reflects the expectations of a program based on the ways that things are done that stem from the program's beliefs, values, norms, and relationships (LeeKeenan & Ponte, 2018). Hence, program leaders must regularly communicate in a way that supports the program's mission, vision, and goals. While a program's culture changes over time due to its evolving needs, there are essential characteristics within the program that support a healthy culture.

First is the establishment of continuous, nurturing relationships. Building a relationship-based community takes time. The director should interact with staff and families on a regular basis (**Figure 11.20**). In general, being open to suggestions enhances the environment and opportunity to build relationships in and between all individuals who participate in the early childhood program environment.

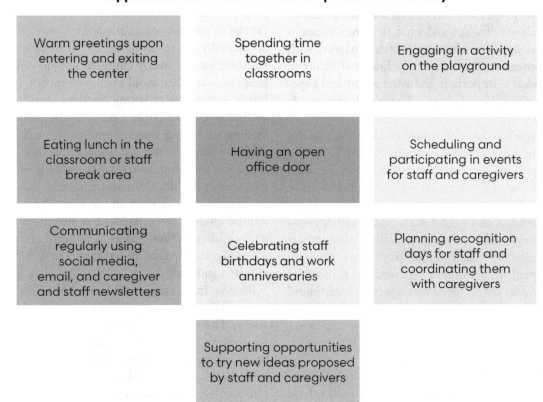

Opportunities to Build a Relationship-Based Community

Warm greetings upon entering and exiting the center	Spending time together in classrooms	Engaging in activity on the playground
Eating lunch in the classroom or staff break area	Having an open office door	Scheduling and participating in events for staff and caregivers
Communicating regularly using social media, email, and caregiver and staff newsletters	Celebrating staff birthdays and work anniversaries	Planning recognition days for staff and coordinating them with caregivers
	Supporting opportunities to try new ideas proposed by staff and caregivers	

Figure 11.20   Having an open-door policy supports opportunities to nurture relationships between staff and families.

Communication

While addressed in multiple chapters, the area of communication cannot be emphasized enough in its importance when being an effective early childhood program leader. Almost all program communications stem from the director, and how the director shares information is just as important as what information they share. Staff and parents need communication that is meaningful, timely, and clear. The program leader must be ready to answer potential questions and address any favorable or unfavorable reactions to the communication. Directors must carefully consider what message they want to deliver. Here are two messages about the same issue:

- *To avoid entrance by outside individuals, please securely latch all gates when entering and exiting the playground areas.*
- *Lock the gates! People are wandering in off the street into the child care area.*

Notice that the first example addresses what is taking place. Then, it provides a respectful solution to resolve the issue. The second example addresses what is taking place, but it lacks clarity and a respectful solution. The first statement could be posted throughout the program using social media, placement within a newsletter, on signs posted by the playground gates, and sent out as a mass email. The message is concise and respectful, and it provides the proper amount of necessary information. Striking a balance of when and what to communicate is also valuable. Avoid overloading staff and parents with so many communications that they find it difficult to determine what is important and what is not and experience communication fatigue (Bloom, Hentschel, & Bella, 2016).

The program's communications need to be positive and shared in a collaborative way. Staff must be valued for their opinions to foster an appreciation between yourself and the staff members and nurture a positive environment. Program directors need to be aware of the different personalities of their staff. Some will appreciate being recognized in a group situation, while others would prefer more subtle kudos from their program leader. The goal when building relationships is to create a level of comfort that is based on respectful, meaningful communications.

Inviting Atmosphere

An early childhood program consists of a large physical space, including hallways, classrooms, work spaces, food service areas, and outdoor areas. These spaces require regular care and should reflect a welcoming and comfortable atmosphere (**Figure 11.21**). Design these spaces to

Rawpixel/iStock/Getty Images Plus

Figure 11.21   When planning for a large physical space, it is important to have a warm and welcoming atmosphere.

reflect the diversity of the children and families that they serve using cost-effective strategies. For example, having children bring photographs of their families, displaying the artwork children create, or playing music that reflects the home languages and cultures of the children provide opportunities to reflect the cultures, languages, abilities, family structures, community, and religions represented within the program.

You should also consider how people move in and out of any space within the center. Is there enough room for groups to pass by one another? Do doors swing freely to accidentally hit someone on the other side? Check that hallways are not overly cluttered and do not create tripping hazards. They should be well-kept and inviting. The hustle and bustle of young children's shuffling feet and excited voices can create a noisy distraction during quiet reading or resting times. Some adults and children are also very sensitive to loud noise and voices. Staff should use soft, soothing tones when talking with children whenever possible. Firm voices should only be utilized in situations when they are needed. Outdoor locations require louder teacher voices but also closer interactions with children in these spaces to be heard and understood. The program director should model these behaviors with children and staff.

Positive interactions and communications are, by far, some of the most complex variables to maintain consistently. The director's role of leading others is complex and begins with how you manage external and internal roles and responsibilities. When operations are going well, your changing roles and responsibilities may be manageable. However, managing program culture, communications, and atmosphere can become stressful and overwhelming. Program leaders in the field have a professional code of ethics to guide them.

Director's Showcase

Taisha

During classroom observations, Taisha noticed the staff implementing the new ideas that they were learning to effectively manage their classrooms and increase their ability to better guide children's misbehaviors. However, a teacher was implementing one of the training's techniques regularly with a child in her class and the practice was upsetting the teachers in the classroom next door. Taisha knew that the strategy was acceptable from a state-licensing perspective and had already discussed and cleared it with the child's parents. However, when the other teachers shared their distress and concerns with the teacher, she was distraught. Taisha had to do something.

Meredith

Meredith worked in her office for several weeks, focusing on the update of the program's policies and procedures. Some of the staff questioned what she was doing and why she was not as present during the day. Wanting to be transparent, Meredith told them that she was completing a major overhaul of the staff and parent policies. Before she knew it, gossip and disagreements had created a major rift among the staff members. Some acknowledged and accepted that changes were necessary, while others were upset and wanted everything to stay the same. What was Meredith to do?

Director's Showcase

Reflect

Have you been a part of a workplace environment where gossip was creating hurt feelings and an unproductive work atmosphere? In your opinion, what should have taken place by those in leadership roles to deal with the issues?

11.4 Utilizing the NAEYC Code of Ethics

Professionals in the early child care and development field share a common **code of ethics**. This code is based on the core values of like-minded professionals in the field. It serves as a guide for proper behavior and making hard decisions involving the needs and rights of children, families, and staff. The National Association for the Education of Young Children (NAEYC) has defined the code of ethics for those working with children in early care and education settings. It clearly spells out ethical responsibilities. The code identifies both actions that must be taken in certain circumstances and actions that must not be taken.

The director influences the general tone of the entire program, which includes serving as a role model for all staff. Part of the professional duty is to be familiar with the code of ethics and to follow its guidance in making program decisions. The administrator's professional, mature, and ethical behavior is vital if the program offers a quality service to children and families (**Figure 11.22**).

In 2006, NAEYC adopted a supplemental section to the Code of Ethical Conduct that specifically applies to early childhood program administrators. In 2011, this document was reaffirmed and updated to assist program leaders with additional guidance that is unique to the ethical issues that arise when leading an early childhood program. The NAEYC (2011) guidance added three core values for administrators:

- Recognition of responsibility to children, families, staff, governing boards, sponsoring agencies, funders, regulatory agencies, the community, and the profession. Above all the primary responsibility is to the children.
- Recognition of the importance to maintain a humane and fulfilling work place for staff and volunteers.
- Recognition of the commitment to professional development for all staff members.

cnythzl/Getty Images

Figure 11.22   Early childhood program leaders must be guided by ethical standards, as they are vital to provide quality services for children and families.

Like the Code, this supplement has ideals and principles that are based on the additional challenges that arise. Those challenges include the children, their families, staff, sponsoring agencies and governing boards, and the community and society overall. This shared framework was created for the purpose of inspiring and guiding the work of early childhood leaders. It is important to recognize when reviewing the document in its entirety, there are some duplicates of the Code that are either repeated or have been revised to reflect the role of administrators within the ideals and principles. Understanding the global expectations in the five areas is essential for the early childhood program leader.

Ethical Responsibilities to Children

The priority for any early childhood leader is to ensure that the program meets the needs of the children. Their health, safety, and nurturance are the focus of everyone who works within the program environment. The leader commits to ensuring that developmentally appropriate activity is provided to the children and that their social and emotional needs are met. Utmost respect is shown to individual differences and thriving within cooperative environments is expected.

Ethical Responsibilities to Families

Program leaders role model and uphold the unique relationship that a parent has with their child. They display ongoing communication, collaboration, and cooperation when talking with a child's family members. Conflicting expectations will occur when it comes to meeting children's needs. The program director must find the balance between what the program can offer and what the parent requests. In addition, staff may also struggle with parent expectations. The director serves as the buffer and voice of what is reasonable based on the state licensing standards and the program capacity.

Ethical Responsibilities to Staff

Staff require a healthy, safe, work environment that provides nurturance and guidance from a professional perspective. The administrator is expected to role-model behaviors and professionalism and hold everyone accountable to the same standards. When the director provides clear policies and procedures as well as system supports such as personnel reviews, staff can thrive and grow as professionals.

SDI Productions/E+/Getty Images

Figure 11.23 For those leading non-profit early childhood programs, board meetings are a monthly occurrence to provide updates on what is taking place.

Ethical Responsibilities to Sponsoring Agencies and Governing Bodies

Typically, not-for-profit programs deal with one or more sponsoring agencies and a board. This means keeping accurate documentation and providing reporting processes that meet deadlines and expectations. Often, a board will meet monthly (**Figure 11.23**). Since board members are not typically at the center on a regular basis, the program director must explain things in an accurate manner and be transparent when tough issues arise. The director is responsible to the sponsoring agency and board and should closely follow the guidance provided by them.

Ethical Responsibilities to Community, Society, and the Field of Early Childhood Education

Working with other professionals in the field of early childhood education and other service agencies is an expectation of the program leader. The director may serve in numerous capacities from identifying children who need additional services to providing referrals for staff members who may be struggling. They must handle issues in a confidential manner and extend empathy and awareness to provide the necessary supports. Building connections with community professionals cultivates positive ongoing working relationships.

An early childhood program leader faces many challenges. Having access to necessary tools like the NAEYC Code of Ethical Conduct Supplemental for Early

Director's Showcase

Both Taisha and Meredith sought out the NAEYC Code of Ethical Conduct Supplemental for Early Childhood Program Administrators. Both program leaders noticed that their staff members were unaware of this resource. They decided that a staff meeting would be appropriate to provide an overview as well as training on the application of the Code of Ethics.

Taisha

Taisha needed to act quickly to address the immediate issue. She consulted the code and determined that utilizing the guidance strategy was appropriate. She further gathered more information about the strategy to share with staff. Rather than reacting defensively, she chose to meet with the staff who were concerned and to include the classroom teacher who directly worked with the child. During the meeting she referenced the code and shared the materials about why the use of the strategy was effective. The classroom teacher was able to share observations of how the strategy was working with the child and that the parents were reporting success at home. The other staff were able to ask questions and at the end of the meeting, everyone agreed that next time the issue arose, being more transparent with each other by seeking credible information was a meaningful first step.

Meredith

Before she began the revision process, Meredith compared a few of the policies that she was concerned about with the Code and with comparable-sized program's policies and procedures. Next, she convened a group of teaching staff to review the revised policies and procedures. She carefully selected a mix of members who were either supportive or critical about the changes. During the groups meetings, she started in the course of the 10-day span to notice that the group discussions were focusing on the reasons for the necessary changes. Within 60 days of initially starting the process, Meredith was able to launch the new personnel and parent policies.

Director's Showcase

Reflect

As you review the NAEYC Code of Ethical Conduct Supplemental for Early Childhood Program Administrators, what were areas of interest to you?

Childhood Program Administrators provides guidance during demanding times. While the answers may not be clear cut, using the proper resources can provide guidance when thinking through possible solutions to issues that arise.

Chapter 11 Review and Assessment

Summary

11.1 Describe early childhood program leadership skills and characteristics necessary to support a quality organization.

- To assume responsibility for a child care program requires leadership skills and characteristics that will motivate others to do the work necessary to care for children of all ages. This includes an awareness of societal issues and influences that will impact the program.
- Program leaders must have vision and problem-solving skills that will determine the future direction of the program. The director must be knowledgeable and concerned about all aspects of the program.
- Directors must hire and retain staff members to support necessary areas to support the program and serve as the mediator and peacemaker in the center.
- Program leaders need interpersonal skills and the ability to communicate clearly. These skills help a group function effectively.
- Early childhood program leaders must create strategies for organizing time to support effective day-to-day operations.

11.2 Distinguish between healthy organizational elements necessary to build a solid climate in which teachers and enrolled families thrive.

- The role of an early childhood leader is complex no matter the size of the program. Responsibilities vary and are separate from everyone else's in the program.
- Making multiple decisions that are program-focused take time, attention, and delegation. Depending on the type of decisions, program leaders must determine at what level they can work with staff to come to solutions or make exclusive decisions due to the circumstance or type of issue.

11.3 Identify roles and responsibilities of the program leader that are unique to the early childhood program environment.

- Leading others can be complicated. In addition, a program leader needs time and confidence to be able to lead others.
- When assuming the responsibility for an organization, a director must have some leadership

skills and characteristics and be able to motivate others to do the work necessary to care for children of all ages.
- The external and internal roles and responsibilities of the program leader build the ongoing health of the organization. The director must display genuine care for the children, their families, and the program staff.
- The roles and responsibilities for a program leader may have some consistency, but a leader must embrace flexibility.

11.4 Utilize the NAEYC Professional Code of Ethics to provide guidance when leading an early childhood program.

- Program leaders may find themselves in compromising situations due to their constant interactions between people. The field of early childhood education has a Code of Ethical Conduct provided by NAEYC.
- Due to the comprehensive responsibilities of an administrator, NAEYC created a Supplemental for Early Childhood Program Administrators to provide guidance to leaders when challenging circumstances arise. Administrators can turn to these guidelines when making the right decision based on the circumstances.

Review

1. Explain how the role of the director differs from that of any other staff member in the center. (11.1)
2. Identify the five essential tasks that must be carried out by an administrator. (11.1)
3. What factors will have an influence when organizing an early childhood program? (11.2)
4. Describe the difference between the Theory X and Theory Y types of management. (11.1)
5. What are three components of successful interpersonal skills? (11.1)
6. What are the 10 dimensions of a healthy organizational climate? (11.2)
7. Describe a group leader's role. (11.3)
8. Identify the six components of careful decision making. (11.2)
9. What is the difference between program culture and climate? (11.3)
10. How is a code of ethics utilized in the field of early childhood education? (11.4)

Showcase Your Skills

As you learned in this chapter, Taisha and Meredith have two different early childhood program environments. All program environments are unique due to the individual personalities of the staff and characteristics of the program.

You have been hired by a not-for-profit board as a consultant for a new program director, Iesha, who has been in place for about six months. She was promoted from master teacher to director. The program is licensed for 60 children and has eight full-time and eight part-time staff. The board identifies several areas that they would like for you to address. The first is to assist Iesha's abilities with managing time. The second is to help her understand the differences between the teacher and director roles. Third, how to better manage difficult situations as a director. For example, there was a family that was having issue with the new teacher hired in Iesha's place. Iesha's recommendation to the board was to terminate the fledgling teacher. However, upon questioning her the only insight she could provide was the family who was not happy with the new teacher.

Based on the information shared in each section of this chapter, it is now your turn to serve in the role of consultant. Write an overview of the strategies to consider when working with Iesha and use the following points as your guide.

1. Read a book that identifies time-management skills for administrators. Provide an overview of the book and identify some ideas that seem especially useful. (11.1)
2. Identify the duties of a director. Make a list of the duties of a classroom teacher. Compare the lists. Talk with an actual director and a teacher to see how closely your duties for each match what they do in a typical work week. (11.3)
3. Access a personnel handbook from a child care program. Using the guidance provided, determine what steps should be taken by the program director when dealing with the family who is unhappy with the new teacher. Also identify any guidance that NAEYC's Code of Ethical Conduct offers that would apply to this situation. (11.4)

Matching

Match the following terms with the correct definitions:

A. advocates
B. climate
C. interpersonal skills
D. networking
E. organizing
F. planning
G. reflective listening
H. staffing
I. Theory X
J. Theory Y

1. Function of management that involves setting goals for the program and identifying methods or strategies for reaching those goals.
2. Qualities and abilities that help one to get along with others and to help them feel at ease.
3. People who speak out or act on behalf of their beliefs.
4. Overall atmosphere and "feel" of the program.
5. Management style in which a manager believes that staff are self-motivated and committed to the organization's goals.
6. Function of management that refers to the recruiting, hiring, and retention of skilled individuals needed to operate a quality program.
7. Management style in which a manager believes that employees have no real commitment to their jobs and cannot be trusted.
8. Repeating the other person's main point using slightly different words to ensure they heard and understood.
9. Developing a group of professional colleagues to interact and communicate with about career issues.
10. Function of management that involves determining an appropriate arrangement of time, people, and space.

SolStock/E+/Getty Images

12 CHAPTER

Supervising and Supporting Program Staff

Learning Outcomes

After studying this chapter, you will be able to:

12.1 Develop and implement necessary personnel policies and activities.

12.2 Design a personnel plan when action needs to be taken.

12.3 Devise strategies for an inclusive and positive working environment.

Key Terms

burnout
grievance procedure
in-service training
personnel policies
self-care

Introduction

A quality child care program begins with quality staff. Empowering staff members is a hallmark of exceptional programs. Staff members feel empowered when they are aware of expectations, have clearly defined roles and job descriptions, and have access to program policies and procedures. Many programs struggle with staff turnover; proper supervision and support of staff will improve employee retention. A program achieves its goal of providing distinctive child care when accomplished staff are able to flourish and grow (**Figure 12.1**).

Continuing to learn and thrive in the child care environment is essential for staff members. A program should provide professional resources and materials, such as books, journals, computers, mobile devices, internet access, assessment tools, and software to all professional staff as well as resources and procedures that support staff wellness, such as referrals for stress management. Teachers and assistants need breaks outside the classroom during the day and the ability to request relief when necessary to support their mental and physical well-being. Providing time to complete curriculum plans and communicate with other professionals or caregivers while not teaching or actively supervising children should be included in program policy.

SDI Productions/E+/Getty Images

Figure 12.1   Quality early childhood programs empower staff and provide clearly defined roles, job descriptions, and access to program policies and procedures.

NAEYC/DAP standards

Standards covered in this chapter:

6c

Director's Showcase

Diwa

Diwa recently accepted the job of director in a small child care program. Her previous position was as director of a large program in a metropolitan area. During her first week at the new program, she noticed a handwritten policy and procedure file that was decades old. Diwa has been very careful not to change things too quickly but has decided that a more formal policy and procedure manual should be at the top of her to-do list. During her first staff meeting, she mentioned updating the manual and was met with resistance from several staff members. She has been told "this is how we have always done things" on more than one occasion.

Kai

Kai has been the director of a medium-sized program for nine years. The owners of the program recently purchased a large child care program in the same city. Kai has been made the director of both programs and facilities. He can hire assistant directors for each facility and has been searching for candidates. In the meantime, he has noticed the large, new program does not radiate a positive environment and has an extremely high staff turnover. He recognizes that he needs to address the culture and staff issues as soon as possible.

Director's Showcase

Reflect

If you were faced with the issues experienced so far by Diwa and Kai, which of the issues would be the hardest one for you to tackle first?

12.1 What Are Personnel Policies?

Personnel policies are the agreements between your center and its employees. The policies should be in printed

shironosov/iStock/Getty Images Plus

Figure 12.2 Personnel policies must constantly be monitored by the director, owner, or members of the board to keep them current and amended as the need arises.

form and distributed to every staff member. When all staff members know what the policies are, each person can feel confident about being treated equally and fairly. Staff members understand what is expected of them and what they can expect from employment in the program. Written policies support a sense of security in new staff. They can feel comfortable knowing what they are supposed to do. All staff can use the personnel policies to identify their opportunities for advancement and recognition, grievance rights, and benefits and to plan their leave time.

The director, owner, or members of the board develop personnel policies for the program and amend them when the need arises (**Figure 12.2**). As the director of the program, you are responsible for seeing that these policies are carried out. If you are the owner of a program, you will need to review personnel policies with a legal counsel or a personnel consultant.

Programs change over time. You may modify the organizational structure as your program becomes more complex. Labor laws and licensing regulations may change. As a result, have your personnel consultant or the personnel committee review your personnel policies at least once a year. If policy changes should be made for a public agency, the committee would recommend action to the full board. If the board approves the revisions, you, as the director, are responsible for the implementation of these changes.

Personnel policies should always include some standard items. Other topics may depend on the nature of your program. Some sections are mandatory for not-for-profit agencies but not for proprietary programs. Personnel policy manuals commonly include

- statement of nondiscrimination;
- description of benefits;
- descriptions of employee responsibilities and conduct;
- grievance procedures;
- health and safety procedures;
- emergency procedures;
- procedures for transfers and promotions;
- probationary employment rules; and
- evaluation procedures.

Statement of Nondiscrimination

A statement of nondiscrimination provides assurance that your center's personnel policies are nondiscriminatory and provide equal opportunity. The specific wording of this statement may vary according to local or state requirements. It must also follow federal regulations. The statement should appear in your personnel policies as well as your job announcements and applications (**Figure 12.3**). If you are not sure how to word it, check with your local employment office or Human Relations Commission.

Description of Benefits

The description of benefits section outlines the benefits staff members receive as a part of their employment. The benefits for which your center is responsible are, in part, determined by law. As an employer, you must provide such items as workers' compensation and social security. Other benefits are determined by what your agency can afford.

Typical benefits offered by programs may include

- *Leave days.* These may include leave for vacation, sickness, bereavement (for death of a loved one), education, jury duty, and military service. Leaves of absence for other miscellaneous reasons may also be granted. Indicate procedures by which employees must request these leave days. Clearly define the difference between paid time off, earned leave, and unpaid leave. Indicate if you require a note from a doctor when an employee misses an extended

School of Creative Play provides equal employment opportunities to all employees and applicants for employment without regard to race, color, religion, sex, sexual orientation, gender identity, national origin, age, disability, veteran status, ancestry and marital status, and other protected classes, in accordance with applicable federal and state laws. School of Creative Play does not participate in visa sponsorship.

In addition, the School of Creative Play complies with applicable state and local laws governing nondiscrimination of employment. This policy applies to all terms and conditions of employment, including, but not limited to hiring, placement, promotion, termination, layoff, recall, transfers, leave of absence, compensation, and training.

Goodheart-Willcox Publisher

Figure 12.3 Developing a statement of nondiscrimination varies according to local or state requirements.

period of work time. Specify when an employee is eligible for bereavement leave.

- *Retirement plan contributions.* Investing pre-tax money into a structured retirement account such as a 401k or 403b.
- *Health insurance.* This may include full or partial payment for health insurance. It may cover the employee only or their family members as well.
- *Group life insurance and disability insurance.* This will pay a policy beneficiary in case of injury or death.
- *Additional benefits.* Dental, vision, or prescription coverage and flexible spending accounts are additional benefits offered separately from basic health insurance.
- *Lunches.* These may be offered if you are providing lunch to the children.
- *Parking.* If your center is located in an urban complex, daily parking can be both expensive and troublesome. A guaranteed space is highly valued.
- *Child care.* Many of your staff may have their own child care needs. You may allow them to bring their children to the center or offer a discounted rate for child care. This benefit may have tax consequences for the staff member.
- *Dues payments for professional memberships.* One way to grow staff is to assist with the payment of yearly dues typically required by early childhood professional groups.
- *Tuition assistance or reimbursements.* Policies should be discussed around tuition for additional classes, training, or conference attendance, as well as reimbursements or subsidization of those classes.
- *Health reimbursements.* Reimbursements for immunizations and/or annual physical exam, as well as any additional reimbursements for gym memberships or health programs.

The description of benefits informs all employees what benefits the center offers. Staff can see they receive more for their work than their paycheck indicates.

Employee Responsibilities and Conduct

The employee responsibilities and conduct section should include information that clearly details what is expected of employees. It should include such items as

- timeliness in arriving for work;
- confidentiality regarding center information;
- description of center dress code, if applicable;
- expectation of respectful attitude toward children, families, and other staff members;
- requirement of commitment to the center's philosophy and practices;

shapecharge/E+/Getty Images

Figure 12.4   Many programs utilizing program software have apps that can put out information and communications to staff on a daily basis.

- expectation of employee's participation in training opportunities; and
- adherence to the center's policies and requirements.

Methods of communication should also be addressed in the policy. If all staff are expected to read daily notices on a staff bulletin board or electronic app, they should be aware of this expectation (**Figure 12.4**). If there is a method through which staff can make suggestions or communicate with each other, include this also. Policies about the use of phones and social media in the classroom should be clearly stated and revisited frequently.

Grievance Procedures

The **grievance procedure** is the process by which employees can issue a complaint if they feel they have been unfairly treated. The procedure should detail first attempting to solve any problem at the lowest level of administration. This usually involves informal attempts to discuss and resolve the problem with the immediate supervisor. For example, an aide who is unhappy about treatment from an assistant teacher should first discuss the issue with the head teacher of that classroom. If the issue is not settled at that level, the employee would be advised to put the concern in writing and present it to the director. If the employee is still not satisfied with the director's handling of the problem, a written complaint could be presented to the board or owner of the program.

Health and Safety

Issues related to health and safety of employees should also be included in the personnel policies. There are two areas of concern in this category. One concern is for the health and safety of all who work in the center. The other concern is the impact that the health or safety practices of employees might have on the well-being of the children in their care.

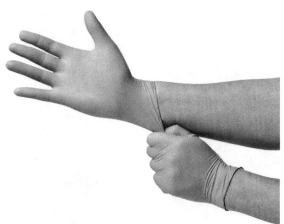

Figure 12.5 From handling potential bloodborne pathogens or other bodily fluids, to knowing how to protect themselves and the children in their care, it is important for staff to comply with state laws and regulations.

Employees should be assured that you are concerned about their welfare. They need to know that the center complies with all laws and regulations that apply to the workplace (**Figure 12.5**). Child care licensing regulations are written to protect the children. These regulations ensure the safety of the adults who work in child care as well.

Government agencies have additional regulations designed to protect the welfare of the adults in the workplace (**Figure 12.6**). The Occupational Safety and Health Administration (OSHA) sets and enforces job safety and health standards for workers. The center should comply with these standards, and staff should be trained in health and safety procedures. Every state has an OSHA office that oversees compliance.

Current laws require a posted notification to staff of any potentially hazardous chemicals, such as industrial

cleaning fluids, or materials used in the workplace. Employers must also post a notification of staff rights regarding a safe workplace. The federal Right to Know laws require that this information be easily visible to employees. Administrators may include this information in the personnel manual or simply list the locations in the facility where the information is posted.

The manual should also include policies outlining when an ill staff member should not report to work. Many employees pride themselves on not missing a day of work or do not want an unpaid day. However, they may not consider how quickly a contagious illness can spread to others in their workplace, especially a child care center. Open, oozing sores, an undiagnosed skin rash, fever, diarrhea, sore throat, or a severe cold are all conditions under which an employee should stay home.

Emergency Procedures

Personnel policies should include the basic emergency procedures for the center. Staff members must understand their responsibility to follow these procedures if the need arises. The procedures must include the following:

- an evacuation and reunification plan in case of fire or other emergency within the building;
- universal precautions necessary when dealing with potential bloodborne pathogens;
- methods for securing the center should a violent situation arise; and
- basic cardiopulmonary resuscitation (CPR), first aid, and abdominal thrusts, also known as the Heimlich maneuver (**Figure 12.7**).

You may also develop additional procedures in relation to your location, hours, or clientele. One center, located

Figure 12.6 Even those who work in early childhood programs are protected by OSHA safety and healthy standards for all staff members.

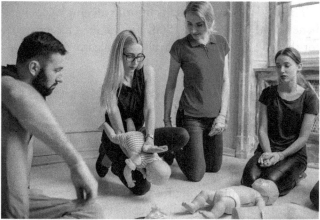

Figure 12.7 All early childhood programs must have basic emergency procedures in place, including certifications for staff in areas such as basic first aid and cardiopulmonary resuscitation (CPR) for infants, young children, and adults.

near a busy railroad track, identified a specific set of procedures to follow in case a train carrying hazardous chemicals derailed. Another center served several families with drug and alcohol dependency problems. The administration developed plans to ensure the safety of both staff and children in case an out-of-control adult entered the center.

Transfers, Promotions, and Probationary Employment

The personnel policies should also address such issues as transfers within the program, how to seek a promotion, and the details of any probationary employment. How will you handle a request by an employee who wants to be moved to a different classroom or center? What is the policy regarding an employee who wants to be considered for a promotion or an administrator position? How long is the probationary period for new hires? Requiring a probationary period of employment benefits the program and the employee. This time at the beginning of employment allows for everyone to determine if the employee is a good fit for the program and vice versa. A 60- or 90-day probationary period allows for an early review of performance and time to address any concerns or problems with the employee or the program.

Evaluation Procedures

Within every agency, there must be a plan for employee evaluations (**Figure 12.8**). Many states require this as a condition of funding and licensing. Evaluations are also a necessary part of the controlling function of management.

hh5800/Getty Images

Figure 12.8   Most states require that employee evaluations take place as a condition of funding and licensing. Regular performance evaluations provide opportunities for staff members to better understand areas of strength and areas that need more work when performing their job role within the early childhood program environment.

You must know how well staff members are performing their responsibilities to understand how well the center is functioning. The program's evaluation procedures should be included in the personnel policies. An evaluation plan should include the following components:

- a timeline that identifies when formal evaluations will occur;
- procedures that will be followed for the evaluation;
- identification of staff members who will have responsibility for evaluation;
- selection of items to be included on the evaluation;
- a procedure for communicating the results of the evaluation to the employee;
- safeguards to ensure that unauthorized persons do not have access to completed evaluations; and
- a list of training options that could be offered to employees who need to improve specific areas of performance.

Developing standard forms that identify the major aspects of successful performance for each job category is useful. Evaluation forms should be consistent with the job description and should be available to the employee. Including definitions of behaviors that indicate a need for improvement, additional space for comments, suggestions, or awards or recognition for outstanding performance can allow each employee's evaluation to be individualized. The completed evaluation must be shared with the staff member and should become the basis for discussing individual and program goals and identifying ways to meet those goals.

Evaluating staff members is often difficult for directors and supervisors. One way to help supervisors feel more confident in this role is to review evaluations before they are presented to staff members. If the supervisor can clearly explain the ratings in advance and is familiar with the content, they will be more successful presenting their evaluations later to those staff members. This pre-evaluation meeting with supervisors ensures that you know what is being suggested to employees and gives you the opportunity to guide and support the evaluator.

Director's Showcase

Reflect

Now that you have read more, where should Diwa focus her efforts to update the personnel policies and procedures at her program? How will Kai deal with the noticeable negativity in the environment and high staff turnover?

12.2 What Kinds of Personnel Actions May Be Necessary?

When staff members are performing their duties satisfactorily, decisions regarding personnel actions are relatively simple. You may have to take no action at all except to file the evaluation in the personnel file. If the opportunity exists for a promotion or salary increase, the evaluation may become a part of that decision. When a staff member is in a probationary status, a favorable evaluation may result in permanent employment status.

When an evaluation has not been satisfactory, the employee is not working out well or struggling in the role. As the director, you will need to consider options regarding this situation. If the person needs additional training, your actions may include the development of an individualized training plan. If the staff member is habitually late, unprepared, or irritable and unresponsive to the children, you should address these concerns. An unsatisfactory employee may be placed on probationary status for a set period. The training plan should stipulate that improvement in the deficient areas may be required for continued employment.

Disciplinary Action

An employee who violates the conduct code may be subject to disciplinary action. Establish a disciplinary action procedure in case a problem arises (**Figure 12.9**). Disciplinary action may involve a simple verbal or written warning. This may be sufficient to serve as a warning that an employee's behavior is unacceptable. An employee who is always late may simply need to be reminded of the inconvenience this causes everyone else. The administrator must handle more serious or repeated violations with stronger action. A disciplinary meeting may result in the creation of a personnel action plan and/or temporary suspension. The last necessary action may result in actual termination of employment. Discipline at this level will require approval by the board or owner of the center.

Document any disciplinary steps taken. When you become aware of a problem with an employee, keep a record of the infractions. Also, keep a written record of any disciplinary actions, even verbal warnings, in the employee's personnel file. If stronger action is required, be sure that you have documented both the reasons and the action taken. The employee's evaluation reports will normally be among those items that provide documentation and rationale for a dismissal action. A disgruntled employee may claim unfair treatment or unjust termination. You must be able to explain the rationale for your

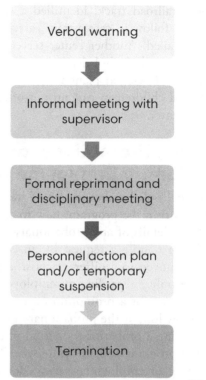

Goodheart-Willcox Publisher

Figure 12.9 Having an established disciplinary action procedure assists should a problem arise with a staff member.

actions and demonstrate that they were not discriminatory. Be sure that all actions you have taken are consistent with your personnel policies.

Termination of Employees

Laws vary from state to state regarding termination of employees (**Figure 12.10**). Seek legal advice when setting up personnel policies in relation to dismissal of unsatisfactory staff members. When an employee's conduct is not satisfactory, there should be several levels of warning given before the individual is terminated.

pablohart/E+/Getty Images

Figure 12.10 Laws vary from state to state and it is important for early childhood program leaders to be aware of policies related to terminating employees.

- *Level 1.* A simple verbal warning that alerts the employee of unsatisfactory behavior.
- *Level 2.* A written warning given to the employee that documents unsatisfactory conduct.
- *Level 3.* A return to probationary status for a particular amount of time. (This carries with it the expectation of dismissal if additional evaluations do not indicate improvement. At this level, suspension may also occur. This means the employee is on leave without pay as a disciplinary measure.)
- *Level 4.* Termination of employment.

Document all disciplinary action at any level in the employee's personnel file. The board of directors or the owner of the center should provide approval for any actions at levels three and four. It is also a good idea to have the disciplined employee sign and date the documentation of the disciplinary action.

As the director, you must determine the appropriate response to more serious disciplinary problems. An employee who abuses a child, violently threatens a coworker, or commits some other serious offense must be dealt with immediately through a higher level of disciplinary and sometimes legal action.

12.3 How Can I Support a Positive Working Environment?

When staff feel supported and stable in their workplace, they are more likely to stay in their job. Your job, as director, involves seeking ways to build job satisfaction among your employees. Many caring staff members remain in their jobs for years. When asked why they stay, they often mention how they love their jobs and how they feel they are doing something important for children. Since high salaries are not the norm in this field and the work can be both physically and emotionally exhausting, the child care director must find other ways to create a positive working environment and support their staff. The atmosphere where a person works is often just as important as the wages that person earns. Many staff members stay in jobs that do not pay well because they love what they are doing. Pleasant working conditions are more important than money for many people. As a director, you can take many steps to create a positive working environment.

Compensation

All employees are interested in the amount of their salaries. Some employees may be adding a second household income, while others may be the sole support of themselves and their dependents. Both the amount of the salary and the assurance that they will be paid consistently are important to employees.

In the child care field, salaries do not reflect the significant influence that preschool staff have in the lives of children. For too long, our society has taken the position that "anyone can do it." As a result, many children are in

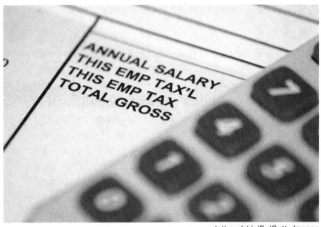

Figure 12.11 Adequate pay for staff is one of the biggest challenges early childhood leaders face while also striving to keep the program financially secure.

situations where the care is inadequate and indifferent. As an administrator, one of your hardest jobs is to figure out how to pay adequate salaries to your hard-working staff, while keeping the program financially secure. The reality of budgeting is that you cannot pay salaries with money you do not have. Whatever your wages are, they must be realistic in terms of the income of the program.

When considering how to establish salary ranges, keep the following points in mind (**Figure 12.11**):

- All salaries must be at or above minimum wage.
- Your program may not always operate at full enrollment.
- Jobs that require more training and have more responsibility should also receive higher salaries.
- Some salary increase should be offered each year to encourage staff to stay.
- Financial benefits are calculated in addition to salary and must be included in the cost of each employee.
- Staff members who are doing similar jobs should be on a similar pay scale.
- Salary increases raise the employee's salary for every year following the increase.
- Bonuses can be given when money is available, but do not raise the base salary.

Most professional staff in child care are aware of the salary picture in the field. They understand that their salaries are connected to enrollment and the cost of tuition. They will appreciate your efforts on their behalf as you work to increase the enrollment at your center and advocate for higher wages across the field as well.

Positive and Respectful Climate

Creating a positive, respectful climate is an important part of building a good working environment. Staff members need to feel they are valued in their workplace.

They must be treated with respect and consideration. You are a role model for this behavior. You set the tone for the center as you treat staff with the same consideration you expect them to show families and children. Greet staff members each day. Let them know you are glad to see them. Encourage a sense of inclusion that helps every person feel they play an important role in providing good care for the children in the program.

A positive climate also involves an open mind toward new ideas (**Figure 12.12**). If staff members' ideas are always met with a "No, we can't do that here!" response, new ideas will not be shared. If things are done a certain way simply because they have always been done that way, stagnation sets in, and the work can become boring. If new ideas are welcomed and applied, the program will be more successful.

Classroom Assignments

As you make personnel decisions, try to place each person in the role where they will work best. For example, certain staff work well with infants, but dislike the more assertive characteristics of preschoolers. Others prefer working with two half-day groups rather than a full-day class. Some may relate better to three-year-olds rather than four-year-olds. If you can place your staff with the age group or in a classroom where they fit best with the children, things will be smoother for them and you.

Pay close attention to the interactions among staff members. Putting two adults who do not get along or have vastly different teaching styles in the same classroom is guaranteed to lead to trouble. Even if the two staff basically like each other, personality characteristics should be considered in organizing work groups. Two strong-willed, assertive individuals may not work well together for long without clashing. Likewise, two mild-mannered, nonassertive individuals working in the same classroom may not make the best team. Staff members with

Figure 12.12 The climate in which the staff works should be positive and respectful. Teachers should feel free to share new ideas with each other.

complementary personalities often are the best match if they balance and support each other.

Schedule Preferences

Staff members also have preferences regarding their schedule. Some like early morning hours and feel invigorated by an early shift. Others may have their own children to get off to school and prefer starting later. When staff can request their preferred shift, you may be pleasantly surprised that all shifts are chosen. While you may not always be able to accommodate individual preferences, the staff will appreciate your efforts to do so when possible. Scheduling decisions can signal to the staff that you view them as individuals and that you are trying to meet their needs. For some staff with complicated family responsibilities or special health considerations, scheduling decisions may make a difference in whether they can work in your program.

Physical Environment

The physical environment of the center is a vital part of the workplace. A clean, pleasant classroom with adequate ventilation and lighting helps staff enjoy their workday. Sanitary bathrooms and kitchens not only present a more impressive environment, they also are important in protecting the health of staff and children.

Within your facility, try to find a space where staff can have a few quiet moments away from the children (**Figure 12.13**). Interesting magazines, soft chairs, coffee or juice, and a brief chance to talk with other adults can provide a relaxing break. Staff can share many valuable ideas with each other during these casual conversation times. A staff bulletin board in the break room can serve as a place to share training opportunities, sign-ups for shared equipment, or humorous cartoons. Available professional journals or a folder containing successful ideas for field trips can stimulate new activity ideas.

Working conditions play a significant role in building staff loyalty to your program as well. Staff members who feel that you are concerned about their well-being, including their working conditions, have a greater commitment to the program. While there will always be some staff turnover, many child care agencies have staff who have remained with their program for many years. Even if you cannot afford to pay the salaries you would like to pay, you can create a center where people feel comfortable, safe, and appreciated.

Motivation and Recognition of Efforts

People usually choose to work in child care because of their love for children and commitment to the field. The work is often physically demanding and emotionally exhausting. The pay is typically low. Extra effort is often unappreciated by parents who are, themselves, exhausted. As director, you must provide a nurturing and supportive atmosphere that will motivate staff and help them grow. They need to feel their efforts are valued by those who understand the nature of the work.

You can recognize staff who have been with the program a long time (**Figure 12.14**). A staff appreciation banquet can give tired personnel a time to relax and socialize with each other. Acknowledge years of service with certificates, award pins, plaques, or small gifts. You could feature a different employee with a brief description in each issue of your center's newsletter. Some centers with limited parking offer an "employee of the week" reserved parking space. When the center has an open house, you could arrange for local newspaper coverage.

SDI Productions/E+/Getty Images

Figure 12.13 Having a comfortable space away from the children for staff to take a break to rest, relax, and share a few laughs with one another supports positive working conditions and a sense of being cared for.

Wavebreakmedia/iStock/Getty Images Plus

Figure 12.14 Time should be planned for staff recognition. This includes recognizing years of service, award pins, plaques, or small gifts.

Staff can be featured in publicity photos as they work with the children.

An important way to recognize staff efforts is for you, as director, to acknowledge them personally. A brief note of appreciation, stopping by the classroom to say "thanks," or a more formal letter of commendation that is placed in the personnel file are usually gratefully appreciated by the staff. Employees may appreciate heartfelt words of gratitude and commendation during a staff gathering or banquet. Mentioning outstanding effort at a board meeting ensures that the commendation will also appear in the formal board minutes as a permanent record of staff effort.

In-Service Training

In-service training refers to training that a person receives while already employed. Pre-service education, such as vocational school, college, skill training seminars, and certificate-focused courses, occurs before employment. Participation in in-service training is usually expected while an individual is employed.

The purposes of in-service training may include the following:

- updating knowledge with new information;
- providing in-depth information on topics covered briefly in earlier training;
- improving specific areas of on-the-job performance;
- presenting new activity ideas;
- providing an opportunity to share ideas and concerns;
- meeting required training hours mandated by funding or licensing agencies;
- giving staff the opportunity for personal advancement;
- strengthening staff understanding of child development principles; and
- renewing enthusiasm and providing motivation and encouragement for staff (**Figure 12.15**).

FatCamera/E+/Getty Images

Figure 12.15 Regularly scheduled in-service training allows for staff to strengthen their understanding of child development principles and effective ways to work with families.

Many states require that child care personnel participate in continuing education each year. The requirements for these training sessions or workshops vary from state to state. Even though training requirements in some states are minimal, some staff will still be unwilling to participate.

Staff who do not work directly with children need to have an opportunity to participate in appropriate professional development as well. If you are purchasing a new computer system, your administrative and clerical staff will require training and support to learn how the new system works. A new receptionist may need training in phone etiquette or how to handle difficult people.

Encouraging Self-Care and Preventing Burnout

After a few years in the child care field, staff members may begin to experience symptoms of burnout. **Burnout** is physical and mental exhaustion that results from prolonged periods of stress or frustration. They are mentally tired and may feel unappreciated and bored with the day-to-day routine. They may be overwhelmed by the latest problems. These feelings can drain the energy of the individual and discourage all who work in the program.

The basic nature of working with children cannot be changed. It is necessary to be actively alert when caring for children. Emotional availability and involvement are a part of what makes the relationship between children and caring adults work well. Interactions with many people on many different levels go on continuously. It often seems that no one notices these efforts. By having an emotionally available director, staff will feel supported and in turn will be more available to the children they work with. Directors can implement an "open-door" policy that allows staff members to schedule time with the director to talk through issues that may arise. The director should also have outside resources available for staff that need to talk to a professional. The toll of stress in the workplace is not limited to staff and employees. Directors and those who work in an administration role will need to attend to their own social and emotional well-being. Self-care is for everyone, —allowing time to take care of personal issues, burnout, frustrations, and stress is imperative for a successful program.

As director, you cannot control your employees' feelings. However, you can focus on self-care and provide opportunities for staff to participate in self-care activities (**Figure 12.16**). **Self-care** means taking care of yourself in ways that keep you healthy, allow you to do your job, and prevent burnout. Providing a quiet space for breaks, planning in-service training about mindfulness and self-reflection, and having a staff meal after hours or on the weekends to bond outside of the program are all ways

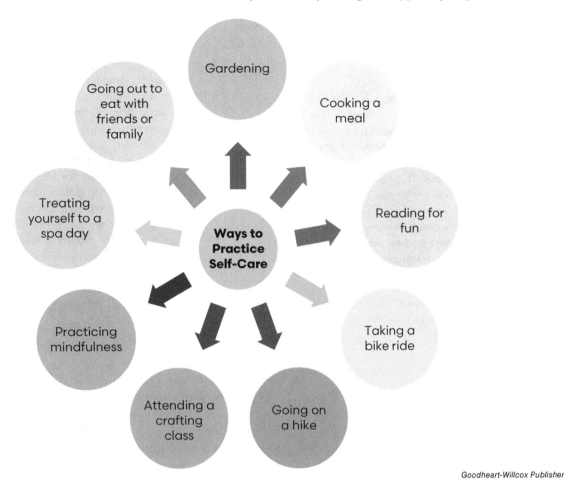

Goodheart-Willcox Publisher

Figure 12.16   Self-care is important for program leaders and their staff to participate in regularly.

to help boost employee morale and create opportunities for reflection and support.

You could form a committee to plan staff activities. Craft classes, nature hikes, or flea market shopping expeditions can all help staff become more comfortable with each other. No one activity will interest everyone, and participation should not be required. Nor should activities be scheduled in such a way that they take time away from the children. Children's museums and library programs are often willing to provide programming on site or low-cost access to their own programming. Finding common interests among staff and having a night out or an in-service day to have fun goes a long way in making connections and reducing stress. It is difficult to be stressed when you are having fun at work.

Once again, your attitudes and behaviors set the tone for the center. If you maintain a sense of humor and keep things in perspective with a touch of lightheartedness, others will do the same. If you are gloomy, frantic, or overwhelmed much of the time, others will adopt that tone. When you participate in activities that renew your own energy, you can encourage others to do likewise. Many of the concerns facing classroom staff are serious, and their importance should not be minimized. At the

same time, being able to "look at the bright side" can help staff address problems more creatively and effectively.

Maintaining a well-qualified staff for the program is one of the director's most important responsibilities (**Figure 12.17**). The quality of the program and the

SolStock/E+/Getty Images

Figure 12.17   One of the program leader's most important responsibilities is to maintain a group of well-qualified staff who provide quality day-to-day experiences for the children in their care.

Director's Showcase

Diwa

Diwa was able to implement a new policies and procedures manual in the program she had just taken over. By asking for input from her staff, they felt heard and validated. Most of the staff are relieved to have procedures in writing to refer to when questions arise. The staff that were resistant to the changes have warmed up to the idea after seeing the new manual and understanding that no big changes have been implemented. Having clearly defined roles and expectations has benefitted everyone in the program.

Kai

After spending time with staff and in the classroom, Kai has implemented ways to address staff self-care. Most of the staff had been facing burn out. He has transformed the break room into an oasis for staff. Instead of a table and hard-back folding chairs, he has added a sofa, ambient lighting instead of fluorescent light, a coffee machine with a variety of coffee flavors, and a radio for music if wanted. He also has scheduled chair massages once a month for his staff. Kai also started providing lunch once a week for staff during which he arranges for staff from different classrooms to eat together and get to know others around the center. He has begun recognizing employee accomplishments on a spotlight board in the front office. He catches staff doing good work and puts their picture up on the board with a short blurb about their work. The feedback from staff members has been positive, and he has observed a positive change in the culture and attitudes of his staff.

Director's Showcase

Reflect

As you start to think about leading others, what would be specific areas would you focus on to establish and maintain a positive working environment?

day-to-day experiences for children are dependent on the staff. Many directors find that this is the hardest part of their job. Motivating staff, helping them get along with each other, and supporting their efforts to do a good job are not easy tasks. As the director, you must accomplish all of this, with a good sense of humor and a "thick skin."

Chapter 12 Review and Assessment

Summary

12.1 Develop and implement necessary personnel policies and activities.

- A quality child care program depends on maintaining a committed, well-trained staff.
- Printed personnel policies help individuals understand their place within the organization and inform them of basic program expectations and procedures.
- Staff members need to know what their duties and responsibilities are as well as how to carry out their job requirements. The personnel policies also inform staff of their rights as employees.

12.2 Design a personnel plan when action needs to be taken.

- The center must have some procedure for evaluating staff. The evaluation should be based on the job description of the individual being evaluated. The format should be made clear to the employee ahead of time.
- Results of the evaluation must be shared with the individual but maintained in confidence. The evaluation should be used as a basis to help the employee grow in the job.
- If the staff member is not performing satisfactorily, the director may have to take action that may lead to dismissal.

12.3 Devise strategies for an inclusive and positive working environment.

- Attention also must be paid to staff compensation and overall working conditions within the program. Many child care workers stay in their jobs because they love what they do.
- Pleasant working conditions, in-service training opportunities, and recognition of efforts encourage staff to stay with the program.
- The director's support and commitment to a positive work environment can be a crucial factor in maintaining program stability.

Review

1. Why are written personnel policies important to your staff? (12.1)
2. Why is it necessary to review and possibly change personnel policies over time? (12.1)
3. What is the purpose of the Right to Know laws? (12.1)
4. What types of basic emergency procedures should be considered to keep staff and children safe? (12.1)
5. What is the purpose of a probationary employment period for a new employee? (12.1)
6. What components should be included in an evaluation plan? (12.1)
7. Why is it important to document any disciplinary action at any level in an employee's personnel file? (12.2)
8. How can classroom assignments affect the morale of staff? (12.3)
9. What are the purposes of in-service training? (12.3)

Showcase Your Skills

1. Visit a child care center. Look at the area surrounding the building. What dangers existing in that environment might present a safety hazard to staff? Would the dangers change depending on whether it was daylight or dark? What kinds of ideas would you have to ensure the safety of staff? (12.1)
2. Contact several center directors and ask to look at a copy of their personnel policies. Examine the policies to see what types of information are included or not included. Report to the class on the differences you found among programs. Discuss how the different policies might affect employees. (12.1)
3. Role-play with another student a situation involving a director and an assistant teacher. Evaluations of the assistant teacher support the concern that the assistant has not been doing the job in a satisfactory manner. The assistant has been placed on a probationary status, but the work has not improved. You are dismissing the assistant from the program. What documents and materials do you need to back you up? How will you discuss this? How will you handle the reaction? (12.1)

Matching

Match the following words with the correct definitions:

A. burnout
B. grievance procedure
C. in-service training
D. personnel policies
E. self-care

1. Agreements between your center and its employees that list what the expectations are for treatment of staff and management treatment.

2. Process by which employees can issue a complaint if they feel they have been unfairly treated.

3. Physical and mental exhaustion that results from prolonged periods of stress or frustration.

4. Training that a person receives while already employed.

5. Taking care of yourself in ways that keep you healthy, allow you to do your job, and prevent burnout.

Serhii Hryshchyshen/iStock/Getty Images Plus

13 CHAPTER

Managing People and Setting Expectations

Learning Outcomes

After studying this chapter, you will be able to:

13.1 Develop insights on the importance of workplace relationships.

13.2 Compare aspects of situations where conflict is viewed in the workplace as negative and positive.

13.3 Implement conflict-resolution strategies that support a healthy workplace environment.

13.4 Establish policies and procedures that support employees and families as they work together for the benefit of the program environment.

13.5 Explore strategies to assist with workplace gossip and bullying.

Key Terms

communication
conflict
conflict-partnership pathway
conflict resolution
gossip
hierarchy
negative conflict
positive conflict
workplace bullying

Introduction

Workplace relationships are key to a healthy organization. Whether a program is large or small, people are still interacting and being together. Working together can support flourishing relationships or create clashes in personalities. An early childhood program environment is very different from most workplace environments because it encompasses people of all ages. Not only do the adults need to get along, but the children need to as well. Whether adult to adult or adult to child, the director of a program must serve as the balance between relationships. This includes being mindful of their own actions and modeling best practices to others. Directors often find managing relationships is one of the most challenging parts of leading an early childhood program (**Figure 13.1**).

There are many ways to manage people. For the purposes of this chapter, the focus will be on managing people and setting expectations that support healthy adult working relationships. When times are good and everyone gets along, it is wonderful! But what happens when people are not getting along? Is it appropriate to allow them to "act out" in front of the children or for an angry

gradyreese/iStock/Getty Images Plus

Figure 13.1 Managing relationships within the early childhood program environment can be one of the most challenging parts of leading others.

NAEYC/DAP standards

Standards covered in this chapter:

2b, 4a, 6b, 6c

1C, 2C

parent to yell at a teacher? The easy answer to these questions is "no." The harder task is getting involved and helping resolve these issues. From program policies located

Director's Showcase

In Chapter 12, Taisha and Meredith had assumed responsibility for two different early childhood programs. How did they begin the complex role of leading others?

Taisha

The program enrolled quickly and necessitated acquiring many new staff members. Taisha had to make many key decisions in a short period of time, including assigning teaching teams. She initially felt good about her choices, but with time, she has noticed quarreling between teachers and teachers dividing into factions. She thought she had made it clear from the beginning that everyone was expected to get along. However, some of the teachers are blaming her for the unrest between staff members.

Meredith

After some time at the program location, Meredith has noticed that some staff members have difficulty communicating with each other to the point that she was observing very little if any communication between certain teachers. Because the previous director spent little time with the staff, Meredith has decided that making herself more available by walking around is an appropriate first step.

Director's Showcase

Reflect

How might Taisha and Meredith begin building relationships with and between teachers at their program sites?

within employee and parent handbooks to conflict-resolution strategies, the program director is responsible for taking the lead in managing these situations. This may include reaching out to community resources to refer a staff member or a family for expertise that can assist with the issue that may be taking place. Having knowledge in these areas is a responsibility of a program leader.

13.1 Workplace Relationships

Workplace relationships do not bloom overnight. In fact, they take months and even years in some cases to develop. The foundation of any relationship begins with trust, respect, and communication. For a group to feel a sense of togetherness, they must be able to speak, listen, and hear each other. This takes time and opportunities for the group to experience good and bad times together, including overcoming times of conflict.

In a work setting, the mediator of this process is the leader (**Figure 13.2**). For an early childhood program director,

Kristen Alexandria

Figure 13.2   Program leaders working alongside their staff gain valuable insight regarding the new staff member's abilities.

this means becoming quite attuned to those around you. Observation and being fully present within the relationship-building process are key. A program director will only know if they chose the "right fit" within the established group by engaging with them on a regular basis. This includes their interactions individually, in the classroom with the children, and with other teaching team members. In addition, keeping a certain awareness of the emotional environment is crucial. If teaching staff are working effectively together, then children's needs are adequately being met and relationships with parents are being fostered.

Trust

Think about some of the closest relationships you have, such as with a parent, sibling, grandparent, significant other, or very close friend. These are long-term relationships that have evolved over years of time together and are based on mutual trust. On the other hand, trust in the workplace must be established quickly and appropriately. The intent is to trust one another to work collectively when caring for young children while also upholding the policies and rules of the workplace. The NAEYC Code of Ethical Conduct states that a commitment to "recognize that children and adults achieve their full potential in the context of relationships that are based on trust and respect" (NAEYC, 2011) is essential.

When there is trust in the workplace, people feel safe. When coworkers feel safe, they are willing to grow and learn together. Teaching teams begin to interact with each other, share ideas, and engage collaboratively. Rather than focusing on "I," the feeling of the team becomes about "we." The more that early childhood program environments nurture trust between staff, the more classrooms radiate a positive emotional climate. Settings with strong leadership trust in each other's strengths and abilities, take responsibility for the greater good, and display good intentions (O'Neill & Brinkerhoff, 2018).

Respect

The field of early childhood care brings together a diverse set of people. As children come to the program environment, they bring their families, cultures, and backgrounds. As an employee comes to the workplace, they bring their own unique ideas, backgrounds, and values, which may or may not "fit" with their coworkers' thoughts or experiences. However, the NAEYC (2011) Code of Ethical Conduct provides guidance related to the equity and diversity that must be supported in the program environment (**Figure 13.3**).

Respect comes from valuing another person no matter what the differences might be. Those who are respectful take the time to listen intently, offer to assist if the other

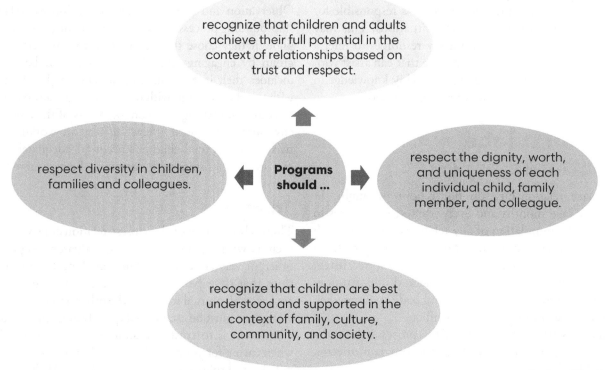

Figure 13.3 The NAEYC Code of Ethical Conduct provides guidance related to equity and diversity for all within an early childhood program environment.

person needs help, value another's opinion even though they may not agree, and empathize with others' opinions. Open and honest communication establishes and conveys respect among colleagues and with children and their families.

Communication

Everything that a person does utilizes some sort of *communication*, whether it be written, verbal, or physical. **Communication** is the process of clarifying the perceptions that people have of each other, and this happens in three ways by listening, sensing, and asking clarifying questions. People combine these three areas when communicating with one another.

Hearing and listening to what someone is saying are two different things. Effective listening requires concentration by both individuals on the words that are being said. Poor listening feeds pressure, especially when emotions are running high. A person may be busy thinking about how they will respond rather than what is being stated by the other person and their intent. Sometimes, because a certain word or phrase is used, a person completely shuts down and does not hear anything past what was said. Further, some people listen poorly so that they can avoid issues or have an excuse to misperceive. Ineffective listening accompanied by an individual's perceptions can be a dangerous combination when trying to communicate with one another (**Figure 13.4**).

Figure 13.4 When people listen poorly, misperceptions take place, which impacts the ability to communicate together.

Our eyes, ears, and other sensory inputs are triggers when communication takes place. This includes things such as tone of voice, a roll of the eyes, crossed arms, or facial expressions. These nonverbal actions send a message to the other person. These reactions can often be perceived in different ways, which can lead to misinterpretation and conflict. If too much attention is given to these types of behaviors, they may be interpreted in a negative way and lead to incorrect assumptions. Asking clarifying questions is important to avoid misinterpretations.

The process of asking clarifying questions helps to make clear what is being said and the meaning behind it.

Asking follow-up questions allows the listener to gather additional information that may not have been stated or addressed. This exchange allows both the speaker and the listener to thoughtfully consider what is being communicated rather than making assumptions of what has been said or understood and the meaning behind it. For example, "I hear you saying that when I start lunch preparation early it disrupts your circle time with the children. How can we plan our class time so that each of us can complete these tasks without disrupting each other?" states the problem and asks a clarifying question rather than providing a confrontational response of "Fine—I'll wait for your circle time to be over. The children can run wild, while I am trying to prepare their lunches and supervise as you take your break." Asking clarifying questions allows for both parties to stop and show interest in what is being said and the intent behind it. By doing this, more information is gathered and a possible resolution to the situation can be sought rather than escalating a conflict. Overall, communication is key when workplace relationships are developing.

Healthy Workplace Relationships

Establishing and maintaining healthy workplace relationships takes time. Relationships affect how the early childhood program environment operates each day.

Trust, respect, and communication are foundations to a successful workplace and the relationships that grow within it. A program leader can send very powerful messages of acceptance and respect throughout the early childhood program with these simple suggestions:

- Be accessible to families and staff by having an open-door policy. This goes a long way in demonstrating care about everyone and their input, needs, and interests.
- Create routines that encourage sharing and working together to solve issues as they arise.
- Coordinate events during which staff can share together over a potluck lunch or families can get to know each other over a dinner hosted by the program.
- Organize staff retreats that allow employees to share professional development opportunities and growth in their working relationships together.
- Provide space for staff to work together outside of the classroom when planning.
- Validate staff with notes or tokens of appreciation. Recognize and spend time talking with parents as they share about their children and time together outside of the program (**Figure 13.5**).

Every staff person, child, and family member should feel like they belong in the program. They should see themselves reflected in the environment and the curriculum and should feel safe, valued, and welcome. When conflict does arise, the program leader must be ready with a resolution.

Director's Showcase

After giving more time for relationships to grow between the staff, Taisha and Meredith observed some concerning behaviors between certain teachers. They needed to do more to address the situations.

Taisha

One afternoon Taisha overheard two staff members raising their voices in the break room. As she stepped toward the doorway, she heard Francesca proclaim, "You are just impossible to talk to!" Taisha had to jump out of the way as Francesca forcefully pushed the door open. Startled, the teacher looked at her and said, "It's a good thing she and I don't work together in the same classroom," pointing to Alia inside the break room and then continued walking down the hall. A little stunned, Taisha was still standing in the hallway watching Francesca walk away as Alia came out of the break room. She met Taisha's gaze and shrugged, "Some days I just don't feel like talking on my break. Obviously, some people just don't get that."

Meredith

An afternoon incident between two preschool classroom teachers resulted in an unsupervised situation with a child. It began when Rico woke up from nap rather grumpy. He insisted he wanted to go home "right now." His teachers reassured him that his grandmother would be there soon at the normal pickup time. While the teachers were busy helping the children prepare for afternoon pickup, Rico bolted out the classroom door and down the hallway into the arms of his grandmother. The teachers were not aware that he had left the room until they turned around to see the grandmother standing at the door with Rico in her arms. She was obviously angry, snatched his things, and left as another parent, Clarissa, was coming in to pick up her son. When all the children had departed, both teachers were still upset and began to argue loudly about who was to blame for the incident. As Clarissa and her son were walking down the hall to leave the center, they overheard the teachers' heated exchange. Once in her car, Clarissa called Meredith—very upset by all that she and her son had seen and heard.

towfiqu ahamed/iStock/Getty Images Plus

Figure 13.5 Leaving notes for staff to show your appreciation validates their work in a very personal way.

Director's Showcase

Reflect

How might Taisha and Meredith work to build workplace relationships based on the issues that are taking place in their program environments?

13.2 Conflict in Healthy Workplace Environments

Conflict, or strong disagreement between two or more people or a difference that prevents agreement, exists in all forms of relationships. Directors may view managing conflicts as difficult and even destructive or as opportunities to learn more and make adjustments to help balance a situation at hand. To successfully achieve healthy conflict, trust within the environment is crucial. Tschannen-Moran (2004) provides a framework specific to educational settings called the Five Facets of Trust:

- *Benevolence*—demonstrating a caring and positive regard for others.
- *Honesty*—admitting mistakes, telling the truth, and honoring agreements between one another.
- *Openness*—allowing opportunities for shared decision making and power, while also listening to others.
- *Reliability*—displaying commitment and dependability.
- *Competence*—being accountable and flexible, and providing a good example (**Figure 13.6**).

Trust takes time; but from a leadership perspective, finding a balance of giving it freely until behaviors show differently is a hard concept for some to embrace.

Five Facets of Trust

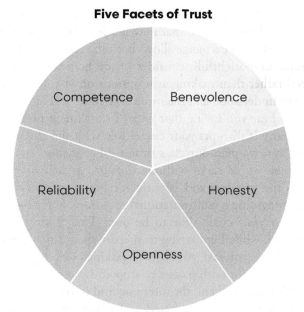

*Based on Tschannen-Moran's 2004 framework.

Goodheart-Willcox Publisher

Figure 13.6 The Five Facets of Trust support healthy relationships within program environments.

Typically, relationships demand that a person earn trust. When leading, trust must be given freely, while also understanding that guidance and ongoing communication will be a part of the relationship-building between staff and leadership.

In managing conflict, directors must also recognize that group dynamics often mirror societal dynamics. For example, consider the hierarchy within a center. A **hierarchy** means that some people within an organization have more power than others. In an early childhood setting, the director is seen as the person with the most power. However, as a leader, you can choose to change this dynamic and empower individuals throughout the organization to work together. You can delegate responsibilities fairly and equitably while recognizing employees' strengths and assigning tasks accordingly. For example, two teachers have modeled their abilities to develop age-appropriate lesson plans. One works with toddlers, while the other works with preschool-age children. The director decides to talk with them about taking lead roles in coaching and mentoring new teachers in the program with their lesson plans. Notice how the director has approached the staff members with the qualities they have shown on a consistent basis and asked them to share their talents with others. In other words, the director is empowering the staff to share with others. Both eagerly agree to take on the extra duty (**Figure 13.7**). However, conflicts may arise if other staff members do not understand the overall intention of the coaching and mentoring. This may be an opportunity for the director to identify and manage positive and negative conflicts.

Mario Arango/E+/Getty Images

Figure 13.7 Rather than doing all of the talking, a director must sit back and empower others to share their thoughts and talents as issues are resolved.

Positive Conflict

Believe it or not there is such a thing as **positive conflict**, which often results from misunderstandings that are quickly dealt with in an open, honest, and consistent fashion. As decisions are made, leaders need to share openly and appropriately. In the situation with the two teachers, this director can seize upon the opportunity to continue to model communication and openness. Once the teachers agreed to serve in the mentorship role, the director put out an email to everyone to explain what it was that each teacher would be doing for the age groups served in the morning, how they were going to aid teaching staff within the program, and when this extra resource would be available. While the majority of staff will read communications, not all will totally understand.

To continue building and maintaining relationships, the director walked around the center and for the next few days followed up with the email communication. This included observing staff's body language as well as expressed feedback. Some seem surprised as it was perceived as a quick decision while others seemed genuinely thankful for the opportunity to work directly with the teaching staff members. For those who showed hesitancy, the director

addressed this positive conflict by talking more with those staff members by patiently answering questions and discussing what mentoring really meant. This included making a mental note to observe these staff members for signs of negative behavior toward the two staff members. Over time, the director observed most staff utilizing the talent and resources provided by the two staff members. However, there was one teacher who showed signs of complete resistance to the decision that was made.

Negative Conflict

Unfortunately, **negative conflict**, or the type of conflict that can reduce opportunities to reconcile issues, can arise even when the best efforts and intentions have been made by a leader (**Figure 13.8**). Observation is key and should be a skill that is always utilized when managing a workplace environment. This includes daily ongoing dialogue with staff members to "check-in" to see how they are doing and to answer any questions that they might have. This is all key to relationship building because it gives the leader an opportunity to see each person for who they are and how they act. Sudden employee behavioral changes are warning signs that negative conflicts are arising.

Kristen Alexandria

Figure 13.8 Program leaders should observe staff as they are working to include regular check-in opportunities to build a strong working relationship and answer questions.

Director's Showcase

Taisha

While both situations were in conflict, Taisha determined that what had taken place in the break room was at some level a positive conflict situation. While it initially felt troubling due to her expectations that everyone should get along, it did create an internal awareness and opportunity that she needed to keep her eye on.

Meredith

Meredith knew that she clearly had a negative conflict situation on her hands. To complicate matters, she was going to need to deal with not only the two teachers but also the child's grandmother and the concerned parent who had reported what she had overheard. Both program directors needed to identify and apply conflict-resolution strategies.

As the director continued to observe and talk with the teacher, she noticed that when she shifted the conversation to her interest in working with the mentoring teachers the conversation ended quickly. After this happened a couple of times, the director decided it was time to confront the situation. While not the result that she had wanted when she had announced the mentoring opportunity, dealing with the issue was important not only to the relationship with the teacher but before negative attitudes began to influence other staff members and impact the program.

13.3 Conflict-Resolution Partnerships

Conflict resolution is a process that aims to not only find a solution to a problem but also improve relationships. Individuals who are in conflict with each other may find it hard to imagine that they could ever possibly "get along" or salvage their relationship. Early childhood leaders need to frame the tricky conflict-resolution process as a partnership between those who are at odds. This strategy reimagines the conflict as a partnership in which the parties focus on needs, perceptions, goals, potential shared power, and commonalities together. The goal of the early childhood leader is to support a **conflict-partnership pathway**, which allows everyone to be heard and supports the development of expectations that will contribute to solutions. The resolution ultimately bolsters a healthy workplace and benefits the staff, children, and their families (**Figure 13.9**).

The first step in the conflict-partnership pathway is to create an atmosphere that is effective. This includes the early childhood leader being prepared to manage the discussion and to determine an appropriate timing and private location and to set the expectation that when opening statements are made by participants, they are factual and provide concrete examples. Consider the following scenario at Little Golden Bear's Child Care.

Martha and Luis exchanged words one morning because Sophia's mother did not bring diapers and wipes. After writing notes to the mother for several days, Martha was concerned that the program's diaper inventory was

Vadym Pastukh/iStock/Getty Images Plus

Figure 13.9 The goal in a healthy workplace is for everyone to be heard and supported as they contribute to solutions.

running very low. As the mother turned to leave, Martha loudly states, "You still haven't brought in diapers and wipes, and now we are just about out. Do I need to text and remind you before you come back today?" Luis was talking with another parent who abruptly ended the conversation and left. Sophia's mom mumbled a reply and quickly departed.

Luis turned to Martha and observed, "Now that was embarrassing. I can't believe you just did that!" Martha snapped, "That's ridiculous! If I hadn't said anything, who knows how long we would have provided diapers and wipes for them. She needs to take responsibility!" Two of the infants started to cry. Luis went to attend to one, while Martha comforted the other. They did not talk to each other except to communicate the children's needs for the rest of the morning. The more Luis thought about it, the more upset he was. He decided to tell the program director what happened during his lunch break.

Once a conflict situation has been shared, remind yourself that conflict is not always negative and that it is not an "I versus you" conversation. The goal is to work as partners to resolve the conflict. When considering the timing and place, there is no "perfect time" to deal with conflict. Based on what has taken place, it can be a quick timeline or there might be a little time for a "cool off" period. This short cooling-off period allows all involved individuals to sort out what it is that they want to say (**Figure 13.10**). Then, a place should be utilized that is away from others who may interrupt and provides privacy—typically the program leader's office works well.

During his lunch break Luis shares what happened with the director, Petra. Petra clarified with Luis his intent for sharing this with her. Did he want her to help in resolving the conflict with Martha or did he feel he could do it himself? Luis replied that he had seen Martha be short

SDI Productions/E+/Getty Images

Figure 13.10   While managing conflict comes at times when least expected, taking a minute to hear the words said and allowing for a "cool off" period creates another opportunity to sort out what needs to be said and done.

with several parents lately and what she said to Sophia's mom was just his breaking point. Petra asked that he put his thoughts down on paper of specific examples and told him she would schedule a meeting for the three of them to discuss the incident further.

Petra made arrangements for coverage in their classroom and sent an email to Luis and Martha letting them know that she wanted to talk with them in her office the next morning at 9 a.m. When Martha was clocking out for the day, she poked her head in Petra's office and observed, "I'm sure this has something to do with Sophia's mom." Petra responded with a reassuring smile, "Yes, it does. I'd like to hear your side of the story in the morning. Have a good evening."

When planning a conflict-resolution meeting, the goal should be to take the time to clarify views on what has taken place. This begins by focusing on each person's needs and then determining if what has been said by each person has a common goal to be shared. This is the beginning of shared positive power. As meeting participants continue to talk, focus on the future and how things

should be handled or done going forward. Discussing the past should be kept to a minimum unless there are lessons learned about what did not work (**Figure 13.11**). Write down options that are generated by both parties to determine action steps and an overall plan. This plan should reflect mutual benefits for both parties involved and next steps when resolving the conflict that took place.

The next morning Luis and Martha were busy welcoming the children and serving breakfast until the staff members covering their classroom arrived. At 9 a.m., Luis and Martha joined Petra in her office. Petra began the meeting by referring to the statement made by Martha the previous evening. "We are here today because of a situation that arose yesterday with Sophia's mom. Martha, since you mentioned it to me last night as you were leaving, I would like to hear your account of what took place."

Martha explained what had occurred and stated that, after thinking about it, her tone probably had been a little sharp with Sophia's mom. Petra then allowed Luis to talk about his thoughts on what had taken place. Luis mentioned how he felt sorry for not only Sophia's mom but the other mom in the classroom, as both were embarrassed. He agreed that Sophia's mom needed to take responsibility

SDI Productions/E+/Getty Images

Figure 13.11   At conflict-resolution meetings, participants should talk and focus on how things should be handled in the future rather than focusing on the past.

Director's Showcase

Taisha

Taisha implemented a similar conflict-partnership strategy as Petra. She determined that an opportunity to discuss communication expectations was needed. She would provide an opportunity for the two teachers to assist in determining how they could best communicate to avoid confrontations with each other.

Meredith

Meredith needed to do a little more work on the conflict in her program. She had few conflict-resolution or grievance policies in place, and she knew that she needed to get a plan fast! Unaddressed for too long, this incident could completely derail the great reputation she had been building within the community. Meredith needed to carefully plan what her next steps were going to be.

for supplying diapers and wipes for her child but thought there could have been a better way to handle it.

Petra expressed appreciation to them both for sharing their sides of the story and then asked, "So, how should we communicate with parents who are not bringing supplies for their children going forward? And how can I help?" Martha and Luis explained their current strategy of writing notes on the child's daily slip. As they discussed what had happened, they realized that Sophia's mom had been allowed to go a full week without bringing supplies. Everyone agreed that this was too long to wait for a response. Petra suggested that after two days of note reminders, either Martha or Luis would email her. Then she or the infant/toddler coordinator would reach out to the parent. Both agreed that this would be the plan moving forward and that they would touch base should other issues arise.

There is no doubt that conflict can be difficult to overcome. A child care administrator must address issues and implement strategies on a regular basis to provide timely reconciliation. In a field based on relationships, conflicts will arise. Everyone involved has their own unique opinions and perspectives on the care of young children. However, the program leader must assist by guiding these conflicts in a productive way that results in the best care of the children and families enrolled in the early childhood program.

Director's Showcase

Reflect

What are some conflict-resolution strategies that Taisha and Meredith might consider to deal with the issues in their programs?

13.4 Establishing Policies and Procedures

A program's developed policies and procedures communicate expectations not only regarding benefits and dress code but should also detail behavior standards and the conflict-resolution process. When conflict arises, an early childhood program's employee and parent handbooks provide a framework of how situations will be managed, typically referred to as grievance procedures. While the intent of all programs is to provide quality services, inevitably there are misunderstandings and personalities that do not mesh. The early childhood program leader must be prepared and have a set of policies and procedures to address such difficulties.

Staff work much more effectively through conflict when there are communication expectations put in place within

an employee handbook (**Figure 13.12**). Understanding that the program expects conflicts and resolutions to occur sends a message that supports a healthy workplace environment. Working relationships will become strained at times. Disagreements will arise due to differing classroom management strategies, frustration with a child's behavior, or addressing the demands of a parent. The possibilities are endless, and developed policies may not support all circumstances. However, having a clear set of procedures paves the way for positive conflict resolution.

Working with parents and families of children can pose several challenges that may lead to conflicts. Parents come to the program with expectations of how their child will be cared for, which may or may not be aligned with the teacher's classroom management style. Parents may also be feeling guilty or anxious about placing their children in the program (**Figure 13.13**).

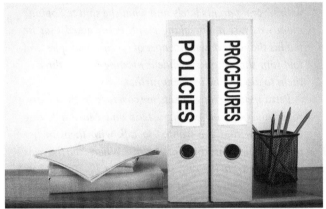

tumsasedgars/iStock/Getty Images Plus

Figure 13.12   Staff work much more effectively when there are established policies and procedures to follow to sort out issues of conflict.

Kristen Alexandria

Figure 13.13   Program directors must help ease the transition for parents who are often anxious to leave their children at an early childhood program.

Little Golden Bear's Child Care Program understands that disagreements between staff members are inevitable. We support a collaborative, mindful workplace environment and expect staff to treat each other with dignity and respect. This includes being aware of those (i.e., children, parents, and other staff members) who may potentially witness a negative encounter between staff members and be affected by disrespectful behaviors. Professional relationships must be upheld at all times. The use of inappropriate language and actions is strictly prohibited and will result in immediate termination.

When disputes or misunderstandings occur, Little Golden Bear expects staff members to discuss and try to work through the conflict together first. Involving unrelated staff members is considered inappropriate and may result in a formal warning. The staff involved staff members should set an appropriate time to talk in private. If assistance is needed to cover a classroom, the site supervisor will make arrangements for classroom coverage. These meetings should take place in 30 minutes or less, and the resolution should be shared with the site supervisor.

Should the first step not result in a resolution between staff members, then dialogue with the program director will take place. Once this meeting is requested, staff members will be asked to write down the issue(s) to be addressed and include at least two suggested ways to resolve the issue. The program director will schedule the time and location of the meeting and will do this in a time frame that is conducive to appropriate coverage for the children in care. Little Golden Bear upholds that conflicts can lead to positive resolutions when everyone comes to the table with respect, trust, and reason.

Little Golden Bear's administrative leadership has the right to intervene, as needed, based on circumstances or additional program policies if the conflict is deemed to be too interruptive to the daily programming of the center or damaging to our healthy workplace environment or the center's reputation.

Goodheart-Willcox Publisher

Figure 13.14   Policies within a developed personnel handbook help to clarify processes and expectations for all employees working within the program.

They need time to build the necessary relationships and to establish trust and respect with the teaching staff. Often parents need reassurance that they are the expert on their child and that working with the program staff is for the benefit of their child. While some parents may be easier than others to engage, establishing good relationships with children's parents or legal guardians must be a priority for every program staff member. A program's employee and parent handbook should detail this expectation as well as behavioral norms and communication procedures to create a groundwork for working together.

Written Policy Considerations

Written policies within employee and parent handbooks are essential when managing the different groups that come and go within the early childhood program environment. While a majority of the policies specific to grievances are guided by state and local regulations that support the licensure of the program, specific policies that best inform staff and parents about conflict resolution are often left to the program's discretion. When creating these policies, a director should seek guidance either from consultants, local Resource & Referral Agency staff, or legal counsel that specialize in conflict resolution.

Staff Policy Considerations

Dealing with conflict between staff members is often less contentious when the employee handbook addresses

clear conflict-resolution expectations. This all begins by addressing the steps in the conflict-resolution process that the program expects all staff to follow in the employee handbook (**Figure 13.14**).

During the orientation of new employees, program leaders should take time to address the policies related to how conflict is managed within the workplace (**Figure 13.15**). This includes reminding existing staff members that when working with the new person, it is their professional responsibility to be patient and explain the program's expectations. With a team-centered approach, staff members should remain focused on the task at hand, which is to provide quality early childhood program services.

SDI Productions/E+/Getty Images

Figure 13.15   During the orientation process, program leaders must take time to go over with new employees how conflict is managed in the workplace.

Parent Policy Considerations

Parents also need to understand that conflicts regarding the care of their child may occur. Stating this up front and including conflict-resolution expectations within your parent handbook provides parents with a clear road map for respectfully handling difficult situations. By mirroring the grievance steps outlined within the staff handbook, staff will understand the process and feel supported as parents are held to the same standard of behavior. Establishing clear, parallel expectations for parents and staff helps to avoid the confusion that often accompanies conflict. A policy within the parent handbook should be clear about any expectations (**Figure 13.16**).

Introducing Policies

During the orientation of new employees or families to the program, the program leader should take time to detail the policies related to how conflict is managed within the program. There is never a guarantee that a staff member or parent fully understands the policies set forth by a program, nor that they will follow them. Most programs require that staff and

families sign a statement acknowledging that they have read and agree with the policies. Updating your handbooks and having parents and staff sign this statement annually reminds them of these policies and the program's communication and behavior expectations (**Figure 13.17**). In addition, program administrators should invite staff and parent input as they review policies each year. As LeeKeenan and Ponte (2018) observe, by involving staff and family, the program director can gain insights on

- suggested topics that might need to be addressed or are not in line with the program's mission statement;
- how staff and parents are understanding certain policies that may need further clarification; and
- additional perspectives on whether the policies and procedures are supportive and inclusive.

These guidelines should reflect the unique diversity within the program's children, families, staff, and community. Overall, the purpose of the process is to recognize that conflict is inevitable and provide guidance to staff and parents on how to handle grievances in a respectful manner.

Director's Showcase

Taisha

Taisha was fortunate in that she had a policy in place that encouraged staff members to work it out together. First, she followed up to see if they needed coverage for their classrooms. The staff members reported that they were able to talk and determined that when Alia stated that she "needed a break," Francesca would respect that she needed some time to relax. Taisha was pleased that the staff were working together to resolve the conflict but disappointed to learn that other staff members were gossiping about what had taken place. One staff had approached her stating that Francesca had used bullying behavior during the incident.

Meredith

Meredith began addressing the conflict situation that took place in her program. She thanked the mother that called in to report what had happened and assured her that making sure that the children were being supervised effectively was taking place. Next, she entered the classroom and checked the current enrollment in the classroom

to make sure that the room was staffed appropriately. She quietly let both teachers know that she had been made aware of the situation by another parent. She made sure they were both okay and offered to have an afternoon teacher come in to assist. Both teachers agreed. Meredith took a brief statement from each of the teachers individually. She then planned a meeting time for the next day. Before they left, she asked that they think overnight about possible solutions to assist with the care of Rico.

She also reached out to Rico's grandmother by phone to let her know that she had been made aware of what happened and would be working with the staff to make sure that a safety plan was in place for him. The grandmother commented that she knew that Rico had been hard to manage lately, but she feared what would have happened if he had gotten out the front door. Meredith reassured her that they would all be discussing steps to ensure the care of Rico the next day, which would probably include updating some of the program policies and procedures. Throughout this Meredith noticed that her assistant director was talking quietly to the other staff that were asking, "What happened?"

Little Golden Bear's Child Care Program understands that disagreements between parents and staff regarding the care of their child are inevitable. We support a program environment that expects all individuals to treat each other with respect and dignity, including being aware of the effect of witnessing a negative parent-teacher encounter may have on children, other parents, and other staff members. The use of inappropriate language and actions by any parent are strictly prohibited and will result in dismissal from the program. Our staff are expected to uphold professional relationships with all children and parents enrolled in our program. Our parents are expected to maintain the same level of respect in their communication and interactions with our staff.

When a disagreement or conflict occurs, the involved staff member(s) and parents are expected to meet and try to reach a resolution together first. Involving unrelated staff, parents, and family members in the situation is considered inappropriate. The involved parents and staff members should find a mutually convenient place and time to meet privately either in person or via videoconference. These meetings should last 30 minutes or less, and their resolution will be shared with the center administration.

Should the first step not result in a resolution between the staff member(s) and parent(s), then a dialogue with the program director will take place. Once this meeting is requested, either by staff member(s) or the child's parents, each will be asked to write down the issue(s) to be addressed and at least two suggested resolutions and share them with the director before the meeting. The program director will work with all involved to schedule a convenient time and location for the meeting. Little Golden Bear upholds that conflicts can lead to positive resolutions when everyone comes to the table with respect, trust, and reason.

Little Golden Bear's administrative leadership maintains the right to intervene, as needed, based on circumstances or additional program policies if a conflict is deemed to be too interruptive to the daily programming of the center or damaging to our safe, healthy education environment.

Goodheart-Willcox Publisher

Figure 13.16   Policies within a developed parent handbook help to clarify processes and expectations for all family members of children who are attending the program.

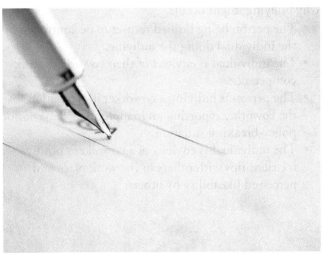

Martin Barraud/Getty Images

Figure 13.17   Requiring parents to read and sign that they have read the program policies upon enrollment and annually reminds everyone of the program expectations.

Director's Showcase

Reflect

What would be some follow-up policies that Taisha and Meredith could put in place to deal with the issues they are experiencing?

13.5 Workplace Gossip and Bullying

Gossip, or telling information that has not been confirmed as true, can be a very destructive force within an early childhood program. Gossip focuses on someone who is not present, is of a personal nature, and is intended to harm the subject's reputation. Staff members who are uncomfortable with direct confrontation may seek support from other coworkers when a conflict occurs (Tannen, 1991). Gossip can be a form of avoiding uncomfortable face-to-face interactions when the person feels unable to express their critical thoughts directly. Gossip creates divisions and misunderstandings in the workplace and, if left unaddressed, can diminish trust among staff and generate a toxic environment for everyone.

Workplace bullying, according to Pontus and Scherrer (2011), consists of incidents of inappropriate actions by an individual or group that are persistent, abusive, threatening, and malicious in nature with the intent to do harm. These behaviors result in significant physical and mental health issues for the people being bullied and as well as the person displaying the behavior. If allowed to take place, these behaviors become a part of the workplace culture, which significantly impacts all employees. Often coworkers are unwilling to report the behaviors out of concern for negative repercussions or from a belief that nothing will change due to ineffective leadership.

Strategies to Create a Gossip-Free Workplace Environment

Early childhood leaders must first look at themselves and their own behaviors. If they are modeling and promoting gossip, then their staff members are likely to display the same behaviors. If the program leader is committed to supporting a gossip-free workplace environment, then they need to encourage the staff that surround them to do the same. They should honor and enforce the NAEYC's Code of Ethical Conduct and encourage staff members to talk about their concerns and hopes to support a workplace environment that does not allow gossip. When the leader promotes this positive environment, staff are relieved to know that this type of behavior will not be tolerated or supported and feel safe to work conflicts out in a healthy, productive way.

Program leaders must utilize other supports to contain gossip within the workplace. Bruno (2007) recommends doing simple things like reviewing and updating job descriptions as needed and including the program's policy regarding workplace gossip within the staff handbook (**Figure 13.18**). Provide staff development on workplace gossip and bullying and give staff examples of statement strategies to say when they feel that a situation may be turning into gossip such as, "I am not comfortable talking about someone who is not here."

Sometimes staff members will push the boundaries. When this happens, Bruno and Copeland (1999) suggest the following process to enforce consequences against those who choose to gossip:

- State the inappropriate behavior.
- State the expected behavior.
- Require that the staff member who has been gossiping take responsibility for what was said and how it will be resolved.

- Create specific action steps.
- Follow up together on the effectiveness to end the gossip that has taken place.

For staff members who are consistently breaking the gossip-free workplace expectation, program leaders will need to implement the disciplinary process outlined within the staff handbook. Personnel policies must specifically name gossip as an inappropriate staff behavior that will not be tolerated within the early childhood program environment.

Strategies to Combat Workplace Bullying

Workplace bullying has become a very prominent topic within the business and management literature. Many news stories have reported bizarre cases of behavior that have led to employees being harassed, hospitalized, and even losing their life due to these types of behaviors. While it is hard to imagine such behaviors by adults who are around children every day, it is a reality. Program leadership is responsible for everyone in an early childhood program, and tackling this issue head-on must take place (**Figure 13.19**).

Program leaders need to understand why individuals choose to bully. Valentino (2008) provides five reasons why bullying might occur:

- The person being bullied refuses to be controlled by the individual doing the bullying.
- The individual is envious of their coworker's work competence.
- The person is bullying a coworker in retaliation for the coworker reporting an inappropriate behavior or policy-breaking situation.
- The individual is envious of a coworker's positive relationships with others in the work place and perceived likeability by others.

designer491/iStock/Getty Images Plus

Figure 13.18 Reviewing and updating job descriptions on a regular basis helps to stop gossip within the workplace.

NicolasMcComber/E+/Getty Images

Figure 13.19 Program leaders are responsible for everyone in the early childhood program environment and should stand up against workplace bullying.

- The person is bullying others because of a cruel personality and possibly an underlying mental illness or past trauma.

No program leader purposefully works to recruit and hire individuals who display bullying behaviors. However, being aware of why people choose these behaviors is a great starting point to stopping them.

Shurtleff-Ainscough (2016) suggests putting in place expectations of behavior with the help of all staff members who work together in an early childhood program environment. Start by asking questions to help staff members define how they expect to act and for others to act when they are at the workplace. Question prompts might include:

- What does living our values statement look like each day when we come together to care for the children, families, and each other?
- What does teamwork that supports young children, their families, and each other look like in our program environment (**Figure 13.20**)?
- How do we define professionalism, and what does it look like each day as we work with the children, families, and each other?
- How do we support each other in actions and words that reflect a supportive workplace environment?

Once these questions have been answered, you use the staff replies to develop a commitment statement to stop workplace bullying before it ever gets started, having each member read through and sign it during orientation or annually. Overall, staff need to understand the importance of holding each other accountable, and the program

leader needs to hold the staff accountable. Just like those who break the gossip-free workplace expectation, program leaders must begin the disciplinary process that may lead to termination. Workplace bullying cannot be tolerated in healthy early childhood program environments.

Director's Showcase

Taisha

Because Taisha had taken the time to address gossip-free work zones when she began leading the program, this was the first real test of her policies. She was able to remind the staff of their agreements not to support workplace gossip and asked that employees refrain from talking about a situation that they were not a part of. However, the accusation of another staff member bullying another was new to her. Taisha did some research and consulted her board to formulate a clear workplace bullying policy. With the improved policy, she was able to address the staff member's concerns regarding bullying and provide her with clarity about the situation and how the program handles bullying. Having a written policy helped Taisha to feel more comfortable moving forward.

Meredith

Having addressed and resolved the concerns of Rico's teachers and grandmother, as well as the other parent, Meredith needed to discuss professionalism with her newly hired assistant director. Because the role was new to her, Meredith decided to approach the issue as a learning opportunity. She discussed at length the importance of supporting a gossip-free workplace and worked with her assistant director to create statements that would allow her to answer staff questions at a level that was appropriate while also protecting the confidentiality of those involved in private situations.

FG Trade/E+/Getty Images

Figure 13.20 Teamwork supports young children, their families, and each other, which results in a healthy and supportive workplace environment.

Director's Showcase

Reflect

What other policies do you think Taisha and Meredith should put in place to combat workplace gossip and bullying?

Chapter 13 Review and Assessment

Summary

13.1 Develop insights on the importance of workplace relationships.

- Healthy workplace relationships are key to a healthy working environment. Programs of all sizes must support positive relationships.
- Trust has been found as the foundation of healthy workplace relationships. This nurtures respect and also provides the ingredients for positive communication between those in a program environment.
- Healthy workplace relationships are time intensive but well worth the investment by program leaders.

13.2 Compare aspects of situations where conflict is viewed in the workplace as negative and positive.

- Conflict is certain when adults work together. Just like children who must be managed in a classroom setting, the same is necessary for program leaders to do with staff members.
- Using the suggested guidance strategies and the use of personnel policies, all are supports for workplace relationship building between staff and leadership. In addition, expectations are set and reviewed on a regular basis.

13.3 Implement conflict-resolution strategies that support a healthy workplace environment.

- Resolving conflict necessitates a focus on needs, perceptions, goals, opportunities for shared power, and collective commonalities. Strategies discussed included avoiding an "I versus you" situation.
- It is important that staff are supported to work as partners when resolving conflict. This takes providing an appropriate private space, time, development of a plan, and opportunities to reflect on that plan as time goes on.
- Program leaders guide productive ways to resolve conflict.

13.4 Establish policies and procedures that support employees and families as they work together for the benefit of the program environment.

- Written policies and procedures for staff and parents are crucial and they must be revisited on a regular basis. These developed items provide a necessary framework of how situations will be managed.

- It is important for early childhood leaders to provide the necessary follow-through on a consistent basis. By embracing these workplace necessities, all individuals within the program environment are informed and held accountable.

13.5 Explore strategies to assist with workplace gossip and bullying.

- Sadly, today's working environment has become a place where bullying is possible. Typically those who participate in these types of behaviors often suffer from mental disorders or previous trauma.
- Carefully monitoring these behaviors and having a plan of action in place is important. This may include reaching out to community resources to refer a staff member for expertise that can assist with the issue that may be taking place.
- Having knowledge when managing people and setting expectations is important for today's early childhood program leader.

Review

1. Explain how the role of the director differs from that of staff members when dealing with conflict. (13.1)
2. Identify and explain the three essential components of a healthy workplace environment. (13.1)
3. How can the Five Facets of Trust establish a healthy workplace environment? (13.1)
4. Describe the difference between positive and negative conflict. (13.2)
5. What factors support a conflict-partnership pathway? (13.3)
6. What are considerations when writing staff and parent policies dealing with conflict? (13.4)
7. Describe a gossip-free zone. (13.5)
8. Identify five factors behind individuals choosing to bully. (13.5)
9. What strategies can a program director use to create gossip-free zones? (13.5)
10. What strategies can be used by program directors to combat workplace bullying? (13.5)

Showcase Your Skills

In the Director's Showcase, Taisha and Meredith had two very different situations that surrounded conflict in the workplace. It is important to understand that all program environments are unique due to the individual personalities of the staff and characteristics of the program. However, in the case of establishing a workplace environment, it is the role of the early childhood program leader to establish and maintain this environment.

You have been hired by an owner of an early childhood program to assist his newly hired director to deal with the unhealthy workplace environment that was created by the previous director. While the owner has spent some time in the location with the newly hired director, he needs to step away to deal with other businesses that he owns. He originally bought the program because he was told it would be a great investment. However, after hiring two directors in the space of six months, he is starting to wonder if he made the right decision. As a consultant, you will spend the next 90 days working side by side with the new director. Your primary task is establishing and maintaining a healthy workplace environment.

1. Based on the information shared in each section of this chapter, write an overview of the strategies to consider when working with the newly hired director. (13.1, 13.2, 13.3, 13.4, 13.5)

Matching

Match the following words with the correct definitions:

A. communication
B. conflict
C. conflict resolution
D. conflict-partnership pathway
E. gossip
F. hierarchy
G. negative conflict
H. positive conflict
I. workplace bullying

1. Allows everyone to be heard and supports the development of expectations that will contribute to solutions.
2. Incidents of inappropriate actions by an individual or group that are persistent, abusive, threatening, and malicious in nature with the intent to harm.
3. Telling information that has not been confirmed as true.
4. Process that aims to not only find a solution to a problem but also improve relationships.
5. Process of clarifying the perceptions that people have of each other by way of listening, sensing, and asking clarifying questions.
6. Results from misunderstandings that are quickly dealt with in an open, honest, and consistent fashion.
7. Type of organization system where some people within an organization have more power than others.
8. Strong disagreement between two or more people or a difference that prevents agreement.
9. Type of conflict that can reduce opportunities to reconcile issues.

Jovanmandic/iStock/Getty Images

14 CHAPTER

Supports for Director Success

Learning Outcomes

After studying this chapter, you will be able to:

14.1 Establish professional boundaries between director and staff and between staff and families.

14.2 Recognize the daily stress of managing programs and the importance of work-life balance by engaging in acts of self-care.

14.3 Analyze factors that support positive mental wellness and healthy environments where staff, children, and families can thrive.

14.4 Apply health and mental wellness community supports and opportunities to support oneself and others in the early childhood program environment.

Key Terms

culturally competent
diversity
domestic violence
employee assistance programs (EAP)
equitable programming
food insecurity
housing insecurity
inclusive program environments
low socio-economic status
microaggressions
mindfulness
professional boundaries
self-care activities
stigma
stress
stressors
zone of helpfulness

Introduction

In previous chapters, you have been given information about the daily directing of a child care program. In this chapter, you will learn about issues that may interfere with your program's success and the importance of understanding professional boundaries. This includes specific relationship boundaries that need to be established between director and staff, staff and families, and how to maintain professional boundaries. The other major focus of this chapter is the importance of work-life balance to help support burnout. In a field with such a high turnover rate, caring for oneself and others within the program is necessary. This includes understanding the multifaceted issues that create stressful circumstances that program leaders often have to manage. To combat

NAEYC/DAP standards

Standards covered in this chapter:

2a, 2b, 4c, 6a, 6e

1E, 4A

this stress is a focus on supporting positive mental wellness and healthy environments for not only the program leader, but the staff, children, and families to thrive.

14.1 Establishing Professional Boundaries

Professional boundaries delineate the personal relationship from the professional relationship. Professional boundaries are used to clearly define expectations and responsibilities between program staff and the families they serve. It is important to plainly state professional roles and expectations in enrollment literature and information for families entering your program.

Professional boundaries differ from ethical boundaries in that professional boundaries are situational (**Figure 14.1**). Ethical boundaries are more regulated and consistent across all child care programs. Confidentiality and health and safety policies and protocols are ethical boundaries. Professional boundaries are unique to a specific child care program, the location or region, and cultural differences, and they can be modified depending on a family's or employee's situation.

Director's Showcase

Kateri

Kateri has just started a child care program in her home. She has enrolled a new family with an infant and a toddler. The mother is raising the two children as a single parent and is working two jobs, one during the week and another on the weekend. Kateri has noticed that mom is late picking up her children almost every evening and has been arriving later and later each day. The extra time that the children are still in her care has diminished the time

Kateri has to spend on program paperwork at the end of her day as well as cut into her personal time.

Sam

Sam is the director of a small child care center. He noticed a teacher in the two-year-old classroom has been bringing a child from her class with her to work on some mornings. When Sam asked the teacher why this was happening, she responded that she had become friends with the child's mother and was just helping out by bringing the child to the center on mornings when the mother was running late.

Figure 14.1 Professional boundaries are clearly defined expectations and responsibilities between program leaders, staff members, and families.

Ingenui/E+/Getty Images

Here are some examples of professional boundary violations in early childhood education. While this is not an exhaustive list, these boundary violations are likely to arise in a child care program:

- Having dual relationships, such as financial involvement with a family.
- Practicing outside of scope where a staff member or teacher is offering unqualified advice.
- Inappropriate use of social media, text, or email with families, coworkers, or staff.
- Lending money to or borrowing money from families.
- Having an intimate relationship with a parent or guardian.
- Having supervisory issues, such as inadequate supervision or delegation and insubordination.
- Pushing religious opinions, including using personal religious expression in the classroom. The exception to this rule would be religious centers that use religious programming and curriculum. This would not be considered a boundary violation.
- Breaching confidentiality.
- Accepting or giving overly generous gifts to children or families.
- Showing favoritism to certain children or families.

Importance of Professional Boundaries

According to the NAEYC Code of Ethical Conduct, early childhood professionals must refrain from personal gain at the expense of families, refrain from actions jeopardizing the child-family relationship, and respect and protect the family's autonomy,

dignity, and privacy (NAEYC, 2020). Professionals working in early childhood programs have a unique relationship with the children and families in their care families. Teachers spend a significant amount of time caring for the children, know confidential information about each of the families in their care, and typically understand child development better than parents and guardians and may recognize children's delays or conditions before a parent does. Earning the respect and trust of families in your programs and working together to the benefit of each child should be the gold standard to which you and your staff hold this profession. When the lines of professional expectations and relationships become blurred, harm can be done to children and families.

Defining the difference between professional relationships and personal and social relationships can be helpful when discussing boundaries with families and staff members. Here are some differences to keep in mind (**Figure 14.2**). Every child should be treated fairly and consistently. Early childhood professionals should build relationships of mutual respect and understanding with all families they serve. Adhering to professional boundaries leads to a healthy and successful early childhood program.

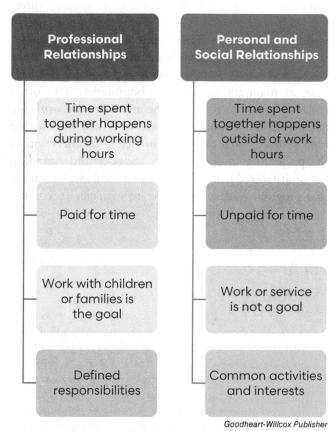

Professional Relationships	Personal and Social Relationships
Time spent together happens during working hours	Time spent together happens outside of work hours
Paid for time	Unpaid for time
Work with children or families is the goal	Work or service is not a goal
Defined responsibilities	Common activities and interests

Goodheart-Willcox Publisher

Figure 14.2 Boundaries are important for staff to have with each other and the families that they work with.

Professional Boundaries Between Director and Staff

The NAEYC Code of Ethical Conduct states that early childhood program administrators commit themselves to the following additional core values. We make a commitment to

- recognize that we have many responsibilities—to children, families, personnel, governing boards, sponsoring agencies, funders, regulatory agencies, the community, and the profession—and that the well-being of the children in our care is our primary responsibility, above our obligations to other constituencies.
- recognize the importance of and maintain a humane and fulfilling work environment for personnel and volunteers.
- be committed to the professional development of staff.

The early childhood program director's main responsibility is to make sure the early childhood program is a safe, healthy, nurturing, and responsive environment for each child. Directors ensure the early childhood program supports children's development and learning; promotes respect for individual differences; and helps children learn to live, play, and work cooperatively (**Figure 14.3**). Early childhood directors ensure that the program promotes children's self-awareness, competence, self-worth, resiliency, and physical well-being (NAEYC, 2017).

It is the responsibility of the program director to provide a healthy, safe, and cooperative working environment for their employees. The early childhood program director leads by example. The director must adhere to professional boundaries and create a community of trust and fairness. Unequal treatment of staff can lead to a competitive and problematic work environment.

Kristen Alexandria

Figure 14.3   Directors ensure that children develop and learn in respectful environments.

The program director can maintain professional boundaries by respecting individual differences; by valuing confidentiality of staff, children, and families; and by creating clearly defined expectations and boundaries. Many successful programs have written professional expectations and boundaries, so every staff member is aware of what is acceptable behavior.

Relationships between the director and the staff must remain professional. It is often difficult to remain professional and not develop friendships with the staff that have many shared interests and values. It is acceptable to have a friendly, nurturing, and supportive relationship with staff, but developing a close friendship with an individual staff member can lead to professional boundary violations and favoritism.

Setting Professional Boundaries with Families

The responsibilities of a director of an early childhood program are many and vast. Directors must strive to provide diverse and inclusive programming and policies, maintain confidentiality, and be a resource for all families they serve. Critical to the efficacy of the child care program, maintaining professional boundaries helps facilitate success.

The director holds a place of power in an early childhood education program. The director knows significant confidential information about children and families in their care. Abusing that power for personal gain is a boundary violation. Finding a level balance between caring too much and becoming enmeshed with a family and caring too little or ignoring a family's needs and becoming too harsh is the goal of the child care administrator.

Consistency in behavior with every family and child is often an unattainable goal for a child care director or staff. Not every family has the same needs as others. However, setting and maintaining consistent boundaries with every family is possible. Setting clear boundaries and informing all families what those are can help a director and staff maintain the proper relationship with families and avoid possible ethical issues that could arise. Inserting a paragraph in the enrollment packet for every family about established boundaries is an easy way for everyone to be on the same page. Listing expectations, such as staff will not receive or provide gifts to children or families, staff will not socialize outside of work with individual children or families, or staff will communicate with families during working hours and not outside of working hours, are a few boundaries that can be set easily.

Using the continuum by Kemp (2014) called the **zone of helpfulness**, this can be used as a guide for early childhood program directors and staff (**Figure 14.4**). This continuum can be used to find balance in professional relationships.

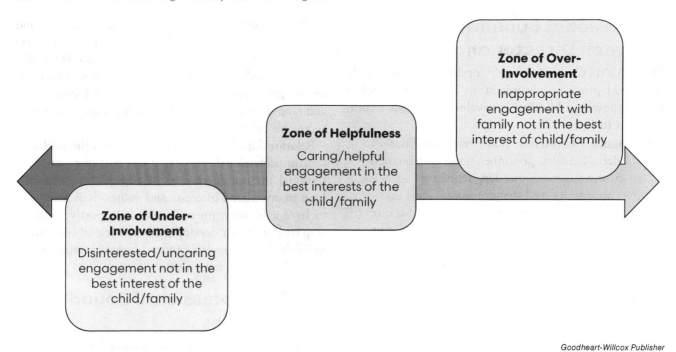

Figure 14.4 The zone of helpfulness guides early childhood program leaders with professional relationships.

Establishing and maintaining professional boundaries with families is critical to the success of an early childhood education program and ultimately the director of the program (**Figure 14.5**). Effectively communicating and promoting professional boundaries to all staff and families in the program can lead to clearer boundaries and expectations. Discussing possible boundary violations with staff before they occur can lead to a rarer occurrence of these violations.

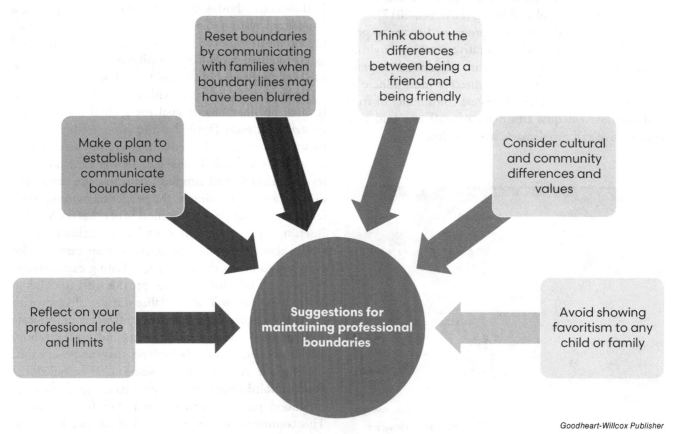

Figure 14.5 Suggestions for early childhood leaders as they work to maintain professional boundaries with staff.

Director's Showcase

Kateri

Kateri decided to introduce the mother who is struggling to pick up her child on time to the other parents during a parent meeting. She asked all the parents about time management strategies without referencing the mother. Two other parents discussed their shared pickup arrangement as they both worked shifts that differed from week to week. They would text each other on Sunday and plan out the responsibility for that week's pickups. When one parent had to work later, the other would pick up both children and would meet the other parent at a designated spot. Kateri encouraged the mother to talk with these parents to discuss their arrangement and her own challenges. When she did, they were happy to include her in their shared pickup arrangement.

Sam

After meeting with the teacher, Sam has decided to move the teacher to another classroom to resolve any boundary issues that may arise with the relationship between the family and the teacher. He met with the parents separately to discuss the changes in staffing and why the teacher was reassigned. By moving the teacher, favoritism and jealousy of the child would no longer be an issue.

Director's Showcase

Reflect

As a new program leader, how would you work to maintain professional relationships separate from personal and social relationships? What would be the main considerations between relationships with staff members and those with children's parents? Do you believe that Kateri and Sam made the right choice based on what took place?

14.2 Recognizing the Daily Stress of Managing Programs

Stress is the deviation of normal function of the body and/or mind. The daily management of an early child care program includes a variety of **stressors**, or the people, places, or things that cause stress. The responsibility of caring for children, managing staff and employees, attending to health and safety concerns, and workforce issues are just a few stressors that a director faces daily.

The health and well-being of early childhood educators is imperative to a successful program. Increased rates of illness and depression have been reported in those working with children (Gooze, 2014). Working in child care often leads to staff illnesses, which lead to inconsistent care for children, staffing issues, and ultimately stress for the director and other staff. Therefore, the director should focus on programs and activities that promote

Director's Showcase

Kateri

During the fall and winter months, Kateri noticed that she was having a more difficult time getting out of bed and sticking to a consistent routine during child care hours. She was more impatient and sometimes harsh with the children. She also noticed that she was falling farther and farther behind with completing daily tasks. This was impacting the children's daily routine and one of her long-time parents asked if she was okay.

Sam

Sam noticed a change in the attitudes and atmosphere in the center. Teachers were short with each other, there were more teachers getting sick, and they were struggling with staffing issues. It seemed that every day there was a teacher who was sick or a problem between teachers. This was beginning to affect the behavior of the children in the classroom. The children were acting out and having meltdowns. Sam was well aware that staff inconsistency was playing a big role in children's behaviors. He started to feel his own frustration with certain teachers on his staff who, typically, were those he could depend on. They were missing deadlines when turning in lesson plans and they seemed distant.

health and wellness among adults and children in the early childhood setting.

Stress can lead to a decrease in mental health (**Figure 14.6**). Depression and anxiety disorders can be a result of unmanaged stress. Mental health issues affect

Figure 14.6 Stress can lead to decreased mental health, depression, and anxiety disorders.

daily living as well as work life. Poor mental health of any administrator can have a great impact on the success of an early childhood program. It can lead to poor communication with staff members and families, decreased performance and productivity, disengagement at work, and incompletion of daily responsibilities.

Burnout is often the first sign of stress. Having a hard time getting out of bed, not wanting to be at work, and not finding joy while at work are a few of the symptoms of burnout (LeBlanc & Marques, 2019). Burnout and stress can lead to health issues such as cardiovascular disease, autoimmune disease, and other health risks. Burnout can also lead to child care administrators leaving the profession.

Determine Acts of Self-Care

Identifying stressors is the first step in building a successful work-life balance and ultimately a successful early childhood program. Recognizing the signs of stress in yourself and in others is important to the overall health of the program. Early signs to watch for are changes in appetite, being easy to anger, headaches or neck and back pain, changes in sleep, or overall tiredness. These are just some of the signs of potential reactions to stress. The second step is to address those stressors and determine acts of self-care. According to the World Health Organization, *self-care* is defined as the ability to promote health, prevent disease, cope with illness or disability, and maintain health without the support of a healthcare provider (WHO, 2022). The goal of self-care is to improve health, prevent or control disease, and preserve overall well-being.

Self-care includes a variety of activities. Focusing on hygiene, exercise, living conditions, social habits, nutrition, personal beliefs, and culture are just a few **self-care activities** (**Figure 14.7**). Finding a balance between work life and personal life can be difficult to

maintain. Bringing work problems and anxieties home to personal space and time can be an obstacle to self-care.

Work-Life Balance

Priorities between work life and home life can be challenging and often bleed over into one another. Problems or stress at work can lead to anxiety and worry when at home. Likewise, problems and issues at home can carry over into the workplace. Work-life balance comes with the right balance between all the many demands and responsibilities in life. These include family, friends, career, hobbies, and other areas that take time and energy.

Finding a balance between work life and personal life can be difficult to maintain. Bringing work problems and anxieties home to personal space and time can be an obstacle to self-care. Learning to leave work issues at work and personal issues at home can go a long way to healthier boundaries and positive mental health. Providing a place for employees to discuss stressors and anxiety in a safe space can aid in keeping a work-life balance. Some programs have access to **employee assistance programs (EAP)**, which are employer sponsored programs that offer free confidential assessments, short-term counseling and referrals, and follow-up services for staff facing personal or workplace problems. Smaller programs often tend to share work concerns among trusted people who are familiar with the situation. All are options that can ease stress and provide opportunities to leave work problems at work. Other ways to lessen daily stress is by helping employees with time-management skills, managing daily stress, and having healthy relationships.

Practicing Mindfulness

Mindfulness has been a buzzword for many years. According to the University of Massachusetts Medical

Figure 14.7 One self-care activity, yoga, has been found to be a great exercise and stress reliever.

School and University of Oxford, "[m]ounting research shows that mindfulness not only reduces stress but also gently builds an inner strength so that future stressors have less impact on our happiness and physical well-being." Understanding the process of mindfulness can be helpful in alleviating stress and anxiety. **Mindfulness** is the state of being conscious or aware of the present moment. During this time of awareness, one can acknowledge personal feelings, thoughts, and sensory sensations. When overcome with stress, mindfulness can be a way to bring back focus to the present and reduce immediate stress. Here are some ways to begin being mindful.

- Watch what you say about yourself and others. Negative words lead to negative thoughts.
- Concentrate on growth. What is happening around you that is improving?
- Think like a beginner. Be gentle with yourself; this is a new way of thinking.
- Focus on what is going right. Find something that you are doing well.
- Create affirmations. Say what you like about yourself or your work environment out loud.
- Take a nature walk or sit outside and listen to sounds around you (**Figure 14.8**).
- Feed your mind.
- Journal or self-reflect daily.
- Take a break from social media.
- Still your mind by meditating or even taking several deep breaths with your eyes closed.

Being mindful is a practice in being present. It takes time and repeated practice to get into the habit of being present in the moment. These suggestions are just a few ways to practice mindfulness. There are many resources available online and in books (**Figure 14.9**). Directors

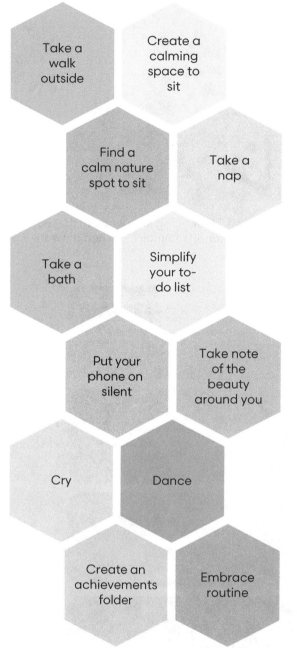

Figure 14.9 More ways to practice mindfulness when taking care of oneself.

and staff who exercise mindfulness report that it takes time and repeated practice to get into the habit of being present in the moment.

Managing Time

As a busy early childhood leader, managing time is one of the most important roles in maintaining work-life balance (**Figure 14.10**). Program leaders with good time-management skills are efficient and productive. They plan their time wisely so they can achieve everything they want to do including caring for oneself. This includes

Maridav/iStock/Getty Images Plus

Figure 14.8 One way to practice mindfulness is by taking a nature walk and listening to the sounds around you.

NicoElNino/iStock/Getty Images Plus

Figure 14.10 Managing time is one of the most important factors in maintaining a healthy work-life balance.

role-modeling time-management skills to the staff and providing professional development opportunities that teach them more.

Many situations arise throughout the day that can quickly monopolize large gaps of time. The result is putting other tasks to the side. Picking up where you left off is sometimes difficult to do. Utilizing different strategies serves as an excellent framework for the program to collectively implement and maintain to support one another (**Figure 14.11**). As a program director, it is important to remember that you are the person who ultimately has control of your time and making yourself a priority. Staff need to see the program leader effectively implementing a healthy work-life balance and displaying appropriate mental and emotional well-being.

Make a schedule and create to-do lists	• Keeps you focused • Avoids forgotten items
Utilize digital devices	• Make scheduling quick and easy • Provide audible reminders when tasks are due
Combine tasks	• Save time and energy by dovetailing tasks, or doing several similar tasks at once
Designate priorities	• Decide which tasks are essential, which are important, and which can be done if time allows • Use A, B, C, or 1, 2, 3 to designate priorities
Avoid procrastination	• Start with the more difficult or complex tasks first • Break a big project down into smaller, more manageable pieces • List all the steps that need to be completed to get a project done
Be flexible	• Schedule some time to deal with any emergencies that may arise • Reprioritize tasks, if necessary • Have a plan for spare time

Goodheart-Willcox Publisher

Figure 14.11 Utilizing time-management strategies supports work-life balance.

Mental and Emotional Well-Being

Mental and emotional well-being has to do with a person's internal sense of self and emotions or feelings. When leading others, it is important to feel a sense of inner confidence while also feeling comfortable with one's self, and not overly anxious or depressed (**Figure 14.12**). Engaging in life and feeling good with that engagement is important when you are in a position that makes major decisions each day.

There are many medical tests that can measure mental and emotional well-being that are no different from other tests that provide further insights into how the body is working. A doctor or psychologist can diagnose mental illnesses and disorders and just like physical illnesses, they are treatable when diagnosed early. Like a diabetic has to monitor their insulin on a regular basis, the same is true with many mental illnesses.

Dealing with so many priorities between work and home life can be challenging. Early childhood leaders must be constantly aware of themselves and listen to those who express concern about their mental well-being. When a person has a balanced work life, it assists with their decision-making abilities, effectiveness when managing stress, and their ability to maintain healthy relationships and manage time.

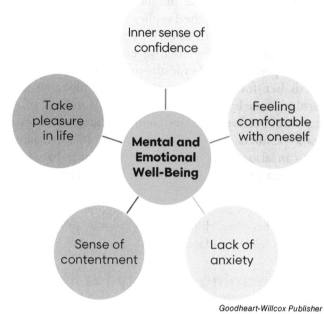

Goodheart-Willcox Publisher

Figure 14.12   Program leaders who maintain their mental and emotional well-being are able to deal with the stress in their lives.

Director's Showcase
Kateri

While Kateri had noticed her lack of consistent routines during child care hours, her husband voiced a concern. As she was disciplining a child one afternoon, he brought to her attention the unusual tone and how loud she was being. Her eyes teared up! She realized she wasn't herself and shared that evening with her husband that one of the parents had asked her if she was doing okay. They decided together to first schedule a medical checkup. In addition, they made arrangements with a family friend to come over on a part-time basis to help out until they could figure out what was going on with Kateri.

Sam

One afternoon, Sam stopped one of the teachers that he depended upon and asked that she meet him for coffee on Saturday morning. She agreed, and they met the next day at the local coffee shop. During their talk the staff member shared how many of the long-term staff were feeling. They were tired of always being the ones asked to stay late when there were other staff members out sick. These long-term staff members had outside commitments and families too! Sam thanked the teacher for her honesty and decided that it was time to call a staff meeting to deal with issues as well as scheduling individual meetings with the staff members whose attendance was poor.

Director's Showcase
Reflect

Based on the information shared in this section, Kateri and Sam have several things to consider. If you were a consultant working with them, what would you recommend as next steps as each deals with the circumstances described?

14.3 Creating a Healthy Program Environment for All to Thrive

Early childhood leaders are responsible for a healthy program environment that staff and children can thrive within. However, this is easier said than done due to a variety of factors that are outside the control of the program director. While the goal is to provide a healthy and stress-free program environment, oftentimes the staff and the families served lack available and affordable health care. They may also live within conditions that have negative environmental factors such as pollution and exposure to toxins. Further, basic needs like food, clothing, and shelter might be very hard to come by. Sadly, the early-child workforce often does not receive adequate compensation, which puts staff members at risk (**Figure 14.13**). In turn, families can also suffer the same consequences based on circumstances outside of their control. This impacts mental and social-emotional health when individuals do not feel safe, that they belong, or hope for the future. These hardships typically become priorities for program leaders to facilitate.

Encouraging Security for Staff and Families

Unfortunately, when people are subjected to **low socio-economic status**, or inadequate financial resources to meet basic needs, they may face potential conditions that put them in social and emotional harm and instability. **Food insecurity** is when adults and children do not have adequate food resources and experience. **Housing insecurity**, on the other hand, is the result of the high cost of housing relative to income,

lolostock/iStock/Getty Images Plus

Figure 14.13 The early childhood profession lacks adequate compensation, which can be difficult for staff members with few resources.

overcrowding, poor housing quality, and/or unstable neighborhoods. Both of these issues create stress about safety and where the next meal will be coming from.

The role of the program leader is to be resourceful, organized, caring, communicative, and objective (**Figure 14.14**). This includes being well-connected with community supports while balancing each situation with respect to protect the person's dignity. Steering them to resources will create more stability and confidentiality

Director's Showcase

Kateri

Kateri was able to talk directly with her doctor and it was determined that medications were needed to deal with her diagnosed depression. At first, Kateri didn't want anyone to know that she was having this issue. She was scared she would lose enrollment if parents thought she was "unbalanced." One day, one of the moms was talking with her and mentioned the name of the same medication that Kateri had been described. The mom talked about the significant difference it had made in her life and ability to deal with day-to-day life. Kateri felt a rush of relief; someone else was experiencing the same thing that she had!

That weekend, she put together a letter to the parents letting them know the emotional struggles she had been having, that she had been to the doctor, and received a diagnosis. That diagnosis had led to daily medications which, as she described in her letter, had significantly changed her outlook on life. That evening after sending the letters home with the children, three of the

families called to say how glad they were that she was feeling better and how much they appreciated her and her honesty.

Sam

As Sam sat each one of the individual teachers down regarding their attendance issues, one in particular was very concerning. This teacher, Ms. Athena, was essentially homeless. As a single mom, she and her preschool-age child were "couch surfing" at family and friends' homes. She went on to explain that her boyfriend had kicked her and the little girl out after the police had come to their apartment due to a domestic violence call made by a neighbor. When the police came, they offered to provide her protection as she gathered a few things, got in the car, and left. Filing charges was worrisome to her and she didn't want to lose her little girl to child protective services. All she had was this job, where she knew that her child would be well cared for, fed, and there was access to bathing opportunities. She just didn't know where she was going to turn next and she began to cry.

Figure 14.14   The role of the program leader is to be resourceful, organized, caring, communicative, and objective.

when dealing with issues is necessary. Oftentimes if support is quickly built around a situation, the person is able to begin making better decisions. These decisions often lead to stabilizing the situation and overcoming barriers.

Program Leader as Presumed Counselor

One of the heaviest responsibilities an early childhood leader has is to manage the multitude of social issues that are brought to their attention. Because of the population served, meaning all human beings—of all ages—circumstances are all different. While being a mandated reporter for any type of child abuse has already been discussed at length, abuse does not just happen to young children. The adults that program leaders work with may have suffered abuse that resulted in lower academic achievement and lifelong mental health issues. Some adults who abuse children were also victims of abuse. While they may not want to be an abuser, the cycle is repeated due to learned behaviors and a lack of knowing another way.

There are many risk factors that early childhood leaders need to be aware of that are directly linked to child abuse and neglect according to the *Centers for Disease Control and Prevention (CDC)* (**Figure 14.15**). Locations where

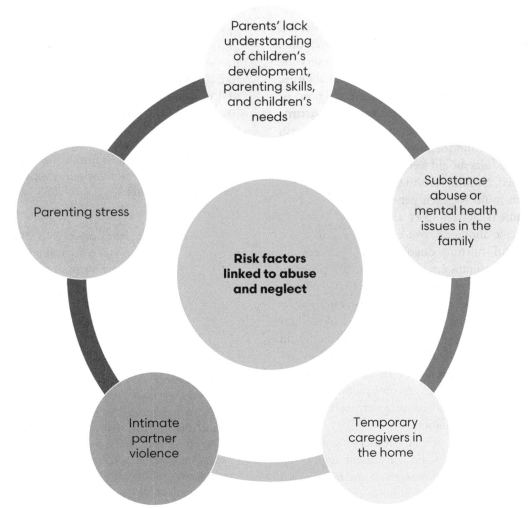

Figure 14.15   The Centers for Disease Control and Prevention (CDC) identifies several risk factors for early childhood leaders to be aware of that are directly linked to child abuse and neglect.

staff or families live also create risk factors. If violence is taking place in a neighborhood, then children are more likely to face abuse. This also increases the possibility of **domestic violence**, or intimate partner abuse, which can be physical and mental. All of these issues result in stress and the need to contact child protective services or other legal authorities. This is a stressful position to be placed in, but, as a mandated reporter, it is the program leader's duty to report the situation and make sure that the concern is taken seriously by the proper authorities. It is not the program leader's responsibility to confront a suspected abuser. In addition, while providing appropriate assistance is important, maintaining boundaries, as discussed earlier in the chapter, must also be considered to avoid dependence upon the program leader. The role is to refer the person(s) to the appropriate counselor or resource, not to become the counselor or resource.

martinedoucet/E+/Getty Images

Figure 14.16 Everyone benefits from strong connections, relationships, and established trust.

Maintaining Diverse, Equitable, and Inclusive Program Environments

The early childhood program environment should feel safe. It should provide a place that is positive for everyone. **Inclusive program environments** accept everyone regardless of physical characteristics, intellectual abilities, gender, race, socio-economic class, culture, religion, or social resources. Each take part in **equitable programming**, which is a fair chance to learn, grow, and flourish for all individuals within the program environment.

Children and adults should feel that they have an opinion that is valued. Skillful, sensitive leaders who have the best interest in mind for each person within their program environment show respect and practice *empathy*, the ability to take another person's perspective, to boost relationships and nurture ongoing trust between all members of the program environment. When program staff feel trust and a foundation of honesty, this works to the advantage of the children and their families. In turn, parents and children feel that the program has their best interests in mind (**Figure 14.16**). Leaders should strive to provide as much diversity as they can within their programs. **Diversity** reflects various cultures, races, socio-economic levels, genders, age groups, and religious backgrounds. This includes the program staff and the families that attend the program.

Finally, early childhood program leaders must be diligent in their awareness of various forms of aggression. Referred to as **microaggressions**, these are the subtle or indirect, often unintentional, comments or actions that express discrimination or a prejudiced attitude against a member of a group of people consisting of different races, people with disabilities, or people of low socio-economic

Director's Showcase

Kateri

Kateri's honest conversation with the families in her care led to more conversations about the importance of mental health and wellness. The parents decided to collectively work together to assist each other with carpooling should one of the parents have to work late. In addition, the families met with Kateri on a Saturday to schedule long weekends, twice a year, where her program could be closed and she could take extended time with her family. As a group, they decided that they all needed to support mental health and wellness.

Sam

After Ms. Athena stopped crying, Sam asked what he could do. He also talked about the importance of making sure that she and the little girl felt safe. They worked out a plan to gain access to the "safe shelter" for victims of domestic abuse that provided temporary housing for up to a year. In addition, the site provided transportation for Ms. Athena so she could get to work. As Ms. Athena began to confide in certain staff members, each reached out to Sam in confidence and a collection was taken up to purchase more clothing since winter was right around the corner. By attending therapy, Ms. Athena and her daughter began to forge their next steps and the social worker at the shelter helped her to secure affordable housing. Throughout all of this, Ms. Athena's confidence and attendance at work increased significantly.

status. Leaders must stop any comments or actions that are offensive and hurtful that devalue a person or group of people. By staying **culturally competent**, a program leader has a keen sense of self-awareness about one's cultural identity and attitudes or views about human differences, while also becoming knowledgeable about the cultural identities of the staff, children, and families—the overall program environment—they are responsible for.

14.4 Health and Mental Wellness Supports

Working as a director in early childhood education is isolating and stressful. Directors often experience burnout and stress and have no one to turn to for support. Discovering health and mental wellness support in the community can serve as a bridge to getting out of the burnout rut and make connections with others in the same circumstances or experiencing similar stress.

It is no secret that all workplaces are impacted by health and mental wellness concerns. Many employers are scrambling to enhance these benefits while also finding support to manage stress and have disabilities such as anxiety and depression treated. Those who work in the field of early childhood are part of the trend of mental health disorders that are on the rise, displaying symptoms of poor mental health that negatively impacts work performance, and the cost is a large financial burden due to lost wages for the staff member, and an absent workforce needed to work with children each day. Program directors must be mindful of strategies to support themselves, and others, in the program environment.

Understand and Act to Support Opportunities to Support Health and Mental Wellness

Many programs across the nation have started providing health and mental wellness training for staff with the intent of increasing awareness and investing in a staff member's well-being. While key for early childhood

Director's Showcase
Kateri
Kateri began practicing mindfulness exercises to address her burnout symptoms. She incorporated deep-breathing exercises into the daily routine and included the children. She set time aside to sit alone with her thoughts after the day ended. Kateri also connected with the local children's museum to find out about programming. She was able to schedule a free play day at the museum and encouraged parents and other caregivers to attend. She also scheduled more time for outdoor play at the park down the street from her home. The children were able to explore nature, and Kateri was able to spend time in a place she loved. She has been able to get out of her burnout rut and has continued to practice mindfulness.

Sam
Sam decided to have staff complete an interest survey. They found that many of the staff shared an interest in art and pottery. They scheduled a time at the local county art center for the staff to have an introductory lesson on art. This was scheduled at the end of an in-service training day. The training was focused on decreasing stress and practicing mindfulness activities. They also added a community bulletin board for sharing ideas to de-stress, events happening around the community, as well as other interests staff might share. There was a notable decrease in stress in the center, fewer staff absences due to illness, and a more enjoyable atmosphere during the work day.

leaders to understand the signs of distress, staff members need to be aware as well (**Figure 14.17**). Everyone within the program environment should be aware of the common warning signs of emotional distress according to the *Substance Abuse and Mental Health Services Administration (SAMHSA)*:

- eating or sleeping too much or too little;
- pulling away from people or things;
- low or no energy;
- unexplained aches, pains, constant stomach issues;
- feeling hopeless and helpless;
- excessive smoking, drinking, use of drugs or misuse of prescription drugs;
- excessive worry and feeling of guilt;
- desire to hurt oneself or others; and
- struggling to adjust in home and work life.

SDI Productions/E+/Getty Images

Figure 14.17 Oftentimes, early childhood leaders are one of the first people to recognize the signs of distress in staff members.

The use of surveys is also another way to collect insightful information regarding the feelings of staff members. Questions could surround the following topic areas:

- feeling support from team members;
- ability to manage their work-life balance;
- feeling their voice was heard;
- breaks and time away are supported; and
- opportunities are available to learn more and take on increased responsibility.

By gaining insights on staff members' perceptions about how they feel in the workplace based on these topic areas, more information can be acquired, meaningful conversations can take place, and change can potentially be made to support the overall workplace environment before issues get out-of-hand.

Program leaders should have a good idea and know each one of their staff members. This means understanding who they are as individuals and what their typical characteristics are like. It is normal for all of us to have "off" days (**Figure 14.18**). However, if they

shapecharge/E+/Getty Images

Figure 14.18 When program leaders notice that a staff member is struggling over several days, it is important to sit down and have a private conversation.

persist, it is important to notice. Should the behavior continue a few more days, it's time to talk to that person. In that private conversation, check to see what needs they might have or just listen. Sometimes venting frustrations to a safe person is the biggest assistance that can be provided.

Providing Access to an Employee Assistance Program (EAP)

There are many opportunities provided within employee assistance programs (EAPs). These programs are typically part of programs providing health coverage or can be delivered through a variety of program types. Sometimes they are hotlines, others have on-site specialists available to teaching staff, and others might be provided by a teacher union. These programs strive to link proactive prevention and health and wellness activities. For example, discounted memberships to health clubs, access to a counselor, financial planner, or attorney are potential services provided by an EAP.

When an early childhood program director is tasked with choosing an EAP, it is important to select one that will meet the specific needs of the organization. SAMHSA provides some basic questions to ask when determining if the EAP provider will meet the needs of the program staff and their family members (**Figure 14.19**).

It will be important to have in mind the budget allocated to cover this cost. Further, EAPs may not understand the level of stress that early childhood teachers are under each day to include the role of the early childhood leader. Be prepared to share specifics so that they better understand the needs of the program. Overall, research studies have shown that the investment in EAPs is a smart choice and often steers individuals to appropriate healthcare options.

Create an Inclusive Health and Mental Wellness Culture

In today's early childhood program workplace environments, it is important to ask staff what they expect from you as a leader. The staff should see their program leader as one who embraces the range of individuals working in the classrooms. Directors should role-model the importance of physical and mental health. Further, they should also be very aware of the **stigma**, or negative or unfair perception, of mental health. Some of the harmful effects of stigma include:

- Reluctance by the person to seek help or treatment
- Social isolation
- Refusal to stay in treatment
- Fewer opportunities for work, social activities, housing

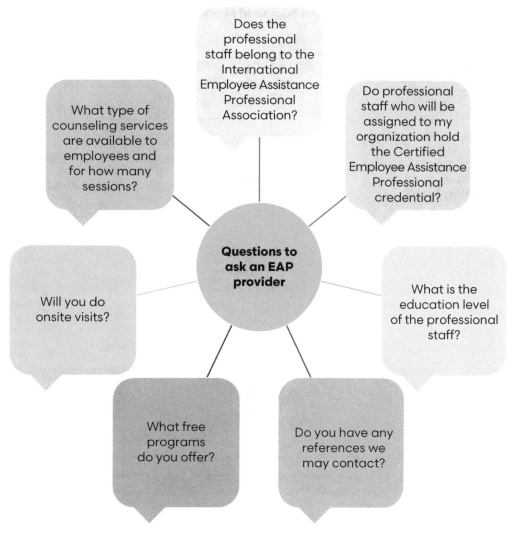

Figure 14.19   Here are some questions to ask when shopping for EAP providers to assist the program.

- Physical violence or harassment
- Reduced hope and lower self-esteem

One of the highlights of the past several years has been celebrities who have shared their own struggles with mental health. Program leaders that speak out and share stories can make a positive impact. They are seen as a credible source and by sharing their own issues, mental health issues become less scary (**Figure 14.20**).

Program leaders should be vocal and decisive so that everyone within the program environment feels protected and empowered to pursue their physical and mental health wellness goals.

NAEYC developed an online platform called "Hello," which serves as a way for early childhood providers, educators, and families to connect with others (**Figure 14.21**). It has interest forums where members can post questions, ask for advice, and share resources with others. This is a simple way to connect with others

any time of day and can be a valuable resource for everyone working with children.

Directors need to explore their community and access programs that can enhance and support their staff and themselves. Identifying community support and opportunities for staff is also a way to decrease stress and increase job satisfaction. Provide transportation to

Director's Showcase

Reflect

Have you or do you know someone that has been impacted by the stigma of mental health? As a program leader, how would you advocate for physical and mental wellness at your program site?

Ways to Reduce the Stigma of Mental Health Issues

Share social media and credible information openly	Share facts and experiences	Remind people that words matter
Encourage equality between physical and mental illness	Be compassionate	Share the facts about treatments
	Choose empowerment over shaming	

Figure 14.20   Ways to reduce mental health stigma with staff as a program director.

Welcome to Hello!

HELLO is the platform for NAEYC's Interest Forums and online communities. Members can use this space to have conversations and create connections with peers around important early learning issues.

Click here to learn more.

Latest Discussions

Figure 14.21   NAEYC has many great online resources to assist members with sharing ideas, seeking advice, and sharing resources.

a community event for staff that would like to attend. Finding new places for staff to explore outside of work, creating a safe space for staff to relax, and providing a place for staff to share community events and programs that may be of interest are all ways to provide connections for your staff.

This work is difficult and demanding and not everyone can do it. The environment that you provide requires adults who are flexible and consistent in their approach—which comes from an immense amount of mental and emotional wellness, patience, and understanding.

You *must* take care of *yourself first*!

Chapter 14 Review and Assessment

Summary

14.1 Establish professional boundaries between director and staff and between staff and families.

- Professional boundaries differ from ethical boundaries in that professional boundaries are situational. Professional boundaries are unique to a specific child care program, the location or region, and cultural differences, and they can be modified depending on a family's or employee's situation.
- The program director's responsibility is to provide a healthy, safe, and cooperative working environment for their employees. The early childhood program director leads by example.
- The director must adhere to professional boundaries and create a community of trust and fairness. Unequal treatment of staff can lead to a competitive and problematic work environment.

14.2 Recognize the daily stress of managing programs and the importance of work-life balance by engaging in acts of self-care.

- The daily management of an early child care program includes a variety of stressors. The responsibility of caring for children, managing staff and employees, attending to health and safety concerns, and low pay are just a few stressors that a director faces daily.
- Learning to identify stress and potential stressors in daily running of the program can lead to greater program success and employee retention.

14.3 Analyze factors that support positive mental wellness and healthy environments where staff, children, and families can thrive.

- Early childhood leaders are responsible for a healthy program environment that staff and children can thrive within. Issues such as the lack of available and affordable healthcare, and negative environmental factors such as pollution and exposure to toxins are a reality. Further, basic needs like food, clothing, and shelter might be very hard to come by.
- Due to inadequate compensation paid to those working within the early-child workforce, this puts staff members at risk.

- Families can also suffer the same consequences based on circumstances outside of their control. This impacts mental and social-emotional health when individuals do not feel safe, that they belong, or hope for the future. These hardships typically become priorities for program leaders to facilitate.

14.4 Apply health and mental wellness community support and opportunities to support oneself and others in the early childhood program environments.

- Striking down stigma, staying aware, and discovering available community support can serve as a bridge to getting out of the burnout rut and making connections with others in the same circumstances or experiencing similar stress.
- Whether it is the use of employee assistance programs or community and access programs that can enhance and support their staff and themselves, directors must be aware of opportunities.
- Identifying community support such as providing transportation to community events for staff, finding new places to explore outside of work, and having a safe place for staff to relax are all ways to help provide a nurturing and healthy work place. This provides opportunities for staff to decrease stress and increase job satisfaction.

Review

1. What is the difference between professional boundaries and ethical boundaries? (14.1)
2. What are the differences between social relationships and professional relationships? (14.1)
3. What are the three zones of helpfulness? (14.1)
4. What are some ways for directors to practice self-care? (14.2)
5. What are five strategies that support mindfulness? (14.2)
6. What is stress and its negative impacts? (14.2)
7. What are the differences between food and housing insecurities and what are the causes? (14.3)
8. What are microaggressions and why are they hurtful? (14.4)
9. What are five common warning signs of emotional distress? (14.4)
10. What are five results of stigma in mental health? (14.4)

Showcase Your Skills

As we discussed in the chapter, Kateri and Sam had specific issues either they themselves or identified staff members needed assistance with. Kateri worked to resolve her own personal issue while being transparent with the families in her care. Sam worked closely with a staff member that came to him with a significant personal issue.

Either program would benefit from a resource book specific to physical and mental health awareness. This resource book would need to include the following items:

1. Expectations of professional boundaries for all staff members including the program director. (4.1)
2. An overview about stress and stress management. Include mindfulness techniques, relaxation exercises, and information about self-care. (14.2)
3. Develop a 10-question survey specific to health and mental wellness for employees of an early childhood program to complete. (14.4)

Matching

Match the following words with the correct definitions:

A. culturally competent
B. diversity
C. food insecurity
D. housing insecurity
E. microaggressions
F. mindfulness
G. professional boundaries
H. stress
I. stressors
J. zone of helpfulness

1. Subtle, indirect, and often unintentional comments or actions that express discrimination or a prejudiced attitude against another person or group.
2. People, places, or things that cause stress.
3. Separates the personal relationship from the professional relationship.
4. Reflecting various cultures, races, socio-economic level, genders, age groups, and religious backgrounds.
5. Occurs when adults and children do not have adequate food resources and experience.
6. Results from the high cost of housing relative to income, overcrowding, poor housing quality, and/ or unstable neighborhoods.
7. Deviation of the normal function of the body and/ or mind.
8. State of being conscious or aware of the present moment.
9. Continuum that can be used to guide early childhood program directors and staff in finding appropriate balance in professional relationships.
10. When a person has a keen sense of self-awareness about personal cultural identity and attitudes or views about human differences, while also becoming knowledgeable about the cultural identities of other they work with or serve.

FG Trade/E+/Getty Images

15 CHAPTER

Program Evaluation to Support Quality Improvement

Learning Outcomes

After studying this chapter, you will be able to:

15.1 Identify program assessment tools utilized to measure how children are benefiting from the early childhood program environment.

15.2 Distinguish between the common program tools that gather important insights and information from families served by the early childhood program.

15.3 Examine how education and experience expectations for administration and staff provide valuable insights when doing professional development planning.

15.4 Evaluate tools that measure administrative expectations in an early childhood program.

15.5 Explain why quality rating systems are important in relation to measuring the quality of care provided to children and families.

Key Terms

Business Administration Scale (BAS)
Certified Child Care Professional (CCP)
Classroom Assessment Scoring System® (CLASS®)
Environment Rating Scales (ERS)
orientation training
professional development registry systems
Program Administration Scale (PAS)
training systems

NAEYC/DAP standards

Standards covered in this chapter:

NAEYC

3a, 3b, 3c, 3d

DAP

3C

Introduction

The evaluation of child care programs has grown in recent years as the demand for not only child care but also early childhood education has increased. Individual states have gone beyond providing standard licensing requirements to meeting basic health and safety requirements when caring for large groups of children. Professional associations, such as the National Association for the Education of Young Children (NAEYC), have established developmentally appropriate practices (DAP) and launched accreditation standards that identify quality practices that programs must follow to be nationally recognized. Research time and funding has been devoted to studying early childhood settings and the brain development of young children. Significant research findings have shown the importance of the quality of children's earliest experiences and having a strong, healthy start in their education and care. For example, research supports how high-quality environments and appropriate relationships between children and adults support children's learning.

Federal and state funding has supported programmatic changes. Enhanced licensing requirements have opened the door for discussions about the cost of quality care within the field of early childhood. Many state systems have adopted program assessment and measurement scales from universities and institutions, including measurements that look closely at the environments that infants, toddlers, preschool, and school-age children engage in daily; the quality of the interactions program staff have with children; and the administrative abilities of a program director. Some states also have created their own checklists to guide their expectations. These efforts have been supported by various program incentives and opportunities, such as facilities and equipment grants, links to services for families, encouraging ongoing staff professional development, and supporting growth for an early childhood program leader. The result has been

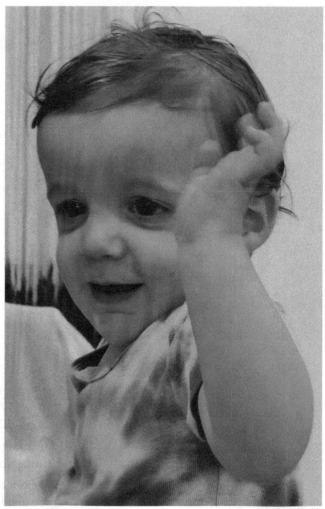

Kristen Alexandria

Figure 15.1 Federal and state funding over the past two decades has been intended to support quality learning environments for young children.

quality rating systems in many states that are intended to support quality learning environments for young children (**Figure 15.1**). The goal of this investment of federal and state funding over the past two decades has been to enhance program quality while also supporting families' needs for child care.

Director's Showcase

Ilya

Ilya is ready to take the next step in her child care program by joining the quality-rating system initiative in her state. Her staff were excited to become the first three-star program in their area. After reviewing the criteria together, they all felt because of the quality programming they were already providing, they would qualify for one of the higher star levels starting out. In their state, a five-star was the highest and obtaining that was the staff's goal. They all saw this as recognition that was well-deserved for all of their efforts when serving the children and families in their program. They were eager to get started!

Maria

Maria, on the other hand, began hearing from other family child care home providers how the extra money they were receiving by being a higher star level in their state system provided a small raise and other benefits. Since she was a larger family child care home provider in her state, she employed two other ladies that worked in her program. Maria wanted to learn more about how the children in her care would benefit, how this would meet the needs of the families that she served, enhance her relationship with the community, and improve her overall program delivery.

Both program leaders reached out to their licensing representative for more information.

Director's Showcase

Reflect

What value do you think that Ilya and Maria will discover as they learn more?

15.1 Program Benefits for Children

As part of the Quality Rating and Improvement Systems (QRIS), better known today as the *Quality Rating Systems (QRS),* programs must participate in some form of assessment that many administrators perceive as intimidating. However, the intent of a program assessment is to engage early childhood leaders and their staff in thinking about continuous improvement of their services. While some states have utilized self-developed checklist criteria that assist programs with this process, others have made larger investments in valid and reliable tools from outside providers. Some states also provide training to professionals with specific credentials and experience who will eventually go out to programs and complete the assessment processes. The following are two assessment tools that are highly regarded, are supported by research, and are valid and reliable.

- **Environment Rating Scales (ERS)**—The scales address the different age groups of infants and toddlers, preschool, school-age care, and family child care. The scales evaluate a variety of categories, including physical environment; basic care; curriculum; interaction; schedule and program structure; and provisions for parents and staff.
- **Classroom Assessment Scoring System® (CLASS®)**—This tool looks at the teaching quality between teacher and child by measuring interactions, which has been linked to children's academic and lifelong success.

Whether a program uses a checklist or an identified assessment tool, the objective is to engage the program staff by completing the self-assessment portion, have opportunities to make changes or adaptations, and learn more about criteria that supports the quality care of young children.

The use of these types of assessment tools is costly. However, many states provide a variety of initiatives to support early childhood leaders and their staff to be successful in the process. Many of the initiatives include incentives for participating programs to receive free copies of the assessment tools, on-site technical assistance by experts in the tools, and mini-grants or stipends to purchase necessary equipment (**Figure 15.2**).

A program may also choose to participate in a national early childhood education accreditation process. The National Association for the Education of Young Children (NAEYC) accreditation has four steps to follow.

1. Enroll and begin the self-study process.
2. Apply and complete the self-assessment.
3. Participate in a site visit.
4. Maintain accreditation.

Director's Showcase

Ilya

Ilya and her staff started to review the tools that would be used for assessment of their program. They learned that the Environment Rating Scales need to be completed in their infant-toddler, pre-school, and school-age program areas. They also found out that they would need a consultant who would provide free, on-site technical assistance for any areas needing improvement once the scales were completed. Ilya and the staff talked about it and decided that they saw this as a learning opportunity.

Maria

Maria found out from her licensing representative that she would need to take part in an environment rating scale designed for family child care home environments. She was relieved to know that special considerations are made for in-home programs and that she, too, would receive free, on-site technical assistance. Maria was interested to find that gathering information from the families that attended her program would be a part of the assessment process as determined by the quality-rating system requirements. She was able to obtain links to local websites shared with her from her licensing representative to begin learning about this next step.

Kristen Alexandria

Figure 15.2 Participation in assessment tool programs provided by state programs can result in mini-grants to purchase identified equipment such as playground equipment.

Other accreditation models are available to be utilized within differing program environments. For programs serving children with disabilities to those who implement a specialized curriculum such as Montessori, each have accreditation available to them (**Figure 15.3**). Family child care homes and school-age programs also have specialized organizations that provide national recognition.

The benefits of participating in an accreditation process are immense for the children served in the program! An accredited program has proven it is safe, well prepared, and intentional in its care and education of young children. The teaching staff and program leadership are accessing the latest research and applying the best practices in the early learning field.

Director's Showcase

Reflect

As a program leader, having outside resources come in to provide a different perspective may be intimidating. How would you feel about having this type of process done at a program in which you were the program leader?

15.2 Meeting the Needs of Families and the Community

Keeping up with the needs of families and what resources they may be interested in is important to the viability of an early childhood program. Consistent parental feedback is a necessary program evaluation tool. Programs can collect this feedback in many ways, including the use of questionnaires and online surveys. As a consumer of the program's services, families are key contributors to evaluating classroom routines and performance, providing insights into the programming being provided to their child, and sharing perceptions and experiences on the program's culture and outreach, such if they feel

Association	Website	Description
National Association for the Education of Young Children (NAEYC)	naeyc.org	NAEYC's mission is to promote high-quality learning for children birth through age 8. They connect research, practice, and policy to reach their goals.
Association for Early Learning Leaders	earlylearningleaders.org	Formerly known as the National Association of Child Care Professionals (NACCP). It is committed to strengthening the skills of program leaders and professionals who work in early child care and education.
National Early Childhood Program Accreditation (NECPA)	necpa.net	NECPA is an accreditation created by the Nation Child Care Association in 1991 to promote quality child care and bring benefits to the children in care programs.
National Afterschool Association (NAA)	naaweb.org	NAA is a professional association for those people who work with children and youth during out-of-school-time.
National Association of Family Child Care (NAFCC)	nafcc.org	NAFCC is a nationwide non-profit organization dedicated to promoting high-quality child care for those who run home-based programs.

Goodheart-Willcox Publisher

Figure 15.3   There are many accrediting organizations that recognize different program environments.

Makidotvn/iStock/Getty Images Plus

Figure 15.4   Providing online surveys allows parents to provide program feedback from the workplace.

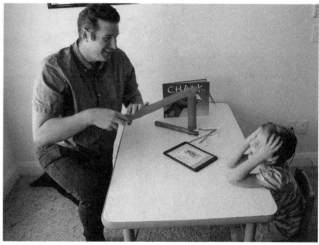

Kristen Alexandria

Figure 15.5   Services to families, such as speech therapy, often welcome work with early childhood programs.

welcome and supported (**Figure 15.4**). Programs could also gather parental feedback on future or past family events, the effectiveness of parent communications, and the utilization of community resources that might be helpful to families and the surrounding community.

Community Connections

Identifying and building relationships with agencies or businesses within the community that are responsive to these identified needs and wants is crucial. Program leaders can stay current with news shared by local outlets, internet sources with city and state data, school district personnel, the community planning agency, a regional

Cooperative Extension office, and the local Chamber of Commerce. Other for-profit and non-profit agencies that provide services to families, such as health, mental health, nutrition, or other resources, often welcome partnering with early childhood programs (**Figure 15.5**). Sharing insights and information can be both beneficial to the community resource as well as to the program.

Early childhood program leaders also need to network together. Many programs closed their doors during the COVID-19 pandemic and never reopened. Those that have stayed in business have increased their waiting lists with names of children for whom there is no room. Program leaders in this situation find it frustrating to know there are children needing care who cannot be placed in their programs. While some program leaders may be threatened by the possible opening of a new program, others focus on the greater need of the community and welcome networking with new and established program leaders within their communities.

Questionnaires and Online Surveys

One of the most frequently utilized ways to gather data from families is through paper questionnaires or online surveys. These helpful tools gather insights from families about their needs. Paper questionnaires can be short and placed at the entryway when parents are coming and going. Staff members can remind parents about how important their feedback is on program issues. Since many parents are technologically savvy, the use of online surveys is also very effective. Surveys can be pushed out through an already-utilized program app or website, survey-specific programs, an email distribution list or program, or a link using social media (**Figure 15.6**). Gathering family opinions on the care their child is receiving, their use of certain community resources, or their ideas on how to better connect the program to support the community

AndreyPopov/iStock/Getty Images Plus

Figure 15.6 The use of program apps and survey-specific programs can gather pertinent information quickly and efficiently from families and staff members.

Director's Showcase

Ilya

Ilya and the staff were excited to find out how willing the parents were to share their needs when asked. Ilya was able to put together an online survey through a free online survey resource, which resulted in over a 75% response rate. With all of the information gathered, one of the main points shared by parents was their desire to learn more about the local school district and area agencies that might provide guidance and assistance in their child's ongoing development. This prompted Ilya and one of her lead staff members to begin collecting the information to share with parents. The other area that they realized they needed to improve was professional development opportunities for new staff members. Several parents noted that new staff often seemed a little lost with implementing programming for the children, especially the afternoon teaching staff.

Maria

Maria utilized a paper and pencil version. She was surprised to find out that the parents were very interested in her educational opportunities to continue increasing her knowledge about young children. This prompted Maria to talk more with the parents about the difficulty of participating in either virtual or weekday professional development opportunities that were offered in her area. Once the parents became aware, they collectively decided to support Maria by setting aside three days per year for her to attend these necessary trainings. Maria was so thankful that the families were willing to support her ability to become a higher-level provider within the quality rating system while learning more by attending more professional development opportunities!

is useful both in assessing current program offerings and planning for enhancements.

Families who choose to participate in questionnaires or online surveys should be expected to do this only on a voluntary basis. When creating these tools, it will also be important to create questions that are sensitive, anti-bias, with a sincere commitment to enhancing the level of care provided by the program. Parents can sometimes feel threatened by questions that feel intrusive into their personal life or that their answers might have consequences for their child. Overall, parents need to be assured that all information gathered is for the purposes of improvement and will be kept confidential. Once the information is collected, compiling the information gives another helpful data point in determining next steps for implementing changes within the program.

Many of the higher levels within quality rating systems require some sort of parent feedback utilizing one of these venues. This data is viewed as valuable to the ongoing quality enhancements taking place at an early childhood program. National accreditation agencies also require some sort of program evaluation component that includes parental input and feedback. Oftentimes, performing this process twice per year is recommended so that program staff are aware of the perceptions of the families they serve.

Director's Showcase

Reflect

As a program leader, why do you think professional development for yourself and others on your staff is so important?

15.3 Supporting Staff in Their Professional Development

As quality rating systems began to evolve in 2000, one area that was identified and lacked significantly was the education and ongoing professional development expectations for those working in the classroom with children. Most states had the expectation that individuals working with children should have a high school diploma or equivalent, and a minimum of 10 to 12 hours of ongoing training per year. Some of these training hours were already committed to CPR and basic first aid training. Very little was then expected for the other hours of training. There were very few expectations for the type or quality of the training,

the speaker, or where or when the training took place. After realizing this gap, states began to identify the need for established career levels in the early 2000s. This included professional development standards, trainer requirements, and overall content review for appropriateness, which has resulted in state registry systems. In addition, state leaders also grappled with what to do with teachers who wanted to earn more formalized education (**Figure 15.7**). This included how they could support the attainment of credentials and formal degrees in early childhood. All of this has resulted in several committees within each state who have worked collaboratively to inform individual state frameworks for professional development.

Established Career Levels

In 2010, the field of early childhood based on the lead by NAEYC worked with professionals across the nation to collectively pull together *Professional Standards and Competencies for Early Childhood Educators*. These standards and competencies have continued to evolve and are informed by

- research and practice;
- early childhood standards and educator standards from other professional organizations; and
- higher education and the workforce in general.

Because early childhood educators work with teachers that serve children through grade 12 in the teaching arena, the established career levels are aligned with the larger education field's understanding of effective teaching. In our field this resulted in the following level titles: ECE I, ECE II, and ECE III. These levels, supported by the NAEYC (2020), are based upon six established standards and competencies for early childhood educators. These standards and competencies

Sam Edwards/Getty Images

Figure 15.7 The field has increased expectations for teachers and program leaders to earn credentials and formal degrees in early childhood education.

allow for individuals to develop the ability to understand, reflect upon, and integrate each of the six areas that include:

- *Child Development and Learning in Context.* This includes a grounded understanding of the developmental period of early childhood from birth through age eight across the developmental domains.
- *Family-Teacher Partnerships and Community Connections.* This incorporates an understanding of family characteristics that values, respects, and responds, while partnering with families to support their young children's development and learning.
- *Child Observation, Documentation, and Assessment.* Teachers recognize that assessment is used to inform instruction and planning, to include understanding the assessment process, use of the data, and its application to development, cultural, and linguistic abilities of each individual child.
- *Developmentally, Culturally, and Linguistically Appropriate Teaching Practices.* Teaching practices should use engaging and supportive relationships with the child. Children are viewed individually when designing universal learning opportunities in the classroom.
- *Knowledge, Application, and Integration of Academic Content in the Early Childhood Curriculum.* The development of curriculum takes into consideration learning standards and other resources when planning, implementing, and evaluating learning experiences for young children.
- *Professional as an Early Childhood Educator.* Early childhood educators should follow the Code of Ethical Conduct when working and communicating to support each individual child in the classroom.

As a program director, you must understand that the field of early childhood will continue to grow and new research will inform these standards and lead to their continuing evolution. These new understandings and societal norms will initiate policy changes as well as inform professional development opportunities.

Professional Development Training Expectations

States now have expectations for those who provide professional development opportunities. Referred to as **training systems**, these systems have determined levels and offer experience in the field for individuals interested in providing learning opportunities for others working in the field of early childhood education. Allocated state and federal funds are utilized to pay contracted individuals who provide approved training to early childhood professionals. The contracted trainers utilize current research and best practices when teaching about the developmental needs of children as well as culturally and linguistically appropriate practices (**Figure 15.8**). The provided training allows the child care professionals to meet the state-determined qualifications for practicing in the early childhood field.

Programs participating in quality rating systems may be required to provide **orientation training** for a new employee, which is content requirements that must be taken within a specified time frame found within state licensing standards. All staff members are required to take ongoing professional development, including the program director, and be aligned with the state's framework for professional development. Ongoing professional development might include topics such as

- health and safety in the child care setting;
- responses to children's challenging behavior;
- the development and implementation of curriculum;
- developmentally appropriate practices;
- engaging families;
- teaching children with disabilities; and
- the screening and assessment of young children.

Training must be delivered by an approved or licensed trainer to ensure that the content is state approved and that the processes and procedures taught are high quality and safe.

Trainer and Training Content Requirements

Most state training systems have levels for trainers. Novice trainers might only have certain topics they are

fizkes/iStock/Getty Images Plus

Figure 15.8 Those who provide educational opportunities must utilize current research and best practices about the developmental needs, including cultural and linguistical appropriate practices.

approved to speak on, while master trainers have more experience, a higher level of education, and an array of training options. These systems recognize areas of need and then create opportunities for those with expertise to offer training in those areas, such as social-emotional learning or teaching with young children with hearing loss. For example, those who provide training for working with children with disabilities or first aid and CPR must have the necessary experience and education to be able to teach others the important concepts within these areas.

The goal of any training system is to improve the quality of learning experiences for those working in the field each day. Quality trainers have the background content knowledge and know how to train adults (**Figure 15.9**). They have the ability to facilitate adult learning by applying knowledge to everyday practices, effectively communicating the information to be shared, and the commitment to strengthen children, families, and communities.

State Registry Systems

States have **professional development registry systems**, or formalized electronic systems that track an individual's education, experience, and professional development training. Not only does this system provide a professional development record for the teacher, but it also supports early childhood programs in meeting state standards. Most licensing representatives have access to accounts that are listed under the name of the

facility, whether it be a child care center or family child care home. Before the licensing visit, the worker will pull the information to check and see if all employees on-site are meeting required training. During the site visit, the worker will address any missing training and the program leader can provide documentation or possibly receive a noncompliance citation.

When a program belongs to the state registry system, the program has the opportunity to earn stipends from funds allocated to enhance child care wages (**Figure 15.10**). Typically tied to the established state-determined career levels, these stipends promote

xavierarnau/E+/Getty Images

Figure 15.9 Those who train adults must have the background and content knowledge to best facilitate effective adult learning opportunities.

Goodheart-Willcox Publisher

Figure 15.10 Many states have online workforce registries that display training opportunities and house an individual's professional development, education, and other information that supports state regulations.

professional development, education, and longevity in the field. They seek to

- enhance a high-quality workforce through professional development and education.
- ensure quality of care by rewarding child care providers who are providing quality experiences in a consistent and stable program environment.
- reduce turnover of staff by offering wage supports for continuity of care at the same early childhood program.

These registry systems often have a nominal membership fee, and a program's membership benefits not only assist the business and its employees, but also serve to contribute important data for state leadership to analyze when making decisions about the allocation of state and federal funding.

Credential and College Education Supports

Many options are available for early childhood teachers seeking nationally recognized credentials or a college education. The Council for Professional Recognition offers the Child Development Associate®

(CDA), and the National Early Childhood Program Accreditation (NECPA) Commission awards the **Certified Child Care Professional (CCP)**. These workforce preparation components provide not only coursework but hands-on work experience. These credentials can be offered either through career and technical education programs or individually. Many community and junior college systems have incorporated these credentials into college credit. While neither are a formalized college degree, these credentials are a competency-based pathway to college and career readiness.

For those early childhood educators looking to continue their education, many states have established incentive programs that offer scholarships to child care teachers and providers (**Figure 15.11**). Typically, these scholarships pay for tuition and books. In addition, many of the participating institutions provide mentors who can assist students in navigating college systems, provide tutoring, and recommend helpful or necessary resources such as those for first-generation college students. The establishment of these types of supports have increased the success rate of early education professionals who are working in the classroom while pursuing a college degree.

Director's Showcase

Ilya

By accessing a variety of resources on the state professional development registry system, Ilya was able to locate a variety of professional development opportunities for her staff and for herself. Ilya piques her staff's interest in the programs by explaining not only the educational benefit but the monetary compensation that could accompany either attending more professional development opportunities or college credit classes. Several of the staff enroll in classes at the local community college and are looking forward to working together toward a college degree.

Maria

With the support of her families in granting extra time for her to participate in professional development, Maria discovered that her state would pay the fees for her to obtain her CDA credential. In addition, because she was pursuing the CDA, the state would provide an on-site professional who would give her free technical assistance to help her through the process. Maria informed her families about her next steps, and they all celebrated her interest and looked forward to supporting her efforts.

PeopleImages/iStock/Getty Images Plus

Figure 15.11 State-funded programs assist early childhood educators with established incentive programs to provide scholarships for books and tuition.

Director's Showcase

Reflect

As you think about future opportunities, what does your state offer to those interested in obtaining more professional development in the field of early childhood?

15.4 Measuring Administrative Success

The responsibilities of a child care facility director or family child care home provider are immense. As program leaders each role deals with multiple areas of responsibility, such as human resources, maintenance and repair, facilities and cleaning services, payroll, and other specialty areas to manage the overall functioning of a business. A successful program leader must have a working knowledge of all parts of the child care program. The list of responsibilities, personality traits, and abilities is lengthy. Two specific tools can be used to assess and measure the quality of administrative, management, and leadership practices within early childhood center-based and home-based programs.

The **Program Administration Scale (PAS)** provides those in leadership positions with valuable information about their program's administrative practices (**Figure 15.12**). The instrument assesses 25 items grouped into nine categories, including human resources; personnel cost and allocation; operations; screening and assessment; fiscal management; organizational growth and development; family and community partnerships; relational leadership; and staff qualifications. The tool's goals are to

- measure administrative tasks, classroom support, and the personality traits necessary to lead;
- provide administrative practices that are inclusive, equitable, and have cultural and linguistic diversity;
- use shared decision making to support quality early childhood program environments;
- promote teacher leadership;
- enhance career development; and
- promote time for reflection, planning, and peer learning.

narith_2527/iStock/Getty Images Plus

Figure 15.12   The Program Administration Scale provides valuable information about an individual's administrative practices, including fiscal management.

The **Business Administration Scale (BAS)** is useful for family child care home providers (**Figure 15.13**). This instrument measures 10 areas: qualifications and professional development; income and benefits; work environment; fiscal management; recordkeeping; risk

Caiaimage/Chris Ryan/iStock/Getty Images Plus

Figure 15.13   Specific to family child care home providers, this tool assists providers with improving business practices.

Director's Showcase

Ilya

As part of the three-star quality rating, Ilya had to make it a priority to participate in the administrative assessment process using the PAS. As she prepared for the assessment, she learned more about how to improve the financial stability of her program and found out about some free financial software support being provided by the Child Care Resource & Referral agency in her area. Consultants were also provided to assist with managing the day-to-day issues that often crop up when working with so many people in a program environment. After completing the PAS, Ilya was able to polish many of her skills and found many helpful resources to strengthen her leadership skills.

Maria

As part of earning the highest star in her state quality rating system, Maria had to participate in a BAS that was provided by a trained local professional that was provided by the state. During the process, Maria was able to learn that there were many areas where she was excelling. This was such a confidence booster for her by learning that her day-to-day administration of her family child care home was meeting quality criteria.

management; provider-family communication; family support and engagement; marketing and community relations; and provider as employer. The intent of the tool is to help providers set goals to improve business practices, support financial stability, and reduce risk when operating a family child care home.

By participating in the assessment process, program leaders in center- and home-based environments gain insights into areas in which goals can be created to enhance the quality of a program. These goals, once identified, determine an action plan that is based on goals and objectives that become the benchmarks of the program leader's progress.

15.5 Quality Rating System Initiatives

Participating in quality state rating initiatives can be beneficial not only for the program but also for the families the program serves. Programs that participate receive higher reimbursement for children who receive subsidy payments (**Figure 15.14**). Families who qualify for subsidy child care may either pay little to nothing for care or may be awarded minimal copayments and are confident that their children are receiving quality care. Participating programs may obtain financial reimbursements that help to offset the true cost of eligible children's enrollment.

States have varying levels of quality criteria for program participants to meet. That criteria may include but is not limited to

- ongoing commitment and compliance to minimum licensing standards;
- functional administrative practices;
- leadership opportunities for staff and ongoing professional development;
- classroom environments that support learning opportunities for all children;

Figure 15.14 The licensed sites that participate in quality rating systems receive higher reimbursement for children who receive subsidy payments which, in turn, provides more money to support the overall needs of the program.

- engagement of families to build a positive environment so children feel more secure and confident; and
- participation in ongoing program evaluation and continuous quality improvement by utilizing assessment practices to regularly improve services and outcomes for the children and families served.

The tools described in this chapter are utilized by many states to determine the level of quality a program is providing. Individual states differ in what tools they utilize and are applied. For example, in some states, programs must earn a certain score on an assessment tool to achieve a higher level and, in turn, increased reimbursements. Assessment scores are typically tied to a time frame, and future assessments are required. On top of maintaining its score, the program must meet basic state licensing requirements. If a program is cited for failing to meet state regulations and is unable to correct the issue, states will demote the program to a lower level until compliance is met. Programs at a higher level are accountable for demonstrating higher-quality practices on a regular basis.

Director's Showcase

Ilya

A year later, Ilya could not be happier with the progress that her program has made. Ilya applied the influx of incentive dollars for more staff training and enrolled herself in a program specific to becoming an administrator of a child development program at the local community college. The staff that started their classes at the community college were still enrolled and on track to graduate in the following spring with their associate degrees in child development. The program had so much interest from the community, that a waiting list had to be started. Ilya and the staff were celebrated by a local business that catered lunch for everyone.

Ilya is so proud of the growth in the program and the investment made by the staff!

Maria

Maria utilized the funds to earn her CDA and aspires to further continue her early childhood administration education. The staff, children, and families have all seen and experienced the benefits of her receiving more education and earning higher levels within the state quality rating system. Maria invested money in more equipment to use indoors and qualified for a grant to have new outdoor playground equipment installed. The children and families are all benefitting from the investment that Maria made in herself and in her family child care program.

kali9/E+/Getty Images

Figure 15.15   Measuring the quality of care by the use of national accreditation has led to greater awareness and commitment to providing quality early childhood programs.

National accreditation is typically the highest level of accreditation for early childhood programs (**Figure 15.15**). A state's quality rating initiative website will include all the accreditation programs it recognizes. NAEYC administers one of the most highly sought-after accreditations for center-based environments. The National Association for Family Child Care (NAFCC) administers accreditation for family child care homes. Both organizations have based their accreditation programs on researched standards that have been developed and reviewed by experts and practitioners in early childhood education and that define the quality interworkings necessary to support children's learning and development.

Many state systems provide potential resources or incentives to help support a program's pursuit of national accreditation. Some of those supports include

- grants to purchase equipment and supplies;
- stipends to assist with the costs tied to accreditation fees;
- onsite technical assistance; and
- reimbursement for professional development training costs.

Measuring the quality of care received by children has been a significant development in the field over the past two decades. State leaders and field professionals have supported research and analysis to help support early childhood programs and their directors. Their dedication has led to a greater awareness and commitment to providing quality child care to families and communities.

Chapter 15 Review and Assessment

Summary

15.1 Identify program assessment tools utilized to measure how children are benefiting from the early childhood program environment.

- Federal and state funding earmarked for quality improvement in child care settings has swept the nation in the past two decades.
- Quality Rating and Improvement Systems (QRIS), or Quality Rating Systems (QRS), are valid and reliable tools that measure the many aspects related to the quality care of young children and are very specific to the differences between the needs of infants, toddlers, preschool, and school-age children. In addition, the quality of interactions between program staff and children has been found to be key in children's development and ability to learn.

15.2 Distinguish between the common program tools that gather important insights and information from families served by the early childhood program.

- Families are excellent contributors to the early childhood program and should be included in the program assessment process.
- From the use of questionnaires or online surveys, parents can provide very helpful insights about the program services and ability to meet the needs of the families whose children attend the program.
- With so many available community resources, early childhood programs are key to identifying and steering families toward opportunities to strengthen the health and wellness of the family unit.

15.3 Examine how education and experience expectations for administration and staff provide valuable insights when doing professional development planning.

- Another large investment has been made in professional development opportunities for both staff and the early childhood program leader. This has resulted in the ability to do professional development planning for individuals who are working at the site. Enhanced education only strengthens the effectiveness of the teacher in the classroom.
- For the program leader, they learn more about best practice when it comes to leading an early childhood program.

15.4 Evaluate tools that measure administrative expectations in an early childhood program.

- The Program Administration Scale and the Business Administration Scale, used in child care centers and family child care homes, measures the unique abilities necessary for an individual leading these two unique program environments.

15.5 Explain why quality rating systems are important in relation to measuring the quality of care provided to children and families.

- Established state rating systems have enhanced the level of quality received in learning environments for young children.
- This investment has supported parents' need for quality child care so that they can be confident about their child's care and focus on their jobs to do them successfully.

Review

1. Explain each of the four environment rating scales used to assess the quality of care received by children. (15.1)
2. Explain why quality rating systems support the type of care children receive. (15.1)
3. List and explain the benefits that parents may potentially receive when providing input on program-provided surveys or questionnaires. (15.2)
4. List and explain the benefits that the community may potentially receive when providing input on program provided surveys or questionnaires. (15.2)
5. What is the purpose of NAEYC Professional Standards and Competencies for Early Childhood Educators? (15.3)
6. Why is ongoing professional development important for individuals who work with young children? (15.3)
7. Explain the differences between a national credential and a college credit course. (15.3)
8. Explain why it is important to measure administrative responsibilities and traits. (15.4)
9. Summarize the advantages of participating in a national accreditation process either in a center- or home-based program. (15.5)
10. List three advantages to the community when a program is quality-rated. (15.5)

Showcase Your Skills

In the Director's Showcase, Ilya and Maria decided to find out more about the quality rating system initiatives in their states to support quality improvement within their programs. To their delight, they found out that there were many resources to utilize. However, they were both concerned as to how their families and staff would respond to partaking in the quality improvement process.

Based on the information shared in each section of this chapter, it is now your turn to serve in the role of the licensing representative who assisted both Ilya and Maria. Your role will be to assist Ilya and Maria with writing letters to better inform the staff at Ilya's program and the parents at Maria's family child care home. Use the following points as your guide.

1. Access a state's quality rating system. Use this state's information for composing the letter for both Ilya and Maria's programs. (15.3)
2. Include the benefits and why they are important to either program and to the staff and parents. (15.2, 15.3, 15.5)
3. Describe the benefits to the care received by the children in Ilya and Maria's program. (15.1)

Matching

Match the following words with the correct definitions:

A. Business Administration Scale (BAS)
B. Classroom Assessment Scoring System® (CLASS)
C. Environment Rating Scales (ERS)
D. orientation training
E. professional development registry systems
F. Program Administration Scale (PAS)
G. training systems

1. Scales address the different age groups and evaluate a variety of categories, including physical environment; basic care; curriculum; interaction; schedule and program structure; and provisions for parents and staff.
2. Assesses 25 items grouped into nine categories in order to provide those in leadership positions with valuable information about their program's administrative practices.
3. Training process that describes program requirements and must be taken within a specified time frame found within state licensing standards.
4. Tool that looks at the teaching quality between teacher and child by measuring interactions, which has been linked to children's academic and lifelong success.
5. Systems that have determined levels and offer experience in the field for individuals interested in providing learning opportunities for others working in the field of early childhood education.
6. Formalized electronic systems that track an individual's education, experience, and professional development training.
7. Tool useful for family child care home providers that measures 10 areas in order to help providers set goals to improve and reduce risk.

References

Chapter 1

Administration for Community Living. (2021, May). *2020 profile of older Americans*. The Administration of Aging, an operating division of the U.S. Department of Health and Human services. https://acl.gov/aging-and-disability-in-america/data-and-research/profile-older-americans

Bump, J., et al. (2018). *US and the High Price of Child Care*. Child Care Aware® of America. https://usa.childcareaware.org/advocacy-public-policy/resources/research/costofcare/

Livington, G. (2018, April 25). *The changing profile of unmarried parents*. Pew Research Center. https://www.pewsocialtrends.org/2018/04/25/the-changing-profile-of-unmarried-parents/

Malik, R. (2019, June 20). *Working Families Are Spending Big Money on Child Care*, Washington: Center for American Progress. https://www.americanprogress.org/issues/early-childhood/reports/2019/06/20/471141/working-families-spending-big-money-child-care/

Matthews, T. J., & Hamilton, B. E. (2016, January). *Mean age of mothers is on the rise: United States, 2000-2014*. Centers for Disease Control, National Center for Health Statistics. https://www.cdc.gov/nchs/data/ databriefs/db232.pdf

Matos, K., Galinsky, E. & Bond, J. T. (2017). *National Study of Employers: 2016*. Society for Human Resource Management. https://www.shrm.org/hr-today/trends-and-forecasting/research-and-surveys/pages/national-study-of-employers.aspx

Motherly. (2019). *State of Motherhood Survey results*. https://www.mother.ly/2019-state-ofmotherhood-survey

NAEYC. (2018) *Staff-to-Child Ratio and Class Size*. https://www.naeyc.org/academy

Panday, S., & Bovino, B. A. (2017). *Declining labor force participation will weigh on US GDP growth—And Fed monetary policy*, S&P Global. https://www.spglobal.com/en/research-insights/articles/Declining-LaborForceParticipation-Will-Weigh-on-US-GDP-Growth-And-Fed-Monetary-Policy

Rnaji, U., & Salganicoff, A. (2014, October 20). *Data note: Balancing on shaky ground: Women, work, and family health*. Henry J. Kaiser Family Foundation. https://www.kff.org/womens-health-policy/issue-brief/data-notebalancing-on-shakyground-women-work-and-family-health/

Schmidt, E. (2018, July 31). *For the first time, 90 percent complete high school or more*. Census Bureau's Social, Economic and Housing Statistics Division. https://www.census.gov/library/stories/2018/07/educational-attainment.html

Thomason, S., Austin, L., Bernhardt, A., Dresser, L., Jacobs, K., & Whitebook, M. (2018, May 22). *At the wage floor: Covering homecare and early care and education workers in the new generation of minimum wage laws*. UC Berkeley Center for Labor Research and Education, UC Berkeley Center for the Study of Child Care Employment, and COWS at UWMadison. https://cscce.berkeley.edu/at-the-wage-floor/

US Census Bureau. (2018). *Median family income in the past 12 months—married couple with children and single female householder with own children*. American Community Survey, 2013-2017 5-year estimates, Table B19126. www.census.gov.

Workman, S. & Jessen-Howard, S. (2018, November 15). *Understanding the true price of child care for infants and toddlers*. Center for American Progress. https://www.americanprogress.org/issues/early-childhood/ reports/2018/11/15/460970/understanding-true-price-child-care-infants-toddlers

Chapter 2

Becker, D., McClelland, M., Loprinzi, P., & Trost, S. (2013). Physical activity, self-regulation, and early academic achievement in preschool children. *Early Education & Development, 25* (1), 56-70. https://doi.org/10.1080/10409289.2013.780505

Bohart, H., Charner, K., & Koralek, D. (2015). *Spotlight on Young Children: Exploring Play*. The National Association for the Education of Young Children.

Bulotsky-Shearer, R. J., Bell, R., Carter, T., & Dietrich, S. (2014). Peer play interactions and learning for low-income preschool children: The moderating role of classroom quality. *Early Education and Development, 25* (6), 815-840. https://doi.org/10.1080/10409289.2014.864214

Cavanaugh, D. K., Clemence, K. J., Teale, M., Rule, A. C., & Montgomery, S. E. (2017). Kindergarten scores, storytelling, executive function, and motivation improved through literacy-rich guided play. *Early Childhood Education Journal, 45* (6), 831-843. https://doi.org/10.1007/s10643-016-0832-8

Cohen, L. E., & Emmons, J. (2017). Block play: Spatial language with preschool and school-aged children. *Early Child Development & Care, 187* (5/6), 967-977. https://doi.org/10.1080/03004430.2016.1223064

Dodge, D. T. (2004). Early Childhood Curriculum Models: Why, What, and How Programs Use Them. *Child Care Information Exchange*.

Frede, E., & Ackerman, D. J. (2007, March). *Preschool curriculum decision-making: dimensions to consider*. NIEER Policy brief. https://nieer.org/policy-issue/policy-brief-preschool-curriculum-decision-making-dimensions-to-consider

Kisiel, J. F. (2003). Teacher, museums and worksheets: A closer look at the learning experience. *Journal of Science Teacher Education, 14* (1), 3-21. http://www.jstor.org/stable/43156305

Langford, R. (2010). Critiquing child-centered pedagogy to bring children and early childhood educators into the centre of a democratic pedagogy. *Contemporary Issues in Early Childhood, 11* (1), 113-127. https://doi.org/10.2304/ciec.2010.11.1.113

Larsen, S., & McCormick, K. K. (2020). Screencasts support early learning in math. *YC Young Children, 75* (4), 24-31. https://www.jstor.org/stable/27011125

Levine, D. G., & Ducharme, J. M. (2013). The effects of a teacher-child play intervention on classroom compliance in young children in child care settings. *Journal of Behavioral Education, 22* (1), 50-65. https://doi.org/10.1007/s10864-012-9163-z

McCrory, E., DeBrito, S. A., & Viding, E. (2014). Research review: The neurobiology and genetics of maltreatment and adversity. *Journal of Child Psychology and Psychiatry, 51* (10), 1079-1095. https://doi.org/10.1111/j.1469-7610.2010.02271.x

Nadelson, L. S., & Jordan, J. R. (2012). Student attitudes toward and recall of outside day: An environmental science field trip. *The Journal of Educational Research, 105* (3), 220–31. https://doi.org/10.1080/00220671.2011.576715

NAEYC. (2018). *Staff-to-Child Ratio and Class Size*. https://www.naeyc.org/academy

National Association for the Education of Young Children. (2021). *The 10*

NAEYC Program Standards. NAEYC. https://www.naeyc.org/our-work/families/10-naeyc-program-standards

National Association for the Education of Young Children. (2020, April). *Developmentally Appropriate Practice (DAP) Position Statement*. NAEYC. https://www.naeyc.org/resources/position-statements/dap/contents

National Center on Early Childhood Quality Assurance. (n.d.). *QRIS Resource Guide*. Retrieved September 22, 2021 from https://ecquality.acf.hhs.gov/about-qris

National Research Council. (2009). *Learning Science in Informal Environments: People, Places, and Pursuits.* The National Academies Press.

Ramani, G. B. (2012). Influence of a playful, child-directed context on preschool children's peer cooperation. *Merrill-Palmer Quarterly, 58* (2), 159-190. https://doi.org/10.2307/23098461

Ramani, G. B., & Eason., S. H. (2015). It all adds up: Learning early math through play and games. *Phi Delta Kappan, 96* (8), 27-32. https://kappanonline.org/early-math-play-games-ramani-eason/

Roskos, K. A. (2009). Play's potential in early literacy development. In *Encyclopedia on Early Childhood Development*, eds. R. E. Trembley, M. Bolvin, R. D Peters, 1-5, Montreal, Quebec: Centre of Excellence for Early Childhood Development and Strategic Knowledge Cluster on Early Childhood Development. www.child-encyclopedia.com/documents/Christie-RoskosANGxp.pdf

Savina, E. (2014). Does play promote self-regulation in children? *Early Child Development and Care, 184* (11), 1692-1705. https://doi.org/10.1080/03004430.2013.875541

Scribner-MacLean, M., & Kennedy, L. (2007). More than just a day away from school: Planning a great science field trip. *Science Scope 30* (8): 57-60. https://www.nsta.org/resources/science-sampler-more-just-day-away-school-planning-great-science-field-trip

Stagnitti, K., Bailey, A., Hudspeth Stevenson, E., Reynolds, E., & Kidd, E. (2016). An investigation into the effect of play-based instruction on the development of play skills and oral language. *Journal of Early Childhood Research, 14* (4), 389-406. https://doi.org/10.1177/1476718X15579741

Tayler, C. (2015). Learning in early childhood: Experiences, relationships and learning to be. *European Journal of Education, 50* (2), 160-174. https://doi.org/10.1111/ejed.12117

Trawick-Smith, J., Swaminathan, S., & Liu, X. (2016). The relationship of teacher-child play interactions to mathematics learning in preschool. *Early Childhood Research Quarterly, 45* (4), 1-17. https://doi.org/10.1080/03004430.2015.1054818

Tunks, K. W., & Allison, E. (2020). Our trip down to the bay: A model of experiential learning. *Young Children, 75* (4), 6-13. https://www.naeyc.org/resources/pubs/yc/sept2020/our-trip-down-to-the-bay

Wenner, M. (2009). The serious need for play. *Scientific American Mind, 20* (1), 1-11. https://www.scientificamerican.com/article/the-serious-need-for-play/

Chapter 3

National Association for the Education of Young Children. (2021). *The 10 NAEYC Program Standards*. NAEYC. https://www.naeyc.org/our-work/families/10-naeyc-program-standards

Chapter 4

Amezquita, R., & Tagawa, D. (2021). Everyone has a place to thrive: Positive perspectives on nature explore outdoor classrooms in the Los Angeles unified school district. *Exchange Press*. http://www.exchangepress.com/article/everyone-h/5025808/

Curtis, D., & Carter, M. (2014). *Designs for living and learning transforming early childhood environments* (2nd ed.) Redleaf Press.

Curtis, D., & Carter, M. (2008). *Learning together with young children: a curriculum framework for reflective teachers.* Redleaf Press.

Copple, C., & Bredekamp, S. (2009). *Developmentally appropriate practice in early childhood programs serving children from birth through age 8* (3rd ed.) NAEYC.

Dodge, D. (2004). *Early childhood curriculum models.* Child Care Information Exchange. https://exchangepress.com/library/5015571.pdf

Dombro, A. L., Colker, L., & Dodge, D. (1999). *The Creative Curriculum for Infants and Toddlers Revised Edition.* Teaching Strategies.

Giles, R., & Tunks, K. (2013). Building young scientists, developing scientific literacy through construction play. *Early Years Journal of the Association for the Education of Young Children, 34* (2), 22-27.

Greenman, J. (2017). *Caring Spaces, Learning Places: Children's Environments That Work.* Exchange Press.

Kisiel, J. (2003). Teacher, museums and worksheets: A closer look at the learning

experience. *Journal of Science Teacher Education 14*, 3-21.

Nadelson, L. S., & Jordan, J. R. (2012). Student attitudes toward and recall of outside day: An environmental science field trip. *The Journal of Educational Research, 105* (3), 220-231. https://doi.org/10.1080/00220671.2011.576715

National Association for the Education of Young Children. (2021, October 27). *10 NAEYC Program Standards*. NAEYC. https://www.naeyc.org/our-work/families/10-naeyc-program-standards

National Association for the Education of Young Children. (2019). *NAEYC early learning program accreditation standards and assessment items.* NAEYC.

National Association for the Education of Young Children. (2015). *Exploring math & science in preschool.* NAEYC.

National Research Council. (2009). *Learning Science in Informal Environments: People, Places, and Pursuits.* Washington, DC: The National Academies Press.

Petersen, S., & Wittmer, D. (2013). *Endless Opportunities for Infant and Toddler Curriculum: A Relationship-Based Approach.* (2nd ed.)

Russell, J. (2018). *Codename: Safe Children: How Secret Service Agents Are Helping Centers Prepare for Emergencies.* Exchange Press.

Scribner-MacLean, M., & Kennedy, L. (2007). More than just a day away from school: Planning a great science field trip. *Science Scope, 30* (8), 57-60.

Schickedanz, J., & Casbergue, R. (2004). *Writing in Preschool: Learning to Orchestrate Meaning and Marks.* International Reading Association.

Tunks, K., & Allison, E. (2020). Our trip down to the bay: A model of experiential learning. *Young Children, 75* (4), 6-13. https://www.naeyc.org/resources/pubs/yc/sept2020/our-trip-down-to-the-bay

Worth, K., & Hya Grollman, S. (2003). *Worms, Shadows, and Whirlpools: Science in the Early Childhood Classroom.* Education Development Center.

Chapter 5

Franco, B. (2015). Five questions asked at every teaching interview. *Teaching Young Children, 8* (4). https://www.naeyc.org/resources/pubs/tyc/apr2015/five-questions-asked-every-teaching-interview

Interlandi, J. (2018, January 9). Why are our most important teachers paid the least? *The New York Times Magazine.* https://www.nytimes.com/2018/01/09/magazine/why-are-our-most-important-teachers-paid-the-least.html

IOM (Institute of Medicine) and NRC (National Research Council). (2015). *Transforming the workforce for children birth through age 8: A unifying foundation.* The National Academies Press.

Main, C., & Yarbrough, K. (2018). *Transforming the Early Childhood Workforce: A Call to Action for the State of Illinois.* https://www2.illinois.gov/sites/OECD/Documents/Transforming%20the%20Early%20Childhood%20Workforce%20IL%20Report.pdf

National Association for the Education of Young Children. (2022). *NAEYC early learning program accreditation standards and assessment items.* NAEYC.

Snyder, B. (2018) The components of high quality child care. *Child Care Exchange.*

Chapter 6

101st Congress. (1989). Military Child Care Act of 1989. https://www.congress.gov/bill/101st-congress/house-bill/1277

National Association for the Education of Young Children. (2019). *Advancing Equity in Early Childhood Education Position Statement.* NAEYC https://www.naeyc.org/resources/position-statements/equity

Chapter 8

Andress, B. (1998). *Music for young children.* Wadsworth.

Berk, L., & Ashkenaz, J. F. (2019). *Child Development* (9th ed.). Pearson.

Fromberg, D. (2002). *Play and Meaning in Early Childhood Education.* Allyn & Bacon.

Greenman, J. (2007). Caring spaces, learning places. *Exchange Press.*

Katz, L. (1987). What should young children be learning? *ERIC Clearinghouse on Elementary and Early Childhood Education.*

Luckenbill, J., Subramaniam, A., & Thompson, J. (2019). *This is play: environments and interactions that engage infants and toddlers.* NAEYC.

National Association for the Education of Young Children. (2021). *The 10 NAEYC Program Standards.* NAEYC. https://www.naeyc.org/our-work/families/10-naeyc-program-standards

National Association for the Education of Young Children. (2020, April). *Developmentally Appropriate Practice (DAP) Position Statement.* NAEYC. https://www.naeyc.org/resources/position-statements/dap/contents

Wittmer, D., & Petersen, S. (2006). *Infant and Toddler Development and Responsive Program Planning: A Relationship-Based Approach.* Pearson.

Yogman, M., Garner, A., Hutchinson, J., Hirsh-Pasek, K., & Golinkoff, R. (2018). The power of play: A pediatric role in enhancing development in young children. *Pediatrics, 14* (2), 2018-2058. https://doi.org/10.1542/peds.2018-2058

Chapter 9

American Academy of Pediatrics (AAP). (2016). *Bright Futures in Practice: Oral Health Pocket Guide.* American Academy of Pediatrics. https://brightfutures.aap.org/Bright%20Futures%20Documents/BF4_OralHealth.pdf

American Academy of Pediatrics (AAP). (2016). *Bright Futures in Practice: Promoting safety and injury prevention.* American Academy of Pediatrics. https://brightfutures.aap.org/Bright%20Futures%20Documents/BF4_Safety.pdf

American Academy of Pediatrics (AAP). (2011). Ultraviolet radiation: A hazard to children and adolescents. *Pediatrics, 127* (3), 599-597. https://doi.org/10.1542/peds.2010-3501

Administration for Children and Families, U.S. Department of Health and Human Services. (2015). *Caring for our children basics: Health and safety foundations for early care and education.* http://www.acf.hhs.gov/programs/ecd/caring-for-our-children-basics.

Centers for Disease Control and Prevention (CDC). (2021, September 16). *Food Safety.* CDC. https://www.cdc.gov/foodsafety/

Centers for Disease Control and Prevention (CDC). (2021, August 10). *When and how to wash your hands.* CDC. https://www.cdc.gov/handwashing/when-how-handwashing.html

Centers for Disease Control and Prevention (CDC). (2016, July 26). *Diaper-changing steps for child care settings.* CDC. https://www.cdc.gov/healthywater/hygiene/diapering/childcare.html

Centers for Disease Control and Prevention (CDC). (2009, December 29). *Guideline for Disinfection and Sterilization in Healthcare Facilities, 2008.* CDC. https://www.cdc.gov/hicpac/disinfection_sterilization/6_0disinfection.html

McConnico, N, Boynton-Jarrett, R., Bailey, C., & Nandi, M. A. (2016). Framework for trauma-sensitive schools. Infusing trauma-informed practices into early childhood education systems. *Zero to Three, 36* (5), 36-44.

National Association for the Education of Young Children. (2021). *The 10 NAEYC Program Standards.* NAEYC. https://www.naeyc.org/our-work/families/10-naeyc-program-standards

U.S. Department of Health and Human Services, Children's Bureau. (2022). *Mandatory Reporters of Child Abuse and Neglect. Child Welfare Information Gateway.* https://www.childwelfare.gov/topics/systemwide/laws-policies/statutes/manda/

Chapter 11

Bloom, P. J. (2012). *Measuring Work Attitudes in the Early Childhood Setting: Technical Manual for the Early Childhood Job Satisfaction Survey and Early Childhood Work Environment Survey* (2nd ed.). McCormick Center for Early Childhood Leadership.

Bloom, P. J., Hentschel, A., & Bella, J. (2016). *A Great Place to Work: Creating a Healthy Organizational Climate* (2nd ed.). New Horizons Educational Consultants and Learning Resources.

Biddle, J. K. (2012). *The Three Rs of Leadership.* HighScope Press.

Hill, L. A., & Lineback, K. (2011). *Being the Boss: The 3 Imperatives for Becoming a Great Leader.* Harvard Business Review Press.

Leekeenan, D., & Ponte, I. C. (2018). *From Survive to Thrive: A Director's Guide for Leading an Early Childhood Program.* The National Association for the Education of Young Children.

McGregor, D. (2006). *The Human Side of Enterprise* (1st ed.). McGraw Hill.

NAEYC Code of Ethical Conduct Supplement for Early Childhood Program Administrators. (2011, May). https://www.naeyc.org/sites/default/files/globally-shared/downloads/PDFs/resources/position-statements/Supplement%20PS2011.pdf NAEYC (2011).

Chapter 12

Bruno, H. E. (2007, September). Problem solving to prevent power struggles. *Young Children. 62* (5): 26-32.

NAEYC. (2022). *NAEYC Early Learning Program Accreditation Standards and Assessment Items.* https://www.naeyc.org/sites/default/files/globally-shared/downloads/PDFs/accreditation/early-learning/2022elpstandardsandassessmentitems-compressed.pdf

NAEYC. (2019). *Advancing Equity in Early Childhood Education Position Statement.* https://www.naeyc.org/resources/position-statements/equity

Shurtleff-Ainscough, R. (2016). Confronting Workplace Bullying. *Exchange.* http://exchangepress.com/article/confronting-workplace-bullying/5022822/

Chapter 13

Bruno, H. E. (2007, September). Problem solving to prevent power struggles. *Young Children., 62* (5): 26-32.

Bruno, H. E., & M. L. Copeland. (1999). If the director isn't direct, can the team have direction? *Leadership Quest, 3* (1): 6–8.

Leekeenan, D., & Ponte, I. C. (2018). *From Survive to Thrive: A Director's Guide for Leading an Early Childhood Program*. The National Association for the Education of Young Children.

NAEYC (2011). *NAEYC Code of Ethical Conduct Supplement for Early Childhood Program Administrators*. https://www. naeyc.org/sites/default/files/globally- shared/downloads/PDFs/resources/ position-statements/Supplement%20 PS2011.pdf

O'Neill, C., & Brinkerhoff, M. (2017). *Five Elements of Collective Leadership for Early Childhood Professionals*. Redleaf Press.

Pontus, C., & Scherrer, D. (2011, April). *Is it lateral violence, bullying or workplace harassment?* Massachusetts Nurses Association. https://www.massnurses. org/2011/04/15/is-it-lateral-violence- bullying-or-workplace-harassment/events/ archive/2011/p/openItem/6082

Shurtleff-Ainscough, R. (2016). Confronting Workplace Bullying. *Exchange*. http://exchangepress.com/article/ confronting-workplace-bullying/5022822/

Tannen, D. (2007). *You Just Don't Understand: Women and Men in Conversation*. Ballantine.

Tschannen-Moran, M. (2014). *Trust Matters: Leadership for Successful Schools*. Jossey-Bass.

Valentino, M. M. *Life Strategies for Dealing with Bullies* [PowerPoint Slides]. Nursing 2015. https://nursing2015.wordpress. com/blue-team/blue-team-documents/ blue-team-ii/

Chapter 15

NAEYC. (2019). *Professional Standards and Competencies for Early Childhood Educators*. https://www.naeyc.org/sites/ default/files/globally-shared/downloads/ PDFs/resources/position-statements/ standards_and_competencies_ps.pdf

For Further Reading

Chapter 1

Bloom, P. J. (2014). *Leadership in Action: How Effective Directors Get Things Done*. New Horizons.

Buckingham, M., & Clifton, D. O. (2001). *Now, Discover Your Strengths*. Gallup Press.

Build Initiative. (2017). Continuous quality improvement in early childhood and school age programs: An update from the field. http://qrisnetwork.org/sites/all/files/session/resources/Continuous%20Quality%20Improvement%20in%20Early%20Childhood%20and%20School%20Age%20Programs%20-%20An%20Update%20from%20the%20Field.pdf

Carter, M., Casio, L. M., & Curtis, D. (2020). *The Visionary Director: A Handbook for Dreaming, Organizing, and Improvising in Your Center* (3rd ed.). Redleaf Press.

ChildCare Aware of America (n.d.). *The US and the High Cost of Child Care: 2018*. https://www.childcareaware.org/costofcare/

Collins, J. (2001). *Good to Great: Why Some Companies Make the Leap and Others Don't*. HarperBusiness.

Feeney, S., & Freeman, N. K. (2018). *Ethics and the Early Childhood Educator: Using the NAEYC Code* (3rd ed.). The National Association for the Education of Young Children.

Institute of Medicine, & National Research Council (2015). *Transforming the Workforce for Children Birth Through Age 8: A Unifying Foundation* (B. B. Kelly & L. Allen, Eds.). The National Academies Press.

Kouzes, J. M., & Posner, B. Z. (2017). *The Leadership Challenge: How to Make Extraordinary Things Happen in Organizations* (6th ed.). Jossey-Bass.

Maxwell, J. (2002). *Leadership 101: What Every Leader Needs to Know*. Nashville, TN. Thomas Nelson.

NAEYC (2011, May). *NAEYC Code of Ethical Conduct*. naeyc.org/sites/default/files/globally-shared/downloads/PDFs/resources/position-statements/Supplement%20PS2011.pdf

Pianta, R., Downer, J., & Hamre, B. (2016). Quality in early education classrooms: Definitions, gaps, and systems. *The Future of Children, 26*(2), 119-137. https://doi.org/10.1353/foc.2016.0015

Sykes, M. (2015). The Role of knowledge in leadership. *Exchange*, 8-10.

http://exchangepress.com/article/the-role-of-knowledge-in-leadership/5022308/

Tonyan, H. A. (2017). Opportunities to practice what is locally valued: An ecocultural perspective on quality in family child care homes. *Early Education and Development, 28*(6), 727-744.

Chapter 2

Barnes, C., & Nolan, S. (2019). Professionals, friends, and confidants: After-school staff as social support to low-income parents. *Children and Youth Services Review, 98*(5), 238-251. https://doi.org/10.1016/j.childyouth.2019.01.004

Crawford, S. K., Stafford, K. N., Phillips, S. M., Scott, K. J., & Tucker, P. (2014). Strategies for inclusion in play among children with physical disabilities in childcare centers: An integrative review. *Physical and Occupational Therapy in Pediatrics, 34*(4), 404-423. https://doi.org/10.3109/01942638.2014.904470

Creating a Yes! environment: Supporting creativity and exploration. *Teaching Young Children, 12*(3), 22-23.

Culkin, M. L. (1999). *Managing Quality in Young Children's Programs: The Leader's Role*. Teachers College Press.

Groves Gillespie, L., & Greenberg, J. D. (2017). Rocking and rolling: Empowering infants' and toddlers' learning through scaffolding. *Young Children, 72*(2), 90-92.

Horn, E., Kang, J., Classen, A. I., Butera, G., Palmer, S., Lieber, J., Friesen, A., & Mihai, A. (2016). *Role of universal design for learning and differentiation in inclusive preschools*. (pp. 55-66). DEC Recommended Practices Monograph Series No. 2.

Humphries, J., & Rains, K. (2017). *A Fighting Chance: Supporting Young Children Experiencing Disruptive Change*. Redleaf Press.

Keyser, J. (2017). *From Parents to Partners: Building a Family-Centered Early Childhood Program*. Redleaf Press.

La Paro, K. M., & Gloeckler, L. (2015). The context of child care for toddlers: The "Experience Expectable Environment." *Early Childhood Education Journal, 44*(2). https://doi.org/10.1007/s10643-015-0699-0

Masterson, M. (2018). *Let's Talk Toddlers: A Practical Guide to High-Quality Teaching*. Redleaf Press.

Maxwell, L. E. (2007). Competency in child care settings: The role of the physical environment. *Environment and Behavior, 39*(2), 229-245.

McMullen, M. B., & Apple, P. (2012). Babies (and their families) on board! Directors juggle the key elements of infant/toddler care and education. *Young Children, 67*(4), 42-48.

Paluta, L. M., Leeann, L., Anderson-Butcher, D., Gibson, A., & Iachini, A. L. (2016). Examining the quality of 21st century community learning center after-school programs: Current practices and their relationship to outcomes. *Children & Schools, 38*(1), 49-56.

Tonyan, H. A. (2017). Opportunities to practice what is locally valued: An ecocultural perspective on quality in family child care homes. *Early Education and Development, 28*(6), 727-744.

Walsh, P. (2019). Making the most of the physical environment. *Educating Young Children: Learning and Teaching in the Early Childhood Years, 17*(3), 14-17.

Chapter 3

(2017). Three Principles to Improve Outcomes for Children and Families. *Center on the Developing Child at Harvard University*. https://www.fatherhood.gov/sites/default/files/resource_files/e000004063.pdf

(2019). From a Nation at Risk to a Nation at Hope: Recommendations from the National Commission on Social, Emotional, & Academic Development. *Aspen Institute*.

ChildCare Aware of America (n.d.). *Choosing Quality Child Care*. https://www.childcareaware.org/families/choosing-quality-child-care/

ChildCare.gov (n.d.). *What Is Child Care Licensing*. https://childcare.gov/consumer-education/child-care-licensing-and-regulations

McGinnis, M. H., Dicker, B. S., & Getskow, V. (2016). The incident report: A discussion about program liability. *Exchange*. http://exchangepress.com/article/the-incident-report/5022832/

NAFCC (2019). *Benchmarks to quality*. National Association for Family Child

Care. https://nafcc.org/wp-content/uploads/2021/03/Benchmarks-2020-English.pdf

National Association for the Education of Young Children (n.d.). *NAEYC Early Learning Program Accreditation Standards and Assessment Items.* https://www.naeyc.org/sites/default/files/globally-shared/downloads/PDFs/accreditation/early-learning/standards_assessment_2019.pdf

Schulman, K., Matthews, H., Blank, H., & Ewen, D. (2012). A count for quality: Child care center directors on rating and improvement systems. *National Women's Law Center & CLASP.* https://nwlc.org/wp-content/uploads/2012/02/ACountforQualityQRISReport.pdf

U.S. Department of Health & Human Services (n.d.). *QRIS Resource Guide.* QRIS Resource Guide. https://ecquality.acf.hhs.gov/resource-guide

U.S. EEOC (n.d.). *Your Employment Rights as an Individual with a Disability.* U.S. Equal Employment Opportunity Commission. https://www.eeoc.gov/laws/guidance/your-employment-rights-individual-disability

U.S. Small Business Administration. (2023, May 3). *10 steps to start your business.* https://www.sba.gov/business-guide/10-steps-start-your-business

Yoshikawa, H., Weiland, C., Brooks-Gunn, J., Burchinal, M., Espinosa, L., Gormley, W. T., Ludwig, J. W., Magnuson, K., Phillips, D., & Zaslow, M. (2013). Investing in our future: The evidence base on preschool. *Foundation for Child Development.* https://www.fcd-us.org/the-evidence-base-on-preschool/

Zaslow, M., Anderson, R., Redd, Z., Wessel, J., Daneri, P., Green, K., Cavadel, E. W., Tarullo, L., Burchinal, M., & Martinez-Beck, I. (2016). *Quality Thresholds, Features, and Dosage in Early Care and Education: Introduction and Literature Review.* Monogr Soc Res Child Dev, 81(2), 7-26. https://doi.org/10.1111/mono.12236

Chapter 4

American Academy of Pediatric. (2014, July 16). *Energy Out: Daily Physical Activity Recommendations.* Healthy Living. https://www.healthychildren.org/English/healthy-living/fitness/Pages/Energy-Out-Daily-Physical-Activity-Recommendations.aspx

Centers for Disease Control and Prevention. (2022, July 22). *Youth Physical Activity Guidelines.* CDC Healthy Schools. https://www.cdc.gov/healthyschools/physicalactivity/guidelines.htm

ChildCare Aware of America. (2017, August 15). *What to Look for in a Quality Afterschool Program.* https://info.childcareaware.org/blog/look-quality-afterschool-program

Elkins, A. (2019). Creating a Yes! environment: Supporting creativity and exploration. *Teaching Your Children, 12*(3), 22-23.

La Paro, K. M., & Gloeckler, L. (2015). The context of child care for toddlers: The "Experience Expectable Environment." *Early Childhood Education Journal, 44*(2). https://doi.org/10.1007/s10643-015-0699-0

Masterson, M. (2018). *Let's Talk Toddlers: A Practical Guide to High-Quality Teaching.* Redleaf Press.

McMullen, M. B., & Apple, P. (2012). Babies (and their families) on board! Directors juggle the key elements of infant/toddler care and education. *Young Children, 67*(4), 42-48.

Norris, D. J. (2017). Comparing language and literacy environments in two types of infant-toddler child care centers. *Early Childhood Education Journal, 45*(1), 95-101.

Tonyan, H. A. (2017). Opportunities to practice what is locally valued: An ecocultural perspective on quality in family child care homes. *Early Education and Development, 28*(6), 727-744.

Walsh, P. (2019). Making the most of the physical environment. *Educating Young Children: Learning and Teaching in the Early Childhood Years, 17*(3), 14-17.

Wang, X. C., Bension, K., C. E., & Lin, B. (2019). A guided, exploration-based visual arts program for preschoolers. *Young Children, 74*(1), 72-80.

Williams, K. E. (2018). Moving to the beat: Using music, rhythm, and movement to enhance self-regulation in early childhood classrooms. *International Journal of Early Childhood, 50*(1), 85-100. https://doi.org/10.1007/s13158-018-0215-y

Chapter 5

Allen, L., & Kelly, B. B. (2015). Transforming the workforce for children birth through age 8: A unifying foundation. *National Academies Press.* https://doi.org/10.17226/19401

Breffni, L. (2017). Enhancing the competence of teacher assistants. *Exchange.* http://exchangepress.com/article/enhancing-the-competence-of-teacher-assistants/5023340/

Click, P. M., & Karkos, K. (2013). *Administration of Programs for Young Children* (9th ed.). Cengage Learning.

Franco, B. (2015). Five questions asked at every teaching interview. *Teaching Young Children, 8*(4).

Heng, A. C. (2019). Hiring the right person. In R. Neugebauer and B. Neugebauer (eds.), *The Art of Leadership: Managing Early Childhood Organizations* (rev. ed.). Exchange Press.

Chapter 7

[Duke University—The Fuqua School of Business]. (2017, December 21). *Walmart CEO Doug McMillon on culture* [Video]. YouTube. https://www.youtube.com/watch?v=c_dxWKQxjIs

[Ed. Flicks]. (2019). *Basic Enrollment Building Strategies* [Video]. Exchange Press Video Clip Library. https://www.childcareexchange.com/ed-flicks/

[Ed. Flicks]. (2019). *Creative Marketing Ideas* [Video]. Exchange Press Video Clip Library. https://www.childcareexchange.com/ed-flicks/

[Ed. Flicks]. (2019). *Standing Out from the Competition* [Video]. Exchange Press Video Clip Library. https://www.childcareexchange.com/ed-flicks/

Kotler, P. (2003). *Marketing Insights from A to Z: 80 Concepts Every Manager Needs to Know.* Wiley.

Maxwell, J. C. (2002). *Leadership 101: What Every Leader Needs to Know.* HarperCollins Leadership.

Wassom, J. (2004). Do they see what you see? Marking to a new generation of child care buyers. *Exchange,* 6-8. http://exchangepress.com/article/do-they-see-what-you-see/5015606/

Wassom, J. (2004). Niche marketing: Branding your early child care and education business without getting burned. *Exchange,* 30-31. http://exchangepress.com/article/niche-marketing/5016030/

Chapter 9

(2021, September 6). *Infant-Toddler Child Care Fact Sheet.* Zero to Three. https://www.zerotothree.org/resource/infant-toddler-child-care-fact-sheet/

[Healthy Futures]. (2020). *Managing Infectious Diseases in Early Education and Child Care Settings: A Learning and Training Tool* [Video]. YouTube. https://www.youtube.com/watch?feature=youtu.be&utm_content=&utm_medium=email&utm_name=&utm_source=govdelivery&utm_term=&v=n83I1uaZuks

Electronic Learning Community (ELC) (2011). *Principles of universal design applied to early learning environments.* Johns Hopkins University School of Education. http://olms.cte.jhu.edu/3868

Lieber, J. (2018, August 14). *Universal Design for Learning Brings Accessibility to Early Childhood Education.* College of Education. https://education.umd.edu/news/08-14-18-universal-design-learning-brings-accessibility-early-childhood-education-0

Masterson, M. (2018). *Let's Talk Toddlers: A Practical Guide to High-Quality Teaching.* Redleaf Press.

Maxwell, L. E. (2007). Competency in child care settings: The role of the physical environment. *Environment and Behavior, 39*(2), 229-245.

McGinnis, M. H., Dicker, B. S., & Getskow, V. (2016). The incident report: A discussion about program liability. *Exchange.* http://exchangepress.com/article/the-incident-report/5022832/

McMullen, M. B., & Apple, P. (2012). Babies (and their families) on board! Directors juggle the key elements of infant/toddler care and education. *Young Children, 67*(4), 42-48.

Nitzke, S., Riley, D., Ramminger, A., & Jacobs, G. (2014). *Rethinking Nutrition: Connecting Science and Practice in Early Childhood Settings.* Redleaf Press.

Shonkoff, J. P. (2016). Capitalizing on advances in science to reduce the health consequences of early childhood adversity. *JAMA Pediatr, 170*(10), 1003-1007.

Tonyan, H. A. (2017). Opportunities to practice what is locally valued: An ecocultural perspective on quality in family child care homes. *Early Education and Development, 28*(6), 727-744.

Walsh, P. (2019). Making the most of the physical environment. *Educating Young Children: Learning and Teaching in the Early Childhood Years, 17*(3), 14-17.

Chapter 10

(2022, July 18). How to Communicate with Parents. Zero to Three. https://www.zerotothree.org/resource/how-to-communicate-with-parents/

Arnold, M. E. (2004). *Effective Communication Techniques for Child Care* (1st ed.). Cengage Learning.

Berger, E., & Riojas-Cortez, M. (2019). *Families as Partners in Education: Families and Schools Working Together* (10th ed.). Pearson.

Click, P. M., & Karkos, K. (2013). *Administration of Programs for Young Children* (9th ed.). Cengage Learning.

Copple, C. (2003). *A World of Difference: Reading on Teaching Young Children in a Diverse Society.* National Association for the Education of Young Children.

Cunningham, B., & Dorsey, B. (2004). Out of sight but not out of mind: The harmful absence of men. *Exchange,* (156), 42-43.

Diffily, D. (2003). *Teachers and Families Working Together* (1st ed.). Pearson.

Dismuke, F., Parks, N., & Jablon, J. (2017). Deepening families' understanding of children's learning in centers. *Teaching Young Children, 10*(4). https://www.naeyc.org/resources/pubs/tyc/apr2017/deepening-families-understanding

Gadsden, V., & Ray, A. (2001). Engaging fathers: Issues and considerations for early childhood educators. *Teaching Young Children, 57*(6), 32-42.

Hearron, P., & Hildebrand, V. (2014). *Management of Child Development Centers* (8th ed.). Pearson.

Hewes, D. W., & Leatherman, J. M. (2004). *An Administrator's Guidebook to Early Care and Education Programs.* Pearson.

Olsen, G. W., & Fuller, M. L. (2007). *Home-School Relations: Working Successfully with Parents and Families* (3rd ed.). Allyn & Bacon.

Scully, P., Stites, M., Roberts-King, H., & Barbour, C. (2018). *Families, Schools, and Communities: Building Partnerships for Educating Children* (7th ed.). Pearson.

Stephens, K. (2004). Sometimes the customer "isn't" always right: Problem solving with parents. *Exchange,* (158), 68-73.

Taylor, B. J. (2001). *Early Childhood Program Management: People and Procedures* (4th ed.). Pearson.

Chapter 12

(n.d.). *Day Care Facilities Emergency Planning Guide.* Bureau of Plans Pennsylvania Emergency Management Agency. https://www.nrc.gov/docs/ML0604/ML060460273.pdf

(n.d.). *School and Child Care Safety.* Pennsylvania Emergency Management Agency. https://www.pema.pa.gov/Preparedness/Planning/Community-Planning/School-Safety/Pages/default.aspx

Click, P. M., & Karkos, K. (2013). *Administration of Programs for Young Children* (9th ed.). Cengage Learning.

Freeman, N., Decker, C. A., & Decker, J. R. (2016). *Management of Child Development Centers* (11th ed.). Pearson.

Hearron, P., & Hildebrand, V. (2014). *Management of Child Development Centers* (8th ed.). Pearson.

Hewes, D. W., & Leatherman, J. M. (2004). *An Administrator's Guidebook to Early Care and Education Programs.* Pearson.

Jack, G. H. (2004). *The Business of Child Care: Management and Financial Strategies* (1st ed.). Cengage Learning.

Russell, S., & Rogers, J. (2005). T.E.A.C.H. Early childhood: Providing strategies and solutions for the early childhood workforce. *Exchange,* (162), 69-72.

Chapter 14

Maravelas, A. (2005). *How to Reduce Workplace Conflict and Stress: How Leaders and Their Employees Can Protect Their Sanity and Productivity From Tension and Turf Wars.* The Career Press, Inc.

Sockolov, M. (2018). *Practicing Mindfulness: 75 Essential Meditations to Reduce Stress, Improve Mental Health, and Find Peace in the Everyday.* Althea Press.

Teasdale, J., Williams, M., & Segal, Z. (2014). *The Mindful Way Workbook.* The Guildford Press.

Glossary

A

accreditation. Officially recognizes that a program meets certain standards of quality and has successfully completed the accrediting organization's evaluation process and met its criteria. (3)

accreditation performance criteria. Activities a program must demonstrate in order to prove it meets the program standards. (3)

ad hoc committee. Committee that reports to the board of directors as an advisory committee that provides advice before making decisions related to health and safety. (9)

administrative staff. Those employees with organizational and planning skills who provide direction for the total program. (5)

advisory board. Board that studies issues and makes recommendations to a program, but those recommendations are not required to be carried out. (3)

advocates. People who speak out or act on behalf of their beliefs. (11)

American with Disabilities Act (ADA). Federal regulation that provides for building access for all persons with disabilities and handicaps, as well as prohibiting discrimination in hiring or enrollment policies. (3)

associate play. Involves interacting with others with limited cooperation necessary. (8)

attachment theory. Bowlby's theory proposes that children are born with an internal need to form attachments with the significant adults in their lives. (8)

atypical development. Abnormal behaviors. (8)

audit. Examines the accuracy of records and verifies expenses. (6)

B

behaviorist. Children's learning is believed to occur as they have more complicated interactions with the environment that is either positively or negatively reinforced in a highly structured and teacher-controlled environment. (2)

behaviorist theory. Theory put forth by Watson and Skinner that states that children's development was based on either positively or negatively reinforced behaviors that a child displays and an adult controls. (8)

blended family. Family type that brings two unrelated families into one household. (1)

block center. Play area that contains blocks of all shapes and sizes that encourages children to create complicated building projects. (4)

bonding insurance. Type of insurance that protects a program against financial loss due to the actions of officers or staff who are authorized to handle program money. (3)

break-even point. Place within the budget that enough money is available to cover basic expenses. (6)

budget. Spending plan. (6)

burnout. Physical and mental exhaustion that results from prolonged periods of stress or frustration. (12)

Business Administration Scale (BAS). Tool useful for family child care home providers that measures 10 areas in order to help providers set goals to improve and reduce risk. (15)

business plan. Plan required by banks or other lending agencies that require significant details about the program's financial planning and the owner's necessary skills to carry it out. (6)

C

cash flow. Movement of money into and out of a program's bank account. (6)

cash lag. Situations when money is owed to the early childhood program but has not yet been received. (6)

cash reserve. Money set aside to cover times when money is not flowing into the program. (6)

center-based care. Care for larger groups of children in settings that have been organized specifically for their use. (1)

Child Care and Development Fund (CCDF). A consolidated fund of multiple federal dollar streams that goes directly to states to support low-income families with child care expenses. (1)

child care centers. Facilities that are licensed by the state in which they operate and provide daily programming of appropriate activities carried out by trained staff members who work within environments that have adequate equipment and safe, healthy routines. (1)

child care cooperatives. New model of child care programs that are sponsored by parents, a business, or multiple businesses interested in providing care for a designated group of children. (1)

Child Care Resource and Referral (CCR&R). State-funded agency used by employers to locate child care services within the community and regions. (1)

Child Development Associate (CDA). Credential approved as acceptable preparation for a variety of early childhood-related jobs according to state-mandated regulations. (1)

Note: The number in parentheses following each definition indicates the chapter in which the term can be found.

child-directed play. Play that allows the child to choose their activities during free play. (2)

child medical and accident insurance. Type of insurance that provides medical and hospital costs for a child who is injured. (3)

Civil Rights compliance. Federal regulation that prohibits discrimination in hiring and other program policies. (3)

Classroom Assessment Scoring System® (CLASS®). Tool that looks at the teaching quality between teacher and child by measuring interactions, which has been linked to children's academic and lifelong success. (15)

class size. All of the children assigned for the majority of the day to a specific teacher or group of teachers within an assigned classroom space. (5)

classroom staff. Those people who work directly with the children. (5)

climate. Overall atmosphere and "feel" of the program. (11)

code of ethics. List of rules that serves as a guide for proper behavior and making hard decisions involving the needs and rights of children, families, and staff. (11)

cognitive development. Refers to a child's brain growth and overall functioning. (8)

cognitive theory. Piaget's and Vygotsky's theory that proposed a set of stages that recognized an adult's interactions assisted with cognitive functioning due to a child's social and cultural upbringing. (8)

cohabitating parents. Individuals who share a biological child, or one person is the biological parent of a child, that live with a significant other but are not married. (1)

communication. Process of clarifying the perceptions that people have of each other by way of listening, sensing, and asking clarifying questions. (13)

conference. Meeting between teacher and caregivers. (10)

conflict. Strong disagreement between two or more people or a difference that prevents agreement. (13)

conflict resolution. Process that aims to not only find a solution to a problem but also improve relationships. (13)

conflict-partnership pathway. Allows everyone to be heard and supports the development of expectations that will contribute to solutions. (13)

consortium model. Child care cooperative that is composed of multiple businesses working together within industrial parks or commercial developments to establish a child care facility as a benefit for the employees within those areas. (1)

constructivist. Children construct their knowledge of the world through having a wide range of concrete experiences in a variety of areas. (2)

contract. Legal agreement signed by the new employee and the program. (5)

controlling. Function of management that includes regularly monitoring and evaluating the program as well as taking action, when necessary, to maintain and improve its quality. (11)

cooperative play. Involves interacting with others due to similar interests in both the activity and the children involved in the playing. (8)

co-pay. Amount still needed for tuition after financial support that is the family's responsibility to pay. (6)

cost coding. Identifying each major budget category with a number code. (6)

cost-per-child analysis. Formula that identifies the costs of providing service to each group on a monthly or daily basis divided by the number of children enrolled. (6)

creative art area. Space where children can engage in multiple types of art activities and create opportunities for creative expression. (4)

culturally competent. When a person has a keen sense of self-awareness about personal cultural identity and attitudes or views about human differences, while also becoming knowledgeable about the cultural identities of others they work with or serve. (14)

culture. Reflects the expectations of a program based on the ways that things are done that stem from the program's beliefs, values, norms, and relationships. (11)

curriculum. Framework that pulls together developmentally appropriate practices for all ages of children cared for in an early childhood program environment. (4)

D

Department of Labor Fair Wage and Standards Act. Federal act that identifies minimum wage and employment conditions. (3)

developmentally appropriate practices. Methods that promote optimal development and learning through a strengths-based, play-based approach to joyful, engaged learning. (2)

directing. Function of management that involves how the director influences others to successfully meet their responsibilities. (11)

directors' and officers' insurance. Type of insurance that covers legal fees in case of a lawsuit. (3)

director's credential. Credential that spells out specific educational requirements for leaders of early childhood programs, including ongoing professional development expectations. (1)

disability insurance. Type of insurance that protects program workers from lost income if they become disabled and cannot work. (3)

diversity. Reflecting various cultures, races, socio-economic level, genders, age groups, and religious backgrounds. (14)

domestic violence. Intimate partner or family abuse that can be physical, mental, emotional, or financial. (14)

dramatic play area. Play area designed to encourage and enhance children's pretend play. (4)

drop-in care. Type of care program often located in or near shopping centers or recreational areas that allows parents to have a few hours to themselves while their children receive care in pleasant, well-supervised settings. (1)

E

Early Head Start. Program launched in 1995 that serves children from birth to three years old and provides the same benefits as the Head Start program. (1)

Early Intervention Program (EI). Federally mandated program that provides specialty services for infants and toddlers with developmental delays. (9)

elementary school. Location that typically services children ages Pre-Kindergarten to fourth grade. (1)

emotional development. How a child learns to recognize their own feelings while also interacting with significant adults and peers. (8)

empathy. Ability to understand how others feel and to recognize their point of view. (11)

employee assistance programs. Employer-sponsored program that offers free confidential assessments, short-term counseling and referral, and follow-up services for staff facing personal or workplace problems. (14)

employee model. Child care cooperative in which a business provides the space and initial financing to make a child care facility operable for their employees. (1)

employment at will. Hiring an employee without using a contract. (5)

encumbered funds. Money for which the program has made a commitment but has not yet paid out. (6)

entrepreneur. Person who is willing to expand an opportunity and invest their own time, money, and skills to get either their service or product in place. (1)

Environment Rating Scales (ERS). Scales address the different age groups and evaluate a variety of categories, including physical environment; basic care; curriculum; interaction; schedule and program structure; and provisions for parents and staff. (15)

equitable programming. Fair chance to learn, grow, and flourish for all individuals within the program environment. (14)

external roles and responsibilities. Direct reach outward from the center and into the community, and engaging with a community in a variety of ways to support and grow a program. (11)

F

Family and Medical Leave Act (FMLA). Act passed by Congress that entitles eligible employees of covered employers to take unpaid, job-protected leave for the birth of a child, to include the care of a newborn child within one year of birth. (1)

family engagement. Developing a relationship with and supporting caregivers. (10)

family style. Takes place when children and teachers sit together to eat a meal. (8)

fiscal year. Set period during which a particular budget or source of grant money is in effect. (6)

fixed expenditures. Expenses to which the program is committed that are predictable and do not vary significantly. (6)

food insecurity. Occurs when adults and children do not have adequate food resources and experience. (14)

for-profit programs. Businesses operated to make a profit for the owners. (6)

free play. Occurs when teachers plan opportunities for children to enhance their creativity, use their imagination, problem-solve age-appropriate tasks, and use their social skills with peers. (8)

G

gossip. Telling information that has not been confirmed as true. (13)

governing board. Legal entity that is authorized to actually operate a program, including making legal and financial commitments for the program. (3)

grievance procedure. Process by which employees can issue a complaint if they feel they have been unfairly treated. (12)

group time. Spending time together as a class. (8)

guarantee. Item purchased is backed by the manufacturer and is expected to last for at least a certain period, and covers repairs if the product is defective or if it breaks under normal use; also known as a warranty. (6)

H

Head Start. Program started in 1965 that receives federal funding and is specifically designed to provide a preschool experience for children from low-income families. (1)

health. State of complete physical, oral, mental, and social well-being, not simply the absence of disease or infirmity. (9)

hierarchy. Type of organization system where some people within an organization have more power than others. (13)

home-based care. Care provided in a home setting. (1)

home visits. Occurs when teachers visit parents and children in their own homes before the children start in a program. (7)

housekeeping area. Play area that contains replicas of familiar items found at home, including kitchen equipment, dolls, plastic foods, and furniture. (4)

housing insecurity. Results from the high cost of housing relative to income, overcrowding, poor housing quality, and/or unstable neighborhoods. (14)

I

I-9 Illegal Aliens Act. Federal act that requires employers to see proof of an employee's citizenship status. (3)

inclusive environment. Environment that enhances the abilities of all children to cooperate and work together in a space that accommodates all abilities and requirements. (2)

inclusive program environments. Programs that accept everyone regardless of physical characteristics, intellectual abilities, or gender. (14)

in-kind support. Items or services received from another source without having to pay for them. (6)

in-service training. Training that a person receives while already employed. (12)

interactionalist. Children develop through their interactions with the environment. (2)

internal roles and responsibilities. All the duties the leader does inside the center on a day-to-day basis, such as scheduling and management, family meetings, tuition collection, and ordering curriculum supplies and food for meal times. (11)

interpersonal skills. Qualities and abilities that help one to get along with others and to help them feel at ease. (11)

J

job description. Spells out the duties, qualifications, and experience needed to perform a position successfully. (5)

K

kith and kin care. Informal care of a small group of children provided by relatives or a friend that is mostly unlicensed. (1)

L

laboratory schools. Programs that exist for the primary purpose of training future teachers and studying child development and education. (1)

labor-intensive. Requires a large workforce for a quality service to occur. (5)

liability insurance. Insurance that protects against financial loss due to a successful lawsuit against the program. (3)

line of credit. Short-term loan that extends a preapproved amount of money. (6)

literacy and writing areas. Quiet spaces that contain an interesting selection of developmentally appropriate books and materials to learn more about the written word. (4)

low socio-economic status. Inadequate financial resources to meet basic needs. (14)

M

mandated reporters. People who work with children and are required to report suspected child abuse to the proper authorities. (9)

marketing. Promotion of your business, including many potential activities that create awareness. (7)

market rate. Typical cost of child care in the area. (6)

matching grants. Grants where for every dollar the program provides the granting agency will match it with additional money. (6)

math and science areas. Spaces that contain materials for engagement that support the foundations necessary when learning math and science concepts in early childhood classrooms. (4)

maturationalist. Children develop according to predictable biological patterns and increase in competence when the environment supports this development. (2)

mentor. Person who serves as an advisor, role model, and friend. (5)

microaggressions. Subtle, indirect, and often unintentional comments or actions that express discrimination or a prejudiced attitude against another person or group. (14)

mindfulness. State of being conscious or aware of the present moment. (14)

Montessori programs. Child care programs that utilize special equipment designed to help children develop their sensory awareness and cognitive skills at their own pace. (1)

N

NAEYC 10 Program Standards. Standards established for all types of early childhood programs to use as guides and to help families be better informed when selecting child care. (2)

NAEYC code of ethical conduct. Offers guidelines for behavior that is responsible and sets a common ground for resolving ethical dilemmas. (1)

national accreditation. The highest level of accreditation of any of the state systems; examples include NAEYC. (3)

negative conflict. Type of conflict that can reduce opportunities to reconcile issues. (13)

networking. Allows professions in the same field to exchange information, offer advice, and provide referrals to other resources within your area or field. (1, 11)

not-for-profit programs. Business legally organized to operate without making a profit, often as a community service; also called a non-profit. (6)

O

Occupational Safety and Health Act (OSHA). Federal act that requires employers to maintain a safe and healthy workplace. (3)

optional expenditures. Wish list expenses for nonessential items or services. (6)

organizational chart. A visual image that indicates job titles and the lines of authority within the program. (5)

organizing. Function of management that involves determining an appropriate arrangement of time, people, and space. (11)

orientation meeting. Meeting that gives new parents in a program a chance to learn more about the center. (7)

orientation plan. Plan with formal and informal ways to help new staff become acquainted with the center and their role in it. (5)

orientation training. Training process that describes program requirements and must be taken within a specified time frame found within state licensing standards. (15)

out-of-school-time care. Type of child care that provides care for children when they are out of school. (1)

P

parent handbook. Basic tool of written communication to which parents can refer with program questions. (10)

parent model. Child care cooperative model that involves parents who have formed a cooperative to provide care for their children. (1)

pedagogical lens. Understanding best practices for teaching and setting up classroom environments. (8)

pedophiles. Individuals who are intent on making inappropriate sexual advances on children. (9)

personnel policies. Agreements between your center and its employees that list what the expectations are for treatment of staff and management. (12)

petty cash. Cash on hand for small, unexpected expenditures. (6)

physical development. Refers to the coordination of small and large muscles to support the child's movement and coordination abilities within the environment.

planning. Function of management that involves setting goals for the program and identifying methods or strategies for reaching those goals. (11)

play. Occurs when children engage in activities with other children, adults, toys, equipment, and materials. (8)

portfolio. Binder or electronic collection of samples of an individual's previous work or work completed within a teacher education program. (5)

positive conflict. Results from misunderstandings that are quickly dealt with in an open, honest, and consistent fashion. (13)

positive guidance. Based on the idea that children are more likely to listen if direction is given in an affirmative way. (8)

positive self-esteem. Knowledge that a person is a good and worthy individual. (5)

preschool care. Programming for children ages three to five years. (1)

probationary employment period. Period of 90 to 180 days that gives an employer the chance to get to know the new employee before making a permanent commitment. (5)

professional boundaries. Separates the personal relationship from the professional relationship. (14)

professional development registry systems. Formalized electronic systems that track an individual's education, experience, and professional development training. (15)

Program Administration Scale (PAS). Assesses 25 items grouped into nine categories in order to provide those in leadership positions with valuable information about their program's administrative practices. (15)

program standard. Defines the level of functioning of a program and sets the expected benchmark in areas that research has found to support high-quality programs for young children. (3)

property insurance. Type of insurance that protects against loss of equipment or building. (3)

proposal. Document explaining what the director wants to do, why there is a need to do it, why the director is qualified to do it, and what kind of help is necessary, usually provided to a grant funder or agency. (6)

protective factors. Attribute in an individual or family that promotes the health and well-being of a child. (9)

psychosexual development. Theory of development pioneered by Freud, who believed that children's development occurs in a series of stages based on pleasure areas of the body that cause conflict and influence adult behavior. (8)

psychosocial development. Theory of development identified by Erikson who believed that social interactions and experiences created points of conflict during identified stages in a child's life that contributed to a child's overall social-emotional development. (8)

public relations. Activities that create an awareness of and a positive attitude toward a business. (7)

Q

Quality Rating Systems (QRS). Federally- and state-funded programs that have built-in criteria that support early childhood programs of all sizes and types with the intent of increasing the quality of care of children beyond basic state licensing requirements. (3)

R

reflective listening. Repeating the other person's main point using slightly different words to ensure they heard and understood. (11)

relationship-focused program environment. Environment in which adults are caring, warm, and respectful and will nurture children's self-concept and confidence. (8)

Right to Know Act. Federal act that requires posted information regarding storage and use of cleaning materials or other hazardous chemicals. (3)

S

safety hazards. Potential source of harm or injury to a person. (9)

self-care. Taking care of yourself in ways that keep you healthy, allow you to do your job, and prevent burnout. (12)

self-care activities. Activities that promote self-care and prevent burnout. (14)

sensory area. Classroom space that allows children to participate in activities involving many types of textures, including sand and water. (4)

separation anxiety. Fears about being away from parents or caregivers. (7)

sick child care. Type of child care that provides supervision for children with mild conditions and low fevers related to illness not allowed within a child care setting. (1)

social development. Child's interactions with significant adults in their lives, peers, and the community in which they live. (8)

social learning theory. Theory from Bandura that states that social engagement with others was the key to their development. (8)

social media savvy. User that is familiar with websites and applications that share content or provide social networking. (7)

sociocultural theory. Vygotsky's theory that expanded on his previous theory with an additional emphasis on actively learning through hands-on experiences and cultural interactions with parents, caregivers, and peers. (8)

sponsor. Person, group, or organization that makes a commitment to provide ongoing support to a program. (6)

staffing. Function of management that refers to the recruiting, hiring, and retention of skilled individuals needed to operate a quality program. (11)

staff-to-child ratio. Number of children compared to the number of adults responsible for a designated group of children. (1, 5)

start-up budget. Budget that covers several months of preparation before a center opens and income is received. (6)

stigma. Negative or unfair perception. (14)

stress. Deviation of the normal function of the body and/or mind. (14)

stressors. People, places, or things that causes stress. (14)

subsidy voucher. Vouchers provided to qualified parents through a state's Department of Human Services as support for part of the tuition but that is typically lower than the rate charged by the program. (1)

supervision. Oversight by teaching staff that includes monitoring the environment and activity to keep all children safe throughout the day. (8)

support personnel. Employee group that provides essential support to program activities, such as administrative assistants, cooks, and maintenance staff. (5)

support system. People in a person's life who help a person when support is needed. (10)

T

tax-exempt. Not having to pay taxes on purchases. (6)

theoretical perspectives. Ideas that have come from a structural framework, explanation, or tool that has been tested and evaluated. (8)

Theory X. Management style in which a manager believes that employees have no real commitment to their jobs and cannot be trusted. (11)

Theory Y. Management style in which a manager believes that staff are self-motivated and committed to the organization's goals. (11)

Title VII of the Civil Rights Act of 1964. Federal law that requires employers to maintain a safe and healthy workplace. (3)

toxic stress. Lasting serious stress experienced by a child without support from a caregiver that can impact brain development. (9)

training systems. Systems that have determined levels and offer experience in the field for individuals interested in providing learning opportunities for others working in the field of early childhood education. (15)

typical development. Normal behaviors. (8)

U

universal precautions. Practices developed by the CDC that require all staff treat every situation as having the potential to spread disease. (9)

Universal Pre-K. No-cost programming and child care funded by the federal and state governments for children ages four to five years old. (1)

V

variable expenditures. Costs paid on a regular basis, but the amount may vary. (6)

vendors. Sellers of the various supplies and equipment that the program needs. (6)

vouchers. Representation of money provided by companies that their employees can use to help pay for care in a program of their choice. (6)

W

warranty. Item purchased is backed by the manufacturer and is expected to last for at least a certain period, and covers repairs if the product is defective or if it breaks under normal use; also known as a guarantee. (6)

workplace bullying. Incidents of inappropriate actions by an individual or group that are persistent, abusive, threatening, and malicious in nature with the intent to harm. (13)

workshop. Events where speakers or educators can share information with caregivers. (10)

Z

zone of helpfulness. Continuum that can be used to guide early childhood program directors and staff in finding appropriate balance in professional relationships. (14)

zoning codes. Rules that specify the types of permitted land use. (3)

Index

10 Program Standards, NAEYC, 26

A

AAP. *See* American Academy of Pediatrics
abilities, 18–19
abuse and endangerment, children. *See* endangerment
    and abuse, children
acceptance of mistakes, 82–83
accessibility, 60–61, 66
accreditation, 53
    long term, 56
    maintaining, 56
    on-site visits, 55–56
    performance criteria, 55
    standards, 55
ad hoc committee, 190
ADA. *See* Americans with Disabilities Act
administrative staff, 85
administrative success, measurement of, 297–98
advertising
    brochures, 130
    flyers, 130
    newspaper advertisements, 130
    social media platforms, 129–30
    use of, 128
    website, 129
    writing and matching to market, 128–30
advisory board, 47
advocates, 228
age-appropriate programming, 34–38
    infants and toddlers, 34–35
    out-of-school-time care, 36–38
    preschoolers, 34–35
agencies, 46
air quality, 173–74
American Academy of Pediatrics (AAP), 171
Americans with Disabilities Act (ADA), 49, 190
analysis, budget, 112–14
applicants, 90–96
    compensation, 94–95
    condition of employment, 96
    criminal background check, 95
    hiring new employee, 94
    interview process, 90–93
    making final selection, 94
    before a new employee can begin, 95
    probationary period, 96
    references, 93–94
    review process, 93

application, 89–90
area child care programs, 8–9
area employment opportunities, 8
areas, classroom, 67–70
assessment, early childhood programs, 51–52
associate play, 155
attachment theory, 147
atypical development, 145
audit, 110

B

background research, 11
bad debts, 115–16
balance, daily schedules, 157
BAS. *See* Business Administration Scale
behaviorist, 27
behaviorist theory, 147
bids, 119
blended family, 6
block center, 68
bonding insurance, 51
break-even point, 114
brochures, 130
budget
    analyzing, 112–14
    developing, 109–12
    fiscal year, 110
    start-up, 109–10
bullying, 263–65
burnout, 246–48
Business Administration Scale (BAS), 297
business plan, 102, 104

C

CACFP. *See* Child and Adult Care Food Program
care
    amount needed, 10
    center-based, 14–17
    drop-in, 16
    home-based, 13–14
    infant and toddler, 14–15
    kith and kin, 14
    out-of-school-time, 15
    preferred types of, 10
    preschool, 15
    sick child care, 17
    types, 12

caregivers
   center activities, 207–9
   communicating with, 200–202
   engaging, 205–9
   perspectives of, 204
   social and cultural influences, 204–5
   supporting, 203–5
carpets, 63
cash flow, 115
cash lag, 115
cash reserve, 115
CCDF. *See* Child Care and Development Fund
CCP. *See* Certified Child Care Professional
CCR&R. *See* Child Care Resource and Referral
CDA. *See* Child Development Associate
ceilings, treatment of, 64
center-based care, 14–17
Certified Child Care Professional (CCP), 296
certified public accountant (CPA), 114
charitable organizations, 106–7
Child and Adult Care Food Program (CACFP), 106, 178
child care
   area programs, 8
   characteristics of quality staff, 81–84
   community considerations, 7–12
   economic considerations, 7–12
   need for, 5–7
   program characteristics, 25–28
   sick, 17
Child Care and Adult Food Program (CACFP), 120
Child Care and Development Fund (CCDF), 5, 106
child care cooperatives, 16
Child Care Resource and Referral (CCR&R), 7, 88
Child Development Associate (CDA), 19, 29
child medical and accident insurance, 51
child predator, identification of, 187–88
child-directed play, 36
children
   difficult circumstances, 137
   ethical responsibilities to, 232
   helping parents help, 134–36
   helping with adjustment, 136–39
   isolating from center, 181
   picking up, 188
   program benefits, 289–90
   recognizing and reporting suspected endangerment
      cases, 186–87
   registering and enrolling, 133–34
   special health needs, 181–83
   in trauma-sensitive classrooms, 189
civil right compliance, 49
clarity, 224
class size, organizational structure, 86

CLASS®. *See* Classroom Assessment Scoring System®
Classroom Assessment Scoring System® (CLASS®), 289
classroom assignment, 244–45
classroom staff, 85
climate, 223
   change implementation, 223–24
   healthy organizational climate, 224–26
   positive and respectful climate, 244
Clinton, Bill, 4
Clinton, Hillary, 4
co-pay, 106
Code of Ethical Conduct, NAEYC, 19
code of ethics, 231
cognitive theory, 147
cohabitating parents, 6
college education support, 296
colleges, 108
collegiality, 224
committees, 47–48, 190–91
communication, 254
   communication-engagement connection, 195–97
   early childhood leader, 230
   strategies, 197–202
   supporting families and caregivers, 203–5
communication options, 137–39
communication skills, 218–19
communication-engagement connection, 195–97
community
   connections, 291–92
   ethical responsibilities to, 232–33
   groups, 107
   meeting needs of, 290–93
   resources, 130–31
community/economic considerations, 7–12
   area child care programs, 8–9
   area employment opportunities, 8
   economic opportunities, 9
   family requirements, 9–10
   information-gathering tools, 10–12
   neighborhoods, 8
company foundations, 108–9
compensation, 94–95, 243–44
conferences, 198–200
confidentiality, 181
conflict, 256
   negative, 257–58
   positive, 257
conflict resolution, 219, 258
conflict-partnership pathway, 258
conflict-resolution partnerships, 258–60
considerations, registering and enrolling children, 133–34
consortium model, 16
constructive play, 154

constructivist, 27
continuity of care, 34–35
contract, 94
controlling, 214
cooperative play, 155
cost coding, 112
cost-per-child analysis, 114
CPA. *See* certified public accountant, 114
creative art area, 69
credit cards, 116–17
criminal background check, 95
culturally competent, 281
culture, 229
curriculum, 74, 145–53
    atypical development, 145
    cognitive development, 145
    considerations, 74–76
    developmentally appropriate practices, 148
    diapering or restroom time, 152–53
    emotional development, 145
    free play, 149
    group time, 149–50
    meeting needs, 148–49
    music and movement, 150
    nap time, 151
    outdoor time, 151–52
    physical development, 145
    reviewing theories, 145–48
    snack and meal times, 151
    social development, 145
    theoretical perspectives, 145
    typical development, 145

D

daily schedule and activities, 35–36
daily schedules, planning, 156–58
DAP. *See* developmentally appropriate practice
debit cards, 116–17
decision making, 226
delivery, 119
Department of Labor Fair Wage and Standards Act, 49
description of benefits, 238–39
development
    atypical, 145
    cognitive, 145
    emotional, 145
    physical, 145
    psychosexual, 145
    psychosocial, 145
    social, 145
    typical, 145
development, budget
    anticipating income, 111–12

fiscal year budget, 110
    formatting, 112
    identifying expenses, 110–11
    start-up budget, 109–10
developmental considerations, 36
developmentally appropriate curriculum. *See* curriculum, supporting
developmentally appropriate practice (DAP), 4, 27–28, 148, 288
diapering, 152–53, 175
difficult circumstances, 137
directing, 216
director
    daily stress of managing programs, 273–77
    director-board relationship, 48
    education and experience levels of, 29
    health and mental wellness supports, 281–84
    healthy program environments, 277–81
    professional boundaries, 269–72
    professional boundaries and, 271
    support, 224
director's credential, 19, 29
directors and officers insurance, 51
disabilities, children with, 132–33
disability insurance, 51
disciplinary action, 242
disease, practices to prevent spread of, 173–76
    air quality, 173–74
    alerting parents, 180–81
    diapering, 175
    disinfecting, 175
    disposable gloves, 174–75
    handwashing, 174
    napping, 175–76
    tooth brushing, 175
disinfecting, 175
disposable gloves, 174–75
diversity, 280
domestic violence, 280
dramatic play area, 68
drop-in care, 16

E

EAP. *See* employee assistance program
early childhood leader, 17–21, 227–30
    communication, 230
    external roles and responsibilities, 227–28
    global responsibilities, 18
    internal roles and responsibilities, 227–29
    inviting atmosphere, 230
    program culture, 229
early childhood programs

care types, 12
center-based care, 14–17
interior elements, 63–64
leaders, 17–21
outdoor elements, 64–66
overall site considerations, 60–63
owning, 20–21
security, 66
Early Head Start, 16–17
Early Intervention Program (EI), 182
education/experience level, 29
educational requirements, 19
EI. *See* Early Intervention Program
elementary school, 7
email inquiries, 131–32
emergencies, preparing for, 183–86
emergency numbers, 184
evacuation plans, 184–85
family notification, 185
first aid, 184
lockouts and lockdowns, 185–86
staff, 184
weather preparations, 185
emergency numbers, 184
emotional development, 145
emotional well-being, 277
empathy, 218
employee assistance program (EAP), 74, 282
employee model, 16
employee responsibilities and conduct, 239
employers, 108–9
employment at will, 94
employment regulations, 88–89
encumbered funds, 116
endangerment and abuse, children
identifying child predators, 187–88
picking up children, 188
suspecting intoxicated parents, 188–89
trauma-sensitive classrooms, 189
engagement, families, 195
enthusiasm for learning, 83
entrepreneurs, 20–21
Environment Rating Scales (ERS), 289
environments, early childhood programs
curriculum considerations, 74–76
equipment needs, 67–70
equipment selection, 70–74
guidelines, 60–67
maintaining inclusive environments, 280–81
planning healthy and safe environment, 169–73
environments, guidelines for, 60–67
interior elements, 63–64
outdoor elements, 64–66

overall site considerations, 60–63
security, 66
equipment
choosing, 70–74
needs, 67–70
equitable programming, 280
ERS. *See* Environment Rating Scales
established career levels, 293–94
ethical responsibilities, 231–33
evacuation plans, 184–85
evaluation procedures, 241
evaluation, child care programs
administrative success measurement, 297–98
family and community needs, 290–93
program benefits, 289–90
support for staff, 293–96
expenditures
fixed, 111
optional, 111
variable, 111
expenses, identifying, 110–11
exploratory play, 154
external roles and responsibilities, 227–28

F
facilities, 37
maintaining, 172
families
blended, 6
center activities, 207–9
child care homes, 13–14, 38–40
cohabitating parents, 6
encouraging security, 278–79
engagement, 195
engaging, 205–9
ethical responsibilities to, 232
family-centered activities, 207
meeting needs of, 290–93
modern structures, 6–7
notification, 185
partnership with parents, 33
professional boundaries, 271–72
requirements, 9–10
social and cultural influences, 204–5
style, 151
supporting, 203–5
two-income, 5–6
values, 204–5
Family and Medical Leave Act (FMLA), 5
family child care home, 74, 76
Family Medical Leave Act (FMLA), 49
family style, 151
federal laws, 48–49

finances
  budget analysis, 112–14
  budget development, 109–12
  financial management, 114–16
  financial planning, 102–4
  for-profit/not-for-profit programs, 105–9
  needed financial services, 116–17
  purchasing decisions, 117–21
  sponsors, 107–9
financial management, 114–16
financial planning, 102–5
  business plan considerations, 104
  funding agency expectations, 103–4
  grant availability, 103
fire codes, 47
first aid, administering, 184
first visits, 133
fiscal year, 110
fixed expenditures, 111
flexibility, daily schedules, 157
flooring, 63–64
floors, treatment of, 63–64
flyers, 130
FMLA. *See* Family and Medical Leave Act
food insecurity, 278
food safety, 177–81
  alerting parents to contagious diseases, 180–81
  confidentiality, 181
  health and safety considerations, 179–80
  isolating from center, 181
  nutritional requirements, 178–79
  safe food handling, 177–78
  special health concerns, 180
food, safe handling of, 177–81
for-profit programs, 105
  fundraising, 105
  sources of income for, 106–7
  tax-exempt, 105
formatting, budget, 112
foundations, 106–7
free play, 149
funding agency, expectations of, 103–4
fundraising, 105, 208–9
fundraising activities, 107
future trends, 12

G
gentleness, 82
global responsibilities, 18
goal consensus, 226
gossip, 263
  strategies for prevention, 264
governing boards, 47–48

governing bodies, ethical responsibilities to, 232
government departments, 108
government program assistance, 120
grants, availability of, 103
grievance procedures, 239
group decision making, 220
group meetings, 135–36
group size expectations, 29–30
group time, 149–50
grouping, 35
guarantee, 119
guidance strategies, 31, 159–64
  addressing needs, 162
  minimizing problems, 160–61
  positive behavior, 162–64
  positive guidance, 161
  redirection and modeling, 162
guidelines, early childhood programs
  interior elements, 63–64
  outdoor elements, 64–66
  overall site considerations, 60–63
  security, 66

H
handwashing, 174
Head Start, 16–17
health, 168
health and mental wellness, 281–84
health and safety, environment
  avoiding safety hazards, 170–73
  committees, 190–91
  establishing policies and practices, 173–76
  family child care, 172–73
  keeping center clean, 169–70
  meeting special health needs, 181–83
  policies concerning child endangerment and abuse, 186–89
  preparing for emergencies, 183–86
  safe food handling, 177–81
hierarchy, 256
hiring process, 90
home visits, 135, 197–98
home-based care, 13–14
home, opening, 38–40
honesty, 84
hours, 37
housekeeping area, 68
housing insecurity, 278

I
I-9 Illegal Aliens Act, 49
illness, signs of, 176
impairment, 188–89

impartiality, 82
in-kind support, 107
in-service training, 246
inclusive environment, 32
inclusive program environments, 280
inclusive programs, 32–33
income
    anticipating, 111–12
    charitable organizations, 106–7
    foundations, 106–7
    fundraising activities, 107
    in-kind support, 107
    matching grants, 107
    private funds, 106
    public funds, 106
    sources of, 106–7
    tuition, 106
income tax, 49
individual decision-making skills, 220–21
indoor environments, guidelines. *See* environments, guidelines for
infant and toddler care, 14–15
    addressing needs, 162
    communication with caregivers, 200
    curriculum considerations, 75–76
    disabilities, 181–82
    elements, 34–35
    elements of programming for, 34–35
    equipment for, 71
    health and safety concerns for, 179–80
    nutritional requirements, 178
    play utilizing their senses, 154
information-gathering tools, 10–12
innovativeness, 226
inspections, 39
insurance protection, 50–51
interactionalist, 27
Internal Revenue Service (IRS), 105
internal roles and responsibilities, 227–29
interpersonal play, 154
interpersonal skills, 217–18
interview process, 90–93
intoxication, 188–89
inviting atmosphere, 230
IRS. *See* Internal Revenue Service
isolation, 181

J
job description, 86–88

K
kindness, 81
kitchens, 62

kith and kin care, 14
knowledge about child development, 83

L
labor-intensive, 91
laboratory schools, 16
lasting impression, 133
leadership characteristics, 214–22
    management responsibilities, 214–16
    management styles, 216
leadership skills, 216–22
    communication skills, 218–19
    conflict resolution, 219
    group decision making, 220
    individual decision-making skills, 220–21
    interpersonal skills, 217–18
    time-management skills, 221–22
legal concerns, 48–51
liability, 49–50
liability insurance, 51
licensing
    child care aspects subject to, 45
    preparation for, 46
    standards, 61
lighting, 64
line of credit, 116
literacy and writing area, 69
local business, support for, 119–20
local ordinances, 46–47
location, 34, 37, 60–61, 65–66
lockdowns, 185–86
lockouts, 185–86
low socio-economic status, 278

M
Main, Catherine, 80
management
    responsibilities, 214–16
    styles, 216
mandated reporters, 186
market rate, 111
marketing, 125
    advertising, 128–30
    community resources, 130–31
    considerations, 128
    informational meetings, 130
    social media savvy, 126
    strategies, 127–28
matching grants, 107
math and science areas, 69–70
maturationalist, 27
mature judgment, 83

meal time, 151
medications, administering, 176
mental well-being, 277
mentor, 96
Military Child Care Act of 1989, 108
mindfulness, 274–75
modeling, 162
modern family structures, 6–7
Montessori programs, 16
Montessori, Maria, 16
motivation, 245–46
movement, 150
music, 150

N

NAEYC. *See* National Association for the Education
      of Young Children
NAFCC. *See* National Association for
      Family Child Care
nannies, 13
nap time, 151
napping, 175–76
national accreditation, 53–56
National Association for Family Child Care
      (NAFCC), 39
National Association for the Education of
      Young Children (NAEYC), 4, 80, 101,
      288, 289
   10 Program Standards, 26
   Code of Ethical Conduct, 19, 231–33
   Standard 1, 31–32
   Standard 2, 31
   Standard 3, 31
   Standard 5, 30
   Standard 6, 29
   Standard 7, 33
   Standard 8, 32
   Standard 10, 30
needed financial services, 116–17
needs
   addressing, 162
   meeting, 148–49
negative conflict, 257–58
neighborhoods, 8
networking, 8, 228
new employee, introducing, 96
newspaper advertisements, 130
not-for-profit programs, 105
notification, families, 185
nursery school, 16
nurturance, 81
nutritional requirements, 178–79

O

Occupational Safety and Health Act (OSHA), 49
offered services, organizational structure, 86
online surveys, 11–12, 292–93
openness to new ideas, 83
optional expenditures, 111
orientation meeting, 135
organizational chart, 85
organizational structure, staffing, 84–86
   development, 85
   influencing, 85–86
organizing, 214–15
orientation plan, 96
orientation training, 294
orientation, parents, 135
orientation, staff, 96–97
OSHA. *See* Occupational Safety and Health Act
out-of-school-time, 73
out-of-school-time care, 15, 76
   elements, 36–38
out-of-state registration requirements, 49
outdoor environments, guidelines. *See* environments,
      guidelines for
outdoor safety hazard, 171–72
outdoor time, 151–52
outdoors space, extension, 70
oversight. *See* regulatory oversight

P

parent meetings, 11–12
parent model, 16
parent-handbook, 197
Parent, Family, and Community Engagement Framework
      (PFCE), 195
parents
   alerting to contagious diseases, 180–81
   conferences, 198–200
   difficult circumstances, 137
   helping with adjustment, 136–39
   helping with helping their children, 134–36
   making program welcome place for, 131–34
   meetings, 206–7
   orientation, 135
   partnership with, 33
   policy considerations, 262
   reassurances and communication, 137
   suspecting intoxication, 188–89
PAS. *See* Program Administration Scale
past experiences, 205
payroll benefit withholdings, 49
pedagogical lens, 144
pedophiles, 187

personal skills, 18–19
personnel actions, 242–43
personnel policies, 237–41
    description of benefits, 238–39
    emergency procedures, 240–41
    employee responsibilities and conduct, 239
    evaluation procedures, 241
    grievance procedures, 239
    health and safety, 239–40
    probationary employment, 241
    promotions, 241
    statement of nondiscrimination, 238
    transfers, 241
petty cash, 119
PFCE. *See* Parent, Family, and Community Engagement
        Framework
physical development, 145
physical environment, 245
physical setting, 226
planning, 214
planning room arrangement needs, 61–62
play
    as social interaction and relaxation, 155–56
    associative, 155
    child-directed, 36
    cooperative, 155
    definition, 153
    importance of, 30–31
    learning for all ages through, 153–56
policies
    health and safety, 173–76
    introduction to, 262
    personnel policies, 237–241
    workplace relationships, 260–62
portfolio, 92
positive behavior, 31
positive conflict, 257
positive guidance, 161
positive self-esteem, 83–84
positive working environment
    burnout, 246–48
    classroom assignment, 244–45
    compensation, 243–44
    in-service training, 246
    motivation and recognition of efforts, 245–46
    physical environment, 245
    positive and respectful climate, 244
    schedule preferences, 245
    self-care, 246–48
predictability, daily schedules, 157
preschool children, 15
    communication with caregivers, 201–2
    curriculum considerations, 76

disabilities, 182–83
elements, 35–36
equipment for, 72
health and safety concerns for, 179–80
modeling, 162
pretend play, 154–55
redirection, 162
private funds, 106
probationary employment, 241
probationary employment period, 96
procedure/goals, explaining, 97
professional boundaries, 269
    between director and staff, 271
    establishing, 269–72
    families, 271
    importance, 270
professional development, 224
    credential and college education supports, 296
    established career levels, 293–94
    opportunities, 29
    registry systems, 295
    state registry systems, 295–96
    trainer and training content requirements, 294–95
    training expectations, 294
Program Administration Scale (PAS), 297
program benefits, 289–90
program culture, 229
program leader as presumed counselor, 279–80
program standard, 55
programs, child care
    age-appropriate programming, 34–38
    characteristics, 25–28
    creating healthy program environment, 277–81
    developmentally appropriate practices, 27–28
    evaluation, 287–99
    family child care home, 38–40
    federal laws and regulation, 48–49
    financial planning, 102–4
    for-profit/not-for-profit, 105–9
    isolating from, 181
    legal concerns of operating, 48–51
    making welcome place for parents, 131–34
    out-of-school-time care, 37–38
    philosophy, 27
    picking up children, 188
    service needs, 10
    sponsors, 107–9
    state laws and regulations, 49
    strategies supporting developmentally appropriate
        curriculum, 145–53
    types, 12–17
    universal practices, 28–33
promotions, 241

property insurance, 51
proposal, 102
protective factor, 189
psychosexual development, 145
psychosocial development, 145
public funds, 106
public relations, 125
    advertising, 128–30
    community resources, 130–31
    considerations, 128
    informational meetings, 130
    social media savvy, 126
    strategies, 127–28
purchasing decisions, 117–21
    bids, 119
    government program assistance, 120
    other considerations, 119–21
    petty cash, 119
    seasonal discounts, 118
    transportation service, 120–21
    vendor relations, 118–19

Q

QRIS. *See* Quality Rating and
    Improvement Systems
QRS. *See* Quality Rating Systems
Quality Rating and Improvement Systems
    (QRIS), 4, 289
Quality Rating Systems (QRS), 4, 19, 29, 44,
    51–54, 289
    initiatives, 298–99
questionnaires, 11–12, 292–93

R

reassurances, 137
recognition of efforts, 245–46
recruitment, 88–90
    application, 89–90
    government employment regulations, 88–89
    hiring process, 90
redirection, 162
reflective listening, 217
regulatory oversight, 44–48
    agencies, 46
    governing boards and committees, 47–48
    licensing, 45–46
    local ordinances, 46–47
relational play, 154
relationship-focused program environment, 160
reliability, 84

Request for Proposal process (RFP), 103
resilience, flooring, 63–64
respect, 253–54
responsibilities, committees, 191
restroom time, 152–53
reward system, 224–26
RFP. *See* Request for Proposal
Right to Know Act, 49
rough-and-tumble play, 154
rugs, 63

S

safety and health, environment.
        See health and safety, environment
safety codes, 47
safety hazards
    avoiding, 170–73
    definition, 170
    facility maintenance, 172
    outdoor, 171–72
safety-net, 6
safety, outdoor environments, 66
SAMHSA. *See* Substance Abuse and Mental Health
        Services Administration
SBA. *See* Small Business Administration
schedule preferences, 245
school-age children
    communication with caregivers, 202
    disabilities, 183
    guidance strategies, 162–64
    health and safety concerns for, 180
    nutritional requirements, 178–79
    positive behavior, 162–64
schools, working with, 38
seasonal discounts, 118
security, 66
self-care, 246–48, 274
sense of humor, 83
sensorimotor play, 154
sensory area, 70
separation anxiety, 134
service, 119
sexual predators. *See* pedophiles
sharing, 207–8
sick child care, 17
sites, considerations for, 60–63
size, 65–66
size of program, organizational structure, 86
Small Business Administration (SBA), 102
snack time, 151
social development, 145

social learning theory, 145
social media platforms, 129–30
social media savvy, 126
sociocultural history, 147
special health needs, 181–83
sponsoring agencies, ethical responsibilities to, 232
sponsors, 107–9
staff
    administrative, 85
    alerting, 184
    characteristics, 81–84
    classroom, 85
    encouraging security, 278–79
    ethical responsibilities to, 232
    job descriptions, 86–88
    organizational structure, 84–86
    orientation, 96–97
    personnel actions, 242–43
    personnel policies, 237–241
    policy considerations, 261
    positive working environment, 243–48
    professional boundaries, 271
    professional development, 293–96
    recruitment, 88–90
    selecting best applicant, 90–96
    space for, 62–63
    special health needs, 181–83
staff-to-child ratios, 12, 29–30
    organizational structure, 86
staffing, 215–16
start-up budget, 109–10
state laws, 49
state registry systems, 295–96
state regulations, organizational structure, 86
state system
    levels, 53–54
    recognition, 53
    reimbursement, 53
statement of nondiscrimination, 238
stigma, 282
storage space, 62
stress, 273
stressors, 273
structured play, 36
subsidy vouchers, 11
Substance Abuse and Mental Health Services
    Administration (SAMHSA), 281
supervision, 148
support personnel, 85
support system, 203
surfaces, treatment of, 66
symbolic play, 154

T
task orientation, 226
tax-exempt, 105
teachers
    behaviors that minimize
        problems, 160–61
    education and experience levels of, 29
    role in preschool care, 36
telephone inquiries, 131–32
termination, 242–43
theoretical perspectives, 145
theories, reviewing, 145–48
Theory X, 216
Theory Y, 216
time-management skills, 221–22
time, managing, 275–76
Title VII of the Civil Rights Act of 1964, 49
tooth brushing, 175
toxic stress, 189
trainer, requirements for, 294–95
training content, requirements for, 294–95
training systems, 294
training, organizational structure, 86
transfers, 241
transportation service, 120–21
trauma-sensitive classrooms, 189
treatment
    ceilings, 64
    floors, 63–64
    surfaces, 66
    walls, 64
    windows, 64
trilemma of child care, 106
trust, 253
tuition, 106
two-income families, 5–6
typical development, 145

U
U.S. Department of Agriculture (USDA), Food and
    Nutrition Service, 178
unemployment taxes, 49
universal practices, programs, 28–33
    curriculum and equipment, 31–32
    education/experience levels, 29
    group size expectations, 29–30
    guidance strategies, 31
    health, safety, and nutrition requirements, 30
    importance of play, 30–31
    inclusive programs, 32–33
    partnership with parents, 33

positive behavior, 32
professional development opportunities, 29
staff-to-child ratio, 29–30
Universal Pre-K, 17
universities, 109
unstructured play, 36
USDA. *See* U.S. Department of Agriculture Food and
    Nutrition Service

V

variable expenditures, 111
variety, daily schedules, 157
vendor relations, 118–19
vendors, 119
visits, 198
volunteer opportunities, 208
vouchers, 109

W

walls, treatment of, 64
warranty, 119
weather preparations, 185
website, 129
Whitebook, Marcy, 80
windows, treatment of, 64

women, work force, 5
work force
    shortage, 7
    women in, 5–6
work-life balance, 274
worker's compensation insurance, 49
workers, shortage of, 7
working alone, 39
workplace bullying, 263
    strategies for prevention, 264–65
workplace relationships, 253–55
    conflict, 256–58
    conflict-resolution partnerships, 258–60
    gossip and bullying, 263–65
    healthy relationships, 255
    policies and procedures, 260–62
workshops, 206
written policy considerations, 261–62

Y

Yarbrough, Karen, 80

Z

zone of helpfulness, 271
zoning codes, 47